**Political Gerrymandering
and the Courts**

This is the third volume in the Agathon series
on Representation.
Series Editor: Bernard Grofman

Previously published:

Electoral Laws and Their Political Consequences
edited by Bernard Grofman and Arend Lijphart

The Federalist Papers *and the New Institutionalism*
edited by Bernard Grofman and Donald Wittman

Political Gerrymandering and the Courts

edited by

Bernard Grofman
University of California, Irvine

AGATHON PRESS
New York

Library of Congress Cataloging-in-Publication Data

Political gerrymandering and the courts / edited by Bernard Grofman.
    p.   cm.
  ISBN 0-87586-092-3 : $36.00
    1. Apportionment (Election law)—United States.   2. Election
districts—United States.   I. Grofman, Bernard.
  KF4905.P65   1990
  342.73'07—dc20
  [347.3027]   89-29830
                                                                    CIP

Printed in the United States

Contents

Preface

This volume is motivated by three concerns. First is the belief that the issue of political gerrymander will play a significant (although far from dominant) role in redistricting litigation in the 1990s and thereafter. In the 1980s, the legislative and/or congressional redistricting plans of all but a handful of states were subject to lawsuits (Grofman, 1985a). Many of these lawsuits involved the issue of racial vote dilution (Grofman, Migalski, and Noviello, 1985). In the 1980s hundreds of local jurisdictions that used at-large or multimember district elections had their electoral system challenged—and most of the jurisdictions under challenge were forced to change their system to a single-member district plan that was not dilutive of minority voting strength (see, e.g., Brischetto and Grofman, 1988). Although partisan gerrymandering is less prevalent than racial vote dilution, in the 1990s we can expect to see challenges to partisan gerrymandering like those in the 1980s to racial vote dilution. In particular, numerous local jurisdictions that use partisan multimember district or at-large elections may be subject to challenge.

Second, in commissioning essays I sought to involve a number of the leading scholars in the field so as to put together a largely self-contained compendium of the major points of view on how issues of partisan gerrymandering are to be litigated. While the ultimate issues in constitutional interpretation are ones that the Supreme Court must resolve, and these will be resolved only after an extensive series of case-by-case adjudications—just as the actual numerical features of the one person, one vote standard evolved only in the decade of litigation after *Baker v. Carr* (Grofman, 1989a)—there is an important role for social scientists to play. Social science testimony proved important in the area of racial vote dilution by aiding courts to interpret the provisions of the Voting Rights Acts (e.g., in defining the operational meaning of terms like *racially polarized voting*; Grofman, Migalski, and Noviello, 1985; Grofman, 1989b). In like manner, I believe that research by social scientists will aid attorneys and the federal courts in specifying manageable standards to define and measure the effects of partisan gerrymandering. I hope this volume will prove instrumental as the beginning of such a dialogue.

The third concern that motivated this volume is my view that egregious partisan gerrymandering is a violation of the Fourteenth Amendment rights of political groups, and that it is both appropriate and necessary for courts to intervene when such rights are significantly impaired. However, I recognize that the courts must steer a careful line so as to avoid encouraging frivolous lawsuits, while at the same time sending a clear message to potential gerrymanders that intentional egregious political gerrymanders, which eliminate competition and are built to be resistant to electoral tides, will be struck down.

Court intervention to end egregious partisan gerrymandering is necessary for a number of reasons.

> First, political parties and the candidate choices they offer voters provide the single most important mechanism for incorporating citizen preferences into public policy decisions. To invidiously discriminate against the candidates of a political party is to effectively disenfranchise the voters who support the positions espoused by the party's candidates, and thus to dilute the importance of their views in the halls of the legislature. Second, it is a fundamental tenet of American democracy that a representative government be responsive to the changing will of the electorate. To create a districting plan which would be largely insensitive to electoral changes that may occur over the course of a decade, because a particular partisan imbalance is "locked in" through the use of dispersal and concentration techniques of gerrymandering, violates this fundamental tenet. Egregious political gerrymandering condemns political groups to permanent minority status almost regardless of their electoral strength or of changes in voter preferences. Third, the central purpose advanced by the Supreme Court in justifying its interventions into the reapportionment process in the 1960s—the need to ensure "fair and effective representation"—has not been achieved, and cannot be achieved, by reliance on the one person, one vote standard. Even if all districts are exactly equal in population, when a districting plan intentionally creates legislative districts in which a class of citizens has had its voting strength distributed in ways that frustrate or significantly reduce its opportunity for effective political participation (for example, by packing or cracking their voting strength), then it cannot be said that "one man's vote . . . is worth as much as another's." Fourth, access to sophisticated computerized districting data bases which can include not just population data but also information about party registration figures, previous election outcomes, and voting and demographic trends, makes it possible for mapmakers to carry out the most sophisticated forms of gerrymandering while at the same time perfectly satisfying any equal population constraints that might be imposed. (Grofman, 1985a, pp. 112–113; footnotes omitted)

B.G.

Acknowledgments

I am indebted to Columbia University Press for permission to reprint excerpts from Peter H. Schuck, "The Thickest Thicket: Partisan Political Gerrymandering and Judicial Regulation of Politics." Copyright 1987 by the Directors of the Columbia Law Review Association, Inc. All Rights Reserved. This article originally appeared as 87 *Columbia Law Rev.* 1325.

This volume could not have been completed without the able assistance of Dorothy Gormick, Michelle Tran, Susan Pursche, and Wilma Laws of the School of Social Sciences, UCI. I have benefited greatly from discussions of redistricting case law and litigation strategy with the many attorneys with whom I have worked as an expert witness. I am also indebted to a number of organizations involved with redistricting issues and related topics for access to information and resources that have facilitated the publication of this volume. These include (in alphabetical order): the American Legislative Exchange Council, Common Cause, Election Data Services, Fairness for the 90s/Lawyers for the Republic, the Lawyers Committee for Civil Rights under Law, Logistic Systems, the Mexican American Legal Defense and Educational Fund, the NAACP Legal Defense and Educational Fund, the National Conference of State Legislatures, the Republican National Committee, the Southern Regional Council, the Southwest Voter Research Institute, and the Voting Rights Section of the Civil Rights Division of the U.S. Department of Justice. My own research for this volume has been supported by grants from the Political Science and Law and Social Science Programs of the National Science Foundation, SES 85-15468 and SES 88-09392. However, none of these organizations is in any way responsible for the contents of this volume, which reflects solely the individual views of its contributors as scholars and citizens.

About the Editor

Bernard Grofman, Professor of Political Science and Social Psychology, University of California, Irvine, is co-editor of *Representation and Redistricting Issues* (Heath, 1982); *Choosing an Electoral System* (Praeger, 1984), *Electoral Laws and Their Political Consequences* (Agathon, 1986), and *"The Federalist Papers" and the New Institutionalism* (Agathon, 1989). He has served as an expert witness or court-appointed consultant in legislative or congressional litigation in eight states and in cases involving local jurisdictions (including Chicago, Boston, and Los Angeles) in several other states. His recent publications on reapportionment include: "Criteria for Districting: A Social Science Perspective," *UCLA Law Review* (October 1985); Amihai Glazer, Grofman, and Marc Robbins, "Partisan and Incumbency Effects of 1970s Congressional Redistricting," *American Journal of Political Science* (June 1987); and Guillermo Owen and Grofman, "Optimal Partisan Gerrymandering," *Political Geography Quarterly* (January 1988).

About the Authors

Charles Backstrom is Professor of Political Science at the University of Minnesota. He is author of "The Practice and Effect of Redistricting," *Political Geography Quarterly* (October 1982), and "Problems of Implementing Redistricting," in B. Grofman et al., eds., *Representation and Redistricting Issues* (Heath, 1982). He is co-author (with Leonard Robins and Scott Eller) of "Issues in Gerrymandering: An Exploratory Measure of Partisan Gerrymandering Applied to Minnesota," *Minnesota Law Review* (January 1987), and "Partisan Gerrymandering in the Post-*Bandemer* Era," *Constitutional Commentary* (Summer 1987). He served on the Minnesota Governor's Bipartisan Commission on Reapportionment in 1964-65 and has been a consultant to counsel litigating reapportionment suits for two decades.

Gordon E. Baker is Professor of Political Science, University of California, Santa Barbara. His books include *The Reapportionment Revolution* (Random House, 1966), and he has served as Consultant to the Special Masters appointed by the California Supreme Court in 1973 to redistrict the State's legislative and congressional districts. His most recent articles on reapportionment include "Whatever Happened to the Reapportionment Revolution in the United States?," in B. Grofman and A. Lijphart (eds.), *Electoral Laws and Their Political Consequences* (Agathon, 1986), and "Judicial Determination of Political Gerrymandering: A Totality of Circumstances Approach," *Journal of Law and Politics* (1986).

Bruce Cain, Professor of Political Science, California Institute of Technology, is author of *The Reapportionment Puzzle* (University of California Press, 1984) and was a Special Consultant to the California General Assembly Elections and Reapportionment Committee in 1981 and a consultant to the Los Angeles City Council in *U.S. v. City of Los Angeles*. His articles on reapportionment include "Simple vs. Complex Criteria for Partisan Gerrymandering: A Comment on Niemi and Grofman," *UCLA Law Review* (October 1985); and Cain and Janet Campagna, "Predicting Partisan Congressional Redistricting," *Legislative Studies Quarterly* (May 1987).

Scott Eller is a partner in the law firm of Best & Flanagan, Minneapolis, Minnesota. His previous publication on reapportionment was Backstrom, Robins, and Eller, "Issues in Gerrymandering: An Exploratory Measure of Partisan Gerrymandering Applied to Minnesota," *Minnesota Law Review* (1978).

Richard L. Engstrom is Research Professor of Political Science at the University of New Orleans. He has served as an expert witness in numerous federal court cases concerning electoral systems and the representation of racial minorities. Among his most recent articles concerning electoral systems are "District Magnitudes and the Election of Women to the Irish Dail," *Electoral Studies* (1987) and "Repairing the Crack in New Orleans' Black Vote," *Publius* (1986).

Thomas Hofeller is Director of Computer Services for the Republican National Committee, Washington, DC. He was also that Committee's Director of Redistricting in the early 80s. He has served as a consultant in redistricting to legislative committees, political parties, and civil rights organizations in the states of California, Washington, Texas, Minnesota, Illinois, Ohio, Mississippi, North Carolina, New Jersey, Maine, and Massachusetts. A former Associate Director of the Rose Institute at Claremont McKenna College, he designed redistricting databases and information systems for various states including California and Illinois.

Samuel Kernell is Professor of Political Science, University of California, San Diego. His books are *Strategy and Choice in Congressional Elections*, co-authored (Yale University Press, 1983, 2nd edition), *Going Public: New Strategies of Presidential Leadership* (CQ Press, 1986), and *Chief of Staff*, co-authored (University of California Press, 1986). He has authored numerous articles in leading political science journals on the U.S. Congressional elections and voting behavior.

Daniel Hays Lowenstein is Professor of Law, University of California, Los Angeles. He is the co-author of Lowenstein and Jonathan Steinberg, "The Quest for Legislative Districting in the Public Interest: Elusive or Illusory?," *UCLA Law Review* (October 1985), and has served as consultant to the Democratic members of the House of Representatives in the California districting litigation throughout the 1980s. Prior to joining the UCLA law faculty in 1979, he served as the first chair of the California Fair Political Practices Commission from 1975-1979.

Michael D. McDonald is Assistant Professor of Political Science, State University of New York at Binghamton. His articles on electoral systems have appeared in the *American Political Science Review* and the *Journal of Politics*. In addition, he has served as a consultant in court cases involving voting rights claims brought under Section 2 of the Voting Rights Act. His most recent work on electoral systems include: Richard L. Engstrom and McDonald, "The Election of Blacks to Southern City Councils: The Dominant Impact of Electoral Arrangements," in L. Moreland, R. Steed, and T. Baker (eds.), *Blacks in Southern Politics* (Praeger, 1987); and Engstrom and McDonald, "Definitions, Measurements, and Statistics: Weeding Wildgen's Thicket," *The Urban Lawyer* (1988).

Richard Morrill is Professor of Geography and Director, Social Science Institute, University of Washington, Seattle. His books include *Political Redistricting and Geographic Theory* (Association of American Geographers, 1981). He was the Special Master to redistrict the congressional and legislative districts of Washington in 1982 and was a consultant to the State of Mississippi (legislative redistricting for racial fairness). Articles on redistricting include "On Criteria and Redistricting," *Washington Law Review* (1973) and "Redistricting, Region, and Representation," *Political Geography Quarterly* (1987). He is a member of the King County, Washington, Boundary Review Board and consultant to the Washington State Local Government Commission.

Richard G. Niemi is Professor of Political Science and Distinguished Professor of Graduate Teaching at the University of Rochester. He has written both about the theory of districting in Niemi and John Deegan, "A Theory of Political Districting," *American Political Science Review* (1978) and in "The Relationship between Votes and Seats," *UCLA Law Review* (October 1985); and about other aspects of districting in Niemi, Lynda Powell, and Patricia Bicknel, "The Effect of Community-Congressional District Congruity on Knowledge of Congressional Candidates," *Legislative Studies Quarterly* (1986) and other articles. He recently served as an expert witness in a districting case.

Leonard Robins is Professor of Public Administration, Roosevelt University, Chicago. In the field of reapportionment he has co-authored with Charles Backstrom and Scott Eller, "Issues in Gerrymandering: An Exploratory Measure of Partisan Gerrymandering Applied to Minnesota," *Minnesota Law Review* (1978), and "Partisan Gerrymandering in the Post *Davis v. Bandemer* Era," *Constitutional Commentary* (1987). He has co-authored with Charles Backstrom, "The Supreme Court Prohibits Gerrymandering: A Gain or Loss for the States?," *Publius* (1987).

Peter Schuck is the Simeon E. Baldwin Professor of Law, Yale Law School. His books include *Agent Orange on Trial: Mass Toxic Disasters in the Courts* (Belknap/Harvard University Press, enlarged edition, 1987), *Citizenship Without Consent: Illegal Aliens in the American Polity* (Yale University Press, 1985, with Rogers Smith), *Suing Government: Citizen Remedies for Official Wrongs* (Yale University Press, 1983), and *The Judiciary Committees* (Viking, 1975). His most recent articles on voting rights are "The Thickest Thicket: Partisan Gerrymandering and Judicial Regulation of Politics," *Columbia Law Review* (November 1987) and "What Went Wrong with the Voting Rights Act?," *The Washington Monthly* (November 1987).

John Wilkerson is a Ph.D. candidate in Political Science at the University of Rochester. His areas of interest include legislative behavior, public policy, and quantitative methods.

Stephen G. Wright is a Ph.D. candidate in Political Science at the University of Rochester. His fields of specialization include electoral studies, political parties, and research methodology. His current research interests focus on electoral systems and party competition.

Introduction

1

Unresolved Issues in Partisan Gerrymandering Litigation

Bernard Grofman

In 1984, in *Bandemer v. Davis*, 603 F. Supp. 1479, a federal district court held (by a 2 to 1 vote) that the 1981 Republican-drawn redistricting plans for both chambers of the Indiana legislature were unconstitutional, because, as intentional partisan gerrymanders, they violated the Fourteenth Amendment rights of the Democratic party (the minority party in the state legislature). In *Davis v. Bandemer*, 106 S. Ct 2797,_____U.S._____(1986), the U.S. Supreme Court affirmed (6 to 3) that partisan gerrymandering was justiciable, but confounded most experts by also reversing (by a 7 to 2 vote) the lower court findings that the Indiana plans were unconstitutional gerrymanders.

Davis v. Bandemer is potentially the most important redistricting case since *Reynolds v. Sims*, 377 U.S. 533 (1964), because it opens to judicial review the only aspect of redistricting that had been seemingly immune from judicial scrutiny, the intentional partisan gerrymander (cf. Baker, 1986b; Engstrom, 1977). Despite its clear declaration that partisan gerrymandering *is* justiciable, *Davis v. Bandemer* has given rise to considerable scholarly dispute over what the test of unconstitutional political gerrymandering will ultimately prove to be.

Because *Davis v. Bandemer* lacks a majority opinion, and because it rejected the District Court claim that both Indiana legislative plans had been shown to be unconstitutional gerrymanders, interpreting the *Davis* ruling is difficult.[1] Headlines in the press proclaimed variously "Court Disallows Gerrymandering" (*Los Angeles Times*, July 1, 1986) and "Justices Uphold Partisan Lines in Districting" (*New York Times*, July 1, 1986). An Op-Ed column in the *Washington Post* (Edsall, 1986) asserted, "As for which party prevails it depends upon whom

3

you ask." There are few features of the *Davis* opinion that most scholars agree on, other than that the evidentiary threshold for establishing a constitutionally invalid districting plan will be quite high.

The contributors to this volume were asked to provide their interpretations of the meaning of *Davis v. Bandemer* and to review its
implications in terms of a theory of democratic representation, in
terms of the constitutional issues it raises; and, in more practical
terms, as to its probable consequences for redistricting in the 1990s
and for partisan balance of power in Congress, state legislatures, and
those units of local and state government that make use of partisan
multiseat elections. There are six key issues that are unresolved.

First, is there a coherent theory of constitutional adjudication of
partisan gerrymandering claims enunciated in *Davis v. Bandemer*? The
most common answer is no. In the words of the *Congressional Quarterly* (July 19, 1986, p. 1641), *Davis v. Bandemer* gave "disgruntled
political groups a hunting license for redistricting plans they dislike,
but left them in the dark as to how to bag one." Most of those who
hold this view believe that we must look to future cases to understand
what *Davis* really means. Grofman (chapter 3) and Lowenstein
(chapter 4) are among the few authors who argue that there is a clear
and consistent interpretation of *Davis v. Bandemer*. However, the interpretations they offer are very different. Lowenstein argues that
Davis v. Bandemer is meant to preserve the status quo ante by leaving
open the possibility of intervention in the most extreme of cases, but
ruling out intervention in any litigation brought by a major political
party. Grofman argues that *Davis v. Bandemer* sets forth a straightforward three-pronged test for partisan gerrymandering: that it be intentional, severe, and predictably long-lasting in its consequences.

Second, is implementing a proportional representation standard
the only viable way to avoid partisan gerrymandering? This claim is
made by Levinson (1985) and by Schuck (1987; chapter 11). It is rejected by Lowenstein (chapter 4, note 1), who is otherwise sympathetic to Schuck's position, and by most of the other authors in this
volume. In my view, in racial vote dilution cases such as *Thornburg v.
Gingles*, 106 S. Ct. 2752 (1986), the courts have been able to specify a
standard for judging racial vote dilution that is not equivalent to
requiring proportional representation, and analogous tests can be
devised in the partisan gerrymandering case (see esp. Grofman,
chapter 3). However, other authors (e.g., Lowenstein and Steinberg,
1985; Lowenstein, chapter 4; Cain, 1985b) argue that no manageable
standards for detecting or remedying partisan gerrymandering exist.

Third, how could the Supreme Court have held partisan gerrymandering to be justiciable and yet have failed to strike down Indiana's legislative plans as unconstitutional gerrymanders (especially the seemingly egregious House plan, including multimember districts that extended beyond the Marion County line)? There are three answers offered to this question. The most common answer is "Beats me!" Most who give this answer would regard even the plurality opinion in the Supreme Court decision in *Davis v. Bandemer* as internally contradictory. The second answer is that offered by Lowenstein (chapter 4). According to him the fact that the Indiana Democrats were not completely "shut out" of the overall political process in the state explains the Supreme Court's unwillingness to consider their Fourteenth Amendment rights to have been violated. My answer is a different one. As someone familiar with the case facts in *Bandemer* (where I was an expert witness for the state of Indiana), I focus in chapter 3 on the evidentiary features (noncompetitive elections, seat losses for the minority party, reliable projections of future results, etc.) that are *missing* from the *Bandemer* trial record. As Justice White said in his plurality opinion in *Davis v. Bandemer*, at 2812:

> Relying on a single election to prove unconstitutional discrimination is unsatisfactory. The District Court observed, and the parties do not disagree, that Indiana is a swing State. Voters sometimes prefer Democratic candidates, and sometimes Republican. The District Court did not find that because of the 1981 Act the Democrats could not in one of the next few elections secure a sufficient vote to take control of the assembly. Indeed, the District Court declined to hold that the 1982 election results were the predictable consequences of the 1981 Act and expressly refused to hold that those results were a reliable prediction of future ones. The District Court did not ask by what percentage the statewide Democratic vote would have had to increase to control either the House or the Senate. The appellants argue here, without a persuasive response from appellees, that had the Democratic candidates received an additional few percentage points of the votes cast statewide, they would have obtained a majority of the seats in both houses. Nor was there any finding that the 1981 reapportionment would consign the Democrats to a minority status in the Assembly throughout the 1980s or that the Democrats would have no hope of doing any better in the reapportionment that would occur after the 1990 census. Without findings of this nature, the District Court erred in concluding that the 1981 Act violated the Equal Protection Clause.

Fourth, how is disproportionality of election results to be measured in the case of political parties? Here there are two standard methods. One is the comparison of election outcomes with the voting patterns in (statewide) baseline elections, as described by Backstrom, Robins, and Eller (1978; chapter 6). The second is the comparison of seat percentages and vote percentages in the actual election at issue (see, e.g., Tufte, 1973; Niemi, chapter 7). Regardless of which comparison we make, we may choose to focus either on bias, which is a measure of symmetry in the treatment of the voters for each party's candidates (see, e.g., Tufte, 1973; Grofman, 1983b; Niemi and Deegan, 1978); or on the responsiveness of changes in seat percentages to changes in the votes received by a party's candidates (or to changes in baseline party strength). One measure of responsiveness is the swing ratio (Tufte, 1973; Taagepera, 1986; Niemi, chapter 7). In my view (Grofman, chapter 3; see also Grofman, 1985b; Owen and Grofman, 1987), both the seats-votes and the baseline method can provide valuable information about the existence of partisan gerrymandering, but both usually need to be supplemented by analysis of the differential treatment of each party's incumbents through techniques such as incumbent displacement. How severe disproportionality must be before it rises to the level of a constitutional violation remains an open question.

Fifth, is gerrymandering to be judged in terms of its methods (e.g., ill-compact districts, violation of political boundaries, unequally populated districts, fragmentation of communities of interest) or its results (the minimizing or canceling out of the voting strength of a racial or political group)? Wells (1981), Horn et al. (1988), and other reformers argue that we can best cure gerrymandering by imposing strict "neutral" standards. While I certainly have no objections to the use of such standards in redistricting, I do not believe that the imposition of such standards can rule out the possibility of gerrymandering. However, like Baker (chapter 2) and Morrill (chapter 10) I believe that violation of neutral districting criteria can provide (prima facie) evidence of gerrymandering and is directly relevant to intent (cf. Justice Stevens' opinion in *Karcher v. Daggett I*, 103 S. Ct. 2653, and Grofman, 1985a). However, for me, it is evidence of the actual or projected partisan (or racial) consequences that is critical.

Sixth, what will be the long-run implications of *Bandemer* for redistricting in the 1990s and thereafter? Mann (1987) suggests that the practical importance of Bandemer has been much exaggerated both by its supporters and by opponents. Because it seeks to rule out only plans whose effect is to "consistently degrade a voter's or a group of voters' influence on the political process as a whole," and because it does not touch bipartisan gerrymandering, Mann argues that, at least for congressional districting, it is likely to be relevant in only a handful of states, such as California. I share this view.

The essays in this volume reflect a range of views, and taken in toto, cover all of the questions discussed above. In the introductory section of this volume, in the essay after this one, Gordon Baker argues that *Bandemer* is the logical culmination of a quest for "fair and effective representation" that began with *Baker v. Carr*. As should be apparent from my earlier remarks, this is a view that I strongly share. Baker also notes that while terms like justice and equality are hard to define, it is often easy to recognize blatant examples of injustice or inequality. In like manner, courts reviewing alleged gerrymandering can confine themselves to striking down only the most egregious instances.

The second section of the book offers several conflicting views of "What Does *Bandemer* Mean?" Daniel Lowenstein argues that the confusion over what *Bandemer* means results not from any deficiency in setting forth "standards," but rather from Justice White's failure to make explicit the conceptual basis for the newly recognized partisan gerrymandering constitutional claim. Consideration of Justice White's opinion and its relation to the malapportionment cases, the racial discrimination cases, and the general framework of Equal Protection doctrine leads Lowenstein to conclude: "*Bandemer* does not make partisan gerrymandering as such unconstitutional, but makes it an unconstitutional weapon when used against certain groups," namely, groups that he characterizes (in the addendum to his essay) as "outcast" political groups.

Grofman, in contrast to most other scholars, argues that there really is a concrete test of partisan gerrymandering outlined in *Bandemer*, and that to understand it one must look in detail at why the Supreme Court majority rejected the lower court finding that Indiana's legislative plans were unconstitutional gerrymanders. In particular, Grofman focuses on the absence of evidence that the Indiana plans were not sufficiently competitive so as to leave open the possibility of a future reversal of partisan control and the absence of any predictions of future election results accepted as reliable by the district court. For Grofman, the key phrase in *Bandemer* is "*consistently* degrade a voter's or a group of voters' influence on the political process as a whole" (p. 2810, emphasis added). Grofman also seeks to demonstrate that it is possible to integrate the Supreme Court and other federal court rulings in racial vote dilution cases with the views of Justice White in *Davis v. Bandemer* so as to develop a coherent theory of both racial and political gerrymandering.

Bruce Cain (Chapter 5) looks at *Bandemer* from the perspectives of the political practitioner, the democratic theorist, and the reformer. A critical point in Cain's chapter is that both *Davis v. Bandemer* and *Thornburg v. Gingles* raise fundamental questions about the role of groups in American democracy.

In the third section, "How to Measure Partisan Gerrymandering," proponents of several different approaches discuss how courts could make practical use of social science tools of analysis to define and measure gerrymandering. Most authors in this section share the belief that this is both a doable task and a desirable one for courts to undertake. Charles Backstrom, Scott Robins, and Steven Eller review and extend the arguments in their influential 1978 *Minnesota Law Review* article to consider how a statewide baseline for partisan voting strength can be established that would provide a standard against which gerrymandering could be judged. Richard Niemi reviews and extends his earlier work on measuring bias in the relationship between a party's share of votes and its share of legislative seats. He also responds to arguments of critics (e.g., Cain, 1985b; Lowenstein and Steinberg, 1985) of this approach.

McDonald and Engstrom draw on their own extensive work on racial gerrymandering to look at related issues in measuring partisan gerrymandering. Gordon Baker, too, draws on the racial vote dilution literature to offer an approach to measuring political gerrymandering analogous to the "totality of circumstances" test that has been used in adjudicating cases brought under Section 2 of the Voting Rights Act (as amended in 1982). Richard Morrill, a leading political geographer, provides another perspective on gerrymandering, as well as a discussion of his recent empirical work on partisan and geographic features of 1980s congressional plans.

Peter Schuck, in contrast, argues that federal courts should have resisted the temptation to meddle with the partisan aspects of redistricting because it is a task for which they are ill-suited and because it forces judges into a "standardless" quagmire, or into reliance on a proportional representation standard foreign to our system of government.

The last two sections of this volume deal with applications to specific state legislative or congressional plans of some of the methodologies discussed in the third section. Richard Niemi and Stephen Wright look at seats-votes relationships under the Indiana legislative plans that were challenged in *Bandemer*. Niemi and John Wilkerson examine the compactness of the challenged single-member and multimember districts in the Indiana House. They look at two distinct aspects of compactness: one perimeter-based and the other based on areal dispersion.

Samuel Kernell and Bernard Grofman look at the consistency of partisan voting patterns in California at the census tract level, over a number of different elections and election types. They argue that, in

California, it is readily possible to identify areas of Republican and Democratic voting strength even in areas as small as the census tract— information that can then be used for purposes of partisan gerrymandering to predict probable long-run consequences of districting plans. Thomas Hofeller and Bernard Grofman consider three different types of compactness measures: perimeter-based, areal-dispersion-based, and population-dispersion-based, and apply them to compactness comparisons of three different California congressional plans, one drawn by a state court and two drawn by a Democratically controlled legislature. They find the court-drawn plan to be the most compact of the three plans under all three compactness measures.

This volume is intended to be a largely self-contained overview of the key issues and the key arguments concerning political gerrymandering. However, the essays in this book are meant to be read in conjunction with those in the October 1985 issue of the *UCLA Law Review*. Articles in that issue, by Richard Niemi, Daniel Lowenstein, and Jonathan Steinberg, and myself, and comments by Bruce Cain and Martin Shapiro, and Sanford Levenson, deal with districting criteria in general and partisan gerrymandering and the District Court opinion in *Bandemer* in particular. Because these essays deal with the state of redistricting case law pre-*Davis v. Bandemer* and pre-*Thornburg v. Gingles*, they provide a useful complement to those in this volume. Other relevant material is contained in the Summer 1985 *PS* "Minisymposium on Political Gerrymandering." The essays in *PS*, most based on expert witness affidavits in *Badham v. Eu* (D. California, 1983), remain among the most sophisticated political science analyses of the partisan gerrymandering issue written to date.

The essays in this volume were written before the U.S. Supreme Court refused in October 1988 to hear an appeal of the dismissal of the *Badham* complaint. The District Court dismissal of *Badham* does not settle any of the unresolved questions about *Bandemer* discussed elsewhere in this essay.

NOTE

1. It may be difficult to separate the views of scholars as to the desirability of judicial intervention to remedy even the most egregious cases of political gerrymandering from their views of what *Davis v. Bandemer* means. I see in *Bandemer* an opportunity to steer a careful course between an inaction that will guarantee abuse of constitutionally protected rights and an overreaction that will embroil the federal courts in a host of petty disputes about "politics as usual."

2

The Unfinished Reapportionment Revolution

Gordon E. Baker

Toward the end of his life, Thomas Jefferson observed that "the generation which commences a revolution rarely completes it."[1] The author of the Declaration of Independence here alluded to the difficulty of translating animating purposes or ideals into practice.

With this in mind, we might ponder the course of the reapportionment revolution in the quarter century since 1962. Now that state legislative and congressional constituencies reflect close (at times almost precise) population equalities, does this indicate that the goals of this major institutional transformation have been fulfilled?

To answer this question, we must first probe the underlying conceptual framework of the decisions that Earl Warren later termed the most significant of his sixteen-year tenure as Chief Justice. Was the point of the one person, one vote rulings simply that of establishing equipopulous districts? A careful reading of these landmark opinions reveals more basic animating purposes, with population equality merely a means to the end.

In a much-quoted passage in the 1964 case of *Reynolds v. Sims*, 377 U.S. 533 (1964), Chief Justice Warren asserted that "the achieving of fair and effective representation for all citizens is concededly the basic aim of reapportionment" (pp. 565–566). But what constitutes "fair and effective representation"? The opinions of Warren and others in 1964 suggest at least three interrelated components: political equality of individual voters; majority rule rather than oligarchy; representative institutions that can reflect significant shifts in public opinion.

The Warren Court's approach to reapportionment revealed a profound judicial reassessment of the relationship between citizens and their state governments. The viewpoint expressed in 1946 (*Colegrove v. Green*, 328 U.S. 549 (1946)) by Justice Felix Frankfurter regarded legislative apportionment as a problem of governmental structure, deeply intertwined with politics, concluding that courts should not interfere with the prerogatives of the states regarding their own institutions (or of a coequal branch in the case of congressional districts). In contrast, the interpretation expressed by the Warren Court majority began at a different point in the political process—the individual. Representative equality is regarded as an aspect of voting rights, as necessary of judicial protection as other guarantees of equality.

Various excerpts from the 1964 reapportionment decisions illustrate this point. The Court applied the one person, one vote principle to congressional districts under Article I, with Justice Hugo Black declaring: "The right to vote is too important in our free society to be stripped of judicial protection." (*Wesberry v. Sanders*, 376 U.S. 1 (1964), p. 7). Four months later, the same basic premise undergirded the Court's disposition of several state legislative cases under the Fourteenth Amendment. In the lead case of *Reynolds v. Sims*, Chief Justice Warren noted, "Undoubtedly, the right of suffrage is a fundamental matter in a free and democratic society. Especially since the right to exercise the franchise in a free and unimpaired manner is preservative of other basic civil and political rights, any alleged infringement of the right of citizens to vote must be carefully and meticulously scrutinized." He added that "the right to elect legislators in a free .and unimpaired fashion is a bedrock of our political system" (p. 562).

While this approach may have seemed new at the time, it actually reiterated conceptions going back to the nation's founding. As early as 1787, the Northwest Ordinance, providing for the future governance of the territory west of the Appalachians, stipulated that its inhabitants "shall always be entitled to the benefits of the writs of habeas corpus and of the trial by jury, of a proportionate representation of the people in the legislature, and of judicial proceedings according to the course of the common law."[2] The second conceptual support for the 1964 decisions is the ultimate reliance on majority rather than minority control of representative institutions. This point is best stated by Warren in these words: "Logically, in a society ostensibly grounded on representative government, it would seem reasonable that a majority of the people of a State could elect a majority of that State's legislators" (*Reynolds*, p. 565). Yet the majoritarian element, as viewed by the Court's majority, must in case of conflict yield to the first principle of equal voting rights for individuals. This was clearly demonstrated in the case decided June 15, 1964, involving

Colorado's legislature, the decision that more than any other focused on the question of majority rule. In all the companion cases the lack of any realistic remedy to malapportionment posed a convincing case for judicial consideration. But the apportionment formula challenged in Colorado was itself the product of an initiative petition ratified in 1962 in all counties of the state, including Denver. Moreover, the new state constitutional amendment established a lower house based on population and entailed comparatively modest deviations from population equality in the Senate. Finally, to make the issue even sharper, the voters at the same election had rejected an alternative amendment that would have based both houses strictly on population.

The decision holding the Colorado plan unconstitutional reflects the newly expressed judicial philosophy that the basic issue at stake in legislative apportionment is the right of the individual to cast an equally weighted vote. As for the fact that Colorado's voters had specifically chosen a less equipopulous districting plan, Warren answered for the Court: "A citizen's constitutional rights can hardly be infringed simply because a majority of the people choose to do so" (*Lucas v. The Forty-Fourth General Assembly of the State of Colorado*, 377 U.S. 713 (1964), pp. 736–737).

A more complex position in the Colorado case was argued by Justice Potter Stewart (joined by Justice Tom C. Clark), who refused to accept the first premise of equal individual voting rights but asserted that the Equal Protection Clause does restrict state legislative apportionments in two ways: They must be rational in the light of each state's own characteristics and needs; and they must not be so constructed as "systematically to prevent ultimate effective majority rule" (pp. 753–754). Applying these criteria, Stewart and Clark dissented from the rulings in Colorado and some other states, while concurring in the results of others.

The third component in the 1964 decisions was the expectation that representative institutions should not be static, but rather should be responsive to shifts in public opinion. In *Reynolds*, the Court put the matter this way: "Since legislatures are responsible for enacting laws by which all citizens are to be governed, they should be bodies which are collectively responsive to the popular will." Indeed, it is this aspect that explains why Earl Warren, in retirement, singled out the reapportionment cases as the most important of his career on the bench. If all citizens had equally valued votes in an apportionment system, he reasoned, then the political process could resolve pressing policy problems (Warren, 1972, p. C43; Warren, 1977, pp. 307–310). Yet the courts must be in a position to determine whether representative equality exists. A recent biography perceptively notes: "Behind Warren's vote [with the majority in *Baker v. Carr*] . . . was a conviction that judicial deference to legislators in reapportionment matters was a sham because those possessing disproportionate power in a legislature had no incentives to surrender it" (White, 1982, p. 237).

These three components of the basic reasoning underlying the 1964 cases are interrelated and reinforce each other, even though they may at times involve potential conflicts. Warren apparently regarded such values as being compatible, stating that "the democratic ideals of equality and majority rule, which have served this Nation so well in the past, are hardly of any less significance for the present and the future" (*Reynolds*, p. 566). Yet some tension between individual voter equality and majority rule was present in the Colorado case. Whether one focuses on Warren's insistence on voter equality whenever the values may conflict, or on the Stewart-Clark formula of "ultimate effective majority rule," the outcome is a conditioned majoritarianism. And this in turn suggests a process of continuing majority formation—an institutional framework that is responsive to changes in public opinion as majority sentiments may shift over the years.

The controlling philosophy articulated by the Supreme Court in *Reynolds v. Sims* left a considerable amount of flexibility in implementing the concept of representative equality. "We realize," said Chief Justice Warren, "that it is a practical impossibility to arrange legislative districts so that each one has an identical number of residents, or citizens, or voters. Mathematical exactness or precision is hardly a workable constitutional requirement" (p. 578). The opinion pointedly disavowed any uniform standard, applicable throughout the nation. "What is marginally permissible in one state," the opinion continued, "may be unsatisfactory in another, depending on the particular circumstances of the case" (p. 578). This note of relativity implies that varying circumstances other than mere population may validly be given some attention by states. A specific example is then provided by the Court:

> A State may legitimately desire to maintain the integrity of various political subdivisions, insofar as possible, and provide for compact districts of contiguous territory in designing a legislative apportionment scheme. Valid considerations may underlie such aims. Indiscriminate districting, without any regard for political subdivisions or natural or historical boundary lines, may be little more than an open invitation to partisan gerrymandering. . . . Whatever the means of accomplishment, the overriding objective must be substantial equality of population among the various districts, so that the vote of any citizen is approximately equal in

weight to that of any other citizen in the State. . . . So long as the divergences from a strict population standard are based on legitimate considerations incident to the effectuation of a rational state policy, some deviations from the equal-population principle are constitutionally permissible with respect to the apportionment of seats in either or both of the two houses of a bicameral state legislature. (*Reynolds*, pp. 578–579).

The highest tribunal went on to express confidence that lower courts could work out specific and appropriate standards in the context of actual litigation on a case-by-case basis. Needless to say, these 1964 Supreme Court decisions yielded less than clear-cut guidelines for others to follow. For example, in the Colorado case, the Court, while finding the total bicameral representation pattern nonseverable, suggested that the lower house, standing by itself, was "at least arguably apportioned substantially on a population basis" (*Lucas*, p. 730). The House districts in Colorado deviated from average population by plus 30% to minus 24.4%. However, to the extent that population percentage deviations were mentioned by lower courts, the most common acceptable range was plus 15% to minus 15% (Baker, 1968, p. 293).

As early as the 1966 term, such an approximate range of population equality among districts encountered difficulty on appeal when the Supreme Court reversed lower court determinations in three key cases. And, whereas the burden of proof had formerly rested with the plaintiff to show that a redistricting plan was invalid, that burden was now shifted to the state to justify any "significant" population inequalities. The late Professor Robert G. Dixon, Jr., gave this perceptive explanation of the shift from apparent flexibility in 1964 to increasingly more stringent expectations:

> Two tactical factors contributed. First, the courts began to insist that all population deviations be justified in terms of a consistent, logical application of identifiable state policies. This was a practical impossibility, both because all law-making, including redistricting, is a compromise and adjustment process and not an exercise in logic, and more importantly, because nonpopulation policies—even a policy of following political subdivision lines insofar as practicable—cannot be made objective. Second, it was always easy for a plaintiff to offer a slightly more "equal" plan than the official state plan (albeit also more palatable to the plaintiff's political interests which motivated his suit). Hence, there was pressure on the state to move in the direction of ever-tighter equality in order to maximize the chances of prevailing in court, but plaintiffs still frequently prevailed with last-minute "tighter" plans. (Dixon, 1980–1981, p. 844)

Soon, the Warren Court split over whether its principal concern should be the goal of "achieving fair and effective representation for all citizens" or the more manageable but misleading exercise of equating representation with equipopulous districts. The latter course may have seemed to some justices to be the logical application of an individual parity suggested by the phrase, "one person, one vote." Yet it ignores important obstacles to achieving anything more than a proximate degree of equality. For one thing, no census can provide a perfect count of population. Births, deaths, and mobility reveal a state of flux rather than a static pattern. Further, some individuals are missed, again beyond complete control, especially in a country as vast and populous as the United States. The Bureau of the Census estimated that in 1970 it had undercounted approximately 2.5% of the nation's actual inhabitants, or 5.3 million persons. Nor was inaccuracy evenly distributed, geographically or racially (nonwhites were undercounted by an estimated 7.7%). In spite of determined efforts by the Bureau of the Census to reduce imprecision to a minimum, it is unclear whether the 1980 Census figures were much closer to reality.[3] Finally, legislative redistricting statutes typically go into effect two or more years after this inexact counting of heads, further compounded by intervening population mobility. Such divergences from "perfect population equality" bulk considerably larger than the variance ranges deemed unacceptable by some members of the Court.

In spite of this, the United States Supreme Court in 1969 rejected a congressional districting plan in Missouri with population deviations ranging from plus 3.13% to minus 2.84%, and an average variation of 1.6%. Writing for the Court, Justice William Brennan insisted that a state must make a good-faith effort "to achieve precise mathematical equality," that any disparities, "no matter how small" had to be justified (*Kirkpatrick v. Preisler*, 394 U.S. 526 (1969), pp. 530–531). In a companion case, a New York congressional districting with population variances ranging from plus 6.49% to minus 6.61% was also invalidated. As a result, both Missouri and New York were ordered to draw new district lines, based on 1960 Census data nearly a decade old, for use in one election only—1970—prior to a new decennial redistricting.

Concern over the Court's approach was thoughtfully expressed by Justice Byron White, in his first dissent in an apportionment case. White reminded his brethren of the earlier caveats in *Reynolds v. Sims* that indiscriminate districting could be an open invitation to partisan gerrymandering. He cogently concluded:

> Today's decision on the one hand requires precise adherence to admittedly inexact census figures, and on the other downgrades a restraint on a far greater potential threat to equality of representation, the gerryman-

der. Legislatures intent on minimizing the representation of selected political or racial groups are invited to ignore political boundaries and compact districts so long as they adhere to population equality among districts using standards which we know and they know are sometimes quite incorrect. I see little merit in such a confusion of priorities. (*Wells v. Rockefeller*, 394 U.S. 542 (1969), pp. 544–555)

The 1972 Term of the Supreme Court marked a significant turning point back to more flexible guidelines in state legislative apportionment. Yet no precedent was overturned, since congressional districting standards remained stringent following the 1969 cases just discussed. Perhaps as important as the four decisions was the judicial mood. While the Court made it clear that legislative districting would remain subject to judicial scrutiny, it made even more evident its hope that such recourse could be minimized, now that the guidelines of tolerable constitutional limits were reasonably clear. In Justice White's words, the high tribunal should recognize the "eminently reasonable approach of *Reynolds v. Sims*" (*Gaffney v. Cummings*, 412 U.S. 735 (1973), p. 749).

In the first of these 1972–73 cases, the Supreme Court overruled a Federal District Court's holding that a recent redistricting of the Virginia House of Delegates strayed too far from the equal population principle, with a maximum overall population variance of 16.4% (plus 9.6 to minus 6.8). The Court found the apportionment to be "within tolerable constitutional limits," since the population deviations resulted from a legitimate state policy of consistently maintaining the integrity of political subdivision (city and county) lines. "While this percentage may well approach tolerable limits, we do not believe it exceeds them," declared Justice William Rehnquist, speaking for the Court (*Mahan v. Howell*, 410 U.S. 315 (1973), p. 329).

Near the end of the term, on June 16, 1973, the Supreme Court handed down the three remaining reapportionment decisions. One involved congressional redistricting in Texas, the other two, state legislative constituencies in Texas and Connecticut. In the latter two cases, the overall percentage variances from precise population equality were smaller than in Virginia—7.8% (plus 3.93 to minus 3.90) in Connecticut and 9.9% (plus 5.8 to minus 4.1) in Texas—but in neither instance was there the rationale of systematically preserving local boundaries as in the Virginia case. "Very likely," the Court suggested, "larger differences would not be tolerable without justification" (*White v. Regester*, 412 U.S. 755 (1973), p. 764)—but such variance ranges alone do not present prima facie instances of invidious discrimination. In the Texas congressional districting case, as in the other three, the Court drew a distinction between the greater population flexibility permitted for state legislative constituencies and the more precise standard ("as mathematically equal as reasonably possible" (*White v. Weiser*, 412 U.S. 783 (1973)) expected for congressional districts.

Indeed, such language by Justice White, writing for the majority in *White v. Weiser*, seems clearly at odds with the contrary views he had expressed so eloquently in dissent in the Missouri and New York congressional cases only four years earlier. Moreover, with several new colleagues who clearly did not share Justice Brennan's penchant for population precision, Justice White seemingly had the votes for more flexibility in congressional districting as well. Yet he may have been reluctant to abandon the doctrine of stare decisis, especially with so recent a precedent. Then, too, the Court majority had carefully emphasized the distinction between congressional and state legislative districting in order to attain a more reasonable standard in the latter category.

These 1973 decisions reflected a return to the animating principles expressed in 1964, with frequent references to the language in *Reynolds v. Sims*. Moreover, Justice White reiterated the basic philosophical concern in the ideal of fair and effective representation, now reformulated as "political fairness." In the Connecticut state legislative case of *Gaffney v. Cummings*, White noted approvingly a state apportionment board's specific use of political data in fashioning a districting pattern designed to achieve political fairness "because it undertakes, not to minimize or eliminate the political strength of any group or party, but to recognize it and, through districting, provide a rough sort of proportional representation in the legislative halls of the state" (*Gaffney*, p. 754). At the same time, White's opinion tempered this idealism with a candid recognition of political realities. In justifying the use of political data in Connecticut, he noted:

> It may be suggested that those who redistrict and reapportion should work with census, not political, data and achieve population equality without regard for political impact. But this politically mindless approach may produce, whether intended or not, the most grossly gerrymandered results. It is much more plausible to assume that those who redistrict and reapportion work with both political and census data. Within the limits of the population equality standards of the Equal Protection Clause, they seek, through compromise or otherwise, to achieve the political or other ends of the State, its constituents, and its office holders. What is done in so arranging for elections, or to achieve political ends or allocate political power, is not wholly exempt from judicial scrutiny under the Fourteenth Amendment. As we have indicated, for example, multimember districts

may be vulnerable, if racial or political groups have been fenced out of the political process and their voting strength invidiously minimizes. (*Gaffney*, pp. 753–754)

This reference to "racial or political groups" in need of judicial protection kept alive the possibility that political maldistricting might eventually be held justiciable, as had racial gerrymandering for a long time (*Gomillion v. Lightfoot*, 364 U.S. 339 (1960)). As early as 1971, the late Robert G. Dixon Jr. had pointed out: "In a functional sense the gerrymandering issue is the same whether the districts are single-member or multi-member—and whether or not a racial factor is present, because racial gerrymandering is simply a particular kind of political gerrymandering" (Dixon, 1971).

Experience following the 1980 Census brought renewed charges of political gerrymandering in several states, again reaching a judicial forum. In 1983, the Supreme Court invalidated New Jersey's 1982 congressional districting, with the plurality decision based on grounds of population inequalities (a plus-to-minus range of less than 0.70% at the extremes, with an average district deviation of less than 0.19%). Speaking for the Court, Justice Brennan echoed his familiar refrain that "the population deviations among districts, although small, were not the result of a good-faith effort to achieve population equality" (*Karcher v. Daggett (I)*, 462 U.S. 725 (1983), p. 727). Noting that the burden of proof lay with the state to justify even small variations in population, the Court elaborated:

> Any number of consistently applied legislative policies might justify some variance, including, for instance, making districts compact, respecting municipal boundaries, preserving the cores of prior districts, and avoiding contests between incumbent Representatives. As long as the criteria are nondiscriminatory . . . these are all legitimate objectives that on a proper showing could justify minor population deviations. . . . The State must, however, show with some specificity that a particular objective required the specific deviations in its plan, rather than simply relying on general assertions. The showing required to justify population deviations is flexible, depending on the size of the deviations, the importance of the State's interests, the consistency with which the plan as a whole reflects those interests, and the availability of alternatives that might substantially vindicate those interests yet approximate population equality more closely. By necessity, whether deviations are justified requires case-by-case attention to these factors. (pp. 740–741)

While the criteria listed are commendable enough, it is also clear that Brennan, at least, had a stringent notion of "minor" deviations. And in any case, legislatures and lower courts dealing with redistricting would invariably regard the kinds of variances in the New Jersey case as excessive.

More revealing and potentially significant was the fact that five justices in that case (Stevens concurring plus four dissenters), *Karcher v. Daggett (I)*, expressed more concern over political gerrymandering than equipopulous districts. The theme of "fair representation" pervaded these opinions. In his concurrence, Justice Stevens insisted that "political gerrymandering is one form of 'vote dilution' that is proscribed by the Equal Protection Clause," adding: "The major shortcoming of the numerical standard is its failure to take account of other relevant—indeed, more important—criteria relating to the fairness of group participation in the political process" (p. 753). Dissenting for himself and three others, Justice White quoted Earl Warren's words in *Reynolds v. Sims* on the basic aim of legislative apportionment, adding: "One must suspend credulity to believe that the Court's draconian response to a trifling 0.6984% maximum deviation promoted 'fair and effective representation' for the people of New Jersey" (p. 766). He reminded his colleagues that phrases such as "as equal as practicable" in 1964 must be understood in the context of the gross malapportionments then existing (e.g., disparities of over three to one among Georgia's congressional districts). Reiterating some of White's views was a separate dissent by Justice Powell, who added: "I do believe . . . that the constitutional mandate of 'fair and effective representation,' Reynolds . . . proscribes apportionment plans that have the purpose and effect of substantially disenfranchising identifiable groups of voters" (p. 788).

In light of the various views advanced in the *Karcher* case, it is not surprising that parties aggrieved by alleged maldistricting should test their claims in court. The time seemed ripe for determining whether political gerrymandering was justiciable. The test came in the 1985 Term of the Supreme Court on an appeal from a Federal District Court decision declaring Indiana's 1981 legislative redistricting an unconstitutional vote dilution by means of a partisan gerrymander. The case was argued on October 7, the first day of the Term, and was not decided until June 30, 1986, shortly before adjournment. Both this long gestation and the written opinions suggest an unusual degree of agonizing on the high tribunal.

Two basic issues were posed in *Davis v. Bandemer*, 106 S. Ct. 2797 (1986), in which Democrats had contended that district lines were drawn by Republicans for partisan advantage: (1) Is political gerrymandering justiciable?; (2) Did the districting in Indiana violate the Constitution's Equal Protection Clause? In a complex division, the

Court answered yes (6-3) to the first question, no (7-2) to the second. The plurality opinion, written by Justice White for himself and three others (Brennan, Marshall, Blackmun), upheld the outcome just noted. Two justices (Powell, Stevens), would have gone further by upholding the justiciability of political gerrymandering claims and applying them to invalidating the Indiana districts. The three remaining jurists (O'Connor, Burger, Rehnquist) regarded such controversies as nonjusticiable and hence upheld the Indiana districts.

The position advanced by Justice Lewis Powell viewed justiciability in political gerrymandering cases as the logical application of the principles found in *Reynolds v. Sims*, with its concern for "fair and effective representation for all citizens" as well as caveats about partisan gerrymandering. Powell's opinion gave attention to Justice Stevens' probing discussion in the recent Karcher case of judicially manageable standards for determining political maldistricting and concluded that the evidence in the Indiana case was sufficient to warrant judicial intervention. At the opposite pole, Justice Sandra Day O'Connor denied the availability of such standards that courts could apply without settling for a form of simple proportionality of party representation. She and Chief Justice Warren Burger (in a brief separate opinion) invoked somewhat nostalgically the spirit of the dissents filed in *Baker v. Carr* in 1962 by Justices Felix Frankfurter and John Marshall Harlan.

The middle position of the plurality group reflected some of the ambivalent concerns earlier expressed by its spokesman, Justice White. On the one hand, he had warned against the Court's becoming "bogged down in a vast, intractable apportionment slough" (*Gaffney*, pp. 749–750) and had insisted that politics could not be extirpated from so political a process as legislative redistricting. On the other hand, he had been attracted by the notion of "political fairness" and had resolutely upheld judicial protection for racial or political groups "if fenced out of the political process and their voting strength invidiously minimized" (pp. 753–754).

The dilemma was resolved by holding political gerrymandering justiciable but attempting to confine judicial scrutiny to boundary manipulation that goes beyond the usual and expected partisanship such as the type apparently indicated by the record in Indiana. White's opinion indicated that "an equal-protection violation may be found only where the electoral system substantially disadvantages certain voters in their opportunity to influence the political process effectively," and that "such a finding of unconstitutionality must be supported by evidence of continued frustration of the will of a majority of the voters or effective denial to a minority of voters of a fair chance to influence the political process" (*Davis v. Bandemer*, p. 2811). The plurality opinion concluded that the mere lack of control of a legislative branch by a statewide majority after a single election does not rise to the requisite level. But, perhaps anticipating an objection that aggrieved voters should not have to wait for additional elections before seeking judicial relief, Justice White carefully noted: "Projected election results based on district boundaries and past voting patterns may certainly support this type of claim, even when no election has yet been held under the challenged districting" (p. 2814).

Reporting of the *Bandemer* decision in various news media may well have conveyed diverse signals to a public unaccustomed to judicial nuances. Some news and editorial accounts stressed the Court's refusal to invalidate Indiana's districting, whereas others focused on the opportunity now open to some contesting boundary manipulation. To this latter group, the Court was apparently indicating that aggrieved parties had to present strong and compelling evidence of discriminatory vote dilution. In the plurality opinion Justice White acknowledged: "We recognize that our own view may be difficult of application. Determining when an electoral system has been 'arranged in a manner that will consistently degrade a voter's or a group of voters' influence on the political process as a whole' . . . is of necessity a difficult inquiry." Yet the opinion did not share Justice O'Connor's "apparent lack of faith in the lower courts' abilities to distinguish between disproportionality per se and the lack of fair representation that continued disproportionality in conjunction with other indicia may demonstrate" (p. 2816). The kinds of circumstances that might be persuasive in the future can be inferred from what was not sufficiently shown in the Indiana case. White noted:

> The District Court did not find that because of the 1981 Act the Democrats could not in one of the next few elections secure a sufficient vote to take control of the assembly. Indeed, the District Court declined to hold that the 1982 election results were the predictable consequences of the 1981 Act and expressly refused to hold that those results were a reliable prediction of future ones. The District Court did not ask by what percentage the statewide Democratic vote would have had to increase to control either the House or the Senate. The appellants argue here, without a persuasive response from appellees, that had the Democratic candidates received an additional few percentage points of the votes cast statewide, they would have obtained a majority of the seats in both houses. Nor was there any finding that the 1981 reapportionment would consign the Democrats to a minority status in the Assembly throughout the 1980s or that the Democrats would have no hope of doing any better in the reappor-

tionment that would occur after the 1990 Census. Without findings of this nature, the District Court erred in concluding that the 1981 Act violated the Equal Protection Clause. (p. 2812)

The Court's caution in extending justiciability to political gerrymandering is understandable, since indentifying excessive boundary manipulation and fashioning remedies are more intricate than dealing with population inequalities. At the same time, Justice White has suggested the kinds of indicators that courts could prudently consider in determining possible vote dilution. A careful judicial weighing of the "totality of circumstances"—an approach that has been utilized successfully in cases of racial gerrymandering—could resolve the more serious threats to "fair representation" (see chapter 9).

That ideal, set forth in *Reynolds v. Sims*, has persisted in subsequent judicial expressions, especially in the *Karcher (I)* case of 1983 and the *Bandemer* decision of 1986. These may well have reflected a heightened sensitivity over increasingly elaborate maldistricting in a number of states. Prior legal prohibitions on breaking county and city lines had already been nullified by the need to construct districts of virtually equal population. The use of computers brought a new degree of sophistication as incumbents drew equipopulous districts for perpetual partisan advantage. The results were likely to be far more durable than the comparatively crude guesswork that formerly characterized even the more professional efforts at political cartography. Hence, the contemporary partisan gerrymander presents an essentially "new" problem rather than simply a venerable practice typically designated in press accounts.

Yet the lofty goal of "fair and effective representation" set forth by Earl Warren in 1964 involves, as do many other ideals, certain internal contradictions. Critics stress the elusive and unattainable nature of "fairness" and the fact that some of its desiderata are incompatible. It must be conceded, for example, that a large number of competitive districts maximizes effective voter choice, but works against such values as rough proportionality of party representation and, often, of communities of interest as well. Is there an effective response to this skeptical approach, an approach that aims to remove "fairness" as an operative ideal at all?

Perhaps we can retain the viability of "fairness" if we approach the question from the opposite direction and look at unfairness. We might take a leaf from the late Edmond N. Cahn's provocative book, *The Sense of Injustice* (Cahn, 1949). Here Cahn pointed to the endless quest for an abstract ideal of "justice" from the early Greek philosophers through more recent natural law theorists. Much like the concept of "fairness," that of "justice" seems incapable of satisfactory definition or application. Cahn imaginatively turned the inquiry around by depicting a series of real-life instances that would evoke a strong consensus—a "sense of injustice."

By the same token, we should approach the question of "fairness" in apportionment by depicting real-world instances that evoke a "sense of unfairness." Even philosopher-kings with the noblest of motives would find impossible the task of designing a districting scheme that is completely fair to all interested groups and individuals. But the impossibility of perfection should not be allowed to paralyze attempts to identify and ameliorate the most egregious gerrymanders, the clearest obstacle to a meaningful concept of representative equality. Hence, examples of blatant boundary manipulation for partisan advantage could produce a "sense of unfairness" among disinterested observers who might find it more difficult to agree on "fairness." Tortuously shaped districts ("bizarre" or "uncouth")[4] have become the hallmark of gerrymandering because they offend the sense of fair play and the desire for representing some approximation of communities of interest.

Focusing on unfairness offers a further advantage in neutralizing judicial apprehension about becoming ensnared in the very heart of the "political thicket" about which Frankfurter had warned in 1962. It can be urged that courts need not ordinarily get into the intricacies of districting "fairness," but only strike down instances of unfairness. It would then be up to the political branches to correct inequities for judicial review, following general guidelines laid down by the Court—for example, proper procedures (public hearings, broad consultation, official justifications of districting plans), adhering to local subdivision boundaries whenever practicable, following traditional (and, often, state constitutional) criteria designed to protect the integrity of geographic regions and communities. Such guidelines could serve as deterrents to more extreme kinds of boundary manipulation. But the Court's stance could be largely negative, striking down unfairness and thus attaining a closer approximation to "fairness."

Extensive gerrymandering can obviously thwart the basic principles that animated the reapportionment revolution at its inception. This reinvigorated dimension of maldistricting can dilute the effective voting power of some individuals and magnify the real power of others, depending on their geographic location. The party in power in the year of redistricting is in a position to determine the fate of the opposition by diminishing its legislative voice. The reapportionment decisions of the 1960s displaced what often amounted to geographically protected oligarchies of rural and small-town legislators. We may now be witnessing the rise of new oligarchies, perhaps no more accountable to the public than the earlier ones. Finally, representational responsiveness to changes in public sentiment can be slowed and even forestalled.

Those who would leave the problem to the give-and-take of the political process overlook the fact that the process itself often resembles a monopoly more than a free market, with little "give" but a lot of "take." A generation ago the problem of malapportionment in the form of vast population disparities among districts was virtually immune from political remedies for much the same reasons. Until the remaining form of vote dilution is also checked by the judiciary, the reapportionment revolution will remain unfinished.

NOTES

1. Letter to John Adams, September 4, 1823, in Padover, 1956, p. 327.
2. I. Stat. 50-2 (1787): An Act to Provide for the Government of the Territory Northwest of the River Ohio.
3. See Bureau of the Census, 1980, especially Nathan Keyfitz, "Facing the Fact of Census Incompleteness," pp. 27–36.
4. Phrases used by Justice Stevens, concurring in *Karcher v. Daggett (I)*, p. 762.

What Does Bandemer *Mean?*

3

Toward a Coherent Theory of Gerrymandering: *Bandemer* and *Thornburg*

Bernard Grofman

In *Bandemer v. Davis*, 603 F. Supp. 1479 (1984), a three-judge federal panel held that partisan gerrymandering did present a justiciable claim and that the 1982 House and Senate plans for the Indiana legislature were unconstitutional partisan gerrymanders. In particular, the District Court found that "the district lines were drawn with the discriminatory intent to 'maximize the voting strength' of the majority Republican party and 'to minimize the strength' of the Democratic party" (p. 1492, references omitted). On appeal, the Supreme Court in *Davis v. Bandemer*, 106 S. Ct. 2797, _____ U.S. _____ (1986) agreed (6-3) with the lower court that partisan gerrymandering claims were justiciable, but reversed (7-2) the lower court's findings that Indiana's legislative plans were unlawful. There are four central issues that this paper will discuss.

First, how is it that the Supreme Court could, for the first time, hold partisan political gerrymandering to be unconstitutional,[1] and yet reject the seemingly overwhelming evidence for intentional partisan gerrymandering that the federal district court in *Bandemer* used as the basis for its finding that the Indiana legislative plans constituted impermissible political gerrymandering? In particular, what facts were either missing or inadequately demonstrated in the factual record in *Bandemer v. Davis* for which the Supreme Court will require evidence if a finding of unconstitutional partisan gerrymandering is to be sustained?

Second, does the Supreme Court plurality opinion in *Bandemer* offer "clear and manageable standards" for determining what constitutes an unconstitutional partisan gerrymander? If it does not, is it in fact possible to draft such standards or, as critics of the opinion have asserted (e.g., Cain, 1985a), is political gerrymandering such a slippery concept that no tractable criteria for judicial decision making can ever be found? Also, are there differences in the appropriate gerrymandering tests for congressional redistricting as compared to state legislative redistricting?

Third, insofar as the Supreme Court did in *Bandemer* set a threshold test for when political gerrymandering rises to the level of a constitutional violation, is that threshold test so high that no partisan gerrymander involving a major political party, no matter how egregious, could ever meet the test, that is, is the *Bandemer* opinion really a dead letter?[2] If the *Bandemer* opinion is not a dead letter, what are its practical implications? In particular, how many existing state legislative and congressional districting plans are likely to be affected by the decision, and what are the long-run implications for changes in the way redistricting will be done in the 1990s and thereafter?

Fourth, what is the relationship between tests for racial vote dilution and those for partisan vote dilution (partisan gerrymandering)? More generally, if we look to the two now leading opinions in each area, both of which were decided on the same day—*Bandemer* and *Thornburg v. Gingles*, a successful Section 2 Voting Rights Act challenge to state legislative districts in a number of North Carolina counties—can we construct from these opinions a coherent theory of what constitutes "fair and effective representation" (*Reynolds v. Sims*, 377 U.S. 533, pp. 565–566 (1964))? I summarize my views on these questions as follows.

First, in a nutshell, the reasons that the Supreme Court failed to strike down the Indiana plans are that (1) for the Indiana Senate there was essentially no evidence of gerrymandering effects, and (2) even for the seemingly egregious House plan, there was no evidence at trial accepted as credible by the district court that the observed skewness in results was anything other than an idiosyncratic result of a single election. Also relevant may have been the fact that in both House and Senate the minority party *gained* seats after the redistricting (six seats in the House, and three in the Senate).

Second, there *is* a clear and manageable standard in *Davis v. Bandemer*—one offered in the plurality opinion. Under it, for partisan gerrymandering to be unlawful, it must be (1) intentional, (2) severe, and (3) predictably nontransient in its effects.

Third, *Bandemer* is far from a dead letter. It was almost entirely the gaps in the evidentiary record that led the Supreme Court plurality to uphold the Indiana plans. Had the necessary evidence in the record been present, the Supreme Court could have corrected the lower court as to the appropriate constitutional test for political gerrymandering and then reaffirmed its conclusion. The Supreme Court plurality in *Bandemer* was walking a tightrope. It wanted to set standards high enough to strongly discourage frivolous suits but low enough so that the most egregious partisan gerrymanders could be overturned by the courts. In my view the Supreme Court has succeeded admirably in that balancing act.

I believe that the practical implications of *Davis v. Bandemer* have been exaggerated by both proponents and opponents of the decision. By rejecting the over-broad test of the district court majority, and replacing it with the three-pronged test identified above, the Supreme Court has narrowed the scope of plausible gerrymandering challenges to those that are the most egregious. Since most state legislative redistricting and congressional plans are bipartisan "sweetheart deals" which appear exempt from attack under *Bandemer*, few such plans are likely to be rejected (see Mann, 1987), although at-large state or local elections where partisan submergence is at issue may well come under successful challenge.

Fourth, there is a direct connection between the test for racial vote dilution enunciated in *Thornburg v. Gingles* and that for partisan gerrymandering enunciated in *Davis v. Bandemer*. That connection draws on the parallels between the predictability of partisan voting patterns on the one hand, and the predictability of levels of racial bloc voting on the other. However, the particular threshold showing required in political gerrymandering cases is derived from the special characteristics of partisan as opposed to racial gerrymandering. In particular, unlike racial identity, partisan affiliation may be mutable. Also, redistricting is inherently a political process. The effect showing in partisan gerrymandering will not be identical to that in racial vote dilution cases, and in some ways it will be stronger (in particular, dilution must be severe).

THE EVIDENCE FOR GERRYMANDERING IN INDIANA

In *Bandemer v. Davis*, Democratic plaintiffs alleged (p. 1482) that plans adapted for the Indiana House and the Indiana Senate in 1982 were intentional partisan gerrymanders that "discriminated against Indiana Democrats" in violation of the Fourteenth Amendment guarantee of equal protection. In the companion case, *Indiana Branches of the NAACP v. Orr* (603 F. Supp. 1479 (1984)), black plaintiffs alleged (*Bandemer*, p.

1482) that the House redistricting plan intentionally fragments black population concentrations in Lake County (which includes Gary) and Marion County (which includes Indianapolis). Democratic plaintiffs prevailed; black plaintiffs lost.[3]

On the face of it, the evidence in the *Bandemer* trial record for the existence of intentional gerrymandering appears overwhelming. Indeed, the trial court held that evidence easily met the three-pronged test for gerrymandering described by Justice Stevens in his concurring opinion in *Karcher v. Daggett (I)*, 103 S. Ct. 2653, p. 2672; 462 U.S. 725, p. 753 (1983). We now look in detail at the district court findings as to intent, the general shape of the plans, and the impact of the plans on Democrats.

Evidence for Intent

The District Court identified a number of findings directly relevant to gerrymandering intent.

(1) The Indiana plans were drawn out of public sight, and initially passed by so-called "vehicle bills," that is, bills that contained no description of actual districts (*Bandemer*, p. 1483).

(2) The actual plans were available for inspection only a few days before final vote on passage (*Bandemer*, p. 1484).

(3) The vote took place the last day of the legislative session (*Bandemer*. p. 1484).

(4) The districting process was completely under the control of Republicans. The governor was Republican as was a clear majority in both houses of the state legislature. Democrats were excluded completely from the districting process. The actual decisions were made in conference committee in which no Democrats were voting members (*Bandemer*, p. 1483).

(5) The Indiana Republican Party spent a quarter of a million dollars to obtain the assistance of a Michigan computer consulting firm to aid Republicans in drafting plans. It was these plans that the Republican legislators on the conference committee adopted, and that then became the state's legislative plans. No Democratic legislators had access to the information provided by the computer consultant firm (*Bandemer*, pp. 1483–1484).[4]

(6) There were no public hearings on the proposed plans (*Bandemer*, pp. 1483–1484).

(7) The majority party felt able to consider redistricting under procedures that were "unashamedly partisan" (*Bandemer*, p. 1484), and informed Democratic legislators that minority party input in the redistricting would not be given any weight (*Bandemer*, p. 1484).

(8) Paralleling the partisan and closed nature of the drafting process, both the House and Senate adopted the legislative plans reported by the conference committee on a vote that went along party lines. Amendments or alternatives endorsed by the Democrats were defeated along party lines (*Bandemer*, pp. 1483–1484).

(9) Democratic legislative leaders admitted that the bill's aim was partisan. House Speaker Dailey, asked in his deposition about the motivations underlying certain districts, responded, "we wanted to save as many incumbent Republicans as possible" (*Bandemer*, p. 1487).

Also, relevant to intent was

(10) "The absence of clear policy statements about the general criteria that shaped the plan from either the debate on the bills or the documents presented to the court" (*Bandemer*, p. 1485).

The Supreme Court accepted the lower court's finding of discriminatory intent (*Davis v. Bandemer*, p. 2808). Indeed, the Supreme Court plurality opinion delivered by Justice White (Part III, joined by Justices Brennan, Marshall, and Blackmun) asserted that "As long as redistricting is done by a legislature, it should not be very difficult to prove that the likely political consequences of the reapportionment were intended" (*Davis v. Bandemer*, p. 2809). Thus, factors (1) through (10) above are *more than sufficient* to establish partisan gerrymandering intent.

Geographic Features of the Plans

The District Court majority identified the "result" of the General Assembly's work as "evident to the Court through a number of exhibits and maps" (*Bandemer v. Davis*, p. 1484). Among the features of the plans singled out by the district court were:

(11) The absence of "nesting" of House districts within Senate districts. The districts for each house of the general were drawn independently of one another (*Bandemer*, p. 1485).

(12) The absence of any "evident pattern to the redistricting plan" (*Bandemer*, p. 1485).[5]

(13) The lack of "any consistent application of 'community of interest' principles" (*Bandemer*, p. 1486).[6]

(14) Unusually shaped districts, especially in the House plan and especially in Marion County (*Bandemer*, p. 1487). No "apparent concern" for compactness of districts (*Bandemer*, p. 1488).

(15) No consideration given to "existing political subdivisions in the districting" (*Bandemer*, p. 1487).

(16) Use of a mix of single-member districts and multimember districts in the plan for the Indiana House. Multimember districts are

confined to urban areas, but "there is no particular pattern which is applied consistently" (*Bandemer*, p. 1489).

Impact on Democrats

In a section on "The Impact of the Redistricting Plan on Democrats" the District Court majority stated a number of additional findings about the Indiana plans.

(17) "In 1982 Democratic candidates for the Indiana House earned 51.9% of all votes cast across the state. However, only 43 Democrats were elected to seats [in the 100-seat house]" (*Bandemer*, p. 1485).

(18) "In the Indiana Senate, 25 seats were up for election. Democratic candidates received 454,849 votes, or about 53.1 percent of the vote. Republican candidates received 402,492 votes or about 46.9%. Thirteen Democrats [52.0%] and twelve Republicans [48.0%] were elected to senate seats" (*Bandemer*, p. 1486).

(19) "46.6 percent of the populations of the House districts which primarily encompass Marion and Allen counties, among the state's most populous, are Democrat, or at least have Democratic voting tendencies. Yet under the plan adopted in 1981–82, and after the 1982 election, 18 Republicans filled the 21 House seats representing these two counties (and those portions of other counties into which the relevant district lines meander). Thus the Republicans enjoy 86% of the House seats apportioned to the populations of Marion and Allen [and the Democrats 14%] of which 46.6% are identifiable as Democratic voters" (*Bandemer*, p. 1489).

(20) "There is no refuting that the Republican majority focused on protecting its incumbents and creating every possible 'safe' Republican district possible, and that this was achieved by either 'stacking' Democrats in districts where their majority would be overwhelming or by 'splitting' any Democratic party power with district lines, thus giving Republican candidates a built-in edge" (*Bandemer*, p. 1488). In particular, "in Marion County, the 51st House district is heavily Democratic and elected three Democrats to the Indiana House seats in 1982. The remainder of the county, while also populated with areas of less heavy Democratic support, was won by Republican candidates in 1982. Those less heavy Democratic pockets have been split by the mapmaker to reduce the influence those voters wield" (*Bandemer*, p. 1487). In Allen County multimember districts are also used, and districts there bisect "Democratic strength in the urban area" (*Bandemer*, pp. 1486–1487).[7]

(21) The majority party has been able to draw lines that will permit it to win close races in certain districts (*Bandemer*, pp. 1485–1486).

Based on findings such as (17) through (21), the District Court concluded that "the figures before the Court, even when looked upon with restraint, would seem to support an argument that there is a built-in-bias favoring the majority party, the Republicans" (*Bandemer*, p. 1486).

In this section of its opinion the District Court also made three general background findings relevant to its decision on the merits:

(22) Indiana is historically a "swing" state (*Bandemer*, p. 1485). Since 1964, there have been years in which Democratic candidates have captured up to 56% of the state's vote, and years in which Republican candidates have captured up to 58% of the state's votes (*Bandemer*, p. 1485).

(23) In Indiana, "given Indiana's history of party-line voting," a competitive seat can be characterized as "a seat in the 45–55 percentage range" (*Bandemer*, p. 1485).

(24) "There is little doubt that a well-programmed computer, full of the most recent election results in Indiana's 4000-plus precincts can aid in the drawing of lines advantageous to the party in power" (*Bandemer*, p. 1486).

Now we turn to how the District Court made use of these findings in shaping its conclusions of law.

The District Court (at 1490) indicated that it had adopted the line of reasoning in Justice Stevens' concurring opinion in *Karcher v. Daggett (I)* (103 S. Ct., p. 2672 (1983)), taken in conjunction with the standard of proof for intentional discrimination as set forth in *City of Mobile v. Bolden*, 446 U.S. 55 (1980).

The first of the three components of the Stevens test requires that plaintiffs prove "that they belong to a politically salient class, . . . one whose geographical distribution is sufficiently ascertainable that it could have been taken into account in drawing district boundaries" (*Karcher v. Daggett (I)*, cited in *Bandemer*, p. 1492). The district court concluded that this first component of the Stevens test was easily satisfied because:

(25) "The Bandemer plaintiffs clearly belong to a politically salient class, those who align themselves with the Democratic Party" (*Bandemer*, p. 1492). Also, "particularly with the computer technology now available, and so utilized by the Republicans in formulating the 1981–82 appointment plan, the geographical distribution of the *Bandemer* plaintiffs and the class they represent is ascertainable from the *voting* records, precinct by precinct, throughout the state" (*Bandemer*, p. 1492, emphasis added).

Just as the Supreme Court plurality did not differ with the District

Court in its finding of intent to discriminate, the Supreme Court plurality accepted the lower court findings that Democrats in Indiana were a cognizable class, and refers to that class as that of "Democratic voters over the state as a whole" (*Bandemer*, p. 2807).[8] The second requirement of the Stevens test is to prove that "in the relevant district or districts or in the State as a whole, [plaintiffs] . . . proportionate voting influence has been *adversely affected* by the challenged scheme" (103 S. Ct., p. 2672, cited in *Bandemer*, p. 1492, emphasis added). Again borrowing language from Justice Stevens in *Karcher*, the District Court plurality asserted that:

(26) "Such a 'vote dilution' may be demonstrated if population concentration of group members has been fragmented among districts, or if members of the group have been over-concentrated in a single district greatly in excess of the percentage needed to elect a candidate of their choice" (*Bandemer*, p. 1492, internal cite to *Karcher v. Daggett (I)*, p. 2672 n. 13).

The District Court then asserted that plaintiffs have provided such evidence, particularly for districts in Marion County and Allen County (see *Bandemer*, p. 1493, see also *Bandemer*, pp. 1485–1486, or numbered items (19) and (20) in the text above).

The Supreme Court plurality opinion agreed with the District Court that, in order to succeed, plaintiffs for a political gerrymandering case are "required to prove both *intentional discrimination* against an identifiable political group *and an actual discriminatory effect on that group*" (*Davis v. Bandemer*, p. 2808, emphasis added). It is with respect to the evidence required to prove discriminatory effect that the Supreme Court and the District Court part company.

Justice White, speaking for the Supreme Court plurality, explicitly rejected the legal appropriateness of the "adverse effect" standard used by the District Court, and in summarizing previous Supreme Court holdings on minority role dilution, asserted that "the mere fact that a particular apportionment scheme makes it more difficult for a particular group in a particular district to elect the representatives of its choice does not render that scheme unconstitutionally infirm" (*Davis v. Bandemer*, p. 2810). A paragraph later Judge White says, "rather, an unconstitutional discrimination occurs only when the electoral system is arranged in a manner that will *consistently degrade* a voter's or a group of voters' influence on the political process as a whole" (p. 2810, emphasis added).

In a paragraph below, this standard is rephrased by Justice White as the requirement that "a finding of unconstitutionality must be supported by evidence of *continued frustration of the will of a majority of the voters or effective denial to a minority of voters of a fair chance to influence the political process"* (*Davis v. Bandemer,* p. 2811, emphasis added). Justice White goes on to say, a few paragraphs further on, that "a prima facie case of illegal discrimination in reapportionment requires a showing of *more than a* de minimis *effect"* (*Davis v. Bandemer,* p. 2811, emphasis added). It is "appropriate to require allegations and proof that the challenged legislative plan has had or will have effects that are *sufficiently serious to require intervention by the Federal Courts in state reapportionment decisions"* (*Davis v. Bandemer,* p. 2811, emphasis added).

I gather two clear messages from the language of the Supreme Court plurality above: If partisan gerrymandering effects are to be held unconstitutional they must be shown to be (1) serious in nature, and (2) likely to be persistent in duration.[9]

Justice White, speaking for the Supreme Court plurality, concludes that "the District Court's findings do not satisfy this threshold condition to stating and proving a cause of action" (*Davis v. Bandemer,* p. 2811).

We will now focus on the key findings *missing from* the District Court opinion that allowed the Supreme Court to uphold the constitutionality of the Indiana plans.

First, there was no clear evidence that the observed disproportionality between Democratic seat share and Democratic vote share in 1982 could be attributed to the 1981 districting plan.[10] In particular,

(27) "The District Court declined to hold that the 1982 results were the predictable consequences of the 1981 Act" (*Davis v. Bandemer,* p. 2812).

(28) "The District Court did not ask by what percentage the statewide Democratic vote would have had to increase to control either the House or the Senate. The appellants here argue, *without a persuasive response from appellees,* that had the Democratic candidates received an additional few percentage points of the votes cast statewide, they would have obtained a majority of the seats in both houses" (*Davis v. Bandemer,* p. 2812, emphasis added).

Second, there was no evidence whatever, accepted as credible by the District Court, that the 1982 Indiana election results could in any way be used to infer predictable consequences for subsequent elections.

The Supreme Court plurality asserted categorically that *"relying on a single election to prove unconstitutional discrimination is unsatisfactory"* (*Davis v. Bandemer,* p. 2812, emphasis added). Several other times in the plurality opinion (e.g., in two separate paragraphs on p. 2814) Justice White repeats the point that data from a single election is insufficient.

In particular,

(29) "The District Court did not find that because of the 1981 Act the Democrats could not, in one of the next few elections, secure a sufficient vote to take control of the assembly" (*Davis v. Bandemer*, p. 2812).

Moreover,

(30) "The District Court . . . expressly refused to hold that these [1982] results were a reliable predictor of future ones" (*Davis v. Bandemer*, p. 2812).[11]

Third, the District Court relied unduly on statewide discrepancies between Democratic candidates' vote share and their seat share without a clear showing that these discrepancies were severe or had significant long-run implications.

In particular,

(31) The District Court made no finding that "the 1981 reapportionment would consign the Democrats to a minority status in the Assembly throughout the 1980s" (*Davis v. Bandemer*, p. 2812).

(32) The District Court made no finding that "the Democrats would have no hope of doing better in the reapportionment that would occur after the 1990 census" (*Davis v. Bandemer*, p. 2812).

Fourth, the District Court unnecessarily and without adequate evidence struck down the Senate plan.

(33) "Even if the District Court correctly identified constitutional shortcomings in the House districting, this did not call for invalidating the provisions for the Senate. The only relevant fact about the Senate appearing in the District Court's findings is that in the 1982 elections to fill 25 Senate seats, Democrats won 53.1% for the statewide vote and elected 13 [52%] of their candidates. That on its face is hardly grounds for invalidating the senate districting" (*Davis v. Bandemer*, p. 2813 n. 16).[12,13]

Fifth, the District Court treated features of the (House) plan such as ill-compact districts and failure of the district lines to adhere consistently to political subdivision boundaries—features that can best be regarded as prima facie indicators of gerrymandering intent—as if they were themselves sufficient evidence for gerrymandering effects.

The third element of the Stevens test is that the plaintiffs must make a prima facie showing that "raises a rebuttable presumption of discrimination" (*Karcher (I)*). Again citing the views of Justice Stevens, the district court held that *Bandemer* plaintiffs met this element of the Stevens test with evidence from "*the shape of the district configurations themselves*" (*Bandemer*, p. 1493, quoting *Karcher (I)*, emphasis added).[14]

In contrast, Justice White takes "the shape of the House and Senate districts and the alleged disregard for political boundaries" as evidence of intent, not effect (*Davis v. Bandemer*, p. 2808), although the plurality opinion also holds that "evidence of valid and invalid configurations would be relevant to whether a districting plan met legitimate state interests" (*Davis v. Bandemer*, p. 2815).

While the evidence in *Bandemer* appeared strong on its face, and it was found more than adequate to prove *intentional* partisan gerrymandering, the Supreme Court plurality held that the District Court had set too low a threshold test for gerrymandering effects and had not found the severe and expected-to-be long-lasting effects needed for partisan gerrymandering to be declared unconstitutional.

It is worth a moment's digression to reflect on the striking peculiarity that, in the Indiana case, it would appear that a gerrymandering claim was made without plaintiffs offering evidence at trial that the plan could be expected to do them long-run damage. In actuality, plaintiffs did offer trial testimony on the anticipated long-run consequences of the 1981 plan, but plaintiffs did not offer *expert witness* testimony on the seats-votes aspects of the case.[15] Plaintiffs' testimony on seats and votes, based in large part on projections from over a decade of statewide election results, was presented by a witness, Mr. Dreyer (with an M.A. in political science), who neither sought (nor received) credentials as an expert witness. Moreover, that witness explicitly refused to claim that his projections had *any* predictive statistical validity.[16] The expert witness for the state of Indiana (myself), in rebuttal, pointed out a variety of flaws in Dreyer's analysis. In reviewing Dreyer's projections the District Court said, "this Court does not wish to choose which statistician is more credible or less credible" (*Bandemer*, p. 1485). Instead the district court chose to rely on simple calculations of votes (and seats) in the 1982 election and *to offer no projections of its own*.

Another interesting fact about the Indiana redistricting was that after the redistricting, the minority party, the Democrats, gained seats in both chambers (6 in the House, and 3 in the Senate). Indeed, across both chambers, a total of 7 Republican incumbents were defeated in the general election. The fact was noted in Appellant's Supreme Court briefs, but was not central in the trial record.

In my view, the reason that the Supreme Court plurality decided to reject the claim that the Indiana legislative plans were an unconstitutional gerrymander is not that they had decided that the plans were not gerrymandered, but rather, quite simply, that the evidence presented at trial and *accepted as credible by the District Court* failed to compel such a conclusion.[17] To appreciate this point required a detailed discussion of the evidentiary bases for the District Court findings and the ways in which the Supreme Court held the District Court findings to be both factually and legally inadequate.

I now turn to the question of whether Justice White's plurality opinion in *Davis v. Bandemer* does indeed offer a clear and manageable standard for gerrymandering.

MANAGEABLE STANDARDS

We learn from *Davis v. Bandemer* that indicia of gerrymandering *intent* are not in dispute, nor is the meaning of the term *gerrymandering* itself. Both the district court majority (*Bandemer*, p. 1488) and the Supreme Court plurality (*Davis v. Bandemer*, p. 2802 n. 6) took the straightforward view that gerrymandering has to do with the way district lines are drawn for partisan advantage, for example, by *stacking* (wasting) votes of one party in districts that they win by large majorities, and/or by *cracking* (dispersing) them in such a way as to be ineffectual. Like most commentators (from Sickels, 1966, to Owen and Grofman, 1987), the Supreme Court plurality took the view that it is partisan consequences that define a political gerrymander, not irregularly shaped districts per se. As Sickels (1966, p. 1300) aptly states,

> Dragons, bacon strips, dumbbells and other strained shapes are not always reliable signs that partisan (or racial or ethnic or factional) interests are being served, while the most regularly drawn district may turn out to have been skillfully constructed with an intent to aid one party.

However, violations of natural communities of interest, ill-compact shapes, or excessive crossings of local jurisdictional boundaries can be seen as prima facie indicators of gerrymandering. For example, Grofman (1985a), like many commentators, identifies them as three of twelve such potential indicators and, as such, they may substitute for direct ("smoking-gun") evidence of gerrymandering intent (See also Morrill, chapter 10; Baker, 1986a, and chapter 2; Niemi and Wilkerson, chapter 12; and Hofeller and Grofman, chapter 14).[18]

There was dispute among the Supreme Court justices as to the threshold level of discriminatory effects that would render a plan unconstitutional. The plurality opted for an effects standard of serious and consistent degradation of influence on the political process as a whole (combining phrases from *Davis v. Bandemer*, pp. 2810–2811).[19] Justice Powell (joined by Justice Stevens), unlike the plurality, would have found the Indiana plans unconstitutional. His opinion in *Bandemer* (like that of Justice Stevens in *Karcher*) took a broad view of how evidence on district configurations could be used. In particular, Justice Powell reiterated that "the merits of a gerrymandering claim must be determined by reference to the configuration of the districts, the observance of political subdivision lines, and other criteria that have *independent relevance* to the fairness of redistricting" (*Davis v. Bandemer*, p. 2827, emphasis added). Also, Justice Powell, unlike Justice White, did not insist on the need for a finding of an anticipated *continuing* disproportionality in election results (see discussion in *Davis v. Bandemer*, p. 2814).

I believe that the gap between Justice Powell and Justice Stevens and Justice White's plurality opinion can easily be exaggerated. As Justice White points out: "The election results obviously are relevant to a showing of the effects required to a political gerrymandering claim under our view. And the district configurations may be combined with vote projections to predict future election results that are also relevant to the effects showing" (*Davis v. Bandemer*, p. 2815). Moreover, with the *Bandemer* precedent of justiciability firmly in place with a 6-3 decision, it is likely that, in the next gerrymandering case, with a different set of case facts, the views expressed by Justice White and those expressed by Justice Powell will begin to meld.[20]

I believe that there are four features of the Supreme Court plurality opinion that are critical in understanding Justice White's approach to specifying manageable standards for gerrymandering effects:

(1) Justice White's insistence that *Bandemer* was a claim that "the 1981 apportionment discriminates against Democrats *on a statewide basis*" (*Davis v. Bandemer*, p. 2807, emphasis added);

(2) Justice White's repeated insistence on evidence that the demonstrated effects must be ones that are not likely to be transient with a single election;

(3) Justice White's reiteration of the Supreme Court's already oft-repeated rejection of "any claim that the Constitution requires proportional representation or that legislatures in reapportioning must draw lines to come as near as possible to allocating seats to the contending parties in proportion to what their anticipated statewide vote will be" (*Davis v. Bandemer*, p. 2809, internal citations omitted); and

(4) Justice White's assertion that a finding of unconstitutionality could be supported by a "continued frustation of the will of a *majority of the voters*" or by "effective denial to a *minority of voters* of a *fair chance* to influence the political process" (*Davis v. Bandemer*, p. 2811, emphasis added).

Statewide vs. District-Specific Gerrymandering Claims

That the *Bandemer* plurality opinion is couched consistently in terms of standards for *statewide* vote dilution is an important but neglected point. It suggests that a political gerrymandering case might be brought seeking a remedy for concentration and dispersal gerrymandering that had affected only a subset of legislative districts, not an entire state. If I am correct about the feasibility of distinguishing statewide and district-specific challenges, a district-specific gerrymandering test would be unlikely to turn upon an analysis of probable *statewide* outcomes, although a severe discriminatory effect would still have to be shown. Also, because *Bandemer* was a statewide challenge to *legislative* plans, it seemed reasonable for Justice White to focus on consequences for control of the state legislature. In a challenge to congressional rather than legislative districting such a focus would be irrelevant.[21]

The distinction between claims of statewide discrimination and district-specific challenges was in fact made in *Davis v. Bandemer*, and the plurality opinion provides support for my view that the appropriate tests for gerrymandering effects would be different for the two types of claims. In Justice White's words, "Although the statewide discrimination asserted here was allegedly accomplished through the manipulation of individual district lines, *the focus of the equal protection inquiry is necessarily somewhat different from that involved in the review of individual districts*" (*Davis v. Bandemer*, p. 2808, emphasis added).

Further support for the legal significance of this distinction derives from analysis of recent vote dilution cases. Vote dilution challenges to single-member districts in a given city or state or to congressional districting plans often focus on a subset of districts in which manipulation of district lines for gerrymandering purposes is alleged to have taken place. For example, in *Ketchum v. Byrne* (740 F. 2d 1398 (7th cir., 1984), *cert. denied* 105 S. Ct. 2673 (1985)), particular Chicago city council districts were attacked as retrogressive and the fragmentation of Hispanic and black population concentrations in certain areas of the city was singled out for review.

In *Major v. Treen* (574 F. Supp. 325 (1983)), although the suit sought to overturn Louisana's congressional districting plan, the district court acknowledged that:

> the *gravamen* of plaintiffs' claims is that Act 20 was designed and has the effect of cancelling, minimizing or diluting minority voting strength by *dispersing a black population majority in Orleans Parish into two congressional districts*. The question posited is whether legislation dividing a highly concentrated black population existing in one geographic and political unit, a parish, into two districts, rather than placing them in a single district in which blacks would constitute a majority deprives Louisiana black voters of the right to effective participation in the electoral process. (*Major v. Treen*, p. 327, emphasis added)

Plaintiffs prevailed on this district-specific claim. Similarly, in *Thornburg v. Gingles* (590 F. Supp. 345 (1984)), although the challenge was to a statewide plan, the *"gravamen* of plaintiffs' claim" had to do with "minority submergence" in six multimember districts and "fracturing between more than one Senate district in the northeastern section of the state of a concentration of black voters sufficient in numbers and contiguity to constitute a voting majority in at least one single-member district" (*Thornburg*, 1984, pp. 349–350, emphasis added).

In *Davis v. Bandemer* the Supreme Court did not make use of any evidence of fragmentation or packing of partisan voting strength. But that was because *Bandemer* was treated as a statewide case, requiring a *statewide* proof of nontransient discriminatory effects. In Justice White's own words (*Davis v. Bandemer*, p. 2815 n. 20): "Given our conclusion that no unconstitutional discriminatory effects were shown as a matter of law, we did not need to consider the District Court's factual findings on the other factors [such as contours of particular districts] addressed by Justice Powell." Cases such as *Major v. Treen* and *Ketchum v. Byrne* show that, in a district-specific political gerrymandering challenge, evidence of fragmentation or packing of partisan voting strength will always be relevant, even though it will not always be determinative. Indeed, in *Ketchum*, the 7th circuit asserted "the ways in which . . . lines are drawn may become independent indicia of discriminatory intent *or result"* (*Ketchum*, p. 1405, emphasis added).[22]

Even in a statewide discriminatory suit,

> If there were a discriminatory effect and a discriminatory intent, then the legislation would be examined for valid underpinnings. Thus, evidence of exclusive legislative process and *deliberate drawing of districts in accord with accepted gerrymandering principles* would be relevant to intent, and *evidence of valid and invalid configuration* would be relevant to whether the districting plan met legitimate state interests. (*Davis v. Bandemer*, p. 2815, emphasis added)

Nontransient Effects

Although Justice White asserts that "a mere lack of proportionate results in *one election"* (*Davis v. Bandemer*, p. 2814, emphasis added) is insufficient to sustain a claim of unconstitutional gerrymandering, Justice White strongly rejects Justice Powell's reading of the plurality opinion (p. 2831, n. 10) as requiring that "more than one election must pass before a successful racial or political gerrymandering claim must be brought" (*Davis v. Bandemer*, p. 2814, n. 17). To the contrary, Justice White asserts that "projected election results based on district boundaries and past voting patterns may certainly support this type of claim, even where *no* election has yet been held under the challenge districting" (*Davis v. Bandemer*, p. 2814, n. 17).[23] This language directly raises one of the central issues for post-*Bandemer* gerrymandering litigation: "Is it possible to project election results with reasonable reliability and, if so, how is this to be done?"

This last question is directly linked to the cognizability of Democrats or Republican voters as a class. While the "ability to determine the distribution of Democratic voters" was not disputed by the defendants [the State of Indiana] in *Bandemer* (p. 1492), in other gerrymandering cases this point is very likely to be a matter of dispute. For example, Schuck (chapter 11) argues that party identification is too evanescent a concept to be used in identifying the members of an aggrieved class and reminds us that individuals sometimes vote for candidates of one party and sometimes for candidates of another depending on the type of election, the characteristics of the candidates, and other exogenous circumstances. However, in my view, this argument as to why partisan gerrymandering cannot be dealt with by judicial inquiry has already been rejected by the Supreme Court. "That the characteristics of the complaining group *are not immutable* . . . may be relevant to the manner in which the case is adjudicated, but . . . do not justify a refusal to entertain such a case" (*Davis v. Bandemer*, p. 2806, emphasis added).

There are two well-established techniques for projecting election results and/or comparing the impact (and fairness) of alternative plans. Method one requires us to establish a baseline measure of (two-party) vote in the districts at issue using votes in some set of election contests that appropriately reflect underlying partisan support propensities (usually statewide ones). This approach has been ably expounded by Backstrom, Robins, and Eller (1978; chapter 6). The second approach involves looking at a party aggregate share of the statewide (two-party) vote in the actual (type of) election contests that are under challenge. In one variant of this approach, ably expounded by Richard Niemi (Niemi and Deegan, 1978; Niemi and Fett, 1986; Niemi, chapter 7; Niemi and Wright, chapter 13) the focus is on estimating expected responsiveness to vote shifts and expected partisan bias. Some variant of method (2) has also been used by a number of other scholars (see, e.g., Tufte, 1973; Scarrow, 1982; Grofman, 1983a,b; Taagepera, 1986; Glazer, Grofman, and Robbins, 1987; King and Browning, 1987; Browning and King, 1987).

The Supreme Court in *Bandemer* was confronted with a divided lower court opinion in that case in which the two judges in the majority calculated baseline Democratic strength by method (1), while the dissenting judge, Judge Pell, obtained a different (and lower) number by amalgamating data from a set of statewide races via method (2). Judge Pell claimed support for his method because Backstrom, Robins, and Eller (1978) had been favorably cited by Justice Stevens in his concurring opinion in *Karcher v. Daggett (I)*. Because the Supreme Court in *Bandemer* did not find evidence from a single election sufficient to meet its "consistent degradation" test, it explicitly refused to decide the question of which of these two methods was the more appropriate (*Davis v. Bandemer*, pp. 2811–2812 n. 15). (Also see Footnote 10 above.)

We believe that both methods (1) and (2) can contribute to determining the existence and effects of gerrymandering. Methods (1) and (2) are useful complements to one another. Method (1) uses the actual sum of the votes received by all candidates of the given party in a set of districts to develop a total vote strength figure for that party. The advantage is that such a sum is a simple and direct measure of aggregate vote strength; the disadvantage is that it is confounded by idiosyncratic district-specific factors such as incumbency. On the other hand, method (2) seems to require careful judgment about appropriate selection of baseline races and thus may be subject to greater controversy. However, we expect that, in practice, if gerrymandering is severe enough, most reasonable selections of statewide races will reveal the extent to which one party's votes have been more packed and more dispersed across the districts than those of the party doing the gerrymandering.[24]

Lowenstein (chapter 4, pp. 75–76) asserts that the question of exactly how a political group's membership is to be identified remains open (see *Davis v. Bandemer* p. 2812, n. 15), and then rhetorically asks whether membership would be identified "By the way they vote? By other political activities? By their political interests?" As I read it, the plurality opinion in *Davis v. Bandemer* (p. 2812, n. 15) recognizes methods 1 and 2 above as the two basic ways to identify partisan voting strength. While the exact nature of the requisite applications of these two methodologies remains to be litigated, like Justice White I do not think it yet necessary to decide between these two methods. Indeed it may never be necessary to pick one or the other, since both have advantages.

Just as the choice among "average deviation," "total deviation," or "electoral percentage" as the best *single* indicator of deviation from "one person, one vote" equality, was not settled (in favor of the "total deviation" as the basic measure) for a number of years after *Reynolds* (Grofman, 1985a; Wollock, 1980), so, too, the choice between a "baseline" and a "votes cast" measure of partisan voting strength need not be resolved yet. Also, even though total deviation is the measure of "one person, one vote" compliance on which courts primarily rely, other measures such as average deviation continue to be used to provide useful supplemental information (see especially *Connor v. Finch*, 431 U.S. 407 (1977), p. 82) and *Holmes v. Burns*, no. 82-1727 (R.I. Super. Ct. 1982), aff'd sub nom *Holmes v. Farmer*, 475 A 2d 976 (R.I. 1984)). Thus, there seems no need, certainly at present, to insist on specifying *the* single measure of partisan voting strength.[25]

Moreover, both methods will need to be supplemented by other indicia of gerrymandering effects. Neither method (1) nor method (2) is perfect at detecting the effects of gerrymanders. In particular, both methods will almost certainly completely miss the use of incumbent-displacement gerrymandering techniques. Method (1) is especially flawed in this regard. Indeed, when there has been incumbent displacement gerrymandering, unless the incumbency advantage is explicitly built in to the equations (as in Cain, 1985a), method (1) will often understate the effects of gerrymandering on the seats-votes discrepancy. The fact that the party that has been gerrymandered against now has fewer incumbents means that it also now has fewer votes, while the party that did the gerrymandering will have more of an incumbency advantage, giving it an expected increase in its vote share. Thus, incumbency displacement will reduce the observed discrepancy between votes and seats by reducing the votes of the party that has its incumbents eliminated by gerrymandering, and thus reduce the appearance of gerrymandering.

Like Schuck (1987; chapter 11) the defendants in *Badham v. Eu* ("Memorandum in Support of the Motion to Dismiss the Third Amended Complaint in *Badham v. Eu*," pp. 36–37), claim that partisan voting strength is inherently unmeasurable, but then go on to suggest that, if there is to be a measure of party strength, it ought to be party registration and not votes cast for the party's candidates. The phrase used by Justice White to identify the plaintiff class, "Democratic *voters over the state as a whole*" (*Davis v. Bandemer*, p. 2800, emphasis added) would seem to largely dispose of this issue. Moreover, there are a number of difficulties in using registration data. Party registration data is not available for all states and its meaningfulness varies from state to state depending on state election procedures (e.g., open versus closed primaries; see Finkel and Scarrow, 1985). Most important, in most states, party registration is a poor proxy for partisan voting strength. In California, for example, vote share for Republican candidates considerably exceeds Republican share of party registration (see Grofman, 1985a; Kernell and Grofman, chapter 15). Thus, if party registration is to be used as an indicator or predictor of party voting strength it must be used with great care, perhaps as one element of a multivariate prediction equation (see Cain, 1985a; cf. Kernell and Grofman, chapter 15).

Even if we agree on a measure of statewide partisan voting strength (and we can, of course, compare the predictive fit of alternative measures in specific cases), we must still determine what to look for to prove gerrymandering. We believe that electoral *bias* (Tufte, 1973; Niemi and Deegan, 1978; Grofman, 1984), that is, asymmetry in the way each party is able to translate its vote strength into seats, is more important than the simple discrepancy between vote share and seat share. Clearly, a 10% discrepancy between votes and seats may be quite reasonable if a party with 65% of the votes gets 75% of the seats. On the other hand, if a party with 45% of the votes got 55% of the seats, there would be considerable grounds for suspicion (cf. Grofman, 1982). In the latter case the *majoritarian criterion* (Grofman, 1985a), that the party with a majority of the votes receive a majority of the seats, has been violated.

Unfortunately, even measures of electoral bias will also miss (or mistake) the effects of incumbency displacement gerrymandering. Thus, I believe that the detection of gerrymandering requires a *combination* of techniques. As I wrote earlier,

> In determining whether partisan gerrymandering has taken place, I would place particular reliance on (1) showing an incumbent-centered partisan bias (i.e., a differential treatment of the incumbents of the two major parties); (2) demonstrating that concentration and dispersion gerrymandering techniques have been used; (3) showing that deviations from compactness and failure to follow political subunit boundaries were systematically linked to probable partisan impacts; and (4) demonstrating that the plan so constrains the probable range of politically competitive seats (in such a fashion) as to create a near certainty of continued partisan unfairness for the foreseeable future. (Grofman, 1985b, p. 155, footnote citation omitted)

IS *BANDEMER* A DEAD LETTER?

In the previous sections I rebutted the frequently asserted claim (see, e.g., Note, 1986, p. 154; Schuck, chapter 11) that *Davis v. Bandemer* fails to identify judicially manageable standards for adjudicating political gerrymandering. In this section I consider the claim that the threshold test set by the plurality opinion in that case is so high that no major political party can ever be found to have had itself unconstitutionally gerrymandered against.

Lowenstein (chapter 4, p. 89) asserts that the only gerrymandering claims the plurality in *Davis v. Bandemer* is prepared to recognize "are claims brought by political groups that have suffered from discrimination to the degree that their status under the equal protection clause is analogous to the status of racial minorities." It seems quite clear to me that this assertion about what *Bandemer* means is wrong, and has explicitly been rejected by the Supreme Court when Justice White said (*Davis v. Bandemer*, p. 2806, emphasis added), "That the group has not been subject to the same historical stigma [as racial groups] may be relevant to the manner in which the case is adjudicated, but [does] *not justify a refusal to entertain such a case.*"

Moreover, if Lowenstein's is a correct reading of *Bandemer*, then the plurality wasted a lot of wood pulp on irrelevant remarks. On Lowenstein's view, all that the *Bandemer* plurality needed to have said is:

> This case is about Democrats; Democrats are a major party in a two-party state; major parties are never discriminated against in the same way that racial minorities are; therefore, even though gerrymandering is justiciable, the Democratic claim must be rejected. Q.E.D.

Another flaw in Lowenstein's interpretation of the *Bandemer* plurality opinion is that it is not easily reconciled with other language (referred to in detail in my discussion above), which shows that it was the lack of a solid evidentiary record (especially as to predictable future consequences) that impelled the plurality to reject the District Court's finding of unconstitutionality, not the mere fact that the case involved a major political party.[26]

There is, however, one passage in Justice White's opinion that, at first glance, would seem to support Lowenstein's interpretation of *Davis v. Bandemer*. That passage is seen by Lowenstein as critical.

> The power to influence the political process is not limited to winning elections. An individual or a group of individuals who votes for a losing candidate is usually deemed to be adequately represented by the winning candidate and to have as much opportunity to influence that candidate as other voters in the district. We cannot presume in such a situation, *without actual proof to the contrary*, that the candidate elected will entirely ignore the interests of those voters. (*Davis v. Bandemer*, p. 2810, emphasis added)

Alfange (1986, pp. 245–246) finds this paragraph largely inexplicable and jarringly out of place with the rest of the opinion. On the other hand, Lowenstein (chapter 4) sees it as the heart of the opinion. In contrast to both, I believe this paragraph must be interpreted in the context of the plurality opinion as a whole. In that context, I would emphasize the phrase "without actual proof to the contrary." I see the role of this paragraph as informing us of yet another evidentiary lacuna in the *Bandemer* trial record, the absence of evidence that Democrats and Republicans behave differently in office, so that it ought to matter from the standpoint of fair and effective representation whether candidates of a particular political party are severely and long-lastingly discriminated against.

Consider two groups of candidates, the "Alphas" (candidates whose last names begin with the letters A through M) and the "Zeds" (candidates whose last names begin with the letters N through Z). Imagine that we find that the votes for "Alphas" do not translate as effectively into seats as the votes for "Zeds." Is this evidence of any sort for partisan gerrymandering? Certainly not, unless the "Alphas" and "Zeds" are more than accidental collections of candidates. There must be at least some evidence that distinct political points of view or groups of voters are being discriminated against. No such evidence was offered at trial in *Bandemer* by the Democrats.

In the case of Democrats versus Republicans, generating such evidence is straightforward, for example, showing partisan alignments on legislative roll calls, or demographic or attitudinal differences in party support in the electorate. Clearly, in the contemporary United States, there are considerable differences in the public policies (and the constituency groups those policies favor) between a Republican party whose presidential nominee is Ronald Reagan and a Democratic party whose presidential nominee is Walter Mondale. Analogous differences exist at the state level, and quite probably may also be shown to exist in particular local jurisdictions. The major political parties are the mediating mechanisms by which voter preferences are translated into public policy. To discriminate against a political party is to discriminate against the policy positions associated with those voters represented by that party and thus against the voters themselves (for more on this point see Hess, 1987).

It is not consistent with the rest of the *Bandemer* opinion, or with the case law on determining the effects of racial vote dilution (see below), to treat *Bandemer* as holding that, unless elected officials totally disregard the voters in their district, no discriminatory effect of a redistricting plan can be claimed. Lack of responsiveness to minority concerns has been an element of proof in some racial vote dilution cases, but it is completely absent from many of the recent leading vote dilution cases (e.g., *Ketchum v. Byrne, Thornburg v. Gingles, Major v. Treen*). Moreover, responsiveness, although mentioned, is not one of the seven major factors singled out as relevant to proof of discriminatory effect in the "totality of the circumstances" test described in the *Report of the Senate Committee on the Judiciary on the 1982 Extension of the Voting Rights Act* (U.S. Senate, 1982; see discussion in Grofman, Migalski and Noviello, 1985, pp. 199–201 and ff. esp. 218, n. 10). Indeed, the Senate report explicitly states that "unresponsiveness is not an essential part of plaintiffs' case" (U.S. Senate, 1982, p. 29).

Furthermore, in Justice Powell's apt phrasing (*Davis v. Bandemer*, p. 2830):

> But (i)t defies political reality to suppose that members of a losing party have as much political influence over state government as do members of the victorious party. Even the most conscientious state legislators do not disregard opportunities to reward persons or groups who were active supporters in their election campaign. Similarly, no one doubts that partisan considerations play a major role in the passage of legislation and the appointment of state officers.

In a 1986 "Memorandum in Support of the Motion to Dismiss the Third Amended Complaint in *Badham v. Eu*," the California Congressional Delegation offers an even stronger version of Lowenstein's stringent reading of *Bandemer*, one in which the requisite test is for a group to be "shut out of the political process" (p. 3). They claim (id., p. 5) that Republicans are barred from an equal protection claim because "Unlike the black plaintiffs in *Rogers v. Lodge* or *White v. Regester*, who had no representatives in the political process, California Republicans have a responsive President, a United States Senator, scores of state legislative representatives, and control of 40% of the state's congressional delegation. The views of Republicans are heard loudly and clearly in Washington, in Sacramento and in local municipalities. The political process works for Republicans." Also, "The Republicans have access to a proven and potent part of the California political process—the referendum" (id., p. 5).

If this view of what *Davis v. Bandemer* meant were correct, *Bandemer* would indeed be a dead letter. The notion that success in, say, state legislative races, exempts a group from successfully proving discrimination at other levels of government is peculiar, to say the least. It is a complete misreading of Justice White's opinion. It is also as a violation of common sense. Remarkably, however, it has been accepted by a federal district in *Badham v. Eu* (1988).

Ketchum v. Byrne, like almost all voting rights cases, relies only on evidence of electoral success *in the jurisdiction at issue* (here the Chicago City Council). Moreover, like many recent racial vote dilution cases, *Ketchum* cannot in any way be characterized as involving a totally excluded minority. The central issue in *Ketchum* was whether an additional two or more black and two or more Hispanic majority city council seats should be created in a plan in which there already were 19 black majority seats and 2 Hispanic majority seats. Furthermore, in congressional cases, even though only the outcome in a *single* seat will be affected, a racial vote dilution claim may nonetheless be sustained (see especially *Major v. Treen*).

Early racial vote dilution cases such as *White v. Regester* (412 U.S. 755 (1973)) were "horribles," that is, cases of nonexistent or virtually nonexistent minority representation; but the first civil rights cases of any type brought to the Supreme Court for remedy usually are "horribles." Minority vote dilution cases subsequent to *White* (e.g., *Thornburg v. Gingles*) did not present such stark patterns of total exclusion, but the Court, nonetheless, held that minorities had been deprived of "an equal opportunity to participate in the electoral process and to elect candidates of choice." The first case in which the Court accepted justiciability, *Baker v. Carr*, was a clear "horrible." Tennessee had not reapportioned for more than forty years, and the discrepancy between the largest seat in the Tennessee House and the smallest seat was on the order of 44 to 1. But reapportionment cases subsequent to *Baker* dealt with deviations from population equality *far* smaller in magnitude—and held those deviations to be unconstitutional. In like manner, the first findings of unconstitutional political gerrymandering to be upheld by the Supreme Court will almost certainly be an acknowledged "horrible"—such as the California congressional plan(s) designed by the late Congressman Philip Burton.

I do not mean to suggest that the *Davis v. Bandemer* threshold is not a high one, but I reject Lowenstein's argument (chapter 4, page 111) that it merely perpetuates a situation in which the Supreme Court plurality sought to "retain the option to intervene" but have "no apparent intention of exercising that option." My earlier work (Grofman, 1985a, pp. 119–123) anticipated Justice White's view that the District Court's majority opinion in *Bandemer* had set such a low threshold for what would constitute an unconstitutional political gerrymander as "to invite attack on all or almost all reapportionment states" (*Davis v. Bandemer*, p. 2811). Justice White goes on to observe that "District-based elections hardly ever produce a perfect fit between votes and representation" (a point I made in my trial testimony in *Bandemer*, see also, e.g., Grofman, 1982). I share fully Justice White's view that "inviting attack on minor departures from some supposed norm would too much enroll the judiciary in second-guessing what has consistently been referred to as a political task for the legislature" (p. 2811).

What is required by *Davis v. Bandemer* are "allegations and proof that the challenged legislative plan has had or will have effects that are sufficently serious to require intervention by the federal courts in state reapportionment decisions" (p. 2811). Justice White chose to require a "showing of more than a *de minimis* effect" (id.). This decision is similar to that made by the Court in *Connor v. Finch*, pp. 430–433, where the Court asserted that a population deviation of less than 10% was "prima facie constitutional." As I have argued elsewhere (Owen and Grofman, 1987), the necessary standard of proof can be met if the gerrymandering is sufficiently egregious and sufficiently sophisticated so as to be durable in its consequences (as is true, e.g., for California's 1982 and 1984 congressional plans: Owen and Grofman, 1987; Grofman, 1985b). Indeed, I regard Justice White's opinion as a remarkable example of views that are both principled and practical—steering a reasonably steady course between the Scylla of encouraging trivial lawsuits and the Charybdis of barring serious ones.

One last point: Is politically gerrymandering "an inherently self-limiting enterprise," as Justice O'Connor (citing Cain, 1985a) asserts (*Davis v. Bandemer*, p. 2804)? The simple answer is that often it is, but sometimes it isn't, depending on the sophistication of those doing the gerrymandering. Some of the time those doing the gerrymandering get too greedy; that is, they draw too many marginal districts in which the majority party's margin of victory may be eroded by electoral tides that change the balance of partisan control in the legislature (Scarrow, 1982). Excess party greed, however, is not inevitable.

"Sophisticated gerrymandering" (Owen and Grofman, 1987) can (a) reduce the number of truly competitive seats low enough that, unless all or virtually all of the marginal seats changed hands, partisan control would be unaffected; (b) lock in a partisan majority in the remaining seats by creating seats lopsidedly safe for the party doing the districting, along with a smaller number of even more lopsidedly safe seats for the minority party; and (c) make use of incumbency displacement techniques to significantly bolster the majority party's long-run advantage (see Cain, 1985a; Grofman, 1985b). Moreover, at least one of the major studies of 1980s redistricting (Born, 1985, p. 309) concludes, "The results suggested no systematic tendency for party fortunes to wane or wax across the course of a districting. Election returns from the initial year a plan is used, therefore, seem representative of the overall partisan impact across the entire period it remains in effect."

LESSONS FROM *THORNBURG V. GINGLES*

Thornburg's Three-Pronged Test

Thornburg provides a test for vote dilution in at-large elections that has three components: (1) minority population sufficiently large and sufficiently geographically concentrated so that there is a single-member district remedy with at least one district in which minority members are the majority; (2) a "politically cohesive minority community as signalled by a general pattern of racial bloc voting among its members"; and (3) "a white bloc vote that normally will defeat the combined strength of minority support plus white crossover votes."

Looking at the *Thornburg* three-pronged test for racial vote dilution suggests the possibility of establishing direct analogues to its components for the case of partisan gerrymandering. As Cain (chapter 5) as well as Lowenstein (chapter 4) emphasize, the partisan gerrymandering cases, like the racial vote dilution cases, turn on the question of group rights.[27] As the late Robert G. Dixon, Jr. pointed out: "In a functional sense, the gerrymandering issue is the same whether the districts are single-member or multi-member—and whether or not a racial factor is present, because racial gerrymandering is simply a particular kind of political gerrymandering." (Dixon, 1971, p. 32; quoted in Baker, 1986a, p. 17)

The direct analogue to racially polarized voting is straight-ticket voting; the direct analogue to crossover voting is split-ticket voting. Thus, in an at-large plan, if Democrats are the minority group, to see if the third prong of the *Thornburg*-derived test were satisfied, we would seek to determine whether there is a Republican bloc vote that normally will defeat the combined strength of Democratic support plus Republican split-ticket voting. This requires looking at expected levels of partisan voting support to see if there is a pattern of partisan political cohesion sufficient to lead with certainty or near certainty to the defeat of candidates of the minority party.[28]

The *Thornburg* test may be adapted to the single-member district context. The only change is in the first element of the test. For challenges to single-member district, I would restate the first prong of the *Thornburg* test as: (1) Is there minority population that has been fragmented to a greater extent than is true for white population concentrations, and that is sufficiently large and sufficiently geographically concentrated to form an effective majority in at least one single-member district?[29] In a single-member district plan, we would need to look at the distribution of partisan support across districts, to see if fragmentation and other gerrymandering techniques had been used to dilute minority voting strength.[30]

However, in addition to the usual analyses of packing and cracking, and so forth, I would also look carefully at the overall treatment of incumbents. Incumbent displacement from the core of his/her old district or the locating of two or more incumbent homes in a single district, if applied in a discriminatory fashion, primarily or exclusively to the incumbents of one party only, is potentially a more powerful tool for obtaining long-run partisan advantage than simple concentration or dispersal gerrymandering. The reason is that, in the United States, incumbents have a considerable reelection advantage. Thus, as noted earlier, eliminating incumbents of the other party (while maintaining or strengthening the seats of one's own incumbents) can considerably increase the ability of a party to translate its votes into seats. Discriminatorily disadvantageous treatment of the incumbents of party out of power is important direct evidence of gerrymandering *effects* (and not merely evidence of intent, although it is that as well).[31]

Projecting Electoral Outcomes

Given the importance attached to projections of (future) election outcomes by the plurality opinion in *Davis v. Bandemer*, how are such projections to be based? A great deal can be learned about how the Supreme Court is likely to answer this question in future cases by examining opinions dealing with racially polarized voting, where analogous issues have arisen.

In the racial vote dilution cases, recent evidence of factors such as racially polarized voting and lack of minority electoral success is taken by courts to be a reliable indicator of the future, absent very strong evidence to the contrary. It is worth quoting Justice Brennan's position, speaking for the Court in *Thornburg v. Gingles* (p. 2770, internal cites omitted), in full on this point:

Because the loss of political power through vote dilution is distinct from the mere inability to win a particular election, a pattern of racial bloc voting that extends over a period of time is more probative of a claim that a district experiences legally significant polarization than are the results of a single election . . . Also, for this reason, in a district where elections are shown usually to be polarized, the fact that racially polarized voting is not present in one or a few individual elections does not necessarily negate the conclusion that the district experiences legally significant bloc voting. Furthermore, the success of a minority candidate in a particular election does not necessarily prove that the district did not experience polarized voting in that election; special circumstances, such as the absence of incumbency, or the utilization of bullet voting, may explain minority success in a polarized contest.[32]

In like manner, I believe, it is *evidence of predictable regularities in partisan voting patterns that are not candidate-specific* that the Supreme Court will demand in future partisan gerrymandering cases. In the racial context, Justice Brennan quotes favorably the views of two leading civil rights attorneys, James Blacksher and Lawrence Menefee: "Racial polarization should be seen as an attribute not of a single election, but rather of a polity viewed over time. The concern is necessarily temporal and the analysis historical because the evil to be avoided is the subordination of minority groups in American politics, not the defeat of individuals in particular electoral contests" (*Thornburg*, p. 2770, internal citation omitted). I believe this analysis applies with equal force to the political gerrymandering context.

Of course there are differences between the political context and the racial one; and, in certain key ways, Justice White's opinion sets a higher threshold for partisan gerrymandering than for racial vote dilution. In particular, in racial cases under section 2 of the Voting Rights Act, either intent *or* effect is sufficient to demonstrate a statutory violation. In contrast, for partisan gerrymandering, intent *and* effect are necessary.[33] Also, certain factors such as history of exclusion from the political process will almost always be absent from litigation brought by a major political party, and proof of other factors will have to compensate. Most important, perhaps, for a statewide case (as distinct from a district case) a political party will have to show *statewide* effects of discrimination. As I read the racial vote dilution cases, no such showing is necessary.

However, future gerrymandering cases, like *Badham* (see note 21) and unlike *Bandemer*, may be brought alleging both a district-specific and a statewide discriminatory effect, or may be brought against congressional plans where district-specific considerations would seem to be of greater relevance. Indeed, I believe that, for challenges to congressional plans, if the effect is to unconstitutionally minimize or cancel out the possibility of control of even a single congressional district, that will prove to be sufficiently "severe" to be justiciable. Certainly, by analogy, cases like *Major v. Treen* support such a single-seat threshold for vote dilution litigation involving *congressional* seats.

Remedy

Levinson (1985) and Schuck (chapter 11), among others, have argued that any test for partisan gerrymandering is simply a requirement for proportional representation in disguise, the Supreme Court disclaimers to the contrary notwithstanding (cf. Thernstrom, 1985, 1987; Niemi, Hill, and Grofman, 1985). If an unconstitutional gerrymander is found, does the plurality opinion in *Davis v. Bandemer* require proportional representation as its remedy? In a word, no.

Justice White (p. 2806) characterizes the claim in *Bandemer* as one that "each group in a state should have the same chance to elect representatives of its choice as any other political group." This is language almost identical to the new (1982) language added to the Voting Rights Act of 1965: Each (protected) group should have "an equal opportunity to participate in the political process and to elect candidates of choice." Thernstrom (1987) and other critics of the Voting Rights Act have charged that this language is tantamount to a requirement of proportional representation. The evidence from the vote dilution cases (especially the Supplemental Opinion in *Gingles v. Edmisten*) demonstrates the error of this view.

The simple fact that must be understood about redistricting done on the basis of single-member districts is that such districting will usually not achieve proportional representation at the group level. The smaller the minority population (and, ceteris paribus, the more scattered it is), the further away we are likely to get from proportionality (see Grofman, 1982, and references therein). In the case of single-member districts, fairness is not the same as proportionality (see, e.g., Backstrom, Robins, and Eller, 1978; Grofman, 1983a; Niemi, 1982; Niemi, chapter 7).

If unconstitutional political gerrymandering is found, just as in the racial vote dilution or equal population cases, the first opportunity for remedy should rest with the jurisdiction, unless the jurisdiction has by its previous history of action forfeited such a right (see, e.g., *White v. Weiser*, 421 U.S. 783, p. 795; *Kirksey v. Board of Supervisors*, 554 F. 2d 139 (5th Cir.) *cert. denied* 434 U.S. 968 (1977)). In most cases, I would anticipate that a plan drawn under neutral principles without intent to discriminate will pass subsequent court muster. If the jurisdiction fails to propose a remedy in a timely fashion, then the Court itself can (either directly or through the appointment of a Special Master) prepare a new plan. Like Lowenstein (chapter 4, page 108, n. 21), I agree that the Court "often does and should strike down practices that can be understood to be wrong when the Court would be unable to specify a practice that is uniquely right." Unlike Lowenstein, where gerrymandering is egregious enough, I believe that the remedy of a redrawn plan, though it may not be guaranteedly better than what it replaces, is nonetheless so likely to be an improvement in eliminating the worst aspects of the unconstitutional discrimination of the previous plan, as to justify judicial intervention in the redistricting process.

CONCLUSIONS

More than two decades ago the U.S. Supreme Court struck down grossly malapportioned districts, many of which had not been redrawn in decades, as a violation of the equal protection clause of our Constitution. The "one person, one vote" doctrine it subsequently enunciated was regarded by many at the time as a revolutionary intervention of the courts in the political process. It has now been sanctified by history, and is generally regarded as a resounding success. In *Bandemer*, Justice White rebutted the argument that, because no simple arithmetic test of political gerrymandering was available, political gerrymandering claims could not appropriately be dealt with by the courts in the way that "one person, one vote" claims had been resolved. As Justice White points out,

> The one person, one vote principle had not yet been developed when *Baker* was decided. At that time, the Court did not rely on the potential for such a rule in finding justiciability. Instead, . . . the Court contemplated simply that legislative line-drawing would be susceptible of adjudication under the applicable constitutional criteria. (*Davis v. Bandemer*, p. 2805)

Justice White asserts "in the light of our cases since *Baker* we are not persuaded that there are no judicially discernible and manageable standards by which political gerrymandering cases are to be decided" (*Davis v. Bandemer*, p. 2805). As by now should be clear, I fully agree with him.

The basis for manageable standards is laid out in the *Davis v. Bandemer* plurality's enunciation of the "intentional," "severe," and "consistent degradation" tests, and in the Supreme Court's resolution of analogous issues of racial vote dilution in *Thornburg*.[34] Like Alfange (1986, p. 179) I believe the ultimate test of *Davis v. Bandemer* will be determined by its ability to provide relief from egregious political gerrymandering without exposing virtually every districting plan to tedious and unnecessary judicial scrutiny. I believe that it will pass that test.

NOTES

1. The Supreme Court dismissed rather cavalierly the claim that it had previously ruled partisan gerrymandering nonjusticiable. Many scholars (myself included) thought that summary affirmances in cases such as *WMCA Inc. v. Lomenzo*, 238 F. Supp. 916, 925 (S.D.N.Y) aff'd per curiam 382 U.S. 4 (1965) vacated 384 U.S. 887 (1966), where the lower court had held partisan gerrymandering nonjusticiable, implied an unwillingness on the part of the Supreme Court to enter what was potentially the deepest part of the "reapportionment thicket." In preparing for trial, the State of Indiana paid more attention to the Indiana NAACP challenge to its legislative plans (in the consolidated case, *Indiana Branches of the NAACP v. Orr* (1984)) than it did to the Democratic party challenge, in part because of a belief that, absent a clear sign from the Supreme Court, the district court would be reluctant to make new case law in the area of partisan gerrymandering. To do so might be seen to fly directly in the face of the Supreme Court's findings in *Whitcomb v Chavis*, 403 U.S. 124 (1971), that Indiana's multimember districts were constitutional and that, even when the minority in question was racial, evidence of electoral disproportionality alone was not sufficient to prove unconstitutionality. As the Supreme Court said in *Whitcomb*, in reversing the lower court findings of racial gerrymandering, "The failure of the minority to have legislative seats in proportion to its population emerges more as a function of losing elections than one of built-in bias against poor Negroes. The voting power of ghetto residents may have been 'canceled out' as the district court held, but this seems a mere euphemism for political defeat at the polls" (403 U.S. 124, p. 153). Indeed this exact language was quoted by Justice White in *Davis v. Bandemer* (p. 2812) as part of his explanation of why the district court's findings in *Bandemer* used an impermissibly low threshold test for partisan gerrymandering (see below).
2. This, too, has been alleged by some critics of the *Bandemer* opinion, sometimes in the same breath that they allege that the screening of partisan gerrymanders would create an impossible and politically contaminating workload for the courts.
3. When the State of Indiana appealed *Bandemer* to the Supreme Court, black plaintiffs in the consolidated case *Indiana NAACP Branches v. Orr* chose not to cross appeal, but instead entered a brief defending the district court's ultimate conclusion that "the challenged plans are unconstitutional in their discrimination against Democrats and blacks as Democrats" (Brief of Appellees Indiana Branches of NAACP in *Davis v. Bandemer*, in the U.S. Supreme Court, October Term, 1985, p. 3).
4. The firm, Market Opinion Research, has strong ties to the Republican Party and was involved in redistricting consulting for Republicans in other states (e.g., Colorado). The district court (*Bandemer*, p. 1485) as-

serted that "Sophisticated computer equipment obviously provided more flexibility to mapmakers."

5. However, the district court majority goes on to say that "the deposition testimony of the legislative principals involved makes clear that Supreme Court guidelines summarized as 'one person, one vote' were carefully followed. The defendants also now state that a policy of 'no retrogression' also guided the decisions made by the legislative mapmakers. 'No retrogression' was an effort to preserve the constituencies for black members of the General Assembly that existed prior to the 1980 Census. The census figures revealed a certain migration of minority citizens from inner city areas in which they commanded considerable voting strength."

6. With this assertion the district court effectively rejected the claim of Senator Bosma that preserving "communities of interest" had been one of the criteria used by Republican legislators. The district court defined "community of interest" as "generally speaking, the inclusion of citizens in a given legislative district who share a geographic area, with similar concerns and needs to be met by their state legislators."

7. The district court went on to hold, "It is obvious that political considerations figured highly in the perpetuation of this sort of districting approach" (*Bandemer*, p. 1489).

8. Justice White, speaking for the plurality, is, however, sensitive to a dispute in the record over how to define the class of Democratic voter, but asserts that since the case has been settled on other grounds, the dispute "need not now be resolved" (*Davis v. Bandemer*, p. 2811, n. 15). I will have considerable more to say about this point in the section on "manageable standards" below.

9. In the "manageable standards" section of this paper I will consider the phrases *consistently degrade* and *non de minimis* in more detail.

10. This was one of the points made by Judge Pell in his stinging dissent in *Bandemer*. According to Pell "(a) comparison between the percentage of Democratic votes cast statewide for legislative candidates and the number of seats actually won, standing alone, fails to prove dilution" (*Bandemer*, p. 1501). Pell went on to observe:

    According to authorities that Justice Stevens cited approvingly in Karcher, "This method of identifying gerrymandering has major flaws . . . (T)he approach fails to account for the fact that the difference between the percentage of votes and number of seats captured may in fact be the result of natural advantages—the inordinate concentration of partisans in one place—rather than any deliberate partisan districting scheme." (*Bandemer*, p. 1501, quoting Backstrom, Robins, and Eller, 1978)

11. In the district court majority's own words: "No party to this lawsuit has attempted to state that the figures [of 1982 votes or election outcomes, by districts and aggregated statewide] have any value as a predictor of future election outcomes, and the Court makes no such reading of the statistics" (*Bandemer*, p. 1486).

12. This is a point I made in my trial testimony in *Bandemer* and in Grofman (1985a, p. 120). I was especially pleased to see it explicitly made in the Supreme Court plurality opinion.

13. The Indiana Senate plan is a staggered plan. The claim was made at trial (by plaintiffs' witness Mr. Dreyer) that, if one looked not just to the districts up for election in 1982 but also to those that would be decided in

1984, the Senate plan should be labeled a gerrymander. In rejecting the possibility of reliable projections of future election results (see fn. 10 above) the trial Court majority effectively foreclosed this line of attack on the Senate plan.

14. In particular, the district court reaffirmed that "the present districting is replete with 'uncouth' and 'bizarre' configurations that beg for some rationale, yet the state has set forth none" (1493) and that "repeated examples exist of bizarre district configurations, drawn with no recognition or adherence to political subdivisions such as municipalities and counties" (*Bandemer*, p. 1493). On pp. 1493–1494 the district court elaborates on examples.

15. My own assessment is that Democratic plaintiffs brought *Bandemer* on a relative shoestring financially.

16. This point was conveniently neglected by attorneys for plaintiffs in their posttrial brief, that made use of charts prepared by Mr. Dreyer, and then provided the attorneys' own interpretations of what the charts meant.

17. I should note, moreover, that my own testimony in *Bandemer* was not that there was no political gerrymandering in Indiana, but rather that the evidence offered by Mr. Dreyer was too flawed on a basis on which to rest a claim of unlawful gerrymandering effects.

18. In most cases there will not be the overwhelming intent evidence found in *Bandemer*. However, a good number of the many indicia identified in *Bandemer* (see, e.g., numbered items 1–16 above) could be missing without ruling out the possibility of intent being shown.

19. "(A)ppellees' claim as we understood it is that Democratic voters over the state as a whole, not Democratic voters in *particular districts*, have been subjected to unconstitutional discrimination" (*Davis v. Bandemer*, p. 2807, emphasis added). References to statewide vote are found elsewhere in the opinion (e.g., p. 2809).

20. Why the Supreme Court chose not to remand the case back to the district court for adjudication under the proper legal standard is a puzzle. My guess is that it may have had something to do with the fact that *Badham* was known to be in the pipeline and might be riper for a more detailed discussion of evidentiary issues. Also, there really was no credible evidence on the record for the unconstitutionality of the Senate plan, albeit the remand could have been for the House only. In particular, the *Bandemer* record did not provide much guidance as to how a remedy should be fashioned to deal with the plan's supposed defects (cf. "We have counselled before against striking down an entire appointment when the constitutional evil could be cured by lesser means," *Davis v. Bandemer*, p. 2813 n. 16, references omitted).

21. In this context it is worth noting that in *Badham v. Eu* (D. Calif, 1984), No. C-83-1126, the Republicans' challenge to California congressional districting in Federal District Court, plaintiffs "claim discrimination both statewide and in individual districts" (Memorandum of Points and Authorities in opposition to Motions to Dismiss Third Amended Complaint, November 21, 1986, p. 18 n. 8).

22. Also see *Rybicki v. State Board of Elections*, 574 F. Supp. 1082, pp. 1108–1112 (N.D. Illinois, 1982), where fragmentation claims were at the heart of a vote dilution suit.

23. We should expect electoral predictions to be probabilistic in nature. Politics is necessarily about probabilities not certainties; nonetheless, as I argue below, sophisticated computer-aided gerrymandering, making use of incumbent displacement and heavy safety margins, can provide a high probability of a lock-in of partisan control for an entire decade. However, we need not wait for the decade. What is needed is evidence that, *if present electoral patterns persist, long-lasting effects of gerrymandering can be expected.*

24. Some scholars who have compared plans in terms of expected long-run effects have made use of computer simulations to determine the range of realistically possible electoral outcomes (Engstrom and Wildgen, 1977; O'Loughlin, 1976, 1982a,b). This can be thought of as a variant of method 1. See also Backstrom, Robins, and Eller (1978).

25. For example, Lowenstein's argument is not consistent with Justice White's view that unconstitutional gerrymandering can be shown by the "effective denial to a *minority of voters* of a *fair chance* to influence the political process" (*Davis v. Bandemer*, p. 2811, emphasis added).

26. Lowenstein (chapter 4) argues that the political gerrymandering cases are not to be adjudicated on the same "principles" as were enunciated in *Reynolds v. Sims* and subsequent "one person, one vote" cases and that these are cases of individual, not group, rights. While true in a narrow sense, this is a misleading statement. Had the principle of judicial intervention to remedy voting rights discrimination in the redistricting process not been established in *Baker* and *Reynolds*, courts would not have challenged redistricting plans that "operated to minimize or cancel out voting strength of racial or political groups" (*Fortson v. Dorsey*, 379 U.S. 433 (1965)). More important, only the politically naive would believe that lack of equal population districts would have ever been the subject of so much concern if it were not that different segments of society, in particular urban versus rural interest, were being differentially affected in their ability to have their views represented in the legislature.

27. Thus, I believe that at-large election plans in which partisan minorities are submerged may be struck down under *Davis v. Bandemer* in the way that racial submergence in at-large plans have been struck down in cases such as *Rogers v. Lodge* (458 U.S. 613 (1982)). In *Rogers* the necessary proof was shown by indirect factors and by the maintenance of a system whose discriminatory effects could be foreseen.

28. In the racial vote dilution minority cases, levels of (voting age) population (discounted for present and past levels of minority registration and turnout) are used to determine makeup of districts needed to provide minorities effective majorities, that is, a realistic opportunity to elect candidates of choice, in situations characterized by racial bloc voting. (See Brace, Grofman, Handley and Niemi, 1988, and case cites therein for details.)

29. Directly analogous are the provisions of parts (a)–(g) of Section 51.59 of the revised procedures for the Administration of Section 5 of the Voting Rights Act of 1965 (28 CFR Part 51, January 6, 1987).

30. In Indiana there was no evidence for differential treatment of Democratic as compared to Republican incumbents.

31. Justice Brennan, in a footnote to this quote (p. 2770, n. 25), remarks that "the number of elections that must be studied in order to determine

whether voting is polarized will vary according to pertinent circumstances."

32. "The requirement of a threshold showing is derived from the peculiar characteristic of the political gerrymandering claims. We do not contemplate that a similar requirement would apply to our Equal Protection cases outside of this particular context" (*Davis v. Bandemer*, p. 2811, n. 14).

33. I have not dealt to any extent with the opinions of Justice Powell or Justice O'Connor in *Davis v. Bandemer* since I believe it likely that in the next case to be decided Justice White's plurality opinion will (after some melding with the views of Stevens and Powell) become the basis for a majority opinion.

34. Egregious political gerrymandering condemns political groups to permanent minority status almost regardless of their electoral strength or of changes in voter preferences (*Reynolds v. Sims*, pp. 565–566, cited in *Davis v. Bandemer*, p. 2806).

Acknowledgments. This research was partially supported by NSF Grant SES# 85-15468, Program in Political Science. I served as an expert witness in four of the cases discussed in this chapter: for the State of Indiana in *Bandemer v. Davis* (603 F. Supp. 1479 (1984), heard *sub nom Davis v. Bandemer* _____ U.S. _____ (1986), 106 S. Ct. 2797 (1986); for the NAACP Legal Defense Fund in *Gingles v. Edmisten* (590 F. Supp. 345 (1984), heard *sub nom Thornburg v. Gingles*, _____ U.S. _____ (1986), 106 S. Ct. 2752 (1986)); for the Republican National Committee in *Badham v. Eu* (N.D. Calif., No. C-83-1126, dismissed for want of a Constitutional claim, 1988); and for the U.S. Department of Justice in *Ketchum v. Byrne* (D. Illinois, 1985). I am indebted to a number of attorneys, including William Evans, Lani Guinier, Michael Hess, James Parrinello, Marguerite Leoni, and Leslie Winner, for making available to me trial transcripts or legal pleadings and briefs in these cases. I am indebted to the Word Processing Center, School of Social Sciences, UCI, for cheerfully typing several drafts of this manuscript from my handscribbled copy, to Michael Migalski for research assistance on projects connected to my expert witness testimony in a number of redistricting cases, and to Dorothy Gormick for bibliographic assistance. The views expressed are solely those of the author.

ADDENDUM: REPLY TO LOWENSTEIN

In the Addendum to his essay Professor Lowenstein accuses me of "wishful thinking" in my interpretation of *Davis v. Bandemer*. Lowenstein's view is that *Davis v. Bandemer* is a case that sets out Fourteenth Amendment protections against some hypothetical future case involving "outcast political groups" subject to McCarthy-era-like discrimination. My view is the commonsense one that a case about partisan gerrymandering involving Republicans and Democrats is a case about partisan gerrymandering involving Democrats and Republicans, and that the plurality opinion (and all the other opinions) refers to just that situation. Since Lowenstein holds the view that partisan gerrymandering ought not to be justiciable (Lowenstein and Steinberg, 1985), it seems clear to me which of us is engaged in wishful thinking; but, of course, only time will tell.

4

Bandemer's Gap: Gerrymandering and Equal Protection

Daniel Hays Lowenstein

In 1962, the decision in *Baker v. Carr* (369 U.S. 186 (1962)) had been "long-awaited," and the "alarums and excursions that ensued in the legal-political world exceeded anything evoked by a Supreme Court decision since 1954" (McCloskey, 1962). Two years later, *Reynolds v. Sims* (377 U.S. 533 (1964)) and its companion cases constituted "one of the most far-reaching series of decisions in the history of American constitutionalism" (Dixon, 1964). "No cases in modern times . . . more sharply provoked . . . disagreement" than did *Wesberry v. Sanders* (376 U.S. 1 (1964)) and *Reynolds v. Sims* (Auerbach, 1964).

By comparison with these redistricting blockbusters of the 1960s, *Davis v. Bandemer* (106 S. Ct. 2797 (1986)), the Supreme Court's entree into partisan gerrymandering, has been a bust. It made the front pages for a day or so, but even then it was overshadowed by the Georgia sodomy case (*Bowers v. Hardwick*, 106 S. Ct. 2841 (1986)) issued the same day. Whatever portion of the public had noticed the gerrymandering case soon forgot about it. Even in the academic journals, as of this writing, attention has been limited to the annual *Harvard Law Review* Supreme Court note, a handful of additional student comments (Anderson, 1989; Crouch, 1987; Holcombe, 1987), commentary by a Republican National Committee staff attorney (Hess, 1987), and a lengthy article by a political scientist (Alfange, 1986).[1] The present volume itself no doubt evidences some interest in the subject, but most of us who have contributed are card-carrying reap-

Acknowledgments. I am grateful to my colleague, Jon Varat, and to the editor of this volume, Bernard Grofman, for their helpful suggestions.

portionment "junkies." Immodestly, we may regard the product of our labor as something more than a mere rounding up of the usual suspects, but our commentaries will not be registered as "alarums and excursions." Additional scholarly commentary will trickle in, but all things considered, a pathbreaking decision of the Supreme Court in a major area of constitutional law scarcely could have provoked less public notice.

The reasons for the nonresponse to *Davis v. Bandemer*, relative to the earlier redistricting decisions, are not difficult to discern. The attack on malapportionment struck a deep and responsive chord in the public mind (McCloskey, 1962, p. 58). Although scholars, politicians, and certain interest groups groused (McKay, 1968, p. 228), generally speaking the American people regarded malapportionment as unfair in both theory and practice, and they were receptive to the "one person, one vote" rallying cry (Cortner, 1970, pp. 144–148). Even critics of *Reynolds v. Sims* have conceded that support for the decision was broad and enduring (Kurland, 1970, p. 95). There is no corresponding public concern about partisan gerrymandering, despite whatever vague recollections our citizens may retain of drawings reprinted in high school civics texts of Governor Gerry's famous salamander. "Proportional representation," gerrymandering's counterpart to malapportionment's "one person, one vote," has no appeal for the American people. Nor are there many Americans who believe an assault on gerrymandering by the Supreme Court can have nearly the effect on their lives and politics that they anticipated and perhaps realized in the case of the malapportionment decisions.[2]

The unstirring subject matter is not the only reason for the figurative yawns that so far have greeted *Davis v. Bandemer*. Another is that the Court upheld the Indiana legislative districts. This result no doubt cooled the enthusiasm of the reformers and muted the opposition of those, like myself, who have believed the constitutionalizing of partisan gerrymandering is unnecessary and undesirable. Still another reason, and the one that will provide the main subject of this chapter, is that no one seems to be quite sure what the decision means.

The confusion, according to critics on and off the Court, is caused by Justice White's failure in his plurality opinion to lay down sufficiently clear "standards" for the adjudication of gerrymandering cases. Justice White erects a "nebulous" standard according to Justice O'Connor (*Davis v. Bandemer*, p. 2817), and Justice Powell believes the plurality altogether "fails to enunciate standards" (p. 2826). In the same vein, one student commentator contends the decision's "practical impact" will be undermined by "the Court's failure to provide lower courts with clear standards by which to adjudicate unconstitutional gerrymandering claims" (Note, 1986, p. 154), and another contends "the standards the Court adopted . . . were ambiguous" (Crouch, 1987, p. 333). Professor Tribe writes that Justice White's approach fails to give "any real guidance to lower courts forced to adjudicate this issue" (Tribe, 1988: p. 1083).

The true source of confusion in interpreting *Bandemer* is not insufficient attention by the plurality to laying down "standards," but an incomplete definition and explanation of the nature of the constitutional violation that may inhere in a partisan gerrymander. The lengthy Part III of Justice White's opinion is devoted entirely to defining the standards that are to apply to partisan gerrymandering cases, and to illustrating the application of these standards by enumerating the deficiencies of the district court's analysis. If these standards are nevertheless unclear, the reason is that Justice White does not moor them to the constitutional principles they are intended to effectuate.

Davis v. Bandemer was argued to the Court primarily in terms of whether an equal protection challenge to a gerrymandered districting plan is nonjusticiable under the political question doctrine.[3] Attorneys on both sides of the case and the justices themselves may have assumed that a decision in favor of justiciability would be tantamount to a holding that an allegation of partisan gerrymandering states a cause of action under the Equal Protection Clause. This assumption is erroneous. Innumerable equal protection claims are filed that are both justiciable and nonmeritorious. A conclusion that a claim is justiciable is a prerequisite to deciding—not a decision of—the question whether the conduct complained of violates the Constitution. Therefore, a finding that a claim is justiciable leaves open the question whether as a substantive matter the claim states a constitutional cause of action. A finding of justiciability creates, and does not obviate, the need to define and explain any constitutional requirements that the claim is found to implicate.

Definition and explanation by the Court of a cause of action being recognized (or explanation of why there is no cause of action) are important attributes of constitutional adjudication, in part because they serve to justify the Court's actions. Of present concern, however, is not whether Justice White gave the *Bandemer* plaintiffs an adequate explanation of why they lost their case, but the question of what *Bandemer* means. The criticism that Justice White's opinion does not lay down sufficient standards is misplaced. Insufficiently explicit articulation of the constitutional principles at stake has given rise to the *appearance* of insufficient or contradictory standards. This is because rules or standards to govern matters of great complexity cannot be precise or comprehensive enough to give adequate guidance in particular cases without an explanation of the principles that those rules and standards are intended to implement.

Justice White may be faulted for not adequately explaining the gerrymandering cause of action, but fortunately the criticism is not a far-reaching one. This is because his opinion contains the necessary clues for us to discern the nature of the contemplated cause of action. In order to interpret *Bandemer* we must work backward from the standards set forth in Part III of the plurality opinion, and seek a coherent conception of the applicability of the Equal Protection Clause to partisan gerrymandering that is consistent with and can illuminate Justice White's specifics.

In this chapter I advance such a conception, and offer it as a guide to the proper interpretation of Part III of Justice White's opinion. My claim for the "correctness" of my interpretation of *Bandemer* is not based on a prediction of what the Court is likely to do in future cases, nor on what Justice White and the other three justices who joined in his opinion may have been thinking.[4] I proceed on the assumption that an interpretation basing *Bandemer* on some articulable conception of the subject at hand is preferable to one that treats its "standards" as arbitrary, random, or contradictory utterances. Here and there along the way I shall be tempted into both criticism and speculation, but in setting forth and defending such a conception, my central purpose is exegesis.

In Part I of this essay, I explain further why the decision in favor of justiciability did not establish that gerrymandering violates the Equal Protection Clause. In Part II, I review the malapportionment cases to lay the foundation for my argument that *Davis v. Bandemer* is based on entirely different constitutional principles. In Part III, I demonstrate existence of a "gap" in *Bandemer*, by describing in some detail the fundamental questions about the gerrymandering cause of action that Justice White does not address directly. Part III also contains a brief description of the doctrinal framework of the equal protection clause within which the new gerrymandering cause of action must be placed. In Part IV, I offer my interpretation of the plurality opinion, concluding that *Bandemer* does not make partisan gerrymandering as such unconstitutional, but makes it an unconstitutional weapon when used against certain groups. In doctrinal terms, I conclude *Bandemer* is a "suspect classification" case rather than a "fundamental right" case.

When Justice White set forth the standards that should govern constitutional challenges to partisan gerrymanders, he spoke for only a plurality of the Court. In Part V, I consider the extent to which the plurality opinion is authoritative.[5] In the Conclusion, I lay aside Lord Tennyson's sound advice and attempt briefly to reason why. Finally, in an Addendum, I respond to Professor Grofman's (chapter 3) criticism of my interpretation.

I. JUSTICIABILITY

In 1849 the Supreme Court was asked to decide which of two competing factions had been the lawful government of Rhode Island during the period of Dorr's Rebellion. Defendant in a trespass action for damages had entered plaintiff's property under authority of the "charter" government, recognized as such by President Tyler, and if that was indeed the legitimate government the entry was no trespass. If the competing Dorr government was lawful, plaintiff was entitled to damages. The Supreme Court held for the defendant but did not apply constitutional principles to determine which faction was the lawful government. To the contrary, the Court, speaking through Chief Justice Taney in *Luther v. Borden* (7 How. [48 U.S.] 1 (1849)), stated that such questions were for the legislative and executive branches to resolve.

Thus was born the political question doctrine.[6] A determination that a constitutional claim presents a nonjusticiable political question is not a determination that the claim fails to allege a violation of the Constitution. Rather, it is a determination that the federal courts will not decide whether the claim alleges a constitutional violation. By the same token, a determination that a constitutional claim is justiciable does not embody a conclusion that the facts alleged by the plaintiff (or any comparable set of facts that could be alleged on the same constitutional theory) describe a violation of the Constitution. It means only that the political question doctrine interposes no preliminary barrier to a determination whether such a violation has been alleged.[7]

The defendants' assertion in *Bandemer* that the constitutional attack on the Indiana legislative districts was nonjusticiable was based on the contention that there was "a lack of judicially discoverable and manageable standards for resolving it" (*Baker v. Carr*, p. 217). The Court rejected this contention and held that the constitutional claim, based on allegations of partisan gerrymandering, was justiciable.[8] This holding in itself implied nothing about whether allegations of partisan gerrymandering ever could give rise to a substantively valid constitutional claim, although Part III of the plurality opinion goes on to answer that question in the affirmative. More important for present purposes, the holding in favor of justiciability implies nothing about the nature of the cause of action recognized in Part III of the opinion.[9]

II. FROM *BAKER* TO *REYNOLDS*

For two reasons, our search for the meaning of *Davis v. Bandemer* begins with a review of the early malapportionment cases. First, this review will demonstrate by example the sort of conceptual foundation that is lacking in the *Bandemer* plurality opinion but that is necessary for understanding of a major new equal protection venture. Second, it will show that the principles underlying the malapportionment cases are dramatically different from those underlying gerrymandering claims, and in so doing will establish that in our search for the meaning of *Bandemer*, we must reject any interpretation that regards the decision as an outgrowth or extension of *Reynolds v. Sims*. This review will also provide the opportunity to correct some widespread and important misconceptions regarding the decision in *Reynolds*.

Baker v. Carr, the first of the malapportionment cases of the 1960s, was ambiguous. It may have done nothing more than open the courts to hear constitutional challenges to malapportionment. But it was susceptible to interpretation as a substantive holding that the Equal Protection Clause prohibited at least some malapportioned districting plans.[10]

Of present interest is not what *Baker* could or should have been interpreted to stand for substantively, but that the Court in its subsequent cases did not rely on *Baker* for any substantive purpose. In the first of *Baker's* progeny, *Gray v. Sanders* (372 U.S. 368 (1963)), Justice Douglas struck down Georgia's county-unit system for statewide elections, citing not *Baker* but the Declaration of Independence, Lincoln's Gettysburg Address, and the Fifteenth, Seventeenth, and Nineteenth Amendments for a conception of political equality that "can mean only one thing—one person, one vote" (*Gray v. Sanders*, p. 381). However much this citation of unconventional authority may have offended some critics (e.g., Kurland, 1964, p. 150), the conceptual basis of the decision was clear enough.

Wesberry v. Sanders extended the one person, one vote concept to Article I, Section 2, governing elections to the House of Representatives. Justice Black wrote for the Court that "as nearly as practicable one man's vote in a congressional election is to be worth as much as another's. . . . To say that a vote is worth more in one district than in another would . . . run counter to our fundamental ideas of democratic government" (pp. 7–8). States drawing congressional district lines would not be permitted to ignore "our Constitution's plain objective of making equal representation for equal numbers of people the fundamental goal for the House of Representatives." Justice Black relied on the original intent of the framers of the Constitution. His history has been sharply criticized,[11] but no one has expressed doubt about the meaning of the principles upon which *Wesberry* is based.

Chief Justice Warren, in his opinion for the Court in *Reynolds v. Sims* extending the one person, one vote rule to state legislative districting, described the applicable equal protection principles more fully than had been done in *Gray* and *Wesberry*. While acknowledging that neither of these cases was dispositive, he drew from them "the basic principle of equality among voters" and the proposition that "the fundamental principle of representative government in this country is one of equal representation for equal numbers of people" (*Reynolds*, pp. 560–561). Then, in a passage some supporters of judicial intervention into partisan gerrymandering have preferred to overlook, he defined the nature of the constitutional claim being adjudicated:

> A predominant consideration in determining whether a State's legislative apportionment scheme constitutes an invidious discrimination violative of rights asserted under the Equal Protection Clause is that the rights allegedly impaired are individual and personal in nature. . . . While the result of a court decision in a state legislative apportionment controversy may be to require the restructuring of the geographical distribution of seats in a state legislature, the judicial focus must be concentrated upon ascertaining whether there has been any discrimination against certain of the State's citizens which constitutes an impermissible impairment of their constitutionally protected right to vote (p. 561)

Attacks on malapportionment could have been conceptualized as claims by the residents of underrepresented districts that as a group they suffered constitutional harm consisting of a discriminatory structuring of the election of the state legislature.[12] In the passage quoted, the Court made it clear that it was having none of this. The Court was invalidating discrimination against individuals rather than groups; it was vindicating voting rights that were "individual and personal in nature"; and the restructuring of electoral institutions that unquestionably would become necessary was a by-product of the vindication of these rights, not a constitutional end in itself.[13]

The discrimination invalidated in *Reynolds* was not contingent on the candidates or parties the voters in underrepresented districts happened to favor, or on the influence a like-minded group of voters could expect to have, as an empirical matter, on the legislative process as a whole. To be sure, Chief Justice Warren wrote that "it would seem reasonable that a majority of the people of a State could elect a majority of that State's legislators" (p. 565). He also cited as evidence against the plans invalidated in *Reynolds* and its companion cases the percentages of the total state populations who resided in the half-plus-one least-populated legislative districts, and who therefore elected a majority of the legislators. In many cases these percentages were far below 50%. But Justice Stewart, dissenting in *Lucas v. 44th General Assembly of Colorado* (377 U.S. 713 (1964)), one of the companion cases, quite missed the point of these figures when he wrote:

> Even with legislative districts of exactly equal voter population, 26% of the electorate . . . can, as a matter of the kind of theoretical mathematics embraced by the Court, elect a majority of the legislature under our simple majority electoral system. (p. 750 n. 12)

In fact, Justice Stewart was embracing an entirely different kind of "theoretical mathematics" from that used by Chief Justice Warren. Justice Stewart's 26% figure is the minimum number of votes that could be received by members of a controlling party or faction in an election conducted in districts with equal numbers of voters. Such a figure is relevant only if actual coalitions of voters and candidates are relevant. Justice Stewart overlooks the Court's emphasis on the individual and personal—as opposed to group or coalitional—nature of the right to vote that is being protected. Nor does it seem reasonable to attribute to the majority—a majority that included a former governor of a major state and a former U.S. Senator—a political analysis requiring, in the words of a commentator who repeats Justice Stewart's error, "absurd assumptions" (Alfange, 1986, p. 183).

Interpreted less perversely, *Reynolds'* statement that a majority of the people should be able to elect a majority of the legislators means simply that a majority of the legislators should represent a majority of the people—in other words, that they should represent districts in which a majority of the people reside, and be chosen in election races in which a majority of the voters vote.[14] The minimum percentage of people capable of electing a majority of legislators was not offered as political analysis—there is no reason to doubt that Chief Justice Warren was as aware of the absurdity of such an analysis as his critics—but rather as one of several ways of measuring the degree of malapportionment that existed.[15]

The passage in *Reynolds* that has given proponents of constitution-alizing partisan gerrymandering the most comfort is the statement that "fair and effective representation" is the aim of a districting plan.[16] If we consider the passage as a whole, it appears they may have drawn more comfort than they were entitled to. The paragraph in which the famous phrase appears is a long one, beginning with the statement we have already considered to the effect that a majority of the people should be able to elect a majority of the legislators. It continues that to conclude otherwise would be to exalt minority rights to excess, and that legislatures should be "collectively responsive to the popular will." Then:

> [T]he concept of equal protection has been traditionally viewed as requiring the uniform treatment of persons standing in the same relation to the governmental action questioned or challenged. With respect to the allocation of legislative representation, all voters, as citizens of a State, stand in the same relation regardless of where they live. Any suggested criteria for the differentiation of citizens are insufficient to justify any discrimination, as to the weight of their votes, unless relevant to the permissible purposes of legislative apportionment. Since the achieving of fair and effective representation for all citizens is concededly the basic aim of legislative apportionment, we conclude that the Equal Protection Clause guarantees the opportunity for equal participation by all voters in the election of state legislators. (pp. 565–566).

Admittedly, the stream of logic in the preceding passage is an elusive one. But it is there, and it can be discerned. Chief Justice Warren has already established that the discrimination in question is one that affects individual and personal voting rights, and that the effect on those rights of creating districts of unequal population is analogous to denying the right to vote altogether (p. 562) and identical to multiplying the votes of some voters during the count. In this context, the first two sentences quoted above assert that under the Equal Protection Clause, voters similarly situated must have equal voting rights and the fact that they may live in different parts of the state does not prevent them from being similarly situated. The next sentence contemplates the possibility that there might nevertheless be some legitimate "criteria" on the basis of which voters would not be similarly situated, so that their votes would not have to be weighted evenly. However, no such criteria could pass muster unless justified by "the permissible purposes of legislative apportionment." And the one "conceded" purpose of legislative apportionment is "fair and effective representation." Since only a purpose justified by this goal of fair and effective representation could justify discrimination among voters, the Chief Justice concludes that no such discrimination is permissible. Apparently "fair and effective representation," whatever else it may be, is not something that is furthered by discriminating among voters.

There are two important points that should be made regarding the term "fair and effective representation" as it is used in this passage in *Reynolds*. First, it is not a constitutional right. Its role in the Chief Justice's analysis is that of a legitimate state purpose, possibly a purpose that is capable of overriding constitutional rights that might conflict with it, but nothing in the passage suggests that "fair and effective representation" itself is a constitutional right.[17]

Second, the term *representation* is notorious for its many different meanings (Pitkin, 1967). To speak of representation that is "fair and effective" does not reduce the range of possible meanings very much. The meaning that the phrase has in *Reynolds* must be discerned from the context. One meaning that it clearly does not have is equality among voters measured by empirical influence on the composition or the product of the legislature. If it had that meaning, the conclusion drawn in the quoted passage would be a non sequitur, since, as an empirical matter, inequality in vote weighting conceivably could offset inequalities in influence elsewhere in the political system.

An alternative meaning of "fair and effective representation" is the representation that results from elections in which all votes are weighted equally. As a proposed interpretation of the phrase as it is used in *Reynolds*, this limited and somewhat formalistic construction has the twin virtues of bearing a close relation to the subject matter of the case and of supporting the conclusion that Chief Justice Warren draws from it.[18] In summary, these points about the malapportionment decisions following *Baker v. Carr* are most important as we turn to *Davis v. Bandemer*.

1. The decisions did not rely on *Baker* for anything other than justiciability. They treated the substantive questions as fresh ones, and although their modes of analysis and their results attracted much criticism, the decisions were grounded in a clear and coherent conception of the Equal Protection Clause and of the rights at stake.
2. The rights protected against discrimination were conceptualized as rights of individuals, not of groups, and were not contingent on any particular patterns of voting behavior.
3. The rights protected against discrimination were conceptualized as voting rights, and can be described as representational rights

only in the sense that the right to vote and have one's vote counted and weighted equally with the votes of others is a part of the system of representation.

Davis v. Bandemer stands in contrast to the malapportionment cases on all three of these points.

III. *BANDEMER'S* GAP

As we have seen, the holding that a constitutional claim presents a justiciable question does not carry the consequence that the claim has any validity on the merits. The generic claim in *Davis v. Bandemer* was that partisan gerrymandering may discriminate against some group in violation of the Equal Protection Clause. The Court ruled against the *Bandemer* plaintiffs, and could have done so by holding that the Equal Protection Clause does not prohibit partisan gerrymandering. It also could have ruled that the Indiana districting plan under attack did not violate equal protection, without reaching the question whether other partisan gerrymanders, different in one or another respect from the Indiana plan, might do so. The plurality took neither of these courses. Instead, it assumed that the Equal Protection Clause does prohibit some partisan gerrymanders, attempted to define standards for judging the constitutionality of plans attacked on this ground, and then showed why the attack on the Indiana plan was insufficient under these standards.

Whether or not Part II of Justice White's opinion, standing by itself, could be interpreted as containing any holding going beyond justiciability makes little difference. What is significant is that Part II no more attempts to define and explain any cause of action under the Equal Protection Clause than did *Baker v. Carr*. As we have seen, this deficiency in Baker was made good in the later malapportionment cases. But *Bandemer* contains no counterpart to the explanation of general principles contained in *Gray v. Sanders, Wesberry v. Sanders*, and, especially, *Reynolds v. Sims*. Instead, the plurality opinion plunges, *in medias res*, into the specifics of the adjudication of gerrymandering claims. It is as if *Reynolds* had *begun* with the observation that "[m]athematical exactness or precision is hardly a workable constitutional requirement" (p. 577). *Reynolds* left open many questions, including how close to exact population equality districting plans would have to come. Without the general explanation of how equal protection principles bore on malapportionment claims, the interpretation of specific standards, such as the statement that mathematical precision was not required, would have been difficult or impossible.

There are several fundamental aspects of the gerrymandering cause of action that are not addressed directly by the *Bandemer* plurality. One is the definition of the group that may be the victim of discrimination and therefore be denied equal protection. This was a straightforward matter in *Reynolds v. Sims*, since a districting statute by definition classifies people into groups residing in various areas of the state. In *Reynolds* the class suffering from discrimination was a class defined by the statute, namely, the residents of statutorily created districts with higher than average populations; this is not true, in a gerrymandering case.

The *Bandemer* plaintiffs were not complaining that the residents of particular districts as such were harmed by the Indiana plan. Their complaint was that the effects of the plan harmed a group that was not defined or singled out explicitly by the districting statute, namely "Democratic voters over the State as a whole" (p. 2807). But the phrase "Democratic voters" does not sharply delineate a group of people. Judges in the lower court disagreed over whether the allegedly disfavored class consisted of persons who voted for Democratic Assembly candidates in a particular election or persons "who could be counted on to vote Democratic from election to election" (p. 2811, n. 15). Other equally plausible definitions of "Democratic voters" are imaginable, such as voters who are registered as Democrats; voters who, when asked by a pollster, will state a preference for the Democratic Party; or persons who vote for Democratic candidates more often than not.

Whatever may be the best definition of "Democratic voter," it appears that the kind of group that may be deprived of equal protection by gerrymandering in the contemplation of the plurality is not limited to voters or partisans of a particular political party. To the contrary, the plurality refers to discrimination against "an identifiable political group" (p. 2808), apparently a much broader category. But the questions regarding how such a group would be "identified" remain. By the way they vote? By other political activities? By their political "interests"?

Justice White stated it was unnecessary to decide in *Davis v. Bandemer* (p. 2812, n. 15) precisely what the group was that allegedly had suffered from discrimination. What he meant, apparently, was that *Bandemer* on its facts was not a close case, so that subtleties of who would be included in the class could have no effect on the outcome. But definition of the group that can suffer an equal protection violation has a purpose well beyond the resolution of detailed factual controversies. Definition of the group would be an important step in articulation of the kind of discrimination that may be unconstitutional.

In *Reynolds* the nature of the discrimination held to be unconstitutional could be simply stated. It was unequal weighting of the votes cast by individuals. The discrimination existed whenever there was an avoidable difference across districts in the ratio of number of voters to number of representatives chosen. What is the nature of the discrimination in a gerrymandering case? Plaintiffs' claim is described as a claim "that each political group in a State should have the same chance to elect representatives of its choice as any other political group" (p. 2806). Are the standards laid out in Part III of the plurality opinion intended as indicators that a political group does not have "the same chance to elect representatives of its choice" as other groups? Or does the plurality have a different conception from that of the *Bandemer* plaintiffs of the type of discrimination that may offend the Equal Protection Clause?

Evidently, gerrymandering claims, unlike malapportionment claims, call for consideration of the political dynamics of legislative elections. In considering discrimination affecting the "chances" for different political groups to elect representatives of their choice, are we to consider the political consequences of the districting plan only, or should we also consider other political factors, such as the access of varying groups to campaign funds and press coverage, the feasibility of different groups entering into political coalitions that are likely to be effective, or the availability of attractive candidates who will support the objectives of various groups?

It is difficult to see how the political consequences of a districting plan could be considered without taking these and many similar factors into account, at least as part of the empirical situation in which the districting plan operates. In assessing the fairness of the actual or predicted effects of the districting plan, should these effects be considered in isolation from the effects of other, possibly offsetting aspects of the system? Or, instead, should we assess the fairness of the districting plan in the context of the fairness or unfairness of the electoral process as a whole? For example, is it relevant to a constitutional gerrymandering claim that the complaining group is benefited disproportionately by other features of the electoral system, say, by the system's reliance on private campaign contributions?

Depending on how the discrimination resulting from gerrymandering is conceptualized, whole new vistas of constitutional restrictions may be placed on the political process. If the underlying right is the right of groups to equivalent chances to elect representatives of their choice, will inequalities in some or all of the other political factors that affect legislative elections constitute violations of equal protection, even in the absence of gerrymandered districts? (see, e.g., Nicholson, 1974.)[19] Or if the underlying right is more general yet, such as a right to "fair and effective representation," do individual voters and groups have an equal protection right to judicial review of the actual effectiveness of the representation they receive? Am I deprived of equal protection if my state legislator is a drunkard, has a high absentee rate, rarely authors bills that are enacted, and is generally regarded as ineffective in committee hearings and elsewhere? Are committee systems, seniority systems, and other legislative procedures that may give one member more influence than another, or that may tilt the legislative process in favor of some interests over others, subject to equal protection scrutiny (see Rae, 1971b, p. 109)?[20] Again, if the ultimate right is the right to equally "fair and effective representation," does equal protection entail a constitutional requirement that the laws and other products of the representational process correlate in some manner with the legislative goals of groups and individuals within the state?

The point is not that by constitutionalizing gerrymandering the Court necessarily places itself on a slippery slope that has no reasoned stopping point short of results that are plainly impossible. Nor is the point that the Court can or needs to provide a comprehensive theory of gerrymandering and the Constitution, grounded in universally accepted political philosophy and containing no loose ends.[21] *Reynolds v. Sims* did not do that much. Neither did *Marbury v. Madison* (1 Cranch. [5 U.S.] 137 (1803)) or *Brown v. Board of Education* (347 U.S. 483 (1954)) or *Roe v. Wade* (410 U.S. 113 (1973)) or any other major and innovative decision of the Supreme Court. But each of these decisions, and every other constitutional decision I can think of that is comparable to *Bandemer* in its novelty and significance, contained at least an attempt to explain the nature of the constitutional claim that was being recognized, the relationship of that claim to established constitutional doctrine, and some reasons for recognizing the validity of the claim.[22]

The plurality's discussion of the standards that must be met by plaintiffs in gerrymandering cases is cast primarily in terms of the requisite discriminatory "intent" and "effects" of plans that will be held to violate the Equal Protection Clause. To see why this is indeed to begin *in medias res* and cannot serve as a basic explanation of the constitutional principles underlying the new cause of action, it is necessary to look briefly at the broader context of equal protection doctrine.

Virtually all legislation draws explicit classifications among people. For example, a progressive income tax explicitly classifies people according to their incomes. In addition, the effects of legislation usually are felt unevenly among groups even when there is no explicit statutory classification. Suppose, as is likely, there is a correlation between level of income and affiliation with one political party or another. Then a change in the progressivity of the income tax tends to benefit as a group the partisans of one party relative to partisans of the other, despite the fact that the statute makes no reference to political parties. Discrimination, then, consisting of both explicit statutory classification and nonuniform effects of legislation across groups, is a normal attribute of legislation.

Only a small fraction of legislative discriminations, tagged with the label "invidious," violate the Equal Protection Clause. Generally speaking, these fall into three categories:[23]

1. A classification that cannot be supported by any rational explanation, however tenuous. See, for example, *New Orleans v. Dukes* (427 U.S. 297 (1976)).

2. A classification drawn along lines that are "suspect," such as race or gender, unless the classification can survive a "heightened" form of scrutiny. See, for example, *Korematsu v. United States* (323 U.S. 214 (1944); *Craig v. Boren* (429 U.S. 190 (1976)).[24]

3. A classification that denies or burdens a "fundamental right" to a particular group, while leaving the right unburdened in others, unless the discrimination can survive heightened scrutiny. See, e.g., *Kramer v. Union Free School District*, (395 U.S. 621 (1969)).

Questions of discriminatory intent and discriminatory effect arise in the second type of case, involving suspect classifications. In the leading case, *Washington v. Davis* (426 U.S. 229 (1976)), passing a written examination was a prerequisite for beginning training to be a police officer. Plaintiffs demonstrated that a lower percentage of black applicants than white applicants passed the test. The Supreme Court held that proof that the test had a disproportionately burdensome effect on black applicants was insufficient to make out an equal protection violation. The Constitution was not violated unless the test also was intended to have such a discriminatory effect.

The questions of discriminatory intent and discriminatory effect are relevant in a case like *Washington v. Davis* because there exists an accepted premise that the Fourteenth Amendment prohibits discrimination on grounds of race in the absence of a very strong justification. When the racial classification appears on the face of the statute, application of this premise is straightforward. *Washington v. Davis* addressed the application of the premise to situations where racial discrimination is alleged in the absence of a racial classification appearing on the face of the statute.

Without such an agreed-upon premise, discussion of discriminatory intent and discriminatory effect is meaningless. Suppose the legislature enacts a special tax credit for makers of open widgets but not for makers of closed widgets. The discrimination between the two classes of manufacturers appears on the face of the statute and clearly benefits one group and burdens the other. Nevertheless, the statute is not unconstitutional, because the Equal Protection Clause does not forbid such discrimination in state taxation. The statute may also have the effect of benefiting the suppliers of raw materials for open widgets and harming suppliers for closed widgets, and although this discrimination does not appear on the face of the statute, it may have been intended. But the showing of such an effect and such an intent avails nothing, because the discrimination does not affront the Equal Protection Clause.

In the case of legislative districting, a plan may have been intended to favor some political groups over others, and may in fact do so relative to alternative plans that could have been adopted. But it is impossible to conduct an accurate search for the relevant intent and the relevant effects without a conception of what it is that makes a discrimination offend the Equal Protection Clause. The plurality's failure to attempt to set forth any such conception constitutes a gap in the reasoning of *Davis v. Bandemer* and accounts for much of the confusion and disagreement about what the decision means in concrete terms.[25] Bridging that gap requires extrapolating from Justice White's definition of *standards* for gerrymandering cases, with the objective of constructing a conception of equal protection that is consistent with all the specifics in the plurality opinion.

IV. BRIDGING THE GAP

In searching for the conception of equal protection that underlies the plurality opinion in *Bandemer*, it will be helpful to begin by recalling that *Bandemer* is not a case with doctrinal roots in *Reynolds v. Sims*. Justice White recognizes the contrast with *Reynolds* in the justiciability portion of his opinion:

The issue here is of course different from that adjudicated in *Reynolds*. It does not concern districts of unequal size. Not only does everyone have the right to vote and to have his vote counted, but each elector may vote for and be represented by the same number of lawmakers. Rather, the claim is that each political group in a State should have the same chance to elect representatives of its choice as any other political group. (p. 2806)

Bandemer, then, unlike *Reynolds*, involves alleged rights of political groups rather than of individuals, and the rights have to do with the outcomes of elections rather than the right to an equally weighted vote. This difference explains the fact that in Part III of the plurality opinion, addressing the merits, virtually no reference is made to the malapportionment cases.[26]

The difference between *Reynolds* and *Bandemer* also raises an immediate question regarding the application of the Equal Protection Clause. In a malapportionment case it is the fact that the districting classification burdens an individual's "fundamental" right to vote that triggers heightened equal protection scrutiny.[27] Only rights "explicitly or implicitly guaranteed by the Constitution" have such a triggering effect (*San Antonio Independent School District v. Rodriguez* (411 U.S. 1 (1973)). Whether or not groups rather than individuals can be the bearers of any rights within this category, it is individuals, not groups, who have the right to vote. The chance of a political group to elect representatives of its choice equally with other groups is in part a function of the right of individual members of the group to vote, but it is not the same thing as the right to vote. Nor is that chance guaranteed, explicitly or implicitly, by the Constitution. It would appear that the claim in *Bandemer* cannot qualify for heightened scrutiny under the "fundamental rights" arm of equal protection analysis.

The key to understanding the plurality opinion is to see that the gerrymandering cause of action it contemplates is one that implicates the "suspect classification" branch of equal protection doctrine.[28] The plurality opinion does not declare gerrymandering, extreme or otherwise, unconstitutional; instead, it declares that the gerrymander may not be directed against groups that are already victimized by pervasive discrimination.

An important indicator that this is the central meaning of the plurality opinion consists of the authorities that it cites in its discussion of the standards that apply to gerrymandering claims.[29] These consist primarily of racial gerrymandering cases, and the only cases cited in which the constitutional claims were upheld were cases of discrimination against racial minority groups. Where such discrimination exists, heightened scrutiny under the "suspect classification" branch of the Equal Protection Clause is plainly appropriate.[30] Many portions of the plurality opinion that have seemed strange or obscure become understandable when it is seen that the gerrymandering claims the plurality is prepared to recognize are claims brought by political groups that have suffered from discrimination to the degree that their status under the Equal Protection Clause is analogous to the status of racial minorities.

For starters, we can make sense out of Justice White's structuring his analysis around the requirements of intent to discriminate and discriminatory effect.[31] These are constitutional standards that have grown up around the concept of "suspect classifications." And although Justice White explicitly places most of the burden of his analysis on the question of discriminatory effect, it is worth pausing to notice the significance of the way he treats the question of intent. The significance arises from the nature of the debate over gerrymandering as it was conducted prior to the *Bandemer* decision.

> A gerrymandering plaintiff must show discriminatory intent, but we think it most likely that whenever a legislature redistricts, those responsible for the legislation will know the likely political composition of the new districts and will have a prediction as to whether a particular district is a safe one for a Democratic or Republican candidate or is a competitive district that either candidate might win. . . . As long as redistricting is done by a legislature, it should not be very difficult to prove that the likely political consequences of the reapportionment were intended. (pp. 2808–2809)

On its face, this language may appear to be a great victory for the supporters of judicial intervention. After all, the erection of a discriminatory intent requirement in *Mobile v. Bolden* (446 U.S. 55 (1980)), a racial discrimination case, was perceived as a major obstacle, and the subsequent amendment to Section 2 of the Voting Rights Act making it clear that discriminatory intent is not required for a statutory claim was regarded as an important civil rights victory. Justice White's expressed willingness to concede discriminatory intent in partisan gerrymandering cases should therefore be a boost for plaintiffs.[32]

The problem that this creates for the reformers is that they have placed at the center of their structure for assailing the gerrymander a variety of "indicators" and "flags," much of whose relevance is directed to revealing the presence of partisan motivation behind districting plans (e.g., Grofman, 1985a). By concentrating on techniques for revealing that gerrymanderers are up to no good, the reformers had obscured the question of precisely what is so bad about the "no good" these gerrymanderers are up to. Once the features of a districting plan that bear on the intent of the plan's authors are declared irrelevant, there is little that can be said about a gerrymander other than some variation on the theme that it does not bring about proportional representation, and Justice White repeated firmly the Court's long-held position that the Constitution does not require proportional representation (p. 2809). The effect on the legal and theoretical case against gerrymandering of Justice White's willingness to concede intent is comparable to what happens to one side in a tug-of-war if the other side suddenly lets go.[33]

It is not surprising, then, that the "indicators," "flags," and other criteria developed by reformers for identifying partisan gerrymanders are notably absent when Justice White turns to his key question, what the discriminatory effects must be if a political gerrymander is to violate the Constitution. No passage in *Bandemer* has received more attention than the statement that

> unconstitutional discrimination occurs only when *the electoral system* is arranged in a manner that will *consistently degrade* a voter's or a group of voters' influence *on the political process as a whole*. (p. 2810, emphasis added)

This statement is indeed central, but the emphasis too often has been on the phrase "consistently degrade," removed from the context of its subject ("the electoral system") and its object ("influence on the political process as a whole"). The passage has been cited by commentators as if it said merely that the districting plan must be such as to "consistently degrade" the chances of the complaining partisan group to elect an appropriate percentage of members to the legislative body in question.[34] This may give the misleading impression that what makes a gerrymander unconstitutional is its being too extreme. If we bear in mind that *Bandemer* is a "suspect classification" equal protection case rather than a "fundamental right" case, our attention will be drawn to the characteristics of the plaintiff group rather than simply to the degree of the burden placed on the group. We are thus led to the other two phrases emphasized above. It is "the electoral system"—not simply the challenged districting plan—that must consistently degrade the plaintiffs' influence on "the political process as a whole"—not simply their ability to elect a certain number of representatives to a legislative body.

Justice White's use of these phrases signifies that the districting plan itself is not the only variable in a gerrymandering case. Equally essential to the plaintiff group's cause of action is the group's political status in general. A districting plan does not violate equal protection because it treats a political group badly or even because it treats the group extremely badly. The plan violates equal protection if the group it treats badly suffers from pervasive disadvantages or discrimination throughout the political system.

The "consistently degrade" passage is not alone in carrying this meaning. The paragraph immediately preceding contains this language, which has seemed implausible to some commentators:

> [T]he power to influence the political process is not limited to winning elections. An individual or a group of individuals who votes for a losing candidate is usually deemed to be adequately represented by the winning candidate and to have as much opportunity to influence that candidate as other voters in the district. We cannot presume in such a situation, without actual proof to the contrary, that the candidate elected will entirely ignore the interests of those voters. . . . Thus, a group's electoral power is not unconstitutionally diminished by the simple fact of an apportionment scheme that makes winning elections more difficult. (p. 2810)

Alfange (1986, pp. 245–246), commenting on this passage, notes that it undoubtedly "came as something of a surprise to the Republican National Committee to be told that whether their candidates are able to win elections is not essentially relevant to the question whether they have been victims of a gerrymander." But the Court's question is whether a political group has been the victim of a denial of equal protection of the laws, and that is a different question.

If we were to assume that *Bandemer* is what the antigerrymandering reformers wanted it to be—a case about the "fairness" of districting plans as between the Democrats and the Republicans under familiar conditions of American politics—then Justice White's statements would indeed be bewildering at best and stupidly disingenuous at worst. But as the reliance on the racial cases and the reference to the "political process as a whole" in the "consistently degrade" passage make clear, the cause of action the plurality is contemplating is not about Democrats and Republicans under normal conditions. It is about a political group suffering pervasive discrimination in the political process. As Professor Alfange (1986, p. 246) acknowledges, it makes an enormous difference to a minority group whether their representatives regard them as "enemies to be overcome or as constituents to be wooed in anticipation of the next election." Democrats represented by Republican legislators ordinarily fall within the latter category.[35] Blacks, communists, and homosexuals are examples of groups that have sometimes fallen within the former category. If the plurality opinion is read as contemplating an action brought by a group suffering from that sort of discriminatory treatment, Justice White's statement about representation for supporters of losing candidates is not bewildering, stupid, or disingenuous after all.

That this is precisely what the plurality contemplates is further evidenced by the citation, immediately following the representation passage quoted above, to footnote 7 of Justice Marshall's dissenting opinion in *Mobile v. Bolden*. That footnote casts considerable light on the showing of discrimination needed to make out a gerrymandering claim, and is worth considering despite its length:

> When all that is proved is mere lack of success at the polls, the Court will not presume that members of a political minority have suffered an impermissible dilution of political power. Rather, it is assumed that these persons have means available to them through which they can have some effect on governmental decisionmaking. For example, many of these persons might belong to a variety of other political, social, and economic groups that have some impact on officials. In the absence of evidence to the contrary, it may be assumed that officials will not be improperly influenced by such factors as the race or place of residence of persons seeking governmental action. Furthermore, political factions out of office often serve as watchdogs on the performance of the government, bind together into coalitions having enhanced influence, and have the respectability necessary to affect public policy.
>
> *Unconstitutional vote dilution occurs only when a discrete political minority whose voting strength is diminished by a districting scheme proves that historical and social factors render it largely incapable of effectively utilizing alternative avenues of influencing public policy.* . . . In these circumstances, the only means of breaking down the barriers encasing the political arena is to structure the electoral districting so that the minority has a fair opportunity to elect candidates of its choice.
>
> The test for unconstitutional vote dilution, then, looks only to the discriminatory effects of *the combination of an electoral structure and historical and social factors.* At the same time, it requires electoral minorities to prove far more than mere lack of success at the polls. (446 U.S., p. 111, n. 7, emphasis added; citations omitted)

The plurality opinion is clear, then, by its language, by the nature of the cases on which it relies, and by the language of Justice Marshall's footnote to which the plurality opinion directs attention, that an essential part of a gerrymandering cause of action is the existence of significant discrimination against the plaintiff group throughout the political system. Significantly, this interpretation harmonizes the plurality opinion with the view expressed by three of the plurality's members in *Karcher v. Daggett (II)* (466 U.S. 910 (1984)), that "[w]e have never concluded, nor in my view should we conclude, that the existence of noncompact or gerrymandered districts is *by itself* a constitutional violation" (Justice Brennan, dissenting, joined by Justices Marshall and White, 466 U.S., p. 917, emphasis added). Although Prof. Alfange (1986, p. 179, n. 20) finds it "surprising" that the justices who took this position in *Karcher (II)* were in the plurality in *Bandemer*, their statement that political gerrymandering "by itself" is constitutional is perfectly consistent with the *Bandemer* cause of action requiring that the gerrymander be employed against a politically oppressed group. The *Karcher (II)* dissent had recognized that "discrimination on racial or religious lines" (*Karcher II*, p. 917) was unconstitutional, and discrimination against politically oppressed groups is a natural addition to such a list.

There have been attempts to read the plurality opinion in a more interventionist vein. One commentator, for example, writes that "[d]isproportionality remains [!] the underlying test of unconstitutionality; the plurality merely adds the requirement that any such disproportion obtain over the long term, not just in a single election" (Note, 1986, p. 161). Such readings are possible only if snippets of the opinion are read out of context. For example, the first sentence in this passage by Justice White, considered in isolation, could support the interventionist reading, but the passage as a whole strongly supports the interpretation I am proposing.

> [A] mere lack of proportionate results in one election cannot suffice in this regard. We have reached this conclusion in our cases involving challenges to individual multi-member districts, and it applies equally here. In the individual multi-member district cases, we have found equal protection violations only where a history of disproportionate results appeared *in conjunction* with strong indicia of lack of political power and the denial of fair representation. . . . In those cases, *the racial minorities asserting the successful equal protection claims had essentially been shut out of the political process.* In the statewide political gerrymandering context, these prior cases lead to the analogous conclusion that equal protection violations may be found only where a history (actual or projected) of disproportionate results appears *in conjunction with similar indicia.* (*Davis v. Bandemer*, p. 2814, emphasis added, cross-reference omitted)

This passage makes it clear that there are two elements to the gerrymandering cause of action contemplated by the plurality. One, as we have seen, is that the plaintiff group must be able to show that it suffers discrimination or disadvantages throughout the political process as a whole. But even a group that is able to make such a showing cannot overthrow a districting plan without showing that it is in fact systematically disadvantaged by the plan in more than an ephemeral way. The recital in Part III-C of Justice White's opinion, setting forth the deficiencies of the trial court's findings with respect to the Indiana plan, shows that in *Bandemer* not even this element of a cause of action was satisfied. To read Part III-C as implying that if these deficiencies had been made good the Indiana Democrats would have been entitled to relief without making the required showing of discrimination throughout the political process as a whole would be to read the plurality opinion as blatantly self-contradictory.

The plurality has no occasion to detail the types of discrimination that would need to exist elsewhere in the political system to satisfy the prerequisite for a gerrymandering claim.[36] We are told that in challenges to particular districts, plaintiff groups have been able to make the required showing by presenting evidence regarding the opportunity of its members to "participate in party deliberations in the slating and nomination of candidates, their opportunity to register and vote, and hence their chance to directly influence the election returns and to secure the attention of the winning candidate" (*Davis v. Bandemer*, p. 2810). Presumably, the "historical and social factors" referred to by Justice Marshall in *Mobile v. Bolden* would be relevant. The ultimate question is whether the controlling political group treats the plaintiff group as conventional political opponents or, instead, the official and unofficial components that collectively make up the "political process" treat the plaintiff group as pariahs and thereby render the plaintiff group unable to enter into political coalitions or use other means for engaging in political competition on a roughly equal basis.

Now this is most of the story of the plurality opinion, but it is not the entire story. I have shown that the plurality says repeatedly there is no gerrymandering cause of action without evidence of discrimination in the political process as a whole against the plaintiff group as well as evidence of systematic harm from the plan itself. Nor does the plurality ever say anything to the contrary. But there are implications that need to be accounted for.

There are three portions of the plurality opinion that, although not inconsistent with the account I have given thus far, are hard to square with it. The first is this statement in the justiciability discussion, which is made in rebuttal to Justice O'Connor's accusation that the plurality improperly reads into the Constitution a preference for proportional representation. Justice White responds that the plurality's preference is "for a level of parity between votes and representation sufficient to ensure that significant minority voices are heard and that majorities are not consigned to minority status" (*Davis v. Bandemer*, p. 2807, n. 9).

The second portion of the opinion that needs explaining is the

emphasized phrase of the following passage, which is otherwise perfectly in tune with the interpretation I have offered:

> [A]n equal protection violation may be found only where the electoral
> system substantially disadvantages certain voters in their opportunity to
> influence the political process effectively. In this context, such a finding of
> unconstitutionality must be supported by evidence of *continued frustration*
> *of the will of a majority of the voters* or effective denial to a minority of voters
> of a fair chance to influence the political process. (*Davis v. Bandemer*, p.
> 2811, emphasis added)

Finally, there is the treatment of the lower court's findings with
respect to the Indiana districting plan. I have shown above that the
cause of action contemplated by the plurality, derived from the racial
gerrymandering cases, has the two elements of discrimination
throughout the political process and serious harm caused by the districting plan under attack. The discussion of the Indiana plan shows
the deficiencies with respect to the second element. Even if the deficiencies did not exist, the first element would need to be satisfied. But
it is fair to ask why Justice White did not make this simple and
obvious point explicitly in Part III-C.

None of these portions of the plurality opinion actually says that a
group can succeed in a constitutional gerrymandering claim without
showing, as part of its case, that it suffers from discrimination in the
political process beyond the alleged discrimination in the plan itself,
and elsewhere the plurality is explicit that such a showing is required.
But these portions of the opinion seem intended to give the impression that a successful gerrymandering claim could conceivably be
brought by one of the major parties against the other without evidence of abnormal discrimination throughout the political system. If
there is any merit in the notion that the plurality declares "extreme"
partisan gerrymanders unconstitutional, it emanates from these portions of the opinion.

The passage from the footnote responding to Justice O'Connor
suggests a twofold concern on the part of the plurality. First, minority
voices are to be heard. Presumably, political groups that suffer pervasive discrimination in the political system will be minority groups.
Second, majorities are not to be consigned to minority status. It is
hard to imagine that a political group attracting majority support
could have the pariah status that could lead to the pervasive discrimination the plurality requires by analogy with the racial cases. Yet the
plurality concedes to Justice O'Connor that its opinion embodies a
preference for protecting majorities, at least under some circum-

stances. There is no stated preference that majorities should be free from all disadvantages or that their majority status should assure them political control. But they should not be "consigned to minority status." The second anomalous passage also suggests that a majority group might be a successful gerrymandering plaintiff, in that it suggests that a part of the plaintiffs' required showing could be "evidence of continued frustration of the will of a majority of the voters."

A plausible explanation of these "anomalous" passages emerges from the following excerpt from the description of the deficiencies in the case made against the Indiana districts:

> The appellants argue here, without a persuasive response from appellees, that had the Democratic candidates received an additional few percentage points of the votes cast statewide, they would have obtained a majority of the seats in both houses. Nor was there any finding that the 1981 reapportionment would consign the Democrats to a minority status in the Assembly throughout the 1980's or that the Democrats would have no hope of doing any better in the reapportionment that would occur after the 1990 census (*Davis v. Bandemer*, p. 2812).

Let us hypothesize a state in which, by any reasonable measure, the A Party enjoys a stable and convincing majority of voter support. However, at the time of the last districting the B Party was in control and was able to enact so overpowering a gerrymandered districting plan that they were assured complete control of state government. Furthermore, the plan is so effective and the geographical patterns of voter support are sufficiently stable that it can be predicted with a high degree of assurance that the B Party's control will last through the next census, in which case they will be able to update their gerrymander in a manner that will virtually assure their continued dominance through the next decade, and so on.

The A Party's hypothesized majority support among the voters should permit it to elect the governor. Accordingly, if the state has typical governing arrangements the B Party, in order to maintain the hypothesized dominance, will need to elect two-thirds of the members of each house of the state legislature. This will permit the B Party to enact legislation over the governor's veto, including the decennial districting update.

Now, suppose the A Party and several of its members challenge this arrangement under the Equal Protection Clause. The Supreme Court would be faced with a self-perpetuating breakdown of the democratic process, comparable to what it faced in many of the early malapportionment cases. The case would not perch neatly on either the "fundamental rights" branch or the "suspect classification" branch of the Equal Protection Clause. But just as the Court blazed new doctrinal trails when confronted with *Baker* and *Reynolds*, the Court should and would, if confronted with the kind of breakdown I have hypothesized, find a way to restore democratic order.

Justice O'Connor expressed a belief that political gerrymandering is a "self-limiting enterprise" (p. 2820). I agree, and the hypothetical case seems to me to be sheer fantasy.[37] But the self-limiting nature of the political gerrymander was not clear to the plurality (*Davis v. Bandemer*, p. 2807), and given the arcane nature of the subject, there is no particular reason why it should have been. Justice White's passages suggesting but not quite saying that a majority group, not suffering from pervasive discrimination, might have a gerrymandering cause of action, are most plausibly read as a hedge against a case like the hypothetical. To call such a case an "extreme" denial of proportional representation would be to speak in euphemisms. The proper description would be a denial of democratic representation.

Now we can bridge the conceptual gap in the plurality opinion. The following skeleton outline for a missing Part Two-and-a-Half of the plurality opinion does no violence to the existing fabric of equal protection doctrine, and leads directly to the specific constitutional standards set forth by Justice White for governing gerrymandering claims. On that basis, I offer it as a guide to the interpretation of *Davis v. Bandemer*.

1. Gerrymandering and similar vote dilution claims brought under the Equal Protection Clause are group claims. As such, they do not implicate the right to vote or any other right attaching to individuals. In the case of constitutional claims brought by minority racial groups, the plan in question will be subjected to heightened scrutiny if the plaintiffs can demonstrate that the plan is intended to minimize their political influence and that it is in fact harmful to them.[38] This follows from the established doctrine that racial classifications are suspect under the Equal Protection Clause.

2. A gerrymandering claim brought by a group not constituted by race or by some other classification that has been recognized as "suspect" for equal protection purposes must demonstrate that the group is the victim of pervasive discrimination in the political process to such a degree that it is reasonable to suppose a districting plan contrary to their interests is the result of prejudice and an animus well beyond the usual bounds of political opposition in our system.[39]

3. There is one additional possibility. If a case should arise in which a partisan gerrymander between established political parties should be so effective as to virtually guarantee a minority group permanent dominance over state government, comparable to the situation that existed in *Baker v. Carr* and some of the other malapportionment cases, that might be unconstitutional as well. It is not necessary to determine whether gerrymandering really is a powerful enough tool to produce such a result, nor to decide exactly what the theory supporting judicial intervention in such a case would be.

V. THE AUTHORITATIVENESS OF THE PLURALITY OPINION

The rationale underlying Justice White's opinion is not binding on the Court in future cases, since it was joined by only a plurality. Nevertheless, the results derived in specific cases by application of the plurality opinion are binding on lower courts to the extent that the results reached under the plurality opinion would be the same as those reached under at least one of the other major opinions in *Bandemer*, those of Justices O'Connor and Powell.[40]

In practical terms, our inquiry is whenever a violation of the Fourteenth Amendment would be found under Justice White's opinion, would the same result be reached under Justice Powell's opinion; and whenever no Fourteenth Amendment violation would be found under Justice White's opinion, would the same result be reached under Justice O'Connor's opinion? If the answer is yes in each case, then we may treat Justice White's opinion as authoritative, since the result it dictates would command a majority of the *Bandemer* court in all instances.

Turning first to Justice O'Connor's opinion, we are presented with the immediate difficulty that she and the justices who joined her would have decided the case in favor of the *Bandemer* defendants on grounds that the case was nonjusticiable. In future cases, she and her colleagues could be expected to acquiesce in the authoritative decision of the Court in *Bandemer*, and accept the justiciability of partisan gerrymandering claims.[41] However unlikely it may be as a matter of psychology, there is no logical inconsistency if a justice believes a type of constitutional claim ought to be treated as nonjusticiable, but then takes an expansive view of it on the merits once its justiciability has been determined.

Justice O'Connor's opinion has indeed been interpreted as not reaching the merits of the equal protection issue (Alfange, 1986, p.

243; Note, 1986, p. 155, n. 13), an interpretation that leaves open the theoretical possibility of Justice O'Connor and her colleagues joining with Justices Powell and Stevens to strike down partisan gerrymanders that would be upheld under Justice White's opinion. But the O'Connor opinion does not confine itself to the justiciability question.

"The Equal Protection Clause," Justice O'Connor writes, "does not supply judicially manageable standards for resolving purely political gerrymandering claims, *and* no group right to an equal share of political power was ever intended by the Framers of the Fourteenth Amendment" (p. 2818, emphasis added). These are two separate propositions, the first sounding in justiciability and the second sounding in a substantive interpretation of the Equal Protection Clause.[42]

Justice O'Connor goes on to quote Justice Harlan's observation in his dissent in *Baker v. Carr* that the same considerations that ought to lead to a conclusion of nonjusticiability in apportionment cases also bear on the substantive question "whether any cognizable constitutional claim has been asserted." Her ensuing discussion of the contrast between individual voting rights, which *Reynolds v. Sims* establishes are protected by the Equal Protection Clause, and group political rights, which she maintains are not protected except when the claimant is a racial group of the sort specially protected by the Fourteenth Amendment; her distinguishing of *Gaffney v. Cummings* (412 U.S. 735 (1973)) on the merits, when Justice White had relied on that case for justiciability; and her deploring of what she foresees as a likely trend toward requiring proportional representation, all make it clear that her concurring in the judgment against the *Bandemer* plaintiffs is based not only on justiciability but on the merits. The author of that opinion cannot consistently find that a partisan gerrymandering claim states a cause of action under the Fourteenth Amendment, even if she acquiesces in the Court's holding that such claims are justiciable.

Next we must consider whether any partisan gerrymander found unconstitutional under Justice White's opinion would also be unconstitutional under Justice Powell's dissenting opinion. This is not an easy question, for Justice Powell's opinion is more difficult to decipher than Justice White's. Justice Powell begins his analysis by accepting a definition of gerrymandering as "the deliberate and arbitrary distortion of district boundaries and populations for partisan or personal purposes." Since the meaning of "distortion" in this context is hardly self-evident, Justice Powell sets forth the following constitutional standard, quoting from Justice Stevens' concurring opinion in *Karcher v. Daggett (I)* (462 U.S. 725 (1983)):

> [G]errymandering violates the Equal Protection Clause only when the re-districting plan serves "no purpose other than to favor one segment—whether racial, ethnic, religious, economic, or political—that may occupy a position of strength at a particular time, or to disadvantage a politically weak segment of the community." (*Davis v. Bandemer*, p. 2827)

Justice Powell cannot be taken literally when he says that in order to be an unconstitutional gerrymander a plan must serve no purpose other than favoritism. Every districting plan serves the purpose of making it possible for the members of the legislature to be elected by separate and relatively small constituencies rather than on an at-large basis. Under *Reynolds* every plan must have the further purpose of weighting votes equally by assuring that the districts are equal in population. Nevertheless, this is not a serious criticism of the Powell decision, because creating legislative districts that are separate and have equal populations is so universally understood as part of the background that these purposes can be accepted readily as implied exceptions to the standard that "no purpose" be present other than favoritism.

A more difficult problem is presented by the fact that Justice Powell would have struck down the Indiana plan notwithstanding his acceptance of the district court's finding that an additional purpose of the plan was to avoid reduction of black representation in the Indiana legislature (*Davis v. Bandemer*, p. 2838).[43] Justice Powell does not suggest that this is the type of favoritism that is suspect, and it can hardly be suggested that maintaining existing black representation is a background purpose inevitably connected to every redistricting plan. Apparently, then, only certain purposes will save a plan from a constitutional claim of gerrymandering.

Justice Powell's standard therefore must be reworded: A gerrymander is unconstitutional if it serves no *adequate* purpose other than favoritism. We shall inquire into what constitutes an "adequate" purpose momentarily, but first we should notice the clear implication of the standard, that a plan serving a purpose of partisan favoritism is valid as long as it additionally serves some other purpose as well, although we have now seen that not just any other purpose will do.

Justice Powell is not prohibiting even the most strongly partisan-motivated plans, as long as they are not *solely* partisan-motivated. Thus, he distinguishes between gerrymandering of the sort he believes should be unconstitutional and "the common practice of the party in power to choose the redistricting plan that gives it an advantage at the polls" (*Davis v. Bandemer*, p. 2827), which he says is "loosely" called gerrymandering but is not unconstitutional. Justice Powell says only a "sensitive and searching inquiry" can distinguish loose gerrymandering from unconstitutional gerrymandering (p. 2827), but in point of fact there is only one difference between the two as he has defined them, and that is the presence or absence of some other adequate purpose. The be-all and the end-all under Justice Powell's opinion, then, is whether a redistricting plan, no matter how much it may favor one party or political group over another, also serves some other purpose he is prepared to recognize.

The purposes that will validate a redistricting plan against charges of gerrymandering are those Justice Powell is prepared to characterize as "neutral and legitimate" (*Davis v. Bandemer*, p. 2828). But these words do not carry their usual meaning. "Neutral" purposes may not only coexist with "loose" gerrymandering, but "[g]roups may consistently fail to elect representatives under a perfectly neutral election scheme" (p. 2832, n. 13). Furthermore, the "most important" of the neutral purposes are said to be creating districts with regular shapes and adhering to municipal boundaries (pp. 2831–2832). As Jonathan Steinberg and I have demonstrated, these criteria are not at all neutral in any normal sense of that term, since they disfavor a party whose voting strength is disproportionately concentrated in compact areas within municipal boundaries, and dispersed at less than majority levels throughout the rest of the state. Either major party can find itself in this plight, in which case Justice Powell's criteria are not "neutral" as between the parties. As it happens, given the political demographics of contemporary American politics, probably more often than not the criteria will favor the Republicans and disfavor the Democrats (Lowenstein and Steinberg, 1985, pp. 21–35).[44]

Justice Powell summarizes his approach by saying that the most important of the factors that "should" (i.e., that must, under constitutional compulsion, if Justice Powell has his way) guide legislators are:

> the shapes of voting districts and adherence to established political subdivision boundaries. Other relevant considerations include the nature of the legislative procedures by which the apportionment law was adopted and legislative history reflecting contemporaneous legislative goals. To make out a case of unconstitutional partisan gerrymandering, the plaintiff should be required to offer proof concerning these factors, which bear directly on the fairness of a redistricting plan, as well as evidence concerning population disparities and statistics tending to show vote dilution. No one factor should be dispositive. (*Davis v. Bandemer*, pp. 2831–2832)

The last sentence must be taken with a grain of salt, for two reasons. First, Justice Powell adds that "[i]n some cases, proof of grotesque shapes may, without more, provide convincing proof of unconstitutional gerrymandering" (p. 2832, n. 12). In these cases, apparently, the one factor of irregular district boundaries will indeed be dispositive. More important, Justice Powell's summary of the "factors" is much less of a "totality of the circumstances" list than may appear at first reading.

The most important factors, as we have seen, are shapes and municipal boundaries. The other four factors Justice Powell mentions are (1) legislative procedures, (2) legislative history reflecting legislative goals, (3) population disparities, and (4) vote dilution, by which Justice Powell presumably means results falling short of proportional representation. The first, second, and fourth of these are all factors that are likely to be present in the case of "loose" gerrymandering, which is not unconstitutional according to Justice Powell. The remaining factor, population disparities, cannot be present in a gerrymandering case, since it would be sufficient by itself to invalidate the plan on malapportionment grounds. As Justice Powell states his position, if the plan in question satisfies his criterion of regular district shapes and/or his criterion of adhering to municipal boundaries, the plan constitutes "loose" gerrymandering and is constitutionally valid. If it does not satisfy these criteria it is unconstitutional.[45]

This conclusion follows from the language of Justice Powell's opinion, but it may nevertheless be too narrow a reading to assume he will limit himself to district shapes and municipal boundaries. When he demands "neutral and legitimate" purposes, he clearly has no intention of inquiring into whether a given purpose actually is neutral or of pointing to a principle, constitutional or otherwise, by which the purpose acquires legitimacy. He probably means simply to refer to the laundry list of purposes long advanced by the opponents of partisan gerrymandering. He might therefore be receptive to such purposes as drawing districts that comprise "communities of interests," or districts that follow geographic features such as rivers or mountain ranges.[46]

Compactness, adherence to municipal boundaries, and similar criteria play no part in Justice White's analysis. As a general proposition, Justice Powell undoubtedly is more willing to strike down a districting plan on gerrymandering grounds than Justice White, and by a considerable margin. Nevertheless, Justice Powell's opinion, by its terms, permits gerrymanders, no matter how oppressive, if their districts satisfy compactness, adherence to municipal boundaries, or, perhaps, similar criteria.

It is therefore possible, though unlikely, for a districting plan to be unconstitutional under Justice White's opinion, but not under Justice Powell's. In such a case the justices who joined the Powell and O'Connor opinions would constitute a majority to uphold the plan. To this extent, then, the plurality opinion is not authoritative in its entirety. A district court presented with a plan that is unconstitutional under Justice White's opinion should nevertheless uphold it if, for example, the legislators who formulated the plan acted not only with the purpose of savaging an oppressed political minority, but also with the purpose of attaining compact districts that coincide with municipal boundaries.[47]

Under Justice White's opinion, the Court will intervene in gerrymandering controversies when there is a genuine civil rights violation against an oppressed group or when there is a breakdown in democratic processes on the order of those presented in the malapportionment cases. Under normal circumstances, the plurality leaves the major parties to their own devices. In contrast, Justice Powell's approach gives no guarantee of a remedy for civil rights violations or democratic breakdowns, but permits intervention in routine partisan disputes between Democrats and Republicans in the name of criteria such as compactness that have little if any theoretical, historical, or practical claim to legitimacy. It is little wonder that Justices Powell and Stevens, who had announced their interventionist approach to gerrymandering in *Karcher (I)*, were unable to win the support of any additional justices in *Davis v. Bandemer*.

CONCLUSION

Serious prejudice and discrimination against political groups is a recurrent theme in American history, but it has been directed against groups with too little electoral support to be affected by legislative districting. And despite vague fears generated by the use of computers in the districting process, gerrymandering provides benefits to the major parties at the margin. Extreme malapportionment was self-perpetuating in many states at the time of *Baker v. Carr*. Gerrymandering is not a potent enough instrument to permit a minority to dominate state government and perpetuate itself from decade to decade—especially not in a state in which an extraordinary legislative majority is required to overcome a governor's veto.

These considerations suggest a final objection to my proposed interpretation of *Davis v. Bandemer*. Why should the justices who made up the plurality have bothered to hold that political gerrymandering presents a justiciable issue and that under some circumstances there might be a gerrymandering cause of action, if the political and social realities make it improbable that a political gerrymandering suit ever will succeed?

One answer might be that practicalities aside, the justices preferred a response that was analytically sound to one that was "simpler" but unsound. Perhaps a more likely answer is that the one constant in American politics has been change. There is little on the American scene now to suggest that serious prejudice and discrimination will be directed against political groups with sufficient electoral support to have a chance of electing legislators, but who can say that such a development sometime in the future is impossible? Similarly, how could the justices feel utterly certain that gerrymandering will never give a minority party or other political group a stranglehold on the politics of a state comparable to that in the malapportioned states of a quarter-century ago?

If the first type of case arose, the Court would be faced with a genuine civil rights problem. If the second arose, the Court might believe it was necessary to restore a state to democratic control. Neither event seems at all likely, but the fact that an exit may never be needed is no reason to bar the door. Why write another *Colegrove v. Green* (328 U.S. 549 (1946))?

There is one additional consideration. In *Fortson v. Dorsey* (379 U.S. 433 (1965)), the first post-*Baker* case involving multimember legislative districts, the Court wrote that such districts were not generally violative of equal protection but might be struck down if they work "to minimize or cancel out the voting strength of racial or political elements of the voting population." This verbal formula has been repeated in numerous cases, and the racial portion of it bore fruit in *White v. Regester* (412 U.S. 755 (1973)). I believe it is fair to say that the "political" part of this formulation was generally regarded, up to the time of *Bandemer*, as nothing more than a dormant possibility. The Court had never barred the possibility of constitutionalizing political gerrymandering, but neither had it ever indicated the slightest affirmative interest in doing so.

Why should members of the Court wish to perpetuate a situation in which they retain the option to intervene when they have no apparent intention of exercising that option? A somewhat cynical answer is that it is in the interest of the justices to maximize their power by retaining as many options as possible. A less cynical and perhaps more plausible answer is that the justices have believed intervention into routine partisan disputes over gerrymandering would require the

Court to make extremely difficult decisions and might cause political embarrassment, but would bring about little if any public benefit. At the same time the justices, recognizing the complexity of the subject, may have been uncertain what abusive practices might be brought to light in the future, and have been reluctant to cut off an avenue for relief if and when relief was needed.

When *Davis v. Bandemer* came along, invited by the separate opinions of Justices Stevens and Powell in *Karcher (I)*, it seemed as if the Court had to fish or cut bait. The District Court had struck down the Indiana plan. If the Court affirmed, restrictions on political gerrymandering were in the Constitution forever. If the Court reversed, it had to say why. Suppose a justice, placed in this position, wanted only to restore the *status quo ante* as nearly as possible. The result might look very much like Justice White's opinion for the plurality.

ADDENDUM: RESPONSE TO GROFMAN

The reader who compares my essay and Professor Grofman's (chapter 3) with our respective contributions to the 1985 *UCLA Law Review* symposium on partisan gerrymandering will be struck by the correspondence between our present conflicting interpretations of *Davis v. Bandemer* and the differences we expressed in our pre-*Bandemer* writings.[48] No doubt this double correlation falls well short of statistical significance, but unhindered as I am by formal training in either the natural or social sciences, I feel free to conclude that something other than sheer randomness is at work here.

The reader who is not already a card-carrying member of either the Grofman or the Lowenstein camp will therefore be well-advised to approach each of our interpretations with more than the normal amount of skepticism. Nevertheless, our essays, however tainted by the appearance or reality of wishful thinking, at least share the virtue of purporting to identify a way of interpreting *Bandemer* to avoid the conclusion of previous writers that the plurality opinion is hopelessly confused and standardless. The only way of arbitrating the differences is by a close testing of our respective interpretations against the text of Justice White's opinion.[49] In this Addendum I attempt to show by a few important examples that, at least in Grofman's case, the emphasis must be on *"wishful* thinking," and that whatever flaws may be present in my own interpretation, they are not the ones that Grofman claims to find.

Grofman is one of a number of able political scientists who have devoted substantial efforts to defining and refining elaborate methods of assessing the "votes-seats" relationship produced by districting plans. It is therefore understandable that before *Bandemer* he advocated incorporation of these methods into constitutional standards for judging the validity of districting plans, and that he now asserts *Bandemer* did precisely what he had urged. This assertion is essential to Grofman's central claim that under *Bandemer* a partisan gerrymander is unconstitutional if it is intentional, severe, and nontransient in its effects. Grofman cannot plausibly impute to the *Bandemer* plurality the view that the "severity" of a gerrymander is of constitutional significance without also imputing to the plurality some conception of what "severity" means.

Grofman begins this portion of his interpretation by asserting that there are "two well-established techniques" for assessing the "votes-seats" relationship. The first technique, associated primarily with Backstrom, Robins, and Eller (1978; this volume), attempts to determine a geographically defined "baseline" two-party vote from selected statewide partisan elections, while the second technique, variations of which have been proposed by Grofman and many other writers, extrapolates changes in the two-party vote within legislative districts on the basis of hypothetical changes in the statewide aggregate party vote.

On Grofman's reading of *Bandemer*, the plurality decided that the constitutionality of districting plans will turn on the questions these social science methodologies are intended to answer, but left open whether the Court will use just one of the techniques or both for finding answers. Thus, Grofman writes:

> As I read it, the plurality opinion in *Davis v. Bandemer* (p. 2812, n. 15) recognizes Methods 1 and 2 above as the two basic ways to identify partisan voting strength. While the exact nature of the requisite applications of these two methodologies remains to be litigated, like Justice White I do not think it yet necessary to decide between these two methods. Indeed it may never be necessary to pick one or the other, since both have advantages. (this volume, p. 45)

The reference to footnote 15 is the only reference to the plurality opinion that Grofman gives in the above passage or anywhere else in his extended discussion of this subject. Footnote 15 deals with a conflict between the majority and minority in the lower court *Bandemer* decision regarding the identity of the plaintiff class of voters. The majority in the lower court thought the group suffering discrimination was the class of Indiana voters who had voted for Democratic Assembly candidates in 1982, even if they voted Republican in other elections. Dissenting, Judge Pell thought the group suffering alleged discrimination was made up of consistently Democratic voters. On the basis of that belief, he applied (actually misapplied) a version of the Backstrom methodology (method 1 in Grofman's terms). Justice White concludes the footnote by stating that whether or not Judge Pell applied this method correctly "need not now be resolved."

Justice White's opinion contains *no* reference to the social science literature regarding "votes-seats" relationships and the various proposed techniques for assessing them. It contains *no* reference, however oblique, to the family of techniques in Grofman's method 2. As we have just seen, it contains *one* reference to Grofman's method 1, namely to note that although the dissenting judge attempted to use it in the lower court, it had no bearing on the decision of the case. Yet, Grofman concludes, Justice White "recognizes methods 1 and 2 above as the two basic ways to identify partisan voting strength." This is wishful thinking, not only with respect to the fabricated "recognition" of methods 1 and 2, but more importantly in its unsupported assumption that Justice White expresses interest in *any* method for identifying "partisan voting strength."

The second aspect of Grofman's interpretation I shall consider, before turning to his criticism of my essay, is the conclusion he draws from Justice White's enumeration in Part III-C of deficiencies in the lower court's specific findings regarding the Indiana districting plans. Findings of the sort that Justice White enumerates as missing are presumably *necessary* for a districting plan to be struck down.[50] The question is whether such findings would be *sufficient* to invalidate a plan. Grofman assumes, without argument, that they would be. The question is a crucial one for the interpretation of *Bandemer*.

Consider, as an example, Justice White's observation that there was no finding that "because of the 1981 Act the Democrats could not in one of the next few elections secure a sufficient vote to take control of the assembly" (*Davis v. Bandemer*, p. 2812). The context suggests, and Grofman agrees, that without some such showing, the Indiana Democrats could not be entitled to judgment. Grofman goes further, however, to conclude that *if* the Democrats had proved the 1981 Act precluded them from controlling the assembly in one of the next few elections, the judgment in favor of the plaintiffs would have been affirmed. This is the converse of Justice White's proposition.

As a matter of formal logic, it is elementary that a statement does not imply the truthfulness of its converse. Legal interpretation is not a matter of formal logic-chopping, however. Often it is quite reasonable to understand a statement to imply the truth of its converse. If I say, for example, "I am taking my umbrella today because the forecast is for rain," it will probably be a correct inference that I would not be taking my umbrella if the forecast were for clear weather. In contrast, the statement "President Nixon failed to serve his entire second term because he resigned" is true, but cannot reasonably be said to imply the truth of its converse, that if President Nixon had not resigned he would have served his entire second term. In ordinary English, as opposed to formal logic, the question whether a statement implies the truth of its converse is a subtle one, depending largely on the context.

Justice White's laundry list of deficiencies in the Indiana findings contains a number of items, some of which might have been cured relatively easily, either in Indiana or in other cases, and others that would be difficult to prove in any circumstances. An example of the first category is the statement that "[r]elying on a single election to prove unconstitutional discrimination is unsatisfactory" (id.). The second category is illustrated by the comment that there was no finding "that the Democrats would have no hope of doing any better in the reapportionment that would occur after the 1990 Census" (id.).

The suggestion that simply remedying *any* of the deficiencies would have resulted in an affirmance in *Bandemer* is untenable. For example, the suggestion that the plaintiffs lost in *Bandemer* simply because they relied only on one year's election results is explicitly negated by Justice White (*Davis v. Bandemer*, p. 2814, n. 17). In another footnote, Justice White says that even if the findings regarding the House were sufficient, this would not support invalidating the Senate plan, because the findings regarding the Senate were weaker (p. 2813, n. 16). If Grofman is correct that Part III-C is intended to imply the truth of the converse of its propositions, it would follow from footnote 16 that the very findings declared insufficient to support the lower court's ruling regarding the House would have been sufficient to support the ruling as to the Senate. This conclusion is absurd and I do not suggest that Grofman would argue for it, but he provides no basis for accepting reasoning by converse with respect to some portions of Part III-C and not others.

Aside from these specific bits of evidence that Part III-C is not to receive the implicatory weight Grofman gives it, there is the more fundamental point that Grofman's interpretation turns Part III-C into a flagrant contradiction of the main thrust of Part III-B and of specific statements elsewhere, that disadvantageous impact of the districting plan on the plaintiff group is a necessary but *not* sufficient part of a gerrymandering claim.[51] To assume, as Grofman does, that Justice

White's opinion implies the converse of each statement in Part III-C would vindicate not Grofman's view, but the more widespread reading of *Bandemer* as contradictory and confused. However, neither logic nor the ordinary use of language compels this conclusion, which is negated by evidence within Part III-C and by the overall structure of the plurality opinion.

If, as I believe, the foregoing shows that Grofman's interpretation of *Bandemer* is untenable, it does not establish the validity of my own interpretation. The remainder of this Addendum responds to each of the criticisms Grofman levels against my interpretation.

First, Grofman attacks my central point that "the gerrymandering claims the plurality is prepared to recognize are claims brought by political groups that have suffered from discrimination to the degree that their status under the equal protection clause is analogous to the status of racial minorities." I based this conclusion on Justice White's frequent statements that seem to mean precisely this (for example, the statement that "the electoral system" must "consistently degrade" a group's "influence on the political process as a whole" (*Davis v. Bandemer*, p. 2810); and the statement that plaintiffs must show disproportionate results "in conjunction with similar indicia," referring to claims by racial minorities that they "had essentially been shut out of the political process" (p. 2814); on the pervasive references to and reliance on the racial discrimination cases; and on the context of equal protection doctrine, within which *Bandemer* is far more plausibly explained as a "suspect class" case than as a "fundamental right" case. Yet, it seems "quite clear" to Grofman:

> that this assertion about what *Bandemer* means is wrong, and has explicitly been rejected by the Supreme Court when Justice White said (*Davis v. Bandemer*, p. 2806, emphasis added), "That the group has not been subject to the same historical stigma [as racial groups] may be relevant to the manner in which the case is adjudicated, but [does] *not justify a refusal to entertain such a case*." (this volume p. 48, emphasis Grofman's)

Grofman apparently has overlooked the fact that the statement he quotes comes from the discussion of justiciability, not the merits of the case. Immediately preceding the sentence Grofman quotes is the statement that merely because the equal protection claim "is submitted by a political group, rather than a racial group, does not distinguish it *in terms of justiciability*" (*Davis v. Bandemer*, p. 2806, emphasis added). Certainly, *Bandemer* holds that gerrymandering claims brought by the major parties are justiciable or, in the words of the passage quoted by Grofman, that the courts will not "refus[e] to entertain such a case." This justiciability holding left open the possibility, made explicit in the very passage, that the differences between major parties and racial minority groups might affect the merits, that is, "the manner in which the case is adjudicated." Part III of the opinion makes it clear that indeed the nature of the plaintiff group has a profound effect on the merits of the claim.

Grofman claims that if my reading of *Bandemer* is correct, "then the plurality wasted a lot of wood pulp on irrelevant remarks." Although there is some force in this contention, Grofman overstates the point because he is looking at the question solely from the perspective of a reformer seeking judicial intervention in major party districting controversies. If there should be a resurgence of some variant of McCarthyism some time in the future, *Bandemer* provides a potential basis for protecting outcast political groups in cases where neither the First Amendment nor the "fundamental rights" branch of equal protection doctrine are available.

Grofman's next point is that my interpretation "is not easily reconciled with other language . . . which shows that it was the lack of a solid evidentiary record" that caused the *Bandemer* plaintiffs to lose in the Supreme Court. Here, Grofman is referring to Part III-C of Justice White's opinion. As we have seen, the language does not "show" that a stronger record would have been sufficient for a finding of unconstitutionality. At most there are statements susceptible of being so interpreted, and it is Grofman's desire to so interpret them that is not "easily reconciled" with the opinion as a whole.

Finally, Grofman quarrels with my interpretation of the passage in Justice White's opinion saying that individuals who vote for a losing candidate are "usually deemed to be adequately represented by the winning candidate" (*Davis v. Bandemer*, p. 2810).[52] He suggests that this is the *only* passage in the plurality opinion that, "at first blush," seems to support my interpretation, a suggestion that is unlikely to impress anyone who reads my essay or, better, the opinion itself. In any event, Grofman finds the first blush misleading, for he maintains that all Justice White meant was that the *Bandemer* plaintiffs forgot to introduce evidence that Republican office holders tend to behave differently in office from Democratic officeholders. As Grofman suggests, if this is all that is needed, filling the gap will be a simple task (e.g., Sabato, 1988, pp. 46–55).

It seems to me very doubtful whether Justice White's requirement, "that the candidate will entirely ignore the interests" of the group of voters claiming a denial of equal protection, can bear Grofman's interpretation that all that is needed is a showing that Republican legislators tend to vote differently from Democrats. It seems even more doubtful when Justice White adds, "This is true even in a safe district where the losing group loses election after election." And it seems utterly out of the question when at the end of the paragraph, Justice White inserts a reference to footnote 7 of Justice Marshall's dissent in *Mobile v. Bolden*. That footnote is quoted at length in the main body of my essay, but it will be recalled that it includes the statement, "Unconstitutional vote dilution occurs only when a discrete political minority whose voting strength is diminished by a districting scheme proves that historical and social factors render it largely incapable of effectively utilizing alternative avenues of influencing public policy." Unless Grofman believes Justice White is given to selecting citations at random, his interpretation of the passage in question is plainly erroneous.

Grofman adds, however, that his interpretation must be accepted to bring *Bandemer* into line with recent racial vote dilution cases, namely *Ketchum v. Byrne* (740 F. 2nd 1398 (1984)) U.S. Ct. of Appeals 7th Circuit), *Major v. Treen* (574 F. Supp. 325 (1983)), and *Thornburg v. Gingles* (106 S. Ct. 2752 (1986)). The first two of these cases were decided by lower courts, and all three of them were decided explicitly under the Voting Rights Act, *not* under the Equal Protection Cause.[53] Is it a mystery why Grofman believes *Bandemer* needs to be reconciled with statutory decisions that it does not cite, while he feels free to ignore equal protection decisions on which Justice White relies heavily? Not when the reason appears so clearly—wishful thinking.

Whether my essay contains errors attributable to the same cause is for the reader to determine. I am content to conclude by referring you to the only source on which such a determination can rest, the text of the Supreme Court's decision in *Bandemer*.

NOTES
1. Peter H. Schuck's article was published as I was completing final revisions for this essay, and therefore is not referred to in the text (Schuck 1987). Schuck is sharply critical of *Bandemer*. Although I agree with many of the points he makes, I do not agree that they make a case against *Bandemer*, which I believe Schuck misreads. Schuck's criticism is based on the premise that *Bandemer* either does or will require proportional representation or something close to it. To the extent this is simply a prediction of what the Court will do in later cases, see 87 *Columbia Law Review* at 1364, I can do no more than express the hope that Schuck is wrong. But

Schuck also makes the claim that the logic of *Bandemer* either calls for this result or at least makes it inevitable. I believe the present essay demonstrates that this claim is erroneous.

Schuck's argument (at 1364) in support of his claim turns on this sentence:

> A court cannot determine whether and to what extent a districting plan "will consistently degrade a . . . group of voters' influence on the political process as a whole"—the plurality's constitutional test—unless the court can compare the group's post-gerrymander representation in the legislature to what the group's "true" representation would be under a "fair" plan.

Schuck is *misquoting* from *Davis v. Bandemer*, p. 2810, for the subject of "will consistently degrade" in Justice White's opinion is not "a districting plan," but "*the electoral system*" (emphasis added). As this essay demonstrates, consideration of the effects on a plaintiff group of the electoral system as a whole, as Justice White's words contemplate, calls for an altogether different sort of inquiry from the one that Schuck soundly criticizes. Schuck appends a footnote (ibid., n. 149) that "[a]lthough the plurality's test speaks in general terms of 'influence on the political process as a whole' (*Davis v. Bandemer*, p. 2810), the test is clearly concerned with representation in the legislature." My essay is written on the hypothesis that the opinions in *Bandemer* do not "clearly" mean something altogether different from what they say.

2. Whether "one person, one vote" has actually made much of a difference has been a point of controversy (e.g., Auerbach, 1971, pp. 87–90; Bicker, 1971). I share Lewis' (1978, p. xii) view that the rule "has made politics more open and more responsive to accelerating change." See also McKay (1968, pp. 230–231).

3. I must accept my share of culpability, since I am a signatory of an *amicus* brief, filed by the California Democratic Congressional delegation in support of the *Bandemer* defendants, whose argument is cast entirely in terms of justiciability. Whether or not it was a wise tactic to forgo the additional argument that partisan gerrymandering does not violate the Fourteenth Amendment, the failure to assert a direct argument going to the merits of the constitutional issue may have played its part in causing what I argue in the text is the major weakness of the plurality opinion.

4. It would therefore be immaterial to this essay if it could be known, for example, that the standards set forth in Part III of Justice White's opinion derive from no overall conception of the subject at all, but represent instead a compromise of differences, necessary to get four justices to join in a single opinion. Except that I have some qualms about the word *objective*, the following statement is applicable to my purpose here:

> My whole scheme of analysis is based on the notion that a higher-court decision should be viewed as authoritative in some sense other than simply as data upon which one might rely in predicting whether subsequent lower-court decisions will be affirmed or reversed by the higher court. In other words, I believe a lower court should generally feel "bound" by the "decision" (which encompasses the dispositional decree and the objective meaning of the language of the opinion) of a higher court even in the face of developments, such as personnel changes or extrinsic evidence of either the true intentions of or changes of heart by key judges, which might radically alter the predictive calculus. (Blasi, 1979, p. 22 n. 6)

5. Part II of Justice White's opinion, holding in favor of justiciability, enjoys unquestioned authority, having been joined by six justices.
6. Some scholars would trace the doctrine at least as far back as *Marbury v. Madison* (1 Cranch. [5 U.S.] 137, pp 163–167).
7. The *Bandemer* Court's recognition of this point is implicit in its repeated citation (pp. 2803–2804, 2806) of *Gaffney v. Cummings* (412 U.S. 735 (1973)) in support of the justiciability of gerrymandering claims. As *Bandemer* recognizes, Gaffney's holding that the gerrymandering claim against the Connecticut districting plan had no constitutional merit was perfectly consistent with the justiciability of that claim.
8. The justiciability of an attack on gerrymandered congressional districts might be questioned on grounds of "impossibility of a court's undertaking independent resolution without expressing lack of the respect due coordinate branches of government" (*Baker v. Carr*, p. 217). In *Wesberry v. Sanders*, a challenge to congressional districts on grounds of malapportionment was held to be justiciable on the authority of *Colegrove v. Green* and earlier cases without reference to the categories of political questions laid down in *Baker v. Carr*. Since no such precedent is available for a gerrymandering claim, explicit application of the *Baker* standards is necessary. To the extent that a finding of unconstitutional gerrymandering may be based on the failure of the elected legislators to represent fairly a group of constituents, gerrymandering claims would raise much more serious doubts about their susceptibility to resolution "without expressing lack of the respect due" Congress than was the case in the malapportionment cases, which were treated as involving denial of individual voting rights, not "fair representation." On the other hand, such analysis is beside the point if *Baker* was correctly characterized as holding "that apportionment problems at wholesale, in all their aspects, [are] justiciable and no longer to be considered as raising political questions" (Bickel, 1971, p. 61). At a minimum, *Bandemer* seems to preclude a contention that a congressional gerrymandering claim is nonjusticiable by reason of "a lack of judicially discoverable and manageable standards for resolving it."
9. The discussion of justiciability in the text is deliberately simplified. The "judicially discoverable and manageable standards" branch of *Baker v. Carr's* test for justiciability is in fact difficult to apply, and under one interpretation would require at least some prejudgment on the substantive issues in order to decide justiciability. Part II of *Bandemer* is noteworthy for apparently rejecting this interpretation. Explication of these points would require space and a level of technical detail beyond what is appropriate in a volume not specifically addressed to a legal audience. The only point about Part II of *Bandemer* that is essential to this essay is that the holding in favor of justiciability says nothing about the nature of the cause of action discussed in Part III of the plurality opinion.
10. For discussion of the ambiguity of *Baker v. Carr*, see Neal (1962, pp. 262–267). For a sampling of views of what *Baker* held, expressed before *Reynolds v. Sims*, see Bickel (1962); Emerson (1962, p. 65); McCloskey (1962, p. 70); Pollak (1962, p. 81). *Baker v. Carr* was briefed and argued twice before the Supreme Court. Archibald Cox, who was solicitor general, moved from arguing that the Court need resolve nothing more than

justiciability, to a position that the Court should also hold at least that completely arbitrary malapportionment would violate the Fourteenth Amendment. See Cortner (1970, pp. 103–104). In later years Professor Cox characterized *Baker* in one lecture series as holding that the Equal Protection Clause gives citizens an individual right to equal representation (Cox, 1968, pp. 114–115), and in another as holding only that a challenge to malapportionment presents a justiciable controversy (Cox, 1976, p. 69).

11. In addition to Justice Harlan's dissenting opinion, see Kelly (1965, pp. 134–136); Dixon (1968, pp. 187–190).

12. I believe the late Professor Dixon was incorrect in distinguishing sharply between *Gray v. Sanders* (372 U.S. 368 (1963)), which he contended was a "franchise" case, and legislative malapportionment cases, which he regarded as "representation" cases. "In *franchise cases*," he wrote, "a voter has an absolute right to equality. *Representation cases* are not franchise cases" (Dixon, 1968, p. 181; emphasis in original). Voting is an important part of the system of political representation, and both voting and representation were at stake in *Gray* and in *Reynolds*. A governor is the "people's representative" as much as are the legislators, and the kind of arguments that were made in defense of malapportioned legislatures could also have been made in defense of the county-unit system. For example, it could have been argued that in a state dominated by one or a number of large cities, some overrepresentation of rural areas was desirable to assure that the governor would have at least some sensitivity to the problems of agriculture. By the same token, voting rights are implicated in legislative malapportionment to a sufficient extent that a case like *Reynolds* cannot be described as a representation case *to the exclusion of* being a voting case. In my view, *Gray, Wesberry*, and *Reynolds* all involved both voting rights and questions of fair representation. The Supreme Court constitutionalized the voting rights infringed by malapportionment and left fair representation to take care of itself.

13. A member of the *Bandemer* plurality has recently characterized the malapportionment cases as resting on individual rather than group rights (Brennan, at 11).

Reading *Reynolds*, as I do, as standing on the individual's right to vote and not on any supposed right to "fair and effective representation," I disagree with those (e.g., Alfange, 1986, p. 194) who have seen a contradiction or tension between *Reynolds* and its Colorado companion case, *Lucas v. 44th General Assembly of Colorado*. In *Lucas*, the state contended that a districting plan containing substantial population inequalities could be validated by the existence of an initiative process that permitted the repeal of any malapportionment perceived as unfair by a majority of voters. Chief Justice Warren, writing for the Court, responded that "[a]n individual's constitutionally protected right to cast an equally weighted vote cannot be denied even by vote of a majority of a State's electorate" (*Lucas*, p. 736).

14. This formulation ignores the fact that districts of equal population need not have equal numbers of voters, so that a majority of people might reside in a set of districts within which fewer than a majority of the votes are cast. The distinction between equal population and equal numbers of

voters across districts is consistently ignored in *Reynolds*. See Lowenstein and Steinberg (1985, pp. 49–50).

15. For the same reason, the late Professor Bickel was mistaken in describing *Reynolds* as relying on "a statistical showing that malapportionment enabled a minority of voters to control a legislature" (Bickel, 1978, p. 109), at least if "statistical" implies any empirical consideration of election returns or voting behavior. More broadly, Bickel's assertion that the majoritarianism reflected in *Reynolds* constitutes a rejection of the Madisonian principle of countervailing groups and factions is without foundation. Compelled redistricting on an equal population basis might have been expected to have some effect on the balance of power among the groups and factions, but what possible reason could there have been to imagine that it would displace the pluralistic system of interest group politics? It would be difficult to maintain, with the benefit of hindsight, that it has had any such effect. Bickel's position has been restated recently with enthusiasm but with no greater persuasiveness by John Moeller (1984).

16. Consider, for example, this statement from the introduction to Justice Powell's dissenting opinion in *Bandemer* (p. 2826):

> Since the essence of a gerrymandering claim is that the members of a political party as a group have been denied their right to "fair and effective representation," *Reynolds v. Sims*, . . . I believe that the claim cannot be tested solely by reference to "one person, one vote."

The implication is that *Reynolds* stands for a generic constitutional right of "fair and effective representation," of which one person, one vote is but one species. For the reasons that follow in the text, I believe citation of *Reynolds* in this manner, however commonplace it has become, is either sloppy or deceptive.

17. Thus, the statement in the Introduction to this volume—that the Court in *Reynolds* "enunciated a justification for its involvement in redistricting, the need to guarantee 'fair and effective representation'"—is plainly incorrect.

18. Admittedly, the Chief Justice played a bit of a verbal shell game. The only reason "fair and effective representation" can be said to be "concededly" the goal of districting is that the term is sufficiently elastic to mean all things to all people. The particular conception of "fair and effective representation" that supports the conclusion drawn by Chief Justice Warren was too abstract and formal to command universal assent. To the contrary, the limited meaning of this term as it was used in *Reynolds* became the focus of a whole school of criticism of the Court's approach to redistricting, with its nearly exclusive focus on population equality. The most extended statement of this criticism may be found in Dixon (1968).

19. In the campaign finance cases Justice White, more than any other member of the Court, has been receptive to legislative efforts to equalize group opportunities in elections. See, for example, his dissenting opinions in *Buckley v. Valeo* (424 U.S. 1 (1976)) and *Citizens Against Rent Control v. Berkeley* (454 U.S. 290 (1981)). It does not necessarily follow that he would be receptive to claims that some such equalization is constitutionally required. However that might be, the questions I raise in the text are not all intended as rhetorical questions with obvious answers in the negative.

The point is simply that recognition of a gerrymandering claim along the lines proposed by the *Bandemer* plaintiffs would implicate these and many similar questions.

20. A claim that constituents of Democratic members of the Arizona House of Representatives had a constitutional right for the Democrats to have membership on legislative committees approximately proportionate to their membership in the House as a whole was greeted with this response by a federal appellate court:

> We have a strong feeling that if this court were to undertake to grant to plaintiffs the relief that they seek, our action would set the sometimes canonized and frequently capitalized Founding Fathers, as well as the Framers and Supporters of the Fourteenth Amendment, spinning in their graves. To us, the picture of a Federal Judge undertaking to tell the Speaker of the Arizona House of Representatives how many Democrats, and perhaps even which Democrats, he is to appoint to the standing committees, and perhaps to each such committee, of the House is startlingly unattractive. (*Davids v. Akers*, 549 F.2d, p. 123)

21. This seems an appropriate spot to disclaim the somewhat similar idea, attributed to Jonathan Steinberg and me by Martin Shapiro, that:

> something cannot be constitutionally unfair, unequal, and wrong unless there is a standard or measure of what is fair, equal, and right. They believe, therefore, that once they have shown that there is no single, objective, neutral set of electoral district boundaries for a given state with a given geography and demography, they will have shown that courts should not concern themselves with the constitutionality of district boundaries. (Shapiro, 1985, p. 227)

Steinberg and I never expressed such an idea, and I join Professor Shapiro in denouncing it. Our criticism of the reformers' so-called public interest criteria was not simply that the criteria fail to point to a uniquely ideal districting plan, but that they are so inadequate that they provide little or no basis for claiming that a districting plan complying with them is any better than a plan violating them. Concededly, the Supreme Court often does and should strike down practices that can be understood to be wrong when the Court would be unable to specify a practice that is uniquely right. Does Professor Shapiro maintain that the Court should strike down practices it has no defensible basis for believing are any worse than their replacements? Steinberg and I emphasized primarily, not the constitutional arguments regarding gerrymandering, but rather what we believe are fatal deficiencies in the claims of reformers that their districting criteria have a valid claim to the title "public interest." Those who would contest our position must do so by rebutting our criticism of these criteria.

Several of Professor Shapiro's criticisms of Steinberg's and my article consist of similar attacks on positions we did not take. For example, he says our arguments against compactness as a public interest criterion "rest essentially on a showing that there is no single, clear standard of compactness" (Shapiro, 1985, p. 236). If that were all, the objection would be cured easily by the adoption of one measure of compactness to the exclusion of the others. Our major arguments were that compact districts have no intrinsic advantages over districts with bizarre shapes, and that compactness fails as a neutral constraint on gerrymandering because it is not neutral (Lowenstein and Steinberg, 1985, pp. 21–27).

In only one major instance is Professor Shapiro's criticism leveled at a position we actually took. He correctly attributes to Steinberg and me the view that protection of the political interests of racial minorities constitutes a valid public interest criterion for assessing districting plans (Shapiro, 1985, pp. 229–236; Lowenstein and Steinberg, 1985, pp. 5–6). Professor Shapiro maintains that by taking this position Steinberg and I rendered ad hoc our arguments against other proposed criteria. As a constitutional matter, a distinction between racial and other criteria can be defended on the basis of the historical fact, recognized by the Court since the *Slaughterhouse Cases* (16 Wall. [83 U.S.] 36 (1873)), that protection of racial minorities is the central purpose of the Fourteenth Amendment. But the history of the Fourteenth Amendment aside, Professor Shapiro correctly identifies the essential point as the fact that "minorities in general and blacks in particular have been so wronged by American society" (1985, p. 231). That a political group might suffer a comparable degree of wrong and yet be large enough to be affected by legislative districting does not seem likely, but protection of such an oppressed group, if one existed, would qualify as a legitimate public interest criterion. This is what the plurality concludes in *Bandemer*, and perhaps it is a just criticism of Steinberg's and my article that we did not consider this possibility. But I cannot see why favoring protection of oppressed groups, when that is necessary, commits Steinberg, me, or the *Bandemer* plurality to protection of the major parties, as Shapiro believes (1985, p. 244).

Perhaps it bears mentioning that although I might have preferred Professor Shapiro to find some medium for expressing his thoughts on this subject other than a sustained bashing of Steinberg's and my collective head based on what seems to me a careless reading of our essay, this detracts not at all from the valuable and strikingly original insights he so characteristically generates.

22. Perhaps the per curiam decisions following *Brown v. Board of Education* (347 U.S. 483 (1954)), extending the equal protection prohibition of segregation beyond education despite the heavy reliance in *Brown* on considerations particular to education, constitute a comparable example. See Wechsler, 1959, p. 22.

23. See *San Antonio Independent School District v. Rodriguez* (411 U.S. 1 (1973)). A number of more recent cases have seemed to chip away at the foundations of the *Rodriguez* structure, which may never have been particularly firm to begin with. These include *Plyler v. Doe* (457 U.S. 202 (1982)), *Metropolitan Life Insurance Co. v. Ward* (105 S. Ct. 1676 (1985)), and *Cleburne v. Cleburne Living Center* (105 S. Ct. 3249 (1985)). If my analysis is correct, *Davis v. Bandemer* may be added to the list. However, in spite of the serious inroads on the division of equal protection into "suspect class" and "fundamental rights" cases that receive "heightened scrutiny," and all others that receive "rational basis scrutiny," it cannot be said that the division is obsolete.

24. The Court has distinguished between "strict" scrutiny, applicable to race cases, and "intermediate" scrutiny, applicable to gender and other "suspect" classifications. For purposes of our consideration of *Davis v. Bandemer*, it is sufficient to ignore this distinction, and use the term "heightened scrutiny" to refer collectively to "strict" and "intermediate" scrutiny.

25. It cannot be suggested that articulation of a well-developed constitutional theory of gerrymandering was unnecessary on the ground that a consensus on such a theory already existed in the work of scholars urging judicial intervention. See Weinstein (1984, pp. 369–373).

26. The only exception occurs in the last paragraph of Part III-B of Justice White's opinion, in which two of the malapportionment cases are cited on a collateral point, not providing the basis for the gerrymandering cause of action.

27. The "fundamental rights" arm of equal protection doctrine had not been articulated at the time *Reynolds v. Sims* was decided. Retrospectively, *Reynolds* was cast as an important step in the evolution of the doctrine. See, for example, *Harper v. Virginia Board of Elections* (383 U.S. 663 (1966)); *Dunn v. Blumstein* (405 U.S. 331 (1972)).

28. *Bandemer's* treatment of a classification burdening a political group that suffers pervasive discrimination throughout the electoral system as "suspect" is a significant doctrinal innovation with uncertain but potentially far-reaching importance. For example, if we were to have a reprise of McCarthyism in the United States, the Equal Protection Clause might provide at least as effective a shield for the group involved as the First Amendment (cf. Blasi, 1985). As Professor Cain discusses in this volume, this aspect of *Bandemer* also has considerable political theoretical significance.

29. A total of six cases are cited by Justice White in the course of his discussion of the merits. Two involved alleged gerrymanders of single-member districts. In *Gaffney v. Cummings*, (412 U.S. 735 (1973)), a claim by Democrats that the plan was unconstitutional because it was drawn with the avowed purpose of giving proportional representation to the Republicans was rejected. In *United Jewish Organizations v. Carey* (430 U.S. 144 (1977)) an equal protection attack by a group representing white voters against a "benign" gerrymander designed to maximize black representation also was rejected. Two of the cases involved challenges to multimember districts. In *Whitcomb v. Chavis* (403 U.S. 124 (1971)) a constitutional claim by a racial minority that its votes were submerged in the large, predominantly white district was rejected, but similar claims were upheld in *White v. Regester* (412 U.S. 755 (1973)). The remaining two cases were challenges by racial minorities against at-large voting in municipalities. The equal protection attack failed in *Mobile v. Bolden* (446 U.S. 55 (1980)) but succeeded in *Rogers v. Lodge* (485 U.S. 613 (1982)).

    Gerhard Casper aptly described *Regester* in terms similar to the interpretation I am proposing for *Bandemer*:

    > *Regester* is a kind of present-day version of the "white primary" cases. Multimember districts, it would seem, violate the Equal Protection Clause, not because they overrepresent or underrepresent pure and simple, but because they do that in a context where all stages of the electoral process have been effectively closed to identifiable classes of citizens, making the political establishment "insufficiently responsive" to (Mexican-American) interests. (Casper, 1973, p. 28)

30. Justice Marshall argued in his dissenting opinion in *Mobile v. Bolden* that the City of Mobile's at-large voting system warranted strict scrutiny as a

"fundamental rights" voting classification rather than as a racial "suspect classification." See 446 U.S. at 113–122. He took this position primarily to avoid the plurality's holding, based on *Washington v. Davis* (426 U.S. 229 (1976)), that the plaintiffs had to show an intent to discriminate against blacks as a precondition of heightened scrutiny on a suspect classification theory. There are several reasons why Justice Marshall might have been willing to reconsider his view that a group claim of vote "dilution" constitutes a voting rights claim, as he seems to have done by joining in Justice White's opinion in *Bandemer*. First, the need to prove racially discriminatory intent in election cases has been obviated by the amendments to Section 2 of the Voting Rights Act, in effect overruling *Mobile v. Bolden*. See *Thornburg v. Gingles* (106 S. Ct. 2752 (1986)). Second, the treatment of the intent requirement in the *Bandemer* plurality opinion and the victory of the plaintiffs in *Rogers v. Lodge* suggest that proving discriminatory intent need not be a major hurdle in gerrymandering cases. Third, Justice Marshall's position in *Mobile v. Bolden* was based on the faulty premise that the requirement of an equally weighted vote for each individual in *Reynolds v. Sims* was "analytically the same concept" (p. 116) as the claimed entitlement to an empirical group equality in voting power in at-large voting or gerrymandering cases.

31. Justice White precedes his consideration of intent and effect with the preliminary characterization of the claim as based on statewide discrimination rather than as directed to particular districts. This apparently reflects a welcome lack of interest on the part of the plurality in constitutionalizing "formal" districting criteria, such as compactness, adherence to municipal boundaries, or "communities of interest" (see Lowenstein and Steinberg, 1985, pp. 21–35). Nevertheless, since the plurality does not consider any claim directed at the characteristics of particular districts, it would be an exaggeration—however tempting—to say that the plurality holds that none of the formal criteria have constitutional force.

32. Justice White warned, however, that the showing of intent does need to be made. In the event of a claim brought by any group other than a political party, there is no reason to believe the intent finding would or should be at all automatic.

33. It seems to me that this phenomenon is evident in this volume in many of the essays by reform-minded social scientists. They remain at their old stand, refining their various indicators for gerrymanders and criteria for districting plans. These pursuits may have academic value, but the writers are distinctly unsuccessful in showing that their efforts have any relevance to the plurality opinion in *Bandemer*.

34. For a representative example of the type of misreading referred to in the text, see the passage from Professor Schuck's article discussed in note 1, *supra*.

35. Only about one in ten Americans says he or she expects his or her representative in Congress would not be helpful if approached with a problem the representative could do something about. As would be expected, there is a positive correlation between the expectation of helpfulness on the one hand and the constituent and the representative being members

of the same party on the other, but the size of the correlation is only moderate (Cain, Ferejohn, and Fiorina, 1987, pp. 54–56).

36. Justice White acknowledges that determination whether a group suffers pervasive discrimination sufficient to satisfy the *Bandemer* threshold necessitates a "difficult inquiry" (p. 2816). That this threshold showing must be made, and that it cannot consist merely of some sort of "votes-seats" relationship, is made explicit in response to Justice O'Connor's expressed concern that the plurality's opinion inevitably would require proportional representation:

> [W]e do not share Justice O'Connor's apparent lack of faith in the lower courts' abilities to distinguish between disproportionality *per se* and the lack of fair representation that continued disproportionality in conjunction with other indicia may demonstrate. (p. 2816, n. 21)

This passage, like others in the opinion, makes it clear that the *Bandemer* requirements are not satisfied by showing that an adverse "votes-seats" relationship will persist over time. For even *"continued* disproportionality" is insufficient. It must be shown "in conjunction with other criteria"—namely, the electoral system's persistent discrimination against the plaintiff group throughout the political process as a whole.

37. See Cain, 1984, pp. 151–159; Lowenstein and Steinberg, 1985, pp. 64–69. Assuming a two-party system and equal numbers of voters in each district, the theoretical minimum number of votes the *B* Party would need in order to win two-thirds of the seats would be slightly more than a third of the total. The *A* Party would win one-third of the seats with 100% of the votes. The *B* Party would win the remaining seats by a margin of one vote each. Since the theoretical mimimum, then, is one-third of the votes, and since the hypothesis requires that the *B* Party command fewer than 50% of the votes, the requirements of the hypothesis are much too close to the theoretical limit to be a realistic possibility. That the effects of partisan gerrymanders tend to dissipate as a decade progresses finds additional support in this volume in the essays by Morrill and by Niemi and Wright.

38. The intent requirement is applicable to an equal protection racial gerrymandering claim (*Mobile v. Bolden; Rogers v. Lodge*). It is not applicable to a claim brought under Section 2 of the Voting Rights Act (*Thornburg v. Gingles*).

39. Once this showing is made, the plurality opinion is ambiguous regarding the burden that would be placed on the state to justify the plan. There is a brief discussion of some of the criteria that would be relevant to whether the districting plan meets "legitimate state interests" (*Davis v. Bandemer*, p. 2815). This is the language of the "rational basis" test. However, the goal of dividing the state into equally populated districts would justify any plan under the traditionally deferential rational basis test. In two recent cases, *Cleburne v. Cleburne Living Center* (473 U.S. 432 (1985)) and *Metropolitan Life Insurance Co. v. Ward* (470 U.S. 869 (1985)), the Court has purported to apply the rational basis test, but in a most undeferential way. In *Cleburne*, Justice White wrote the majority opinion but the other members of the *Bandemer* plurality, Justices Blackmun, Brennan, and Marshall, dissented in part on the ground that they believed heightened scrutiny was being applied in fact and the Court should have admitted as much. In *Metropolitan Life*, Justices White and Blackmun were in the ma-

jority, whereas Justices Brennan and Marshall were among the dissenters. The ambiguity in *Bandemer* regarding the appropriate standard of review probably reflects these doctrinal differences among Justice White and his colleagues. Justice White and, perhaps, Justice Blackmun are reluctant to add to the list of "suspect classifications," but are willing to apply the rational basis test in an undeferential way in favor of non-"suspect" groups that seem to need some protection. Justices Brennan and Marshall are reluctant to modify the deferential character of the rational basis test but are willing to add new classifications to the "suspect" category.

The doctrinal differences among the members of the plurality make little difference in the gerrymandering context. No supposed public interest criteria for drawing a set of district lines one way rather than another, assuming compliance with one person, one vote, have nearly enough merit to justify a genuine civil rights violation of the magnitude needed to cross the *Bandemer* threshold. At least, that is the burden of my previous writing on this subject (see Lowenstein and Steinberg, 1985).

40. Chief Justice Burger, as was his frequent custom, added an opinion of his own saying that he agreed with the opinion to which he was signing his name, in this case the opinion of Justice O'Connor. The Chief Justice added a grunt that, if taken seriously, cannot be read as anything less than a renunciation of *Baker v. Carr*. This is a noteworthy position for a chief justice to take in a two-paragraph opinion issued during the last week of his last term on the Court, not to mention its inconsistency with Chief Justice Burger's posture in cases such as *Chapman v. Meier* (420 U.S. 1 (1975)) and *Connor v. Finch* (431 U.S. 407 (1977)).

41. References to future cases are not intended as predictions, but simply as statements of what the justices are or are not committed to in the future if they are to act consistently with the opinions they have written or joined in *Bandemer*.

42. The propositions are not only separate, they are probably inconsistent. If challenges to partisan gerrymanders are based on claims of a "group right to an equal share of political power," if no such group right was intended by the framers of the Fourteenth Amendment, and if Justice O'Connor's reference to the intent of the framers implies she thinks their intent should be adhered to; then it follows that the Equal Protection Clause supplies the most manageable standard imaginable for judicial resolution of purely political gerrymandering claims, namely, that such claims do not allege violations of the Fourteenth Amendment and therefore ought to be dismissed.

43. Admittedly, Justice Powell demonstrated skepticism of the lower court's finding, by adding a remark that the court "further determined that the impact of the redistricting fell most harshly on black voters who predominantly are Democrats" (*Davis v. Bandemer*, p. 2838). The opinion might therefore be interpreted as meaning that the purpose of protecting black representation would have been sufficient to defend the Indiana plan had not the fact that the plan as a whole favored Republicans over Democrats negated the likelihood that protecting black representation was a genuine purpose of the plan. This would lead to the conclusion that Democratic gerrymanders accompanied by the purpose of maintaining black representation should be upheld, while Republican gerrymanders accompa-

nied by the same purpose should be struck down—an unlikely conclusion to attribute to Justice Powell.

44. Gordon Baker has challenged our conclusion on the ground that it is "not based on any concrete evidence but rather on abstract theorizing based on partisan population distribution" (Baker, 1986a, p. 6). In fact, we did cite concrete evidence (Lowenstein and Steinberg, 1985, p. 25 n. 69). If that evidence is insufficient to satisfy Professor Baker, he does not explain why. In any event, when both "abstract theorizing" and such evidence as does exist tend to support the proposition that the criteria in question systematically favor one major party and disfavor the other, it is fair to ask Justice Powell or others who wish to read those criteria into the Constitution *in the name of "neutrality"* to come forth with evidence demonstrating that the criteria have no such effects. More important, even if our empirical conclusion is incorrect and in fact the criteria of compactness and adhering to municipal boundaries disfavor Republicans and Democrats randomly from state to state, the essential point that within a given state the criteria are not neutral would be unaffected.

45. Justice Powell's approach in *Davis v. Bandemer* is structured somewhat differently from the approach he and Justice Stevens stated in separate opinions in *Karcher v. Daggett (I)* (Stevens, p. 760; Powell, p. 788). In those opinions, the justices took the position that the plaintiff in a gerrymandering case would make a prima facie showing, among other things, by demonstrating that the districts have irregular shapes or fail to adhere to municipal boundaries. Under Justice Powell's *Bandemer* approach such a showing, together with the background circumstances that would otherwise constitute loose gerrymandering, resolves the lawsuit in favor of the plaintiff. Under the *Karcher* opinions the state would still have the opportunity to provide some "adequate" or "legitimate" explanation of the plan. The dropping in *Bandemer* of what amounts to a "rational basis" test under which a districting plan may be defended following a prima facie showing of its unconstitutionality is an improvement in the Powell-Stevens position, for reasons that were well stated a quarter of a century ago by Phil C. Neal:

> Taken seriously, the suggestion that apportionment must conform to "a rational plan" is really a refusal to recognize or accept as legitimate the process by which reapportionment or unsuccessful efforts to reapportion have characteristically been carried out. That process is compromise. To any legislator who has participated in a legislative struggle over districting, Mr. Justice Clark's sense of outrage [in *Baker v. Carr*] at the vagaries of the Tennessee apportionment must appear ludicrous or feigned. To ask for explanation of all the apparent "inconsistencies" or "discrepancies" in such a legislative act is to demand reconstruction of the details of a complex political battle; to look for "principled" explanations is to expect the impossible. (Neal, 1962, pp. 280).

See also Dixon (1963, pp. 378–380).

46. Like compactness and adhering to municipal boundaries, such criteria have been put forward under an undefended claim of neutrality and under vague or contestable contentions that they serve good government purposes (Lowenstein and Steinberg, 1985, pp. 21–35).

47. It bears repeating that my statement in the text is not a prediction of what the Supreme Court would do if confronted with such a case. Under Justice White's opinion, a partisan gerrymander is not unconstitutional

unless it seriously harms a group that suffers from pervasive discrimination in the political process as a whole. In other words, such a case would present a civil rights violation of the sort that commonly and properly stimulates judicial intervention. In such a case, I do not doubt that Justices Powell and Stevens, and possibly some or all of the justices who joined in Justice O'Connor's opinion, would provide relief to the oppressed plaintiff group. The conclusion in the text is based simply on the logic of the opinion that Justice Powell actually wrote.

48. I wrote my chapter and sent it to Professor Grofman before he wrote his (chapter 3), and therefore he was able to incorporate criticisms of my interpretation of *Bandemer*. Although it would be possible for me to integrate my responses into my own essay, this would create the prospect of an almost endless regress of revisions and responses between Professor Grofman and myself. It has therefore seemed preferable to keep my original essay in the form Professor Grofman saw it (with the exception of some minor editing and updating) and to set forth my response in this addendum.

49. The early returns from the judiciary are distinctly favorable from my point of view. In *Badham v. Eu.* (109 S. Ct. 829 (1989)), the Supreme Court summarily affirmed (i.e., affirmed without conducting a hearing or issuing an opinion) the dismissal by a three-judge district court of a challenge to the California congressional districting plan. Acting several months after an earlier version of this chapter was presented to the 1987 annual meeting of the American Political Science Association, the district court had adopted an interpretation of *Bandemer* quite similar to the one I propose. See *Badham v. Eu.* (694 F. Supp. 664 (N.D. Cal. 1988)). The Supreme Court's summary affirmance has precedental force with respect to the result in *Badham*, but does not necessarily endorse the district court's reasoning.

50. Perhaps this is overstated. Justice White is giving examples of the sort of findings that are needed but that were not made in the Indiana case. There is no reason to assume every one of them must be present in a given case, if the overall findings are strong enough. My central disagreement with Grofman is not over how strong the findings have to be with respect to the districting plan in question, but over whether any such findings are sufficient, in the absence of a showing that the plaintiff group suffers pervasive discrimination in the political process.

51. Several such statements appear in Part III-D of the opinion. Thus, in racial cases,

> the racial minorities asserting the successful equal protection claims *had essentially been shut out of the political process*. In the statewide political gerrymandering context, these prior cases lead to the analogous conclusion that equal protection violations may be found only where a history (actual or projected) of disproportionate results appears *in conjunction with similar indicia*. (*Davis v. Bandemer*, p. 2814, emphasis added)

Later, the crucial passage from Part III-B is repeated:

> Determining when an electoral system has been "arranged in a manner that will consistently degrade a voter's or a group of voters' influence on the political process as a whole," [citation] is of necessity a difficult inquiry. (pp. 2815–2816)

It should be noted that the subject of the key clause, "electoral system," is *not* included within the quotation marks but *is* repeated. Those who-believe Justice White "really" meant to refer to the districting plan under attack rather than to the electoral system must explain why he made this error not once but twice. Finally,

> [W]e do not share Justice O'Connor's apparent lack of faith in the lower courts' abilities to distinguish between disproportionality *per se* and the lack of fair representation that continued disproportionality *in conjunction with other indicia* may indicate. (p. 2816, n. 21, second emphasis added)

52. Grofman asserts that this passage "is seen by Lowenstein as critical." I can find nothing in my essay that could create this impression. The passage is not so much "critical" as "indicative." My point in discussing it was that it has proved bewildering to commentators who have wanted to interpret *Bandemer* as providing expansive judicial license to intervene in major party districting controversies, but that it becomes perfectly sensible when *Bandemer* is understood as protecting outcast political groups.

53. See *Ketchum v. Byrne*, p. 1410; *Major v. Treen*, p. 342; *Thornburg v. Gingles*, p. 2758.

5

Perspectives on *Davis v. Bandemer:* Views of the Practitioner, Theorist, and Reformer

Bruce E. Cain

Much of the commentary immediately before and after the ruling in *Davis v. Bandemer* (106 S. Ct. 2797 (1986)) focused on legal issues primarily, such as the justiciability of partisan gerrymandering, the meaning of equal protection claims for groups, and the existence of manageable standards for judging the fairness of district boundaries.[1] For the most part, political scientists have only played a technical role in this controversy, advising the legal community on possible measures of gerrymandering and analyzing the electoral effects of various redistricting plans.[2] Even so, after a number of sometimes heated academic exchanges and legal skirmishes, the single piece of wisdom our discipline could agree on was that no one indicator completely and unambiguously captured the meaning of "fair representation." Beyond that simple point, there was, and unfortunately still is, little consensus. Some political scientists continue to believe that a laundry list of separately inadequate measures can collectively suffice to identify "invidious gerrymandering" (Grofman, 1983a, pp. 545–549; 1985a), while others assert that the quest for objective measures of political fairness is futile (Lowenstein and Steinberg, 1985; Cain, 1984).

The Court disclosed its long-awaited opinion on these issues in June 1986, ruling in *Davis v. Bandemer* that partisan gerrymandering claims are justiciable and establishing standards for partisan vote dilution that resemble those for racial vote dilution. However, the legal consequences of this decision are still ambiguous. As Professor

Lowenstein has argued in chapter 4, the Court may retain the theoretical right to consider the constitutionality of allegedly partisan redistricting plans, but in practice will rarely, if ever, do so. This interpretation of *Davis v. Bandemer* seems to have been adopted by the Northern California District Court in *Badham v. Eu* (N.D. California, No. C-83-1126, dismissed April 21, 1988, certiorari denied for want of jurisdiction by the U.S Supreme Court, October 1988), a case involving the 1982 California congressional redistricting. In that decision, the district court argued that the Republicans failed to satisfy "the second prong of the 'effects test'" (i.e. "strong indicia of lack of political power and the denial of fair representation"), and dismissed the Republican challenge. If *Badham v. Eu* is any indication of the Court's likely future posture on these matters, then Professor Lowenstein's prediction about the infrequency of Court intervention will almost certainly come true.

Rather than reiterate Lowenstein's able discussion, I propose a different perspective on the Bandemer case, or, to be more precise, three different perspectives: those of the political practitioner, the democratic theorist, and the reformer. Each brings a unique concern to his or her reading of the case. Politicians, technical consultants and staff—those I call political practitioners—must inevitably think of the specific consequences of *Davis v. Bandemer* for future redistrictings: How will it constrain the way they draw district boundaries in 1991, and who will benefit from this decision? Practitioners will be largely uninterested in the niceties of what seem to them arcane legal arguments and more concerned with trying to figure out what they will be allowed to do in 1990. To borrow from Laswell, their question will be who gets what, when, and how as the result of this decision (Laswell, 1951)? Will it mean that majority parties have to be more respectful of minority party demands? Which other racial, ethnic and political groups will now qualify, or think they qualify, for equal rights protection in redistricting?

In sharp contrast to the down-to-earth concerns of the practitioner, those of the democratic theorist are distinctly abstract. Is the right to proportional representation (even the "loose" sort proposed in *Bandemer*) inherent in a representative Democracy? Do groups have claims to fair representation, and if so, why, and what are the implications of this? Whereas the linedrawer necessarily focuses on the practical difficulties of implementing legal guidelines, the democratic theorist contemplates how the court's position on redistricting relates to the philosophical underpinnings of the American system of representation. Since the traditional concerns of democratic theory have been for the stability, legitimacy, and efficacy of representative systems, the relevant question raised by *Davis v. Bandemer* is whether the explicit acknowledgment of group rights to representation furthers or lessens these goals.

Then there is the perspective of the institutional reformer. The court has in effect defined an interval of permissible action for redistricting and the formulation of electoral procedures generally (e.g., multimember versus single-member districts). Within this legally sanctioned interval, many institutional options and redistricting procedures are possible. If the court finds itself unwilling or unable to resolve all of the problems inherent in U.S. electoral arrangements, then the role of the institutional reformer is to ask how redistricting can be made "better" working within the nonlegal political realm. The first step, as we shall see, is deciding what one means by "better." Then, and only then, can we think of institutional changes that might accomplish this goal.

In general, my theme will be that both the *Davis v. Bandemer* and *Thornburg v. Gingles* (Slip Opinion) cases raise fundamental questions about the role of groups in American democracy. Practitioners will wish that these rulings had given them more explicit guidance about the nature of and qualifications for group voting rights. In the absence of clear instructions, they will most likely assume that Democrats and Republicans are not going to be protected by this decision, but that other hitherto excluded groups may be protected. The democratic theorist will see that these cases constitute a move away from formal electoral individualism and toward a more group rights and compensatory approach. Support for the different types of representation probably varies across segments of the U.S. electorate. Finally, the reformer will have the chance to design mechanisms for redistricting that can further the representational goals implicit in this decision.

BANDEMER AND *GINGLES* TOGETHER

It is useful to consider the *Davis v. Bandemer* and *Thornburg v. Gingles* decisions together, not only because they were issued on the same day, but also because the Court clearly attempted to make the reasoning about the constitutional claims of racial and political groups consistent. Prior to these rulings, thinking about racial and partisan gerrymandering seemed to be developing independently, with only a handful of observers arguing for the need for some unifying principle.[3] Then, the surprising decision in *Karcher v. Daggett (I)* (462 U.S. 725 (1983)) revealed that some members of the Supreme Court were interested in exploring the constitutionality of partisan gerry-mandering.[4] It had been widely assumed up to that point that the Court would avoid ruling on these matters if it could, because the issues of party redistricting were so inherently political. But having entered the political thicket on a number of racial vote dilution cases since the sixties, the Court found itself in the logically, and perhaps even politically, uncomfortable position of holding that some groups were entitled to protection against vote dilution but not others without ever having justified this discrepancy in legal treatment. The logical question to ask was whether political gerrymandering was really so different from racial gerrymandering: If the votes of racial minorities could be diluted by gerrymandering techniques, if there were manageable empirical ways to make this determination, and if racial groups could be constitutionally protected from vote dilution, then why not apply the same logic to political groups? As indicated in his concurring opinion in *Karcher v. Daggett (I)*, one member of the Court, Justice Stevens, had already concluded that there was in fact no reason to treat various groups differently in this regard:

> There is only one Equal Protection clause. Since the Clause does not make some groups of citizens more equal than others . . . its protection cannot be confined to racial groups. As long as it proscribes gerrymandering against such groups, its proscription must provide comparable protection for other cognizable groups of voters as well. (p. 154)

At the same time, the 1982 revisions in the Voting Rights Act had challenged the Court's position in *Mobile v. Bolden* (446 U.S. 55 (1980)) on racial vote dilution. In its comprehensive report on the bill, the Senate indicated that it wanted the Court to focus on the discrimina-tory effects that electoral arrangements might have on minority vot-ing power, not on the discriminatory intent of those who devised the electoral arrangements. The intent standard, the Senate Report main-tained, was "unnecessarily divisive," "inordinately difficult" to prove and, in any event, not "the right question to ask" (U.S. Senate Report (1982) p. 36). This forced the Court to reconsider the position it es-tablished on the question of discriminatory effects in *Mobile v. Bolden*.

Together, the 1982 revisions in the Voting Rights Act and the de-cision in *Karcher v. Daggett (I)* set the stage for a reexamination of the Court's views on racial and partisan vote dilution. In *Davis v. Bande-mer*, the Supreme Court was asked to consider the constitutionality of an Indiana redistricting plan that allegedly diluted the votes of Dem-ocrats through unfair boundary design and multimember districting.

TABLE 5.1. Court Options in Retrospect

		Racial Group Standard		
		No Constitutional Claim	Vote Dilution Plus	Vote Dilution Only
Political	No constitutional claim	S1	A1	A2
Group	Vote dilution plus	A3	S2	A4
Standard	Vote dilution only	A5	A6	S3

The District Court had invalidated the Indiana legislature's plan, relying heavily as evidence on the disproportionality of the seat to votes ratio in the election following the 1981 redistricting. The challenge in *Thornburg v. Gingles* also involved a redistricting plan with both single and multimember districts. The contention of the plaintiffs in this case was that the plan violated Section 2 of the Voting Rights Act by "impairing the opportunity of black voters 'to participate in the political process and to elect representatives of their own choice.'" Both cases, in other words, dealt with the claim that a particular districting arrangement unfairly diminished the voting power of a particular group in the electorate. The important difference, of course, was that in the one instance the group in question was racial and in the other it was a political party.

Setting out the possible options the Court could have pursued with respect to the equal protection claims of racial and political groups suggests in retrospect that many courses of action were not feasible. Table 5.1 displays schematically those various options. There were three proposed positions the Court could have taken on vote dilution. The first was to deny constitutional protection against gerrymandering (i.e., labeled "no constitutional claim" in the table). A second, and very much opposite position, was to grant constitutional protection against electoral arrangements that substantially dilute voting power regardless of any evidence of systematic political exclusion (i.e., labeled "simple vote dilution"). And the third was to apply a more stringent test that looked at the overall pattern of exclusion from participation in the political process in addition to evidence of vote dilution, which is the position the Court ultimately adopted in both the *Davis v. Bandemer* and *Thornburg v. Gingles* cases (i.e., labeled "vote dilution plus" in the table).

The other equally important aspect of the Court's choice was whether to treat racial and political groups the same way or not (i.e., symmetric or assymetric treatment of racial and political claims). Table 5.1 has nine options altogether, six of them asymmetric and three of them symmetric. Four choices could be ruled out immediately as not being feasible. In the light of the Voting Rights Act and the general civil rights thrust since the sixties, the Court could not seriously consider options that denied constitutional claims to racial groups (i.e., A3, A5, and S1), or adopt a standard for racial groups that was more stringent than the one it had for political groups (i.e., A6). In addition, options A2 and A4 would have made the racial vote dilution standard easier to prove than the one Congress itself had recommended and considerably easier than the Court's own standard in *Mobile v. Bolden*. Given the reluctance of the Court to set the threshold for intervention into gerrymandering cases too low and its present composition (i.e., leaning toward more judicial restraint), the Court was unlikely to go in this direction.

Thus, the feasible options were S3 (racial and political groups on a simple vote dilution standard), S2 (both on a vote dilution plus standard), and the status quo A1 (racial groups protected by a "dilution plus" standard and political groups with no valid constitutional claim). The status quo option was espoused by some of the Justices in their concurring opinions. Justice O'Connor, for instance, argued that the Court should be interested in individual voting rights primarily, and that racial claims were an exception justified by "the greater warrant the Equal Protection Clause gives the Federal Courts to intervene for protection against racial discrimination" (*Davis v. Bandemer*, p. 8). In the end, however, the plurality rejected the status quo position, because, in principle at least, it did not want to foreclose the possibility that political as well as racial groups might have legitimate constitutional claims against vote discrimination. As a consequence, racial group voting rights are no longer special exceptions to the rule of individual voting rights, but rather they are the only applications so far (and possibly ever) of a rule against group vote dilution. In the terms of Table 5.1, by putting racial and political vote dilution on the same legal footing, the Court has moved from asymmetric to symmetric treatment of group equal protection claims.

Even so, there were two options remaining. S3, as espoused by Justice Stevens, would have drawn the Court into an attempt to end the "discriminatory treatment of groups of voters" that occurs when districting arrangements "serve no purpose other than to favor one segment—whether racial, ethnic, religious, economic, or political—that may occupy a position of strength at a particular point in time, or to disadvantage a politically weak segment of the community"

(*Karcher (I)*, p. 153). His suggestion was that if a racial or political group had been adversely affected by a redistricting plan, if a districting plan had contorted lines and split cities, and if the new lines did not serve "the neutral, legitimate interests of the community as a whole," then the Court could say that a plan violated the equal protection guarantee.

The plurality in *Davis v. Bandemer* rejected this option, holding that (1) a "mere lack of proportional representation will not be sufficient to prove unconstitutional discrimination"; (2) a group will have to show that its vote has been "consistently degraded"; and (3) there must be a conjunction of "strong indicia of lack of political power and the denial of fair representation" as is required in the racial gerrymandering cases (*Davis v. Bandemer*, pp. 20–21, n. 28). Similarly, in *Thornburg v. Gingles*, the Court stuck closely to the Senate Report on the Voting Rights Act, maintaining that the existence of "an allegedly dilutive electoral mechanism and the lack of proportional representation alone does not establish a violation." Groups must "demonstrate that, under a totality of circumstances, the devices result in unequal access to the political process" (*Thornburg*, p. 13). In other words, the Court will require proof of other circumstances indicating exclusion when considering the validity of the claims by either racial or political groups; that is to say, not just disproportionate results in an election, but vote dilution plus evidence of other factors indicating that a racial or political group has been excluded from the political process. Why did the plurality choose symmetric "dilution plus" over symmetric "simple dilution"? Primarily, because it did not want to constitutionalize a right to proportional representation for groups in the electorate, and because it wanted to limit its involvement in the inevitably political task of redistricting. A low threshold, the plurality feared, might invite "judicial interference in legislative districting whenever a party suffers at the polls" (*Davis v. Bandemer*, p. 31).

Thus, S2 seems to have been a compromise between the need on the one hand to put racial and political groups on equal constitutional footing and the desire on the other to limit the court's involvement in redistricting to the greatest extent possible. Assuming that this is the correct interpretation of where things stand, what are the implications of the Court's position for the practitioner, the theorist, and the institutional reformer?

PRACTITIONER'S PERSPECTIVE

Someone will actually have to draw district lines in 1990. And legislators at various levels of government will experience firsthand the practical implications of the Court's decision when the next round of reapportionment occurs in 1991. Leaving aside the question of whether practitioners are themselves the cause of redistricting problems, and whether, as some hope, there might be a more technical and neutral way to conduct the process,[5] the fact is that practitioners have a unique and valued perspective. Above all, they—more than lawyers, judges, and academics—are sensitive to the problems of trying to implement the Court's rulings.

Most incumbents would prefer as little Court involvement in redistricting as possible, because in the United States system of redistricting incumbent legislators possess, and very much desire to retain, a high degree of control over the final outcome, even in commission settings (Balitzer, 1979). It is quite understandable, of course, that they would want to retain such power. In addition to determining whether an incumbent has an unopposed seat to run for in the next election (i.e., the basic issue of survival), redistricting affects the particular mix of constituents in a district, the number and kind of fundraising sources available for campaigns, and the incumbent's access to such district assets as baseball stadiums, amusement parks, and favorite restaurants.

Rulings by the Court on redistricting issues constrain the degree of control legislators have over this process and hence their ability to secure outcomes that are most sensitive to their needs and preferences. Even more to the point, the courts in many states are the ultimate redistricting body when the legislature or redistricting commission cannot come to agreement. The threat of losing control over the process in this sense is a powerful incentive for compromise.

This is not to say that rulings such as "one man, one vote" have prevented legislators from accomplishing what they want, since formal criteria do not have any close bearing on partisan outcomes. However, these decisions have limited districting alternatives in important ways. Plans with wide population disparities or that split racial communities are no longer viable options. Further Court rulings, particularly on the treatment of other political minority groups, could potentially complicate the task of redistricting by increasing the number of individuals and groups whose needs must be satisfied.

If the Court must intervene in redistricting, the practitioner will generally prefer clear and explicit rulings to vague ones. When the Court demands equally weighted votes, the practitioner will want to know exactly what the phrase "equally weighted" means (i.e., how close to absolutely equal?): Is a 1% population deviation permissible, and if not, what is? Or, if groups are to be protected, which ones, and what exactly are they entitled to? In short, practitioners look for de minimis standards, concrete guidelines that will allow them to get on with the business of adjusting district boundaries. I suspect, therefore, that many of them found the Court's ruling in *Karcher v. Daggett (I)* deeply disturbing: If a plan that had less than a 1% deviation in the population of the largest and smallest congressional districts can be ruled unconstitutional because it did not represent a good faith effort to achieve population equality, then any congressional plan is vulnerable in principle. To the practitioner, this kind of uncertainty is troublesome.

It is equally predictable that if practitioners are given a de minimis standard, they will do no better than what they are required to do unless it serves their interests to do so. In this sense, a less explicit (or even a vague) standard can sometimes produce a higher degree of compliance than an explicit one. Risk-acceptant individuals or groups might choose to test the limits of the law, but most incumbents are risk averse when it comes to redistricting matters. There is simply too much at stake for them to be cavalier about the process. If redistricters do not know exactly what the Court's standard is, and if they only know that the Court sometimes intervenes when it sees something that it does not like (as was the case in Karcher), then redistricters may become cautious in order to avoid Court intervention—more cautious, perhaps, than they need to be. Under these circumstances, having a vague standard might lead to a higher level of compliance than having an explicit standard.[6] This may especially apply to redistrictings that affect Blacks and Hispanics in the 1990s—that is, instead of incurring the risk of going to Court over minority districts, legislative linedrawers may take special care in the 1990s to appease minority group districting demands (see Cain and Campagna, 1987).

The "who" in "who gets what" from redistricting is particularly critical since the demand for constitutional protection is potentially unlimited. I recall, for instance, that shortly after accepting the job as technical consultant to the California legislature's redistricting in 1981, I was besieged by redistricting requests from all sorts of groups, including not only the NAACP, various Hispanic groups, and local party organizations, as one might expect, but also groups such as NOW and Planned Parenthood. Since redistricting is a geographical exercise, it was not immediately obvious to me why nongeographical groups like Planned Parenthood felt threatened by redistricting, but, as it turns out, they were interested in protecting the incumbents who had loyally supported their causes over the years. The inference I drew from this experience is that it is virtually impossible to overestimate the number of groups who will become interested in districting and electoral arrangements if given the chance.

Who, then, must be protected against unconstitutional vote dilution? In theory, almost any identifiable political group could be. However, it is unlikely that practitioners will need to worry much about the vote dilution of Democrats or Republicans under the *Bandemer* standard since it will be hard for either Democrats or Republicans to show that they have been systematically excluded from participation in the political process. Ironically, the most obvious places to look for systematic political exclusion are in one-party states, but, in general, partisan redistricting disputes are less likely in noncompetitive, one-party than in competitive, two-party states; and in the latter, the issue is rarely one of exclusion or even "loose proportionality," to use the Court's own term, as it is "exact proportionality," which is a right the Court does not want to constitutionalize. Even so, linedrawers in one-party-dominant states may want to take special care not to dilute the votes of their opposition.

While the ruling in *Davis v. Bandemer* may do very little for the Democrats and Republicans, other political parties such as the Libertarians or Peace and Freedom Party may derive some protection in the future. Typically the problem for minor parties is that their support is evenly distributed across the state and hence never sufficiently concentrated to control one seat regardless of the districting arrangement. But a regionally based minor party that can show a pattern of discrimination and exclusion against it might have a legitimate claim against a hostile redistricting plan. Also, traditionally discriminated-against groups such as the homosexual community may have a basis to claim protection under the decision, although obtaining accurate measures of the size of the homosexual vote would be difficult. In general, however, I do not think that the *Bandemer* ruling presents practitioners with as much challenge in 1990 as *Thornburg v. Gingles*.

The practical implications of the ruling on racial vote dilution in *Thornburg v. Gingles* are potentially important for several reasons. Blacks were successful in using the courts to obtain more favorable districting arrangements in the seventies as were the Latinos in the eighties.[7] An upsurge in non-European, nonwhite immigration into the United States has resulted in the growth of new groups who will also want the full protection of the law in redistricting matters. The problem for the linedrawer in 1990 and 2000 will be to decide which of these groups are to be protected and which are not. The recent Voting Rights challenges to the Chicago and Los Angeles city council redistrictings and the decision in *Thornburg v. Gingles* will, in all likelihood, encourage some of the newer ethnic groups—for example, the Koreans, Filipinos, and recently immigrated Chinese—to demand more representation. As set out in the *Gingles* decision, they will have to show that: (1) they are sufficiently large and geographically compact to constitute a majority in a single-member district; (2) they are politically cohesive; (3) there is white bloc voting against their candidates; and (4) the majority is usually successful against them. This will neither be trivial nor impossible to demonstrate. Here too, the practitioner would prefer more explicit guidelines than the Court seems willing to give. In the absence of de minimis standards from the Supreme Court, informal expectations evolve nonetheless—for example, a 65% black or Latino seat provides a fair opportunity for a black or Latino candidate to win, or a racial voting correlation over 0.7 is evidence of polarized voting—but they are not guaranteed to prevent Court intervention. As I said before, the overall uncertainty about whether a particular racial or ethnic group can win in court may lead some risk-averse redistricters to make concessions to these groups that they might otherwise not have made.

The "what" part of the "who gets what" in the *Davis v. Bandemer* and *Thornburg v. Gingles* cases is what is owed to various eligible groups. At one point in the plurality opinion in *Davis v. Bandemer*, Justice White states that the plurality does not have "a preference for proportionality per se but a preference for a level of parity between votes and representation sufficient to ensure that significant minority voices are heard and that majorities are not consigned to minority status" (*Bandemer v. Davis*, Slip Opinion, p. 14, last part of n. 9). This is another example of what will seem to the practitioner as a vague standard: What exactly is a "sufficient" level of parity between a party's seats and votes? Assuming that a political group can qualify under the "strong indicia of lack of political power test," the experience with racial vote dilution cases suggests that the standard will de facto become something very close to equality of seats and votes. Rules of thumb for redistricting have to be simple and practical, and, as I have argued elsewhere, that excludes so-called vote symmetry measures (Cain, 1985b, pp. 217–219). It is safe to predict that whatever the Court's intention, a group's right to fair representation will inevitably become a right to PR in the minds of group members as least.

Another likely area of controversy is the inevitable ambiguity over voters' rights and incumbents' rights. The Voting Rights Act and the racial vote dilution cases, for instance, focus on the ability of racial groups to elect representatives of their own choosing rather than a given number of incumbents from that racial group per se. In short, the rights protected by the Fourteenth Amendment belong to voters not incumbents. Insofar as incumbents have rights, it is only because of their "status . . . as the chosen representative of a particular racial group" (*Thornburg v. Gingles*, p. 34). In a real redistricting dispute, however, this distinction gets blurred very quickly, because often the key indicator in the minds of many group members as to whether they have been given a fair opportunity to elect a representative of their own choosing is whether a representative from that group actually wins the election.

In political cases, this problem could become even more complicated, especially since what happens to incumbents per se in redistricting can very much affect the outcome of the next election (see, for instance, Cain, 1985a). If, as Justice O'Connor suggests, the plurality is really expressing a preference for bipartisan over partisan plans, this would be generally favorable to incumbents since, as the Court has itself acknowledged, it would require "creating as many safe seats for each party as the demographic and predicted political characteristics of the state would permit" (*Bandemer v. Davis*, p. 19). It is possible that the *Bandemer v. Davis* decision could be used by incumbents in the 1990 round of redistricting to justify anti-competitive or noncompetitive bipartisan gerrymanders, which will likely displease many reform-minded people.

THE DEMOCRATIC THEORIST'S INTEREST

Apart from the significance of *Davis v. Bandemer* and *Thornburg v. Gingles* for redistricting per se, they are both important cases from the standpoint of democratic theory. A critical aspect of both decisions for the U.S. system of representation is the Court's explicit recognition of group voting rights. The "one person, one vote" principle of *Baker v. Carr* (369 U.S. 186 (1962)) and *Reynolds v. Sims* (377 U.S. 533 (1964)) sought to protect an individual's right to an equally weighted vote. By comparison, the partisan and racial gerrymandering cases deal with the right of groups to "fair representation." As set out by Congress, a section 2 violation of the Voting Rights Act occurs when "the political processes leading to nomination or election in the State or political subdivision are not equally open to participation by members of a class of citizens protected by subsection (a)."[8] In *Thornburg v. Gingles*, the Court acknowledged that minority groups with a special history of discrimination against them had a right to their fair share of representation, and in *Davis v. Bandemer*, it extended this constitu-

TABLE 5.2. Types of Representative Systems

Type of System		
Individual formalist	Individual rights to representation	Legal equality of individual political rights
Individual compensating	Individual rights to representation	Rights vary with individual circumstances
Group formalist	Group rights to representation	Legal equality of group political rights
Group compensating	Group rights to representation	Rights vary with group circumstances

tional protection to politically cohesive groups who could demonstrate that they too suffered substantial political exclusion.

Many political and legal ideas about representation in the United States are, at least implicitly, individual and formal in orientation. They are individual in the sense that they assume that the electorate is composed of autonomous individuals who independently acquire information and formulate preferences about relevant candidates and policies, and then choose between alternatives (i.e., vote).[9] Voting mechanisms, according to this view, are methods of aggregating individual preferences into collective decisions. In addition to being individual, this approach is formal or institutional in the sense of focusing on the rules that govern elections, the criteria that determine the composition of the electorate, and the formulae for counting votes. A voting system is formally fair if its rules are applied uniformly to the electorate and if the aggregating mechanisms assign equal weight to all voters. The "one man, one vote" ruling is an exemplar of such formal equality for individual voters. This approach assumes nothing about the various attributes of the electorate—that is, that some are rich and some are poor, some are well educated and some are not, and so forth. Voters are essentially regarded as black boxes, to use the language of social science "positive theory," and thus the empirical fact that differences in attributes confer advantages to some voters over others is not relevant to a consideration of the formal equality of the voting system per se.

At the opposite end of the spectrum, a second approach to representation focuses on groups as opposed to individuals and compensates for nonlegal or informal inequalities in the resources of various groups. Instead of regarding individuals as separate voting entities, it recognizes them as being linked by common ideologies, group affiliations, or racial and ethnic characteristics. Some groups will have advantages over others in the competition for power in a democracy, especially groups with greater wealth and education. An electoral process can be formally fair in the sense that the same rules and procedures apply to everyone in the electorate, but informally unfair if the impact of those rules and procedures is more advantageous to certain classes of individuals than to others. An at-large electoral system, for instance, can be formally fair in the sense that individual voters retain an equally weighted opportunity to affect the outcome of an election and simultaneously unfair in the sense that certain groups are systematically disadvantaged under those rules because they are poor (hence, lack the resources to conduct city-wide campaigns), undereducated (hence susceptible to low turnout), and nonwhite (hence subject to white backlash and voter discrimination). A compensating group approach to representation gives special voting protection to groups that are disadvantaged in these ways. An example of this, as we have already noted, is the Voting Rights Act, which provides remedies for designated protected classes.

Other approaches to representation are also possible, as Table 5.2 illustrates. A system of formal group representation assigns shares of representation by group classification. Some examples of this are the designation of Scottish seats in the British Parliament, list PR, and the power-sharing arrangements between religious groups in pre-War Lebanon and Northern Ireland. There has historically been little sentiment for this approach in the United States, and I doubt that this will change in the near future.

A further possibility would be a system of compensating individual representation in which disadvantaged individuals are given special protection or consideration by the political system. Theoretical examples of this might be allowing individuals of a certain income level or educational background to register on voting day, or a weighting scheme for poor voters offsetting the influence that moneyed interests have on candidates. However, I am hard-pressed to think of any real world applications of this approach, because, I suspect, such schemes would be cumbersome to administer, vulnerable to strategic manipulation, and potentially offensive to many people.

There is no one single American ideal of representation, and consequently, American electoral laws and institutions reflect a hodge-podge of viewpoints. I would conjecture that members of the white middle class in America (from the Progressive movement to contemporary good government groups like Common Cause) favor (implicitly, at least) the formal, individual approach and that lower income, nonwhites more likely favor group compensating approaches for the obvious class-interested reasons, but I have no systematic evidence on this point. Since both the *Davis v. Bandemer* and *Thornburg v. Gingles* cases shift the representational emphasis away from formal individual equality and toward compensating group representation, I would expect that middle America, to the extent that it is aware of these cases, is less enthusiastic about the Court's current views on representation than MALDEF or the NAACP are.

The democratic theorist's question, however, is how does one kind of approach to representation as opposed to another relate to the legitimacy, stability and efficacy of a system based on the consent of the governed—that is, the fundamental concerns of democratic theory. Without trying to resolve the long-standing differences between the formal individual and group compensating approaches, it is useful to place the arguments for them in the context of these traditional issues. For instance, a common justification for a democratic form of government is that because its authority derives from the consent of the governed, democratically produced decisions are perceived to have greater legitimacy.[10] By this logic, institutions that strengthen the connection between what the people want and what the government does add to the system's perceived legitimacy. Thus, pure town hall democracy with a unanimity principle has a stronger claim to legitimacy than, say, American national government, which operates on neither a unanimity principle nor a direct democracy mechanism. Moreover, when a republican form of democracy is combined with single-member, simple plurality voting rules, voters are often faced with a situation of being represented by someone they did not vote for, and whose views they do not agree with. Whether it is rational for them to feel this way or not, people in this situation regard their vote as "wasted" and the electoral system as unfair.[11]

Those who take a group compensating approach favor voting mechanisms that either minimize the number of people who cast losing ballots (i.e., so-called homogeneous districts) or aggregating procedures that more equitably reflect voting strength in seat representation (i.e., proportional and semiproportional systems). On the other side, individual formalists believe that a democratic system requires that individuals have an equally weighted share in the election process not in the electoral outcome per se. Whether one or another system best promotes systemic legitimacy depends on a number of other factors such as whether voters see themselves as autonomous individuals or as members of groups, and whether they believe that there is one common public interest revealed by aggregating voter preferences or just competing interests with inevitable winners and losers.

For instance, an individualist who believes that there is a discoverable, common, and nonpartisan public interest will be more inclined to look favorably on an at-large electoral mechanism because of its median voter properties. Such a person will tend to be offended by the idea that minorities can best represent other minorities, or that women can best represent women. Another strand of individualist theory is antipartisan. For instance, Progressive reforms, especially city manager forms of government and nonpartisan ballots, were meant to remove policy making from divisive partisan politics. By comparison, a compensating group perspective tends to be skeptical of public interest claims, noting that the so-called public interest often shortchanges minority interests. A properly gerrymandered district system, or proportional and semiproportional electoral mechanisms, they would argue, more accurately reflect inevitable differences of electoral interests and therefore give minorities more representation than the at-large systems introduced by the Progressives. Not surprisingly, contemporary racial and ethnic groups do not like, and are seeking to overturn, many of the allegedly neutral reforms introduced by the distinctly white and middle-class Progressive movement. Thus, the nature of the electoral mechanisms a particular democratic system uses—or more generally, the kind of general approach to representation that a polity adopts—can affect public perceptions of its legitimacy. If a particular rule works to the systematic disadvantage of one group over another, members of that disadvantaged group are less likely to think the rules, and any policies produced by them, are legitimate.

The second fundamental concern of democratic theorists is stability. The problem of democratic stability was considered extensively in the Federalist papers.[12] Madison's historical studies had convinced him that divisions of opinions and interests were inevitable in politics, and that conflicts would occur as one faction tried to gain domination over another. These forces, Madison feared, could ultimately undermine a democracy.[13] Madison's apprehensions about excessive factionalism and his "extended republic" solution have been enormously influential to contemporary pluralists.[14] They, in turn, have extended Madisonian logic to argue that competition between groups is a healthy democratic force as long as coalitions are fluid and groups have the opportunity to influence policies that matter to them intensely.

The stability issue arises in the context of electoral procedures also. The relevant question is, does the formal recognition of a group's right to representation destabilize a democracy—that is, is it a step in the direction of the "excessive factionalism" of such countries as Northern Ireland, Canada, and Lebanon? The formal individualist will likely think that it is for several reasons. First, it could be argued, the explicit recognition that a particular group has a right to something may encourage potential group members to think of themselves as actual members. For instance, if the Voting Rights Act designates Asian-Americans as a protected class, then this might encourage them to think more along group lines than they would otherwise, because it would be politically and legally advantageous to do so. By conferring a benefit on groups (i.e., a constitutional right to representation), the Voting Rights Act may actually be creating an incentive for people to think along group lines, thereby unwittingly encouraging potentially destabilizing factionalism and group conflict. Second, the formal individualist might argue, group-based representation will reflect actual interests and intensities in the electorate less well than formal individual representation. Political organizations tend to serve their members less well than their leaders, and in any event, the configuration of preferences within the minority communities is far too complex for there to be a single black, Latino, or Asian interest. As if that were not enough, the formal individualist would argue, once these group rights are conferred, it will be difficult, if not impossible, to unconfer them if they are no longer appropriate.

Proponents of the group compensating position are likely to answer that the fears of the formal individualist are unfounded. To begin with, societies with a much more explicit recognition of group representation rights, so-called consociational democracies, have proved to be highly stable.[15] The images of policy paralysis in the French Fourth Republic and constant government turnover in Italy are offset by the less tumultuous experiences of Belgium, the Netherlands, and West Germany. More important, perhaps, instability as measured by the rise and fall of governing coalitions may be less important than instability measured by the degree of voter alienation. Two-party democracies, fostered by single-member simple plurality rules, are vulnerable to crises of voter disaffection, because new political movements must overcome very high barriers to entry. When voters find that their choices on the ballot are too far from their ideal points, they can become "alienated," or when the choices are too narrow, they can become "indifferent" (Riker and Ordeshook, 1973). In either event, voters may feel that it is not worthwhile to participate in the political process, leading to lower voting rates and higher levels of public cynicism. Recent experience in Britain and the United States has led observers in both countries to rethink the previously unthinkable notion that PR rules are better at accommodating complex configurations of electoral preferences than the traditional Anglo-American district system.[16] Perhaps, the argument goes, a step toward greater acknowledgment of group rights to representation will increase rather than decrease democratic stability in the long run.

Finally, in addition to legitimacy and stability, there is the consideration of efficacy—that is, how well does a democracy work. Mill's justification of democracy was that it fostered a better informed, more concerned electorate (Mill, 1975). Others have suggested that a democracy is more likely to produce "good" decisions than other forms of government, because it receives wider input from those affected by government decisions (Nelson, 1980). The issue of group representation can be put in similarly utilitarian terms—that is, does the recognition of group representation make for better or worse public policy?

Once again, the formal individualist will think that group representation is detrimental rather than helpful. A compensating approach to representation makes political participation easier for less well-educated, lower-income groups. Some might regard this as undesirable. Establishing barriers to participation, it could be argued, serves to screen out the apathetic and uninformed, and thereby improves the quality of decision making in the policy. Assuming that the better informed make better policy decisions, it is entirely possible, the individualist could argue, that less well-informed people would be better off if only knowledgeable people were allowed to make public policy decisions for them. Perhaps, all the uninformed do is add statistical noise to the system. These ideas might initially seem radical, but to the contrary, proponents might argue, they are quite traditional. The fact that the Founding Fathers restricted the voting franchise to property-owning white males indicates that the principle of screening the populace for the proper qualifications to make public decisions is firmly embedded in the traditions of American democracy.

Proponents of group-compensating representation will not see things this way. Questions of public policy, they will point out, depend only partly on facts and to a greater degree on values and perspectives. Voters who are better informed factually are not necessarily better attuned to the values and perspectives of others in the electorate. Participation is a guarantee that minority values and perspectives are heard. Second, they might say, public interest in and information about public policy-making is not exogenous and fixed. Drawing people into the electorate and giving them representatives from their groups can be an inducement for the disadvantaged to become better informed.[17] A representative system that does not take into account informal advantages and disadvantages among individuals may simply play into the hands of the upper-income and middle class, and will tend to produce class biased policies.

The point of all this is that the court's decision implicitly touches on some profound considerations of representation and democracy. I regard it as unlikely that the Court or anyone else could come up with a single theory of representation that will please all viewpoints in the United States. More likely, the Congress and the Courts will pursue some moderate, compromising course that tries to reconcile individual with group rights to representation. This seems to be what the White plurality opinion had in mind in the *Davis v. Bandemer* decision, but there is substantial question in the minds of others about whether a moderate course of action in this matter is a stable equilibrium. Will it be possible in a democracy, some ask, to give representation rights to certain groups and not others? And does the Court itself contribute to the problem in *Davis v. Bandemer* by destroying the legal firebreak between the rights of racial and political groups. This fear is best expressed by Justice O'Connor when she said in her concurring opinion that there "is simply no clear stopping point to prevent the gradual evolution of a requirement of roughly proportional representation for every cohesive political group" (p. 4).

In principle, I see no reason why the Court cannot prevent the predicted slide into a PR system. In practice, however, I know from my own experiences that there are certain inexorable pressures that will push the system in that direction. One such force, as I indicated earlier, is cognitive: Political people will be forced to come up with clear and simple rules for why certain groups should be given special consideration and not others, or why a particular discrepancy between seats and votes is tolerable and another is not. Based on my own experience in the Los Angeles City redistricting lawsuit in 1986, the tendency to think of proportionate results as fair is very strong. It is far too complex to calculate the political influence a minority group might have in any terms other than the number of districts it controls (i.e., has a majority in) and the percentage of legislators who belong to that group.

Moreover, as Pitkin has suggested, there may be several types of representation (Pitkin, 1967), and while groups can be well represented in many senses by someone who does not share their racial, ethnic, or party affiliation, they may not regard themselves as well represented in other ways. Members of minority groups, for instance, complain that nonminority incumbents are not in close touch with their communities nor do they understand as well the special problems facing minorities. Minority constituents may be more reluctant to bring their problems to white representatives than to one of their own. These difficulties are multiplied with respect to partisanship. Democrats are unlikely to feel that they can be well-represented (at least in a policy sense) by Republicans and vice versa. Even in such nonpolicy aspects of representation as casework and project solicitation, constituents can be influenced by partisanship.[18]

Thus, I suspect that the pressure for greater proportionality in representation is going to be with us for some time. The influx of new immigrant groups and the emergence of other geographically based interest groups (e.g., gays, environmentalists, rural preservationists) will test the determination of the Court to hold the line of compromise between individual and group rights to representation. In my opinion, it is the job of the political system, not the Courts, to accommodate the demands that nonracial groups have for "fair representation," which leads us to the third perspective—that of the institutional reformer.

INSTITUTIONAL REFORM AND CONSENSUS

The fact that the Court has chosen to limit its intervention in redistricting and electoral design issues does not exclude the possibility of improvement. The Court, by its recent decisions, has defined a wide interval of permissible action for states and municipalities, broad enough to accommodate many different institutional rules and representational values. Adopting a high threshold for constitutional intervention does not necessarily imply condoning current U.S. redistricting practices. If there are redistricting outcomes that seem unfair but are not unconstitutional, then it will be up to the political system to reform itself. While I do not believe that it is possible to devise a method of redistricting that is "objectively" fair, I do believe that it is possible for a community to arrive at an approach that a consensus or majority think is fair. As long as boundaries adhere to the "one man, one vote" principle and the electoral system does not exclude disadvantaged minorities, there is no reason why a given state or municipality cannot choose between competing representational values. There is also no reason to expect, or even think it desirable, that every community will choose the same set of values, or that a community's ideal of representation will stay constant over time. The key to this, a "subjective" approach to fair representation, is to define the values that enjoy the broadest consensus and try to design institutions and rules that implement them.

The problem of designing institutions to achieve representational goals is the perspective of the reformer. I hesitate to use the term since many recent efforts at redistricting reform have given it a bad name. If reform is to be successful, it must, I think, do several things. First, it must have realistic assumptions about how the political system works and how various political actors will behave under different rules. While it is impossible to anticipate such things with complete certainty, some behavioral assumptions are more plausible than others. Second, the various representational goals should be spelled out clearly, and potential conflicts between them should be identified. Finally, there should be clear connections between the proposed institutional mechanisms and the postulated goals and behavioral assumptions.

Since there is no one perfect approach to redistricting, I will not propose a solution per se, but it might be illustrative if I put forward some ideas based on my own experiences in California. Some of these will not be universally applicable, but others could be widely useful. They fall into three categories: plausible behavioral assumptions, goals that are sensible from a pluralist perspective, and some institutional changes that might further these goals.

With respect to behavioral assumptions, my advice is as follows: Do not assume that those who redistrict must be angels. Some degree of trustworthiness and public-regardingness is required, but on the whole, it is too much to expect members of redistricting commissions or the legislature to put aside their interests and prejudices completely. The idea that a "neutral" commission of experts, scholars, and persons of exemplary probity can redistrict in the public interest is naive and creates a situation that is ripe for abuse and hypocrisy. Many different groups and individuals, not just legislators, have an interest in redistricting. Taking redistricting out of the hands of legislators may insulate the process from certain kinds of incumbent interests (although there is no guarantee of this), but not from general partisan, parochial and self-interested concerns. This is especially a problem in the United States, because it lacks the tradition of an independent civil service and judiciary found in many Commonwealth countries.

Do not assume that ignorance leads to fairness. It is sometimes proposed that redistricting be entrusted to people who do not know the political landscape, or even to an automated computer system, and that lines should be drawn without reference to political data. I have dealt with this elsewhere at some length (Cain, 1984). Basically, one can never be sure that those in charge are really ignorant of effects, but even more important, procedural neutrality does not necessarily lead to substantive fairness or to district lines that make sense from the perspective of important representational values. The latter will occur only if districts are consciously designed that way.

The check of public opinion is especially limited in redistricting matters. The general public is both ignorant about and indifferent to redistricting. It is hard for them to see how their lives are affected by decennial changes in district lines. Redistricting discussions are perceived as technical, complicated, and boring. As so frequently happens in such situations, public opinion on redistricting is easily manipulated, and complex issues of equity and representation are reduced to simplistic themes. However, particular interest groups, party activists, and local organizations can sometimes provide useful information about the effects of proposed plans and sometimes suggest better ways to design districts.

Assume that self-interested motives lurk behind most representational values. Compact districts benefit some more than others, as do equally populated districts, regard for communities of interest, and the preservation of city boundaries. The rhetoric of redistricting will center on representational values, but the incentives of redistricting will usually be self-interested. Institutions and rules should be designed to use these parochial incentives in a Madisonian way to protect worthwhile representational goals. An approach that is insufficiently "realistic" in its assumptions about human behavior will be susceptible to manipulation and hypocrisy. On the other hand, it is a mistake not to foster some public-regarding incentives in the process. In the end, a prudent approach steers a middle course between the extremes of institutional design.

Bearing in mind how the participants in redistricting are likely to behave, the next task is to decide what it is that needs to be accomplished by redistricting—that is, what values or goals of representation should be implemented—and which particular institutional mechanisms or redistricting rules will promote those ends? One goal, for example, might be to increase the chances of a bipartisan agreement to any redistricting plan. The *Davis v. Bandemer* case raised the question of whether it is fair for one party to take advantage of another in the redistricting process. One "objective" approach to this problem might be to define a neutral plan as one with a seats to votes ratio that is close to one, but the problems with this measure have been discussed elsewhere at length (see Lowenstein and Steinberg, 1985; Cain, 1984). A "subjective" approach is to say that fair is what the two parties agree to when both have equal bargaining power in the redistricting process. What was unfair about the Republican plan in Indiana, from this perspective, is that the Democrats did not have equal say over the redistricting process and were forced to accept a plan that was less to their liking. The essence of a subjective approach is introducing redistricting rules that induce consensus by ensuring that both parties have an equal say in the final outcome?

Given my assumptions about the behavior of various political actors, a "subjective" bipartisan solution must involve (1) meaningful input by both parties in the redistricting process, and (2) a supermajority rule that gives a minority party leverage over the final outcome. The first is critical because we want to avoid putting too much faith in the fair-mindedness of redistricters, and the supermajority rule serves to make it necessary for the majority party to get the consent of the minority party in order to pass a plan through a legislature. A frequent objection to a supermajority voting rule is that the redistricting body may find itself deadlocked and incapable of coming up with any redistricting plan whatsoever. This, however, does not seem an insuperable problem to me. For instance, one solution might be introducing some incentives into the negotiations that encourage bipartisan agreement by invoking common incumbent interests. In the case of a legislative redistricting, this could be a rule prohibiting incumbents from using the franking privilege or even being designated as incumbents in the next election unless a redistricting bill is passed with a supermajority vote by a certain date. For a commission, it could be a lottery that removes one member from the commission at random if a plan is not passed on time.

A second goal, especially for communities with a substantial minority population, might be to increase minority representation by lowering the threshold of votes needed to gain a seat. There are various ways to do this. One is is to transform single-member systems into more proportional systems by wantonly disregarding compactness, thus preserving a geographically based system while making it easier for racial and ethnic minority candidates to get elected. This is the path that many cities and states have followed recently. The second option is to adopt one of the European proportional representation formulae (i.e., highest average, largest remainder, Hare, etc.). While the Court has made it clear that there is no constitutional right to proportional representation, it is constitutionally permissible to adopt PR rules. However, as I mentioned earlier, I think it is unlikely that many U.S. communities will adopt PR for fear that it will make it harder to achieve a working majority and lead to the proliferation, rather than the moderation, of groups' interests and demands. A third alternative that has not been much explored in this country is multimember districts with semiproportional properties such as a limited vote (i.e., voters have fewer ballots than there are candidates to elect). Semiproportional systems tend to produce the kind of loose proportionality that the *Bandemer* plurality seems to want to encourage.

Finally, one might seek to subject the process to greater public scrutiny. However, given assumption number three about public ignorance and indifference to redistricting matters, a more realistic goal is to get input from the groups and individuals who are most likely to care about the outcome. The Commonwealth model of redistribution, for instance, involves extensive public hearings throughout the country and revisions based on what is learned from them. Some British commentators believe that the process in their country is too drawn out, but it seems to work well in Australia, New Zealand, and Canada (see Butler, 1963; Waller, 1983; Barnes, 1985; Ward, 1967; McRobie, n.d.) A useful reform for the United States might be to require two rounds of hearings before a plan is passed. In the first, the plan is presented and objections are heard. In the second, revisions in response to those objections are shown publicly; and, if no revisions are made in response, then the redistricting body would be required to explain publicly why it did not do so. In so far as the electoral incentive and voter accountability can act to moderate redistricting disputes, more has to be done to bring the issue to the public consciousness. This might, on the margin at least, constrain some of the more imaginatively self-regarding redistricting proposals.

CONCLUSION

The issue of group representation will not disappear no matter how the *Davis v. Bandemer* decision is ultimately interpreted. The evolutionary development of group voting rights in the law has occurred in response to a growing sensitivity in the United States to the disadvantages that certain groups face. The appearance of large sprawling cities and suburbs has partially undercut the regional and neighborhood focus of political interests in the United States: People in urban settings are more likely to define their political identity in terms of sex, race, or occupation than in terms of where they live per se. However, single-member, simple plurality systems still have certain undeniable advantages over PR systems (e.g., the exaggerated majority effect tends to make governance easier), and the Madisonian fear of excessive group factionalism that is pervasive, if not always explicitly acknowledged in the American middle class, will probably prevent any wholesale transition to proportional representation in any case. Also, as we have seen from the futile attempts of the Liberal-SDP alliance to alter the electoral rules of the British system, single-member systems have a strong inertial force centered on a most powerful human motive—that is, the desire of incumbent politicians to stay in office. Incumbents are unlikely to give up the system that elected them for the uncertainty of a more proportional world. Resistance to abandoning SMSP is also likely to come from regional and local interests, which tend to flourish under single-member simple-plurality rules. Thus, given these forces, institutional shifts toward proportional rules are likely to happen very slowly, if at all.

In the meanwhile, the Court has indicated by its decisions in *Davis v. Bandemer* and *Thornburg v. Gingles* that it will maintain a high threshold of intervention, giving the political system much leeway to deal with the demands of various groups for fair representation. Formally constitutionalizing group claims to proportional representation may be bad law, but informally accommodating various groups may be good politics. In any case, it seems that the recent redistricting decisions have given political entities enough leeway to find out for themselves.

NOTES

1. Before the decision was issued, a number of legal scholars and political scientists discussed *Davis v. Bandemer* and *Badham v. Eu* at a conference at UCLA law school. The papers that were written for this symposium were subsequently published in the *UCLA Law Review*, volume 33, number 1, 1985. Since the decision, a number of articles have been written on the meaning of the *Bandemer* ruling, including various contributions in this volume and Gottlieb (1987) and Maveety (1987).
2. The best examples of this are Niemi (1985), Grofman (1985a, b), and Cain (1985b).
3. One person who raised the question is Shapiro (1985). Also, Grofman's proposed tests for political gerrymandering were clearly influenced by his familiarity with the "totality of circumstances" approach the Court and the Congress set out for racial gerrymandering cases.
4. See especially, the concurring opinion of Justice Stevens in *Karcher v. Daggett (I)*.

5. This cause is most fervently espoused by Common Cause (see Common Cause, 1977).
6. A description of the Burton Plan's merits on city splits and population deviations can be found in my declaration in *Badham v. Eu*.
7. Descriptions of the progress of blacks and Latinos in one state, California, can be found in chapter 5.
8. Section 2 of the Voting Rights Act, as amended, 96 Stat. 134.
9. These premises are most clearly seen in the spatial model literature. See, for instance, Riker and Ordeshook (1973), and the seminal work in this area, Downs (1957).
10. A good critique of the various arguments for democracy can be found in Nelson (1980).
11. The argument that losing votes are wasted votes is actually portrayed as a democratic dilemma in Wollheim (1986).
12. For a recent review of the Federalists from the perspective of Democratic Theory, see Grofman and Wittman, eds. (1988).
13. The classic statement of this fear is in the Federalist 10.
14. Dahl (1956) is actually a detailed inquiry into Madison's thinking about factionalism and the relationship between majorities and minorities.
15. For a sympathetic view of this kind of democratic system, see Lijphart (1976).
16. A variety of perspectives on this question can be found in Lijphart and Grofman (1984).
17. This idea derives from the idea of participation as education in Pateman (1970).
18. This is less true in the United States than in other countries. See Cain, Ferejohn, and Fiorina (1987), pp. 164–165.

How to Measure
Partisan Gerrymandering

6

Establishing a Statewide Electoral Effects Baseline

Charles Backstrom, Leonard Robins, and Scott Eller

The Supreme Court in *Davis v. Bandemer* (106 S. Ct. 2797 (1986)) established, over the objections of Justices O'Connor, Rehnquist, and Burger, that partisan gerrymandering was justiciable. At the same time, however, the Court upheld, over the objections of Justices Powell and Stevens, the constitutionality of the Indiana state redistricting plan that was at issue. Since many students of the subject of partisan gerrymandering (ourselves included) were uncertain that partisan gerrymandering would be declared justiciable, but had little doubt that the Indiana districting plan constituted a classic partisan gerrymander, the result was, to say the least, surprising.

The controlling plurality—Justices White, Brennan, Marshall, and Blackmun—clearly want the courts to eliminate the evil of excessive partisan advantage in districting, but did not enunciate a simple but sound measure and standard for measuring it. Additionally, the plurality opinion was, as we will demonstrate, both confusing and contradictory.[1] Thus, the future evolution of the law on partisan gerrymandering is highly uncertain. Legislators or other state authorities who will soon have to redistrict again, and federal district courts who will have to adjudicate challenged districting statutes have not had their work made easier by *Davis v. Bandemer*.

The resolution of this controversy that ultimately emerges will have to follow one of the following three scenarios: First, after much protracted litigation and difficulty in developing guidelines for testing for the presence of gerrymandering, the Court decides it cannot develop an effective test and reverses the *Davis v. Bandemer* holding that partisan gerrymandering is justiciable (the O'Connor solution). Second, the Court opts to consider that a number of traditional "factors" adequately demonstrate the presence of gerrymandering and tests individual districting plans according to the number of factors on which they are deficient and the extent of the deficiencies—that is, essentially decides each case on an ad hoc basis (the Powell/Stevens solution). Or third, the Court builds on its central thrust of requiring a political test for partisan gerrymandering, but moves away from the unworkable and unwise assortment of requirements mentioned by Justice White toward a more feasible measure and standard of partisan gerrymandering (our solution).

As to which of these scenarios is more likely, it seems to us that the Court is highly unlikely to reverse itself on justiciability. This would fly in the face of the juridical history of the past fifty years. Although only two justices embraced the "factors" approach in *Davis v. Bandemer*, we can envision several more justices coming around to this position in order to avoid essentially vacating justiciability if no partisan gerrymandering cases ever survive the White tests.[2] The third option is developing an *effective* political test, and we contribute to this effort by setting out a specific standard and measure of partisan gerrymandering. Since any of these scenarios is possible, we now consider them *seriatim*.

JUSTICIABILITY OF GERRYMANDERING

Those who oppose granting justiciability for partisan gerrymandering do so on several grounds. They object because they believe that (a) partisan politics does not matter in state legislative races or actions and therefore the allegation of a political gerrymander is irrelevant to public affairs;[3] (b) districting is inherently and irremediably, or even beneficially, a matter of political judgment; (c) courts would be hurting themselves politically if they tried to alleviate gerrymandering; or (d) there is no appropriate measure for partisan gerrymandering. We will attempt to refute each of these allegations in turn.

Significance of Political Parties

All of the justices took for granted that partisanship is important in legislative matters. But the question was whether the plaintiff Indiana Democrats as a group constituted a body that could be hurt by discriminatory legislative action on districting. Justice White declared that an individual voter gains significance in elections only through collective strength as a supporter of a political party. Although Justice

O'Connor also strongly values the two-party system, she denied that a political party is an entity that could be harmed. She stated that people at the polls vote for individual candidates and not for the statewide party, and categorized *Baker v. Carr*, 369 U.S. 186 (1962) as turning on an individual's right to vote, not a group right. She asserted that an individual cannot be harmed by the statewide outcome of an election that is the result of happenings outside his or her own district, ridiculing that concept by posing the congressional analogy, which she said would be asserting that voters in one state were harmed by election results in another state.

That partisanship is weakening has scholarly support. Political scientists have noted the decline in partisan identification among voters, and the willingness of voters to support incumbent Congressmen who have served them in a personal way irrespective of party (Mayhew, 1974; Fenno, 1978; Crotty, 1984). Yet party identification remains the most salient cue for voters in races where they have little other information (Crotty, 1984, p. 210). All party candidates prefer to run in a district where more of their fellow partisans are concentrated because it gives them a base of trust and confidence from which to build.

Further, once legislators are in office, they form party caucuses to advance their personal and program goals. The majority caucus will usually control all leadership positions and install all committee chairs, thus dominating the rules and agenda. It is true that voting in state legislatures does not always follow party lines, but there is likely to be considerable ideological distinction between the center of gravity of the two major parties. Additionally, the legislative caucuses often raise funds collectively to assist their members to win reelection, and some opposition members will be targeted for defeat in hopes of gaining or retaining a working majority. With all of this partisan activity in the election of and the operation of legislatures, it is our view that eliminating partisan unfairness in legislative elections is a legitimate public interest.

Although there are now many independents among voters, at the polls they almost always must choose between the Republican and the Democratic candidates. And whatever their motivation for supporting a particular candidate on election day, voters—independents along with avowed partisans of various intensities—will likely end up with a partisan member, or one who at least must operate in the highly partisan milieu of legislative caucus politics. We think that the choice of the voter between the parties should have a fair chance of being effectuated to the degree that his or her choices are joined by other voters making similar selections in what amounts to an election-day partisan coalition.

Finally, a little common sense seems in order on this issue. If district drawing is irrelevant to partisan outcomes, why do legislators and state political activists go through such agony and pyrotechnics on this issue? They obviously believe it to be vital to election outcomes and legislative action. Absent overwhelming evidence to the contrary, it would seem foolish for courts to disagree with this assessment.

Gerrymandering Is Wrong

Justice O'Connor does not see partisan gerrymandering as an evil that needs to be dealt with by the courts. First she argued that gerrymandering is one of the spoils of the majority party, which should not be judicially denied. Then she noted that parties can fend for themselves without judicial aid, since political gerrymandering is self-limiting because the majority party could overreach by dangerously weakening its hold on some seats if it draws the lines so that too many of its partisans will be put into adjacent districts in an attempt to control them.

Popular acquiescence in and support for laws in a democracy, however, depends on the faith on the part of the losers in this legislative election that they have a fair chance to be the victors in the next. If gerrymandering has unfairly made much more likely an erstwhile majority's ten-year control of the legislature, this consensus would be lost, and the result would be corrosive of the political compact.

The assertion that parties can fend for themselves implies that a true majority purposely weakened to minority status can protect itself from continued damage. This is merely the updated version of Justice Frankfurter's futile option in *Colegrove v. Green* (328 U.S. 549 (1946)) that the remedy for population inequalities was for the voters to "sear the consciences of their lawmakers." What actually happened was that as population inequalities widened, the advantaged groups hung more tightly onto them rather than gave them up in a generous desire to share power.

Nobody contends that gerrymandering can perpetuate a controlling group's power under all circumstances, but it does provide a controlling group with significant unfair advantage. This violates Equal Protection, and a remedy should be available.

Remedying Gerrymandering Would Not Be a Political Liability

It appears to us that Justice O'Connor's main reason for rejecting judicial involvement in partisan gerrymandering is her belief that it is a risky area for judicial action, a political thicket that courts would be well advised to avoid.

In *Baker v. Carr* Justice Brennan's opinion adumbrated several criteria for political questions that would make judicial action unsuitable in any case. These included intrusion on separation of powers, the lack of discernible and manageable standards a court could use to settle an issue, the necessity for a court to make a prior public policy choice before reaching the question at issue in the particular case at bar, or the need to avoid the confusion that would result if a court did not adhere to a political decision already made.

Whatever language is invoked to define "political question," we believe that the Supreme Court can label any issue a political question on which it is not inclined to rule for whatever reason. Justice White for the majority in *Davis v. Bandemer* carefully distinguishes between *political questions* to be avoided and *political cases*, which should not be dodged just because they are difficult cases to deal with. Indeed, careful analysis will show that losses of prestige for the courts are not a function of the toughness of the issues. Instead they arise from one of the following: (1) a problem that the courts are not good at solving—or at least are even worse at than some other branch, in this instance the legislature; (2) a problem on which court action could have no effect; or (3) a problem that can cost the courts political support and credibility.

Under these criteria, partisan gerrymandering is not a thicket because:

(1) The courts *are* actually more suitable than legislatures to handle reapportionment for two reasons. First, handling partisan gerrymandering requires the development of standards prior to drawing specific districts. Courts are better suited to develop and follow standards than the legislature, where the way business is done is to seek short-term, specific, ad hoc solutions. Second, the judges are free from conflict of interest involving the security of their own jobs, whereas if legislative reapportionment is left to the legislators without judicial supervision, that task must be done by officials with a monumental conflict of interest.

(2) As to the efficacy of court action on gerrymandering, the courts have shown they can have an effect on reapportionment: They can

void elections, make legislators redraw a plan, or draw a better plan themselves.

(3) The courts will not suffer politically from correcting gerrymandering because, as in population redistricting where opposition blew over quickly, there will be gainers as well as losers. Unlike the "Little Federalism" argument defending population inequalities that almost negated *Baker v. Carr* through the Dirksen Amendment (see Congressional Quarterly Service (1969), pp. 423–434) what possible rational argument could be made to favor unfair partisan advantage? Avid partisans no doubt are elated to receive a special advantage in elections, but they cannot claim gerrymandering is fair, and therefore cannot openly urge it.

Measures Can Be Developed

A final objection by Justice O'Connor to justiciability for partisan gerrymandering was that there can be no appropriate measure for it.

Justice White for the majority pointed out that standards do not have to be available at the very moment a constitutional evil is identified. The question in *Baker v. Carr*, after all, was not whether unequal population representation was unfair, but whether the courts should step in and decide whether it was unfair—in plain words, whether the issue was justiciable. *Baker v. Carr* turned on this issue alone; the significance of the case was that the Supreme Court agreed to deal with the issue of comparative legislative district population; the application of actual measures of inequality and the setting of standards of equality were left to *Reynolds v. Sims*, (377 U.S. 533 (1964)) and its progeny (*Kirkpatrick v. Preisler*, 394 U.S. 526 (1969)); *Wells v. Rockefeller* (394 U.S. 542 (1969)); *Mahan v. Howell* (410 U.S. 315 (1973)); *Karcher v. Daggett (I)* (462 U.S. 725 (1983)). Justice White argued that the Court, in *Davis v. Bandemer* as in *Baker v. Carr*, ruled only that the subject—here partisan gerrymandering—is justiciable. He appeared confident that a similar evolution would ensue after *Davis v. Bandemer*, namely that a suitable measure of partisan gerrymandering will be developed in subsequent cases. In fact, the cases are not parallel. Although *Baker v. Carr* indeed set up no specific standard of population equality, in *Davis v. Bandemer* the plurality, by speculating on what it might take to demonstrate a partisan gerrymander, appeared to establish a series of standards that, if literally applied, would be impossible to meet.

The courts do obviously need assistance in developing clear criteria for detecting and measuring partisan gerrymandering. This is essential for ultimate acceptance of a judicial remedy.

TRADITIONAL FACTORS AS A TEST FOR PARTISAN GERRYMANDERING

Justices Powell and Stevens believe that the traditional measures of partisan gerrymandering are sufficient to identify partisan gerrymandering and to adjudicate cases alleging its presence. Since these "factors" are widely accepted as constituting the core of a partisan gerrymander, they deserve careful consideration. The factors can be classified as matters of either *process* or *structure*.

Procedural Indicators of Gerrymandering

Justices Powell and Stevens believe that unfair procedures in districting indicate the presence of a partisan gerrymander. In Indiana, according to the facts set out in *Bandemer v. Davis*, these included exclusion of all Democratic legislators from the committees drawing the districts; utilization of the state Republican committee headquarters for the data work done by a consultant (rather than the legislative research department on the grounds that it was prohibited by statute from doing partisan work); bringing the bill to the floor on the last day of the session without opportunity for the Democrats to examine it; and the open admission that the aim of the majority party was to secure for themselves every possible seat.

The plurality justices, in contrast, consider procedural issues to be superfluous for establishing intent, believing that where the subject is legislative districting, partisan intent on the part of legislators is inevitable. We need not discuss procedural matters further beyond stating our view that redistricting should not alone, of all subjects, be excluded from fair legislative process norms. But fair procedures will not alone guarantee a gerrymander-free districting act.

Structural Indicators of Gerrymandering

Several technical or mechanical choices confront those who actually draw legislative districts—whether to use single-member districts, how neatly to outline the districts, and how much consideration should be given to following other governmental lines already on the map. These "structural" tests, in contrast to procedural matters, have both intrinsic bearing on the quality of a redistricting plan and utility as constraints against partisan gerrymandering. But we disagree with Justices Powell and Stevens, who elevate structural measures to be the major constitutional tests for a partisan gerrymander.

(1) Multimember districts. The district court in *Bandemer v. Davis*

(603 F. Supp. 1479 (1984)) held that *inconsistent* use of multimember districts was ample evidence of intent to gerrymander. The Supreme Court plurality disagreed, and although they showed continued suspicion of multimembered districts, they did not find them *per se* constitutionally impermissible. Instead, they perversely reasoned that the very fact that Indiana had not used multimember districts in every metropolitan area in the state showed that there couldn't be a statewide discriminatory effect. This ignores the realities of how gerrymandering is done in practice: to design districts of one type where the controlling party can win them, and to avoid that type where it will be to that same party's disadvantage.

In our opinion, the Court passed up a good opportunity to strike down a districting technique that, *when used inconsistently*, is almost surely a discriminatory practice. Courts should, in addition, be suspicious of changes from single-member districts to multimember districts in a new districting act. In these circumstances the burden should be on the district creators to prove that they have not intended to or in fact have not gained an unfair partisan advantage by mixing district types.

(2) Uncompactness. The classic gerrymander—Governor Gerry's salamander-shaped district—is an area that twists and turns and reaches to include or exclude certain sub-units. It is not compact. The district court in *Bandemer v. Davis* found numerous horrific examples in Indiana that helped persuade it that a gerrymander had been perpetrated. It did not use any rigorous measurement of compactness, relying instead on an optical test—the districts simply looked bad.[4]

It is, in truth, hard to develop a powerful case for the intrinsic value of having compact districts: If the representative lived at the center of a compact district, he or she wouldn't have to travel any more than absolutely necessary to campaign door-to-door or meet with constituents, but other than that, uncompactness does not seem to affect representation in any way.

Compactness in districting has, however, a symbolic virtue, precisely because the long emphasis on visual standards for districts has elevated compactness to be of preeminent value to the public. But the public cares for symmetry beyond mere esthetics; crooked districts lead the public, often correctly, to suspect crookedness by someone manipulating the districting process in order to gain unfair advantage. This shows the importance of requiring compactness; it is a constraint on gerrymanderers, but of course does not itself guarantee fair districts. Those who rely on compactness alone as a test for gerrymandering are not aware of how easy it is for district drawers to come up with a compact-looking plan that still is a fearsome partisan gerrymander. Compactness then can become a snare that encourages judicial acceptance of partisan gerrymandering while ostensibly prohibiting it.

We favor the retention of a standard of compactness for its own merit, and because it would constitute an additional constraint on district drawers' ability to seize partisan advantages, but warn against relying on it as a constitutional test for partisan gerrymandering.

(3) Cutting subdivision lines. The majority district court judges in *Bandemer v. Davis* noted that the Indiana districting plan they voided cut county and municipal lines unnecessarily if the only goal was to achieve population equality. Justices Powell and Stevens went further and found the excessive cutting was a measure of how much gerrymandering had been done. We agree that needless splitting of subdivision lines is usually done to achieve partisan advantage.

Attempting to judge districting plans on how much they respect local government boundaries is, however, not easy. How many splits are too many? Is a little split from a single unit as bad as a big split? Are all units equally sacrosanct—are counties more sensitive to state legislation or more pertinent to voter identification than municipalities? The only "method" that can be used is to compare several plans to see which one cuts fewer sub-unit lines.

(4) Breaking communities of interest. The district court in *Bandemer v. Davis* focused on rural areas being conjoined with parts of Indianapolis to illustrate how the district drawers ignored community of interest as they sought to gain more partisan advantage.

The goal of preserving communities of interest comes into play when larger units must be cut in districting, or smaller ones combined to make an ideal-sized district. Within a large unit of government that is entitled to more than one legislative district, how the unit is cut can leave together people of similar interest, possibly making them a sufficient majority to elect one of their own to the legislature, whereas if the line is run another way, they might be split below a critical mass. Likewise, if several smaller units must be combined to make legislative districts, representation would be fairer if those communities with interests in common were aggregated rather than some being thrown in with very unlike components.[5]

Except for race and ethnicity, community of interest is hard to identify,[6] and in any event, preservation of these other communities of interest is more of a hortatory goal for those designing district plans than a constitutional principle for judging districts.

In summary of this section, we believe that the factors employed by

Justices Powell and Stevens, while having some intrinsic value, do not rise to the constitutional level as proof of discrimination, as they do in total for those justices.

Specifically, the problems with these structural measures are, first, that Justices Powell and Stevens do not set out unambiguous measures or standards for application in other cases. No judge could know how much compactness is required, how few subdivision lines must be split, the criteria for making tradeoffs required by simultaneously applying multiple and quite possibly conflicting criteria, or even how much perfunctory participation the controlling legislative caucus must allow the minority before it marshalls its members and passes its districting bill.

But the main problem with all of Justices Powell and Stevens' "factors," as Justice White points out, is that they do not prove that the minority party has been hurt. They therefore do not rise to the constitutional level as proof of discrimination. Finally, as we have shown elsewhere (Backstrom, Robins, and Eller, 1978) all of these techniques could be avoided, compact districts could be created, few subdivision lines be could cut, and yet a grievous gerrymander could be created.

If, however, measures and standards of acceptability can somehow be created for these factors,[7] they each do serve as constraints on the district drawers' self-interested partisan gerrymandering, a reality the plurality justices ignored. We would be delighted if all districting plans tried to implement them. But in the last analysis, a political problem such as partisan gerrymandering requires that a political measure be central to its detection and resolution.

THE COURT'S POLITICAL TEST FOR
PARTISAN GERRYMANDERING

The Supreme Court plurality in *Davis v. Bandemer* rightly recognized the primacy of an effects measure for partisan gerrymandering. They got right to the heart of the issue in demanding that someone be hurt before the courts will intervene. In partisan gerrymandering the injury is to a political party and its adherents.

But the Supreme Court did not devise a workable, practicable measure for gerrymandering. The Court looked at the single political measure on which the Indiana district court relied, and rejected it as inadequate. Justice White noted that Chief Judge Pell—in dissent in district court—applied a measure of party strength (our measure incorrectly used) but that his conclusions were not challenged at the district court level. Although the appellees used our measure correctly to answer Judge Pell, the Supreme Court found this record not ripe for resolution (*Davis v. Bandemer*).[8]

In truth, most political measures that have been suggested by various scholars are flawed by their impracticality, their irrelevance because of being available too late, or their contamination by other events. In contrast, we believe our proposed measure and standard are pertinent and practical and therefore useful in helping to detect and remedy gerrymandering.[9]

In the record that came before the Supreme Court, the Indiana judges had relied on the results of the 1982 legislative elections, which were run on the challenged plan passed by the legislature the previous year. The district court compared the percentage of aggregate vote received by all legislators of each party with the percentage of seats each party had won. This showed that while the complaining Democrats had received 51.9% of the votes cast for state House candidates, they won only 43% of the seats (*Davis v. Bandemer*, p. 2801). This type of measure is commonly referred to as a "seats/votes" ratio.

The plurality of the Supreme Court correctly found that the seats-votes ratio used by the district court in *Bandemer v. Davis* was not an adequate measure of unconstitutional partisan gerrymandering, but their reasons for rejection were problematic. Reasons were that (1) analysis of the effects of a districting act must be based on several years' elections; (2) a districting act must be predictive of future election results; and (3) the electoral system must have been "consistently degraded" (*Davis v. Bandemer*, p. 2810) by the districting act.

Are Results of a Single Election Sufficient?

The Supreme Court plurality faulted the district court for basing their decision on results of a single election. Perhaps in the next election the disadvantaged party would do better, they suggested, or if not, maybe that party would be in the majority after the next census and could dictate their own districting plan.

This requirement is onerous. How long does discrimination have to persist before it becomes remediable? As already pointed out, policymaking is proceeding each year in the legislature, and who is in charge matters greatly as to what that policy will be. As to waiting until the next census, a decade is essentially forever in the career of the average legislator and his or her partisan supporters. But even worse, gerrymandering is cumulative; the party that ensconces itself in control for a decade will also probably be the one that is entitled to draw the districts after the next census. This is a textbook example of justice being denied by being delayed.

There are also serious conceptual problems with the use of legislative *results* to test for partisan gerrymandering that were not mentioned by the Supreme Court.

First, it is Monday-morning quarterbacking to rely on results of legislative election contests conducted after the challenged redistricting plan has been put into effect. To be of any practical use, a measure of partisan gerrymandering must be available *before* the next election of legislators. As they begin their task, district drawers must have on hand objective guidelines with which to test various plans that are under consideration. Without this they have no way, even with the best of intentions, to tell whether they have drawn a fair plan. How can someone be held to an unknown standard? A seats-votes analysis by its nature cannot be applied until an election has been held under the new plan, at which time the percentage of legislators elected from one party can be compared with the percentage of aggregate votes for all legislators of that party.

Moreover, while court intervention may never be eliminated altogether, there is no judicial economy in a system that ensures litigation in every state after every redistricting, which would be a certainty since the losing party after each election would claim they lost because of the way the districts were drawn.

A further flaw in using election results of legislative elections to test for partisan gerrymandering is that this would neutralize the effects of quality candidates and targeted campaign efforts in the legislative contests. What would be the incentive for a party to engage in careful candidate recruitment and vigorous campaigns if their victory might be countermanded because their efforts were too successful?

Can Election Results Be Predicted from a Districting Plan?

Justice White noted that the district court in *Bandemer v. Davis* declined to address the question of whether a districting plan itself would inevitably produce certain election results, implying that such effort was not made, although the district court had shown at length how various district-drawing techniques had been used to achieve unfair advantage.

It is true that election results will differ for other reasons besides the nature of the districts. Candidates have differential personal appeal, the effectiveness of campaign efforts vary, and some different issues are salient. But the partisan gerrymandering issue should deal with only the partisan voting component of the complex voter calculus.

And there is a substantial demonstrable partisan component in every race where party labels appear on the ballot, an element that is relatively stable over time.[10]

Any districting plan will have some districts more favorable to the election of one party's candidates than to those of the other party. This is because of differing concentrations of voters with a certain partisan identification. These district characteristics *can* be evaluated by a study of the proposed districting plan. But the search for a partisan index to test for gerrymandering should not have to overcome the burden of nonparty components of the vote for specific legislative candidates, which is what happens if legislative seat totals are used to evaluate a districting plan. Instead, a measure that reflects the partisan element is more appropriate.

Is the Electoral Process Degraded?

According to the *Davis v. Bandemer* holding, even if the results over the long term, or projected results, did show serious partisan discrimination, that may not be sufficient evidence to void a districting plan. It is not enough, Justice White added, to show that election of a party's candidates has been made more difficult; there must be "consistent degradation" of the electoral process.

Very dubious is the plurality's assertion that minority party voters may not be hurt by a partisan gerrymander because they are not shut out of any consideration by the majority party officeholders. This is the rationale for "virtual representation," which should have been laid to rest by the American Revolution. What is an election about if it is not between candidates who offer somewhat different policy alternatives on at least some questions? Parties matter in elections, and parties matter in legislative decisions. It is simply not true that a legislator gives equal weight to the views and needs of his supporters and his opponents. In racial cases, Justice White says, consistent degradation meant plaintiffs were excluded from slating, endorsements, nominations, even from casting a vote.

But requiring the aggrieved in a partisan gerrymandering case to produce proof about the perception of persons who did not surface for endorsement, or fashion tests for what constitutes a representative slate for nominations in order to prove discrimination, is inappropriate. The analogy is not applicable to partisan gerrymandering, because while blacks might be able to prove that they were discriminated against within a party in its operations, why would members of the party in control use a districting act to interfere with the internal processes of the other party if they can rig the electoral system through a partisan gerrymander in such a way that it is highly unlikely that their opponents would take control?

Justice White acknowledged that a different formulation of evidence for consistent degradation would have to be applied in partisan gerrymandering cases than in racial cases. The question for him is whether a partisan group "has been unconstitutionally denied its chance to effectively influence the political process. . . . [T]he inquiry centers on the voters' direct or indirect influence on the election of the state legislature as a whole" (Davis v. Bandemer).

We interpret this to mean that the electoral process is consistently degraded if the voting and nominating process of the supporters of one political party are subverted because those voters are unfairly denied the chance to effectuate their choices through potential victory because of a partisan gerrymander that will be the law for ten years. This is what our test measures.

To summarize this discussion of the Court's suggested measures of gerrymandering: The plurality correctly focused on requiring a political measure for a political problem—a measure of partisan strength to identify unfair partisan advantage—but then seemed to require as well an overwhelming pattern of political discrimination that denies people their elementary right to participate in the electoral process. They have rejected the total-legislative-seats-won/aggregate-state-legislative-vote ratio used by the district court in Indiana to strike down that plan, but they did not reject it for its principal weaknesses—lack of uniformity, ad hominem contamination, and post hoc untimeliness.

The Supreme Court's plurality was groping for a formula that would establish discriminatory political effects of a districting plan, but did not define the issues clearly enough to detect on what a reasonable test might be based. It is encouraging that Justice White focused briefly on the redistricting act itself, rather than exclusively on legislative results, and later modified the consistent degradation proof as well as abandoned the initially posed requirement of several post hoc elections by indicating receptivity to using some race prior to the enactment of a districting plan to estimate partisan voting strength in its districts.[11] These understandings are the openings toward what we believe to be the only appropriate measure of gerrymandering—one that neither has to await results of elections subsequent to passage of the districting plan, nor gets entangled in the multifarious components of all legislative elections in a state.

A PROPOSED TEST FOR PARTISAN GERRYMANDERING

We now proceed to lay out what we believe "political effects" should mean and then to present what we consider to be an appropriate measure and standard for identification and remedy of a partisan gerrymander.[12]

Political Effects Defined

The Supreme Court plurality was correct to require the demonstration of discriminatory political effects of a districting plan in order to classify it as a partisan gerrymander. But they went on to discuss political *results*, which commonly means the actual outcomes of elections. *Effects* and *results* are not the same. We distinguish between these terms. Partisan effects in elections are only a portion of the total factors that determine outcomes of an actual election. The party identification of the voters in a district, which influences their perceptions of candidates and issues and to some extent cues their responses to party labels at the polls, has a significant effect on election outcomes. But other factors—personality appeal, issue salience, and campaign activities—can also influence election results. Thus any attempt to test for partisan gerrymandering must isolate the long-term partisan component of elections from other short-term elements.

This is why using the results of the aggregated legislative elections in a state is an unsatisfactory proxy for political effects. And that is why our measure, explained below, is an effects measure that does not guarantee any foreordained results of an election.

Measure and Standard Defined

Although the term *measure* has been used by most commentators to encompass everything the Court must now do to deal with partisan gerrymandering, it is helpful to recognize that there are in reality two concepts involved that should not be confused: measures and standards.

A *measure* is a device or method of detecting and calibrating disparities. A *standard* is how great that disparity must be to constitute an inequity (a somewhat value-laden word) or a discrimination (implying an intolerable degree). Using the population analogy may make this difference clear. The most commonly used *measure* of population disparity is the deviation of extreme districts from the ideal, while the required *standard* of population equality for congressional districts is one person, one vote.

Thus in dealing with partisan gerrymandering, the Court will have to first adopt a measure to ascertain whether and to what degree a disparity is present, and then choose a standard of how much disparity is acceptable before a specific districting act will be overturned.

A Proposed Measure and Standard

Succinctly, our measure of partisan effects is the number of districts in which the majority party adherents dominate, as indicated by the results of a base race. Our standard of impermissible gerrymandering is whether that number of districts in which the majority party dominates is other than 50% plus one of all districts. The measure is developed and the standard applied in several steps, which are listed here and then explained in some detail: (1) ascertaining majority party strength in each district; (2) setting majority rule as the primary value in assessing the fairness of a districting plan; (3) indexing the majority party's actual strength to 50%; (4) counting the number of districts in which the majority party is dominant. If the total is other than just over half the districts, the plan is a partisan gerrymander, unless irremediable under given standards of population and possibly some structural constraints; (5) order substitution of a fair districting plan.

Step 1: Ascertaining majority party strength. To measure the partisanship of individual districts and thereby to calculate the degree of overall dominance of a party in a state requires some kind of index. Our first step in that analysis is choosing an appropriate *base race* for determining party strength.

A partisan base race is a previous statewide election in which the choice between candidates appears to have been largely determined by partisan sentiments of the voters rather than transient issues or grossly dissimilar charismatic personal appeal of the candidates. The vote on this race within each proposed legislative district will be an estimate of underlying partisan adherence in that district. Such partisan adherence, as emphasized in the discussion of partisan effect, will *affect* the outcome of the subsequent legislative elections conducted in the several districts, but will not solely determine the subsequent *results* of the legislative races, either individually or in the aggregate.

That is why we use a statewide base race—an election presenting an identical choice of candidates everywhere in the state. In contrast, each legislative race has unique candidates, and typically some candidates are unopposed; both factors make it impossible to compare the partisan characteristics of precincts at the borders of districts as they are traded back and forth in trial districting plans.

All sides in the lower court in *Bandemer v. Davis* embraced our concept of a base race, although there were differences in how to calculate it in Indiana. What is a suitable base race to estimate partisan strength will not be the same in every state. In some states it may be a largely "invisible" contest (such as state superintendent of public instruction), where individual candidates never mount a major media campaign, and the voters have few cues to guide them in their vote except the party label on the ballot. In other states, it may be a major race in which candidates are relatively evenly matched in name familiarity and personal appeal, leaving partisanship to be the principal difference between the candidates.

The aim is to arrive at a previous election that represents a kind of "normal vote."[13] It should be noted that a base race does not have to be equivalent to the estimated normal vote of a state to be useful. As long as whatever race is picked correlates highly with other partisan races—that is, it rises and falls proportionately in various parts of the state rather than exhibits unique fluctuations in various parts of the state—it can be used in our measure, which reduces the actual statewide proportion to 50% before being applied.

Because the *Davis v. Bandemer* plurality shied away so strongly from a single indicator of partisan strength, courts may prefer using as the base an average of several statewide races in a single year. We have demonstrated that a single race that correlates highly with other partisan races is equally acceptable.[14] But to the general public and to judges averse to statistics a multiple-race amalgam may be a more persuasive index.

Another possibility—averaging several races over several years—is less suitable because assumptions about the effect on individual districts of rising and falling total vote operate only at one point in time (Scarrow, 1982). Moreover, the difficulties of matching redrawn precincts between different elections over the years poses an immense practical burden on the data gatherers.

Courts should not be reluctant to use a base race as a test for gerrymandering. After all, the political party organizations in a state and the legislative district drawers are using exactly that—some kind of base race—to estimate partisan effects on subsequent legislative races in various configurations of districts they draw and evaluate. That is what the expensive computer consultants use for data in advising on how to draw districts. Why shouldn't a court review the data and computer calculations that the controlling party in the legislature used as its indicator of partisan strength, adopt that measure if it is persuasive, and then determine whether the way it was used to draw districts resulted in an egregiously unfair plan?

Step 2: Choosing a standard of fairness. Agreement on a base race as the measure of partisan strength is only the first of four steps in identifying a gerrymander. Next, a standard must be chosen for determining a fair distribution of partisan advantage.

We strongly believe in an electoral system that is supportive of a two-party system and majority rule. This requires that a majority party's supporters be dominant in a majority of the legislative districts. To us this is the "fair representation" Justice White is seeking, which he was confident creative district judges could come up with in subsequent partisan gerrymandering cases (*Davis v. Bandemer*).

An important support for a majority-rule electoral system is the use of single-member districts. Every justice in *Bandemer* insisted that proportional representation must be avoided. Justice O'Connor viewed the whole idea of a district system for representatives as a compromise between winner-take-all and proportional representation. She fears that testing the aggregate outcomes of district elections will inevitably lead to a proportional representation standard, which would be fatal to the two-party system in this country.

But the application of a proportional representation standard for judging partisan gerrymandering would have another consequence endangering majority rule. This is because of the tendency of the majority to gain more than a proportionate share of seats for each increment of additional statewide vote. We term this the "balloon effect" (Backstrom, Robins, and Eller, 1978, p. 1134, n. 10). The balloon effect occurs because, in a single-member district system, any additional votes that one party gets will first make a difference in several marginal districts, tipping them more rapidly into the majority party's column than the proportion by which that party's statewide vote has risen. The courts seem now to understand this "law" and to be willing to live with it. The danger of applying a pure proportional representation standard to statewide results (either aggregate legislative or some base-race totals) is that it will inevitably take from the majority party some of the extra seats they gain through the balloon effect. If at the time of districting the majority party's statewide strength was, say, 54%, and the number of districts dominated was set at 54%, and then in a subsequent election its statewide total fell (but remained above 50%), the downward operation of the balloon effect would drop the majority's proportion of districts dominated to below 50%. We believe it is intolerable that a majority party be districted into minority status, so we propose an adjustment at the outset to ensure that this does not occur. We cannot emphasize too strongly that our measure does not guarantee any party any specified *result* after an election. The goal being sought is fairness of *opportunity to be elected* (from a partisan base standard) granted in a districting plan before an election has been held under it. This is the "level playing field" argument.

Step 3: Indexing majority party strength to fifty percent. In not every state will a statewide party base race be exactly at or very near 50%. Where it is not, there must be an adjustment of the data to produce a usable index. In those circumstances the actual statewide base race percentage of a majority party must be adjusted downward to 50% overall, with concomitant reductions in the base race percentage for each proposed district, in order to avoid penalizing the majority party by negating the balloon effect.

This process consists of adjusting the actual vote in each precinct by a uniform figure—the difference in percentage points between the actual statewide base race and 50%. In the example in a previous article, where the statewide base race was 54% we subtracted 4 percentage points from the actual base race percentage in each precinct in the state to yield an index percentage. That number was then multiplied by the actual total raw votes cast in that precinct for the base race candidates to come up with a new "vote" total for the majority party. Lastly, these new precinct "votes" were added together for each proposed district and the district's index percentage was computed.[15]

Because legislative districts are apportioned on full population count rather than on numbers of eligible voters, or registered voters, or actual voters, and because political measures are typically based on actual votes, using statewide vote totals underweighs the effect of low-turnout districts. One scholar urges compensating for this by aggregating the base race *percentages* on the base race in each district to a statewide total and then averaging them. This yields a mean district vote percentage for each party, rather than pooling raw votes and then figuring a statewide percent, as we have done. This adjustment would have the effect of treating all districts equally in the calculation of a statewide base race percentage, just as they are drawn equal in population (Lowenstein and Steinberg, 1985. This approach is also adopted by McDonald and Engstrom in chapter 8.) But it can be argued that while districts are and should be equal in entitlement to a representative, they should lose or gain potential impact in partisanship by their actual turnout. Since children and nonvoters are now counted in apportioning representatives, averaging district percentages rather than adding actual turnout of voters to the state levels would in effect be counting them twice. We emphasize, however, as this scholar himself acknowledges, that either methodology is fully compatible with our overall approach (Lowenstein and Steinberg, 1985, p. 52).

Step 4: Deciding whether a plan is a gerrymander. The final step in deciding whether a districting plan is a gerrymander is to count the number of districts in which each party dominates (measured by the indexed base race). If this is other than one over 50% of the districts, a gerrymander is present, unless further adjustments of district lines are impossible.

Step 5: Substituting a fair plan. If the districting plan gives unfair advantage to one party, the appropriate remedy is to draw a new plan that is less unfair. Not always, however, will it be possible to draw a completely fair plan. It could be that the residential concentration of one party's adherents in a state is such that their strength cannot be spread among more districts without violating accepted standards of compactness. In such instances, the best surviving plan, even if still somewhat unfair, should not be judged a gerrymander that requires correction. We do not, however, believe this would be a common problem; we have shown earlier that it is relatively easy to make minor adjustments in districting lines to achieve a fair plan (Backstrom, Robins, and Eller, 1978, n. 12).

DECISION RULES

By way of summarizing our argument, here are decision rules for ascertaining the presence of partisan gerrymandering: (1) Test a plan before enactment, or if an act under judicial challenge, before an election has been held under it. (2) Allow no partial or new use of multimember districts. (3) Test the districting plan by an adequate political measure—such as the one we have outlined above—and, if the plan does not meet the standard of base majority rule, declare it unconstitutional. (4) If no alternative plans are fair, judged by the same criterion, the court should direct that a plan be developed that meets the standard.

In summary, our test relies centrally on a political index, as the Supreme Court plurality requires. But our index is independent of individual legislative election results. Our test is forward-looking, as permitted by the Court, rather than retrospective. Our standard is that of majority rule. It gives the majority party dominance in a majority of districts but does not penalize the majority for the bonus it will receive in a single-member district system as it would in a crude proportional representation standard. But our measure also does not guarantee any victories to one party or the other in the subsequent election. It has, instead, provided a fair starting point from which parties can vie for advantage in the first election under the plan.

CONCLUSION

Solving partisan gerrymandering is perhaps not as tractable as rectifying population inequalities turned out to be, but it is a necessary accompaniment to the one person, one vote accomplishment to make sure that election procedures are truly fair.

The *Davis v. Bandemer* decision announces that it is time to move toward an acceptable measure of partisan gerrymandering. There is at present no Supreme Court majority for any one measure of partisan gerrymandering. The Justices' statements may be seen either as (at best) a cry for assistance to develop an acceptable measure or (at worst) a Catch 22 that outlaws gerrymandering, but establishes criteria that will allow no measure to meet the threshold of unconstitutionality. Our hope is that decisions in subsequent individual cases will move in the former direction—creative development of effective measures and standards for handling partisan gerrymandering— rather than in the latter direction—closing the door to effective relief in this matter.[16]

Tackling gerrymandering is technically difficult, but it is not a thicket. With careful thinking, the theoretical framework to deal with gerrymandering can be understood, and a practical measure and standard mastered. No one can seriously defend gerrymandering, and the media and the public will support antigerrymandering strictures.

Courts may not yet be ready to give any specific political test constitutional status. This is not discouraging. Even population disparity measures, which now seem so simple, took many years to develop to their present level of acceptability. We should expect at least as difficult a search before full agreement is reached on a specific test of partisan gerrymandering. But we have no doubt that the test that will ultimately be adopted must be of the *type* we first presented in 1978— a political measure for a political problem.

Justice White conceded that it was not likely that the equivalent of the arithmetical one person, one vote standard could be achieved in partisan gerrymandering cases. But in very few judicial matters are standards transparently obvious. Courts are frequently faced with degrees of uncertainty and conflicting testimony. There is no reason to hold partisan gerrymandering cases to higher standards of certainty and agreement. The gravity of the evil, and the inability to obtain redress elsewhere, requires judicial action to fulfill the promise of relief announced in *Davis v. Bandemer*. Moreover, there will be no respite for the Supreme Court if it chooses to backtrack on this issue, because the public is so intolerant of partisan gerrymandering that case after case will arise seeking to redress this unfairness.[17]

Cogent standards on gerrymandering will improve the whole process of redistricting. If clear fairness standards exist, legislators will be more hesitant to breach them, resulting in a lessened need for judicial intervention. Moreover, redistricting is not inherently a legislative function. If there were less partisan advantage to gain, legislators, in the states where they are the exclusive districting authority, would be more willing to delegate that power to nonlegislative reapportionment commissions. But we do not believe that a fair districting plan is automatically guaranteed because it is drawn by a neutral source. Courts must retain the ultimate right to apply appropriate standards to test contested plans for fairness to the major political interests of the state.

An earlier, more extensive presentation of this subject appeared under the title "Partisan Gerrymandering in the Post-*Bandemer* Era," *Constitutional Commentary*, Vol. 4, No. 2 (1987), pp. 285–318.

NOTES

1. Perhaps the best evidence for the confusion engendered by the White opinion is the radically different ways in which it is interpreted by several authors in this volume—authors who collectively constitute most of the leading experts on the subject of partisan gerrymandering. For example, Daniel Lowenstein basically argues that Justice White requires evidence of a degree of "oppression" of partisans essentially equivalent to that suffered by blacks prior to the passage of the Voting Rights Act before he would invalidate a plan as constituting a partisan gerrymander (see Lowenstein chapter 4). Bernard Grofman, by contrast, argues that White is calling for only the presentation of evidence that a districting plan would *over time* unfairly disadvantage a party and that the partisans of that party are disadvantaged when there is an "overrepresentation" of elected officials from the other party. He indicates that a more effective evidentiary presentation by future plaintiffs could prove that that was happening (see Grofman, chapter 3). Our own interpretation is contained herein. We believe that this enormous variance in interpretation of the White opinion indicates confused writing, rather than confused readers.

2. Although their perspective obtained the least support from the Court initially, some observers believe that the inherent problems in the approach of the plurality will ultimately result in the Court's turning to the traditional factors ("The Supreme Court—Leading Cases," *Harvard Law Review* 100 (1986), pp. 153–163).

3. Peter Schuck in chapter 11 makes the argument that party identification has less and less impact on voting. Nobody in this volume, however, argues that the party composition of the legislatures or Congress has no impact on policy.

4. The simplest measure of overall district compactness (the one we used in 1978) is the ratio of the actual area of the district to the area of the smallest circle that can be drawn around the district (see Roeck, 1963). (A circular district would have a ratio of 1.00—the ideal—and a sprawling district somewhat less.) Presumably, guidelines to regulate violations of compactness could be adopted that required the average ratio to be greater than some set figure: 0.4, according to one authority (see Hacker, 1964). Of course, since averages do not point out single egregiously noncompact districts, a measure of the range between the most compact and the least compact districts could be used, but if all districts were noncompact, very bad districts would not seem so extreme. One author cites seven published tests of compactness, including the circle test, points out the faults of each, and proposes his own: minimizing the number of neighboring basic population units assigned to different districts by counting the number of edges cut—in fact, a measure of the extent to which "neighbors are assigned to different districts" (see Young, 1988).

5. These considerations have arisen most strongly when the community of interest is a single racial or ethnic group, for example, blacks and Hispanics. We should add that leaders of these two groups sometimes pursue different strategies. Blacks typically prefer to be concentrated heavily to ensure election of a black representative, whereas Hispanics sometimes seek to spread their population in order to have a significant presence in a greater number of districts (Cain, 1984).

6. Some scholars maintain that television market areas are today's communities of interest (see Campbell, Alford, and Henry, 1984).

7. We began this task in an earlier article (Backstrom, Robins, and Eller, 1978, p. 1145, n. 9, 12).

8. Additionally an exhaustive analysis of the Indiana redistricting plan that applies our methodology conclusively demonstrates that it was a gerrymander in favor of the Republicans (see Cranor, Crawley, and Scheele, 1986).

9. Comments on our general approach, first presented in Backstrom, Robins, and Eller, 1978: n. 12, are offered by Grofman (chapter 3) and by McDonald and Engstrom (chapter 8).

10. The concept of the normal vote was developed by Philip E. Converse (see Campbell, Converse, Miller, and Stokes, 1966). The concept was to be the division between the major parties in a hypothetical race in which *only* the partisan factor was operative.

11. In his words: "*Projected* election results based on district boundaries and past voting patterns may certainly support this type of claim, even where

no election has yet been held under the challenged districting" [emphasis original] *Davis v. Bandemer*, p. 2814, n. 17.

12. For the earliest formulation of this test, see Backstrom, Robins, and Eller (1978, pp. 1128–1139).

13. The normal vote in a state is often developed with the use of survey research findings of statewide party identification distribution. Survey data is not, however, suitable for establishing base-race data for each proposed legislative district needed for a measure designed to identify gerrymandering, because it is prohibitively expensive to conduct adequate surveys in each tiny subarea of a state. Techniques have been developed to estimate distributions of individual voter characteristics within small geographic areas by noting the relationship of various attitudes to certain demographic characteristics statewide, and then using small area census figures to find out how many people of those census types reside in the area, assuming they exhibit the same attitudes as their statewide cohorts. But this statistical procedure rests on assumptions and manipulations that are too sophisticated for easy judicial and popular acceptance.

Another possible database on which to estimate party identification is registration data. In the states that require preregistration by party choice, some information is available. If this data is used, it would be necessary to ignore registered independents. When actual voting results are used, most of these independents have sorted themselves out by choice between the major-party candidates. In fact, the party registrants are under no compulsion to vote in accordance with their registration, so the voting figures reflect also their actual partisan behavior (see Campbell, Converse, Miller, and Stokes, 1966, n. 21).

14. Our calculations for Minnesota have shown an incredibly high correlation (above *r* = .90) between the race we selected for use and other statewide races the same year and in previous years. This being true, no improvement would be gained by using an index that melded other similar races with the leading one (Backstrom, Robins, and Eller, 1978, n. 12).

15. This uniform percentage reduction is not represented to be a statement of historical outcomes in the United States. Rather, it is an index at one point in time that shows a party's base race percentage. If a party were to drop by a certain number of percentage points, the calculation shows in how many districts that party would no longer be in the majority.

16. A suit, *Badham v. Eu* (N.D. California, No. 3-83-1126, dismissed April 21, 1988), certiorari denied for want of jurisdiction by the U.S. Supreme Court, October 1988, challenging California's congressional districting was set aside until *Davis v. Bandemer* was settled, and now has been reactivated. That the next partisan gerrymandering case to come through the court system is on congressional rather than state districting is unfortunate. A number of special aspects of congressional districting could induce courts to retreat from fashioning an effective remedy for that kind of gerrymandering and thereby impede progress toward solving the more straightforward issue of state legislative gerrymandering.

Congressional districting involves different law, motives, tactics, and impacts.

First, justiciability of congressional districting could be challenged—although the present Supreme Court seems unlikely to agree—on the ground that the narrow definition of "political question" as affecting separation of powers prohibits the federal judiciary from interfering with the election procedures of its coequal branch, Congress (Daniel Lowenstein, Congressional Reapportionment and the Party System, paper delivered at the meeting of the American Political Science Association, Washington, D.C., August 19, 1986).

Second, congressional districting is derivative and decentralized, while state legislative districting is primary and self-contained. That is, the state legislators, in most states, district for themselves, while the state legislators and not the congressmen themselves district for congressional seats. This means that state legislators have a fundamental conflict of interest in the state instance, necessitating greater outside scrutiny.

Third, as mentioned previously, incumbency is an even larger factor in congressional than in state elections, and hence differential treatment of incumbents is a more prominent tactic in congressional than in state gerrymandering.

Fourth, the whole state legislative policy machine is built through one districting act by a legislature, while the overall membership of Congress comes as the result of fifty separate congressional districting acts. No one state legislature can determine, or even substantially affect, the partisan balance in Congress. (An effort has been made to examine the overall effect of gerrymandering on party composition in Congress, concluding that the effect has been slight. This is because pro-Democratic gerrymandering in states under Democratic domination has been roughly balanced by pro-Republican gerrymandering in states under Republican domination (King and Browning, 1987). Further, if a legislature is gerrymandered, control of the next redistricting for itself and for Congress could also be affected, whereas if a legislature is fairly districted, that state's congressional districting is likely to be more fair, and a change of control for the next districting for both legislators and congressmen is more possible.

Our *measure*—the base race domination of individual districts—applies in testing a congressional districting plan as well as a legislative plan. But our *standard*, given the generally many fewer congressional seats, becomes lumpy (in a three-seat state having only 100%, 67%, 33%, and 0% of the seats to aim for). Of course, our standard of majority dominance could apply only to state delegation by state delegation, rather than addressing the important question of overall control of the U.S. House of Representatives.

It would indeed be unfortunate if the special problems involved in handling congressional gerrymandering were to impede the development of a measure and standard to correct the more important and more tractable problem of state legislative gerrymandering.

17. This important insight was expressed by the leading scholar of reapportionment as early as 1968:

It is unlikely that the issue of justiciability of political gerrymandering will be laid to rest until the Supreme Court speaks specifically to the point. In the light of past reversals of Court position, it also is unlikely that seriously aggrieved parties with a provable case will cease suing even if the Court's first explicit response is to leave political gerrymandering by single-member districting within the "political thicket." Indeed, how can parties so aggrieved rest, so long as both multimember district gerrymandering and racial gerrymandering remain justiciable? (Dixon, 1968: p. 493).

7

The Swing Ratio as a Measure of Partisan Gerrymandering

Richard G. Niemi

In a previous paper (Niemi, 1985) I argued that if the Supreme Court is to consider squarely the question of political gerrymandering, "sooner or later it will have to take a position on the significance of the relationship between votes and seats won by each political party" (p. 191). If in doing so the Court holds to its frequently stated argument against proportional representation (reiterated in *Davis v. Bandemer*, 106 S.Ct 2797 (1986), p. 2809), then facile comparisons—that a party won 58% of the vote but only 52% of the seats—are inadequate. So the question arises, how can one look at the seats-votes relationship without reducing it to a question of proportional representation?

Political scientists have developed such a way—now generally referred to as the swing ratio. Though the idea originated as the "cube law" some 40 years ago, the swing ratio is a relatively new concept as it is applied to political districting, and there are a number of problems about its use in this context. But because the seats-votes relationship is at the heart of the gerrymandering issue, I continue to pursue its possible applicability. In this paper I describe the swing ratio, drawing heavily on a previous description (Niemi, 1985), but showing for the first time the swing ratio for the New Jersey legislature at the time of *Karcher v. Daggett*. I then discuss the applicability of the concept to tests of political gerrymandering.

THE SWING RATIO: A DESCRIPTION

The swing ratio is the rate at which seats change as votes change. More formally, it is the change in the proportion of seats won by a

TABLE 7.1. Democratic Percentage of the Two-Party Vote in New Jersey
Congressional Districts in 1982, Ordered from Highest to Lowest

Percentage Democratic	District	Percentage Democratic	District
84.1	10	63.2	3
76.9	14	53.5	9
73.7	1	46.9	4
71.2	8	43.6	7
68.6	2	39.7	13
68.5	6	33.9	5
64.9	11	32.6	12

Source: Congressional Quarterly Weekly Report, February 19, 1983, p. 391.

party when there is a 1% change in the votes won by that party. There are several ways of measuring the swing ratio (Niemi and Fett, 1986), but most ways require the use of data from a number of previous elections and measure the swing ratio in the past. Since assessment of districting plans is usually made after only one election (or even prior to an election), only one measure is suitable in this context: a hypothetical measure of what the change in seats would be if votes changed in some specified manner (usually uniformly) across districts. An assumption of uniform changes across districts is surprisingly appropriate, because the hypothetical swing ratio is designed to measure the structural characteristics of a districting plan. The assumption will not be true in any actual election, but it is useful precisely because it measures what the swing would be if there were no district-level effects such as particularly attractive or unattractive candidates.

Some measure of the statewide two-party vote and of the two-party vote in each legislative district is needed as a starting point. The swing ratio is calculated for one party only, but in a strictly two-party system (or if only the two-party vote is used), it will be identical for each party. In an earlier paper I illustrated the calculation by using the Indiana State House election for 1982, (that is, the election and districting involved in Davis v. Bandemer (106 S. Ct. 2797 (1986)). Here I use the New Jersey congressional plan litigated in Karcher v. Daggett.

First, the Democratic percentage of the two-party vote in each district is calculated. These percentages are shown in Table 7.1. Consider the seat with the largest Democratic vote—that of Representative Rodino, who won with 84.1% of the two-party vote in his district. If the statewide Democratic vote fell uniformly across districts, it could have fallen by 34.0% (from 56.9% to 22.9%), and Rodino would still have won the district. Similarly, the next-most Democratic district would have been won by Representative Guarini even if the statewide vote fell uniformly by 26.8% (to 30.1%), and so on. For each district, we can find the percentage of the statewide vote at which the district would have been just barely won by the Democratic candidate. Since each of the 14 districts represents 7.1% of the total, we can say that at each of the percentages we have calculated the Democrats would win 7.1% more of the legislative seats.

Having found the percentage of the statewide vote at which the Democrats would win each additional legislative seat (or 7.1% of the 14 seats), we can graph this relationship, as in Figure 7.1. Note that the Democrats would win no seats until the statewide vote reached 22.9%; they would win another seat when the vote reached 30.1%, and so on.

In some respects the seats-votes curve traced in Figure 7.1 suggests an admirable result. There is clearly what I have referred to elsewhere as a wide range of responsiveness. If the election results changed dramatically but uniformly across districts, the Democrats would win a seat even if they won only 23% of the statewide vote; they would win all of the sets only if they won 75% or more of the vote. The rate at which seats change hands as votes change is also smooth over fairly wide ranges. This is quite evident in the figure, especially between 30% and 45%, where the curve approximates a straight line.

Yet the plan is not neutral between the parties. The Democrats could win 50% of the seats with as little as 42.1% of the statewide vote; for the Republicans to win half of the seats, they would need at least 56.4% of the vote. There are also large "flat spots" near the actual election result. If the Democrats had lost 13% of the vote, for example, they would have lost but a single seat. To put this possibility in its most dramatic form, note that with 56% of the statewide vote, the Republicans would have won 43% of the seats, a greater disproportionality than the 1982 Indiana results litigated in *Bandemer*.

The line in Figure 7.1 representing the gain in seats for each percentage gain in the vote is the extensive form of the swing ratio. Often, however, it is convenient to have a statistic that summarizes the overall seats-votes relationship, just as one sometimes uses the mean value to summarize an array of numbers. What we want to know is, as votes change, what is the "average" change in seats? The most common summary measure for this sort of situation is the "re-

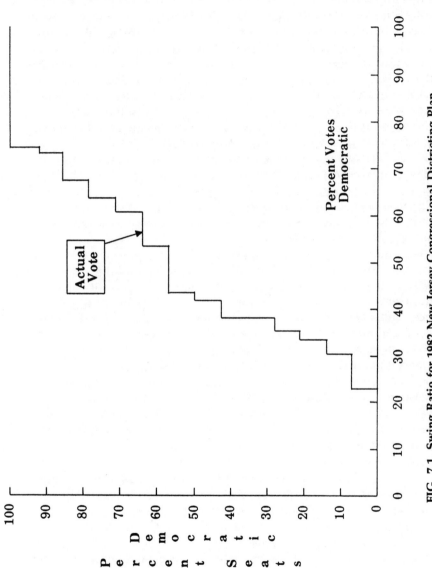

FIG. 7.1. Swing Ratio for 1982 New Jersey Congressional Districting Plan

gression line" (of seats on votes)—the line that best fits a set of points. In this application we typically would not want to calculate the best-fitting line over the entire range. Since most election results fall within a fairly small percentage range, we might be interested in the line that best fits the points within five percentage points on either side of the actual election results. For the New Jersey case, this yields a swing ratio of 1.17.

A swing ratio of 1.17 means that for every 1% gain in votes, the Democrats would have gained an average of 1.17% more seats. Historically, in the U.S. and elsewhere, considerably larger swing ratios have been the rule, with values frequently in the 2.0–3.0 range (Tufte, 1973, p. 543). In fact, such swing ratios are imperative if the majority party is to win proportionately more seats than votes and if the system is to be neutral.

The Karcher swing ratio is also low strictly by New Jersey standards. Tufte (1973, p. 543) found that the swing ratio in New Jersey was 2.10 from 1926 to 1947 and 3.65 from 1947 to 1969. In 1980 the swing ratio was 1.94. The 1982 New Jersey value is also lower than that found for the 1982 Indiana House, where it was 1.48 (Niemi, 1985, p. 198). Even recent swing ratios for the U.S. Congress, which have been criticized as especially low, have dipped as low as 1.17 only once, and have typically been 1.60 or higher (Tufte, 1974, p. 212; Niemi and Fett, 1986, p. 81).

Of course, it is important to notice exactly what the swing ratio tells us and what it does not tell us. It does not tell us what the proportionality is between votes and seats. The swing ratio might have been the same if the Democrats had won 50%, 55%, 60%, or even 70% of the seats. What the swing ratio does tell us is that, whatever their proportion of the seats, the Democrats in New Jersey could have expected to win or lose approximately 1.2% of the seats for each percentage point gain or loss in votes. Thus, the swing ratio tells us about changes in votes and seats, not about the static ratio of seats won to votes won.

APPLYING THE SWING RATIO: TESTING FOR POLITICAL GERRYMANDERING

As noted at the outset, political gerrymandering revolves centrally around the seats-votes relationship, succinctly summarized by the swing ratio. While this suggests that the swing ratio may provide a powerful test for the presence of gerrymandering, a number of problems arise.

First, even in an abstract model, assuming away some of the practical problems, it is impossible to fulfill all the criteria that one would like. Elsewhere I have argued that one might ideally wish for a districting plan that is neutral between the two parties (treats both parties alike in allocating seats per given vote totals), has a high range of responsiveness (a party will win at least a few seats even if its statewide vote is relatively low), has a more or less constant swing ratio (so that whenever a party wins more votes it gains seats and whenever it loses votes it loses seats), and has a relatively high number of competitive districts (ones with two-party vote of, say, 45% to 55%). It turns out that these goals are mutually incompatible (Niemi and Deegan, 1978; Niemi, 1982). Achieving a high degree of competitiveness, for example, might require that one violate neutrality, and vice versa; achieving a constant swing ratio while maintaining competitiveness works against wide responsiveness; and so on. There are some more or less satisfactory compromises, but the incompatibilities indicate that perfect districting is a myth even in the simplest of worlds.

A more significant challenge is Cain's (1985b, p. 218) argument that it is "ludicrously impractical" to think of fine-tuning a districting plan in order to determine the exact size and characteristics of the swing ratio. He is right, of course, in pointing out that it would be impossible to refine the district lines so that, for example, the swing ratio is a smooth function across the entire 0–100% range. Even with the assistance of computerized mapmaking and elaborate databases, achieving the near-perfection of the abstract models is an impossibility.

On the other hand, if one adopts a result-oriented perspective, one can observe the effects of a (real or proposed) districting plan to see what the swing ratio is. If the swing ratio shows that the districting plan is far from neutral, makes seat changes very unresponsive to vote changes, has a very low range of responsiveness, or has very few competitive seats, one might well question the validity of the plan.

There is still an additional problem, that for the swing ratio itself there is no agreed-upon "zero-point" from which to measure deviations (as, for example, deviations of population are measured from exact equality of district size). One can, however, see whether the swing ratio associated with a particular plan is particularly low in comparison with historical experience in the jurisdiction in question and in other legislative settings, much as we have done above for the 1982 New Jersey congressional districts.

These complications do mean that the swing ratio approach is unlikely to yield a unique, simple, and easily interpretable measure, such as exists for population equality. Nonetheless, as one measure of districting quality, to be used alongside other measures, it may prove useful. And, as I have argued elsewhere in this volume, with Stephen Wright (page 277), one needs to interpret the strength of the evidence. A swing ratio of 1.5 where it has historically been 1.6 is weak evidence of a discriminatory effect, whereas a value of 1.2 where it has previously been 2.9 offers stronger support for a discrimination claim.

Assessing the strength of the evidence rather than expecting decisive indicators may also resolve some of the problems that have been pointed out previously (Niemi, 1985, pp. 201–208; Cain, 1985b, pp. 217–218). For example, flat spots in the swing ratio can be taken more seriously the larger the number of districts involved; with very few districts, as in some states' congressional delegations, the swing ratio is necessarily a step function. Similarly, if the swing ratio is low, using several measures rather than only one measure of the underlying vote or using both a random-district and actual vote baseline, support for a gerrymandering claim is that much stronger. Results would also be stronger if they were invariant to assumptions about the uniformity of the change in partisan votes across districts.

Finally, there may also be other imaginative ways in which the swing ratio or very similar notions can be applied. The proposal in Niemi and Wright (chapter 13) is one such possibility. The important point now—precisely because there is so much ambiguity about the whole question of political gerrymandering and about how the Court will handle it—is to recognize that the seats-votes relationship is a vital concern, if not the "ultimate question," for political gerrymandering. If this point is indeed recognized, political scientists and other interested parties will continue to study whether the swing ratio or some other approach is the best way to operationalize that concern.

Acknowledgments. This research was supported by National Science Foundation Grant No. SES-8421050.

8

Detecting Gerrymandering

Michael D. McDonald and Richard L. Engstrom

The issue remaining to be resolved in the post-*Bandemer* era is whether there are any manageable standards by which gerrymandering can be detected. While six justices in *Bandemer* agreed that allegations of gerrymandering are justiciable, they split over the question of a manageable standard for detecting that phenomenon (*Davis v. Bandemer*, 106 S. Ct. 2797 (1986)). A majority confidently maintained, however, that this issue of a standard could be, as the malapportionment issue had been after *Baker v. Carr*, 369 U.S. 186 (1962), "subsequently resolved" (*Davis v. Bandemer*, p. 99), or that it "can and should be developed" (*Davis v. Bandemer*, p. 126, Justice Powell concurring). Moreover, that majority did reach agreement concerning two values on which the standard is to be constructed. First, the standard must be contained within a district electoral system (*Davis v. Bandemer*, pp. 103, 104, 131–132). Second, the fundamental constitutional value at stake is equality, specifically "that each political group in a state should have the same opportunity to elect candidates of its choice as any other political group" (*Davis v. Bandemer*, p. 100).

Our purpose here is to demonstrate that the Court's confidence is not misplaced. Given the two value premises, we propose a clear, precise, and manageable standard for distinguishing what is from what is not a gerrymander.

THE PROBLEM

Gerrymandering is the drawing of electoral district lines so as to assign unequal voting weights to cognizable political groups. It is a noxious political practice. In one form, a gerrymander is arranged by *packing* a group's members into a relatively small number of districts so that the group is virtually assured of winning with overwhelmingly large majorities in those few districts but of losing in the others. Another form of gerrymandering is arranged by *cracking* a group's members so that it has large but inefficacious minorities in most or all of the districts. Just identifying the two methods exemplifies the problem of inherent conflict. When packed the group members are too concentrated; when cracked they are too dispersed. Attempts to combat one form are made by moving in the direction of the other.

The concentration versus dispersion conflict is only one, and a narrow one at that, of the numerous conflicts involved in the gerrymandering issue. When viewed more broadly, the gerrymandering question is reminiscent of the way Justice Frankfurter framed the issue of malapportionment: "What is asked of the court in this case is to choose among competing bases of representation—ultimately really, among competing theories of political philosophy" (*Baker v. Carr*, p. 755).

For gerrymandering, as well, it has been observed that generally its offenses are contrary to so many desired values that a remedy designed to achieve one particular value will conflict with some other value (Cain, 1984, 1985b; Lowenstein and Steinberg, 1985; Polsby, 1985; see also Niemi and Deegan, 1978, on the general issues of trade-offs in districting). There is a serious irony here: The breadth of values that gerrymandering offends may be used as an important element in the argument against taking remedial action.

To appreciate the range of concerns and the difficulty practitioners and scholars have had in agreeing on a standard prior to the Court's adoption of the equality value in *Bandemer*, perhaps the best place to start is in the middle. Imagine a political cartographer is standing in front of her computer terminal as the results of all 10 million possible districting plans are rolling by on the screen. A chilling reality sets in: Knowing what is possible is far removed from knowing what is preferable. She calculates that there are nearly 50 trillion pairs of districting plans to be compared (1st vs. 2nd, 1st vs. 3rd, . . . , 1st vs. 10 millionth, 2nd vs. 3rd . . .). Should she select the one that maximizes the competitiveness of a set of districts (Engstrom and Wildgen, 1977; Niemi and Deegan, 1978; Niemi, 1985)? Or should she select any one from among the many which is typical of the number of districts in which each group constitutes a majority (Engstrom and Wildgen, 1977; O'Loughlin, 1982a)? Then, again, maybe the symmetry of the group percentages across districts should be maximized (Erikson, 1972; Niemi and Deegan, 1978). But one may not want to ignore the group percentages required to control a majority of the districts (Backstrom, Robins, and Eller, 1978). Alas, this wondering about desirable values says nothing about the practical concerns of such matters as protecting incumbents.

A miniature version of the cartographer's quandary can be entertained by considering what might be done in the highly simplified world portrayed in Table 8.1. There we have 900 voters who belong to either one of two political groups, the Blues (47%) and the Greens (53%). There are nine geographical areas, each with 100 persons, that serve as building blocks for three districts. The task is to arrange the three districts with 300 voters each and that, when formed, cover three contiguous areas (with contiguity requiring junction at more than one point—that is, more than corner to corner—so that the combinations of 1-5-9, 1-5-6, etc. are not allowed). In this case there are ten possible districting arrangements, A through J, shown beneath the grid in Table 8.1.

The most competitive set of districts is in plan H. This plan, however, is quite atypical in regard to the number of districts in which each group constitutes a majority. In six of the ten plans, the Blues have a majority in one district and the Greens have majorities in two. In plan H, the Greens, atypically, are a majority in all three. Furthermore, plan H is the least symmetrical plan among the ten, as indicated by the skewness statistic (see Table 8.3 below). On the other hand, plan H is one of the four (along with C, D, and I) most acceptable arrangements based on the Backstrom, Robins, and Eller preference for having each group control a majority of seats when it has, hypothetically, a majority of the jurisdictionwide vote. In short, there appears to be no guide as to how one can select the "best" without also selecting the "worst."

Nor is any semblance of a resolution provided by examining probability calculations. These calculations normally ask whether the chosen plan is among those most likely to have been selected through a random drawing. In the abstract, each plan is equally likely in that picking any one has a probability of selection, in the example, of one in ten. If the probability calculations are prescribed to specify a likelihood of selection in regard to some characteristic—for example, degree of competitiveness or any of the others—then the conflicting values are reintroduced.

Clearly, having complete information about all possible plans is not enough. The point, quite simply, is that one cannot start in the middle. Rather, one must start with the questions: In the end what is the standard supposed to do? And where does one begin the construction of such a standard?

TABLE 8.1. District Possibilities in a Hypothetical Jurisdiction

29*	95	46
Block 1	2	3
24	22	80
4	5	6
12	71	44
7	8	9

	Block Combinations			No. of Blues in Districts[a]		
Plan	Dist 1	Dist 2	Dist 3	Dist 1	Dist 2	Dist 3
A	1-2-3	4-5-6	7-8-9	<u>170</u>	126	127
B	1-2-3	4-5-7	6-8-9	<u>170</u>	58	<u>195</u>
C	1-2-3	4-7-8	5-6-9	<u>170</u>	107	146
D	1-2-5	4-7-8	3-6-9	146	107	<u>170</u>
E	1-4-7	2-5-8	3-6-9	65	<u>188</u>	<u>170</u>
F	1-4-7	2-3-5	6-8-9	65	<u>163</u>	<u>195</u>
G	1-4-7	2-3-6	5-8-9	65	<u>221</u>	137
H	1-2-4	3-5-6	7-8-9	148	148	127
I	1-2-4	3-6-9	5-7-8	148	<u>170</u>	105
J	1-4-5	2-3-6	7-8-9	75	<u>221</u>	127

*Cell entries are the number of Blue group members; (100 − cell entry) equals the number of green group members. Totals: Blues = 423 or 47%; Greens = 477 or 53%.
[a]The underlined entries are districts in which the Blue group is a majority.

ENDINGS

The end sought here is a clear, precise, and manageable standard for detecting a gerrymander.[1] Clarity is needed so that legislators can be aware of what is and is not permissible. In that way all elections following a decennial census can be arranged fairly. Even in simple arithmetic terms, it does only half as much good to find out about unfair districting practices five years into a decade. Precision is needed so that the logic of the standard rests as impenetrably as practicable on a single guideline. On this count the search for evidence on the basis of the totality of circumstances approach, attractive to both Grofman (1985a; chapter 1) and Baker (chapter 2), proves inadequate. That approach to gerrymandering, developed apparently as an analogue to the Senate's directive to the courts' want for evidentiary standards on the 1982 amendments to the Voting Rights Act, will not be of much assistance to legislators during the process of choosing lines, inasmuch as the totality can almost always be debated. What is more, even for the courts, the approach is liable to foster the ambiguity and possible capriciousness Judge Wisdom warned about when he wrote that as "a court must consider a laundry list, an 'aggregate' of factors, some pointing one way and others pointing another way, the case turns on the attitude of the trial judge and the appellate judges" (*Nevitt v. Sides*, 571 F. Supp 209 (1978), p. 233). Finally, clarity and precision are necessary but not sufficient conditions for manageability. To have a clear statement of precise rules without any arguable flexibility is more a kin of developing a dogma than of developing a standard.

BEGINNINGS

Electoral System Premise

Gerrymandering, as originally coined by Benjamin Russell and as used in common parlance today, refers to political manipulation within the process of drawing district boundaries. Through the years, application of the term has expanded to describe a great variety of electoral mechanics. Nevertheless, given the value focus on equality, a post-*Bandemer* analysis is restricted to establishment of a standard capable of distinguishing between the drawing of district lines so as to assign unequal versus equal group voting weights. The desire to promote equality while using districts creates an easily recognized constraint: Equal opportunities to elect candidates of each group's choice is far more straightforwardly achieved by changing the electoral system (see, e.g., Dixon, 1980–81: pp. 840–841) than by changing the line drawing guidelines of the district system.

The so-called trinity of elements for districts is that they be equipopulous, contiguous, and compact (Hacker, 1964, p. 49). The "one person, one vote" rule is well established and is a precondition for judging districting arrangements. Contiguity is virtually a necessary condition for geographical districting and has been an issue in only a few isolated instances, usually concerning the question of connecting territories bordering a body of water (see Mayhew, 1974, pp. 252–253; Grofman, 1985a, p. 84), and therefore has not required much attention. Compactness appears to be the least consensual element of the three. Some have portrayed it as the touchstone criterion of gerrymandering (Henderson, 1982; cited in Grofman, 1985a, pp. 90–91; see also Morrill's [1987, pp. 249–251, 259] more cautious statement). But the fact that cognizable political groups do not necessarily reside in circles, squares, and other conveniently compact residential patterns has prompted others to question its relevance (Engstrom, 1981, p. 214; Grofman, 1985a, pp. 89–92; see also Young, 1988, concerning problems in measuring compactness). It has been argued that if one could ignore compactness (and moreover contiguity) the lines could meander so as to encompass the groups in a more "fair" manner (e.g., this was a defense argument in *Gaffney v. Cummings*, 412 U.S. 735 (1973); see Engstrom, 1981, pp. 220–221). Surely the contrary argument holds as well; the relaxation would also open the way for unfair aggregation of groups' voters (see Engstrom, 1981, 210–211). Although the federal constitution has not been interpreted to require that districts be compact (*Kirkpatrick v. Preisler*, 394 U.S. 526 (1969); *Bandemer v. Davis*), some state constitutions and local government charters do require that districts conform to this principle (see Grofman, 1985a, pp. 84–86; Lyons and Jewell, 1986, p. 76). The standard for detecting gerrymanders must be constructed after *Bandemer*, therefore, on an equality of opportunity foundation, which is corralled within a districting system reflecting the principles of equipopulous, contiguous (and in some instances compact) districts.

Value Premise

Fixing one value as the focal point for evaluating gerrymandering, and thereby dispatching others to a less central position, is a significant development. It precludes undermining a standard with arguments that begin by observing: "Well that takes care of _____, but what about _____?" Still, the focus on *equality of opportunity* is not self-defining. No gaggle of political or language philosophers has fallen in behind any single notion. This is because, as Douglas Rae and his students tell us, the concept to be defined is not equality but *equalities* (Rae et al., 1981). For purposes of identifying gerrymanders, it is imperative that one know "to whom?" "to what?" and "to what degree?" the equality is to be applied.

The "who?" of gerrymandering places emphasis on equality of voters as affiliates of groups, as opposed to voters as individuals. This is an explicit departure from the concern in malapportionment cases, where the idea has been to provide each eligible voter within a political jurisdiction with a vote equal to the vote of every other voter in that jurisdiction. Taking propensities of political preference into account, as they must be taken in order to consider gerrymandering, the only way to achieve equality of individual vote weights is through systems of at-large plurality or proportional winners (cf. Still, 1981; and Grofman, 1981). That is, as long as the winner-take-all district system is used and different districts have different political propensities (e.g., 25% favor Blues in district 1 and 60% favor Blues in district 2), each individual voter's chance to elect a candidate of his or her choice cannot be equal to each and every other individual voter's chance.

Furthermore, the group weights are to be compared on a system-wide basis and not within individual districts. Justice White was correct, in fact and logic, when he wrote that the alleged discrimination in Indiana refers to "Democratic voters over the State as a whole, not Democratic voters in individual districts" (*Davis v. Bandemer*, p. 102). This prompted some commentary concerning the possibility of scrutinizing, as an evidentiary procedure, certain features of individual districts (*Davis v. Bandemer*, p. 129, Justice Powell dissenting, in part). The evidentiary procedure is not to be confused with the general principle, however. Equally effective votes cannot refer to within-district comparisons. Robert Dixon's remark is irrefutable: "All districting discriminates on the grounds of residence, even if population is equal—that is, it arbitrarily qualifies the right to vote at the payoff level, by discounting utterly the votes of minority voters" (1971, p. 19). In sum, the "who?" to which the inequality of gerrymandering refers is the cognizable political group, not individuals, compared on a systemwide basis, not district by district.

The "equal what?" refers to each group's equal chance to elect a candidate of its choice. The meaning of those words appears to be plainly obvious, but they can mean different things, depending on how one chooses to define the precise outcome of interest and on what information is used at the time the groups' chances are formulated.

Lowenstein (chapter 4) and Schuck (chapter 11) argue that *Bandemer* grants rights that refer to outcomes. Their interpretation misstates the issue. Outcomes have a role in the equality value but only as part of a relationship, wherein equal resources hold the expectation of equal prospects. Because votes are sought as the currency to be translated into seats, two groups have an equal chance of winning seats when for any particular, hypothetical vote percentage the expected percentage of seats won is the same for both groups. If 45% of the vote is expected to yield 35% of the seats for Blues, then a 45 to 35 correspondence is what is to be expected for Greens. This is what Erikson means when he says "the perfect absence of a gerrymander would occur if the distribution of the votes across districts is symmetrical, such as with the normal distribution" (Erikson, 1972, p. 1237). And this symmetry is what Niemi and Deegan (1978, p. 1304) refer to as the neutrality condition of districting. As well, symmetry is the essence (though malapportionment is also implicitly referenced) of what Grofman and Scarrow refer to as discriminatory districting when they define "aggregate gerrymandering as occurring *only* when some group or groups is discriminated against compared to one or more other groups in that a greater number of votes is needed for the former to achieve a given proportion of legislative seats than is true for the latter" (Grofman and Scarrow, 1982, p. 454, emphasis in original; see also Grofman, 1985a, pp. 154–155 n. 320). In brief, equal resources—meaning votes—hold equal prospects—meaning seats (see Rae et al., 1981, pp. 64–81).

Symmetry attacks only half of a gerrymander's potential to offend. Its concern is differential packing. Where one group finds that its members comprise a far larger district majority than it needs to win, say 95%, symmetry requires that another district have a similarly oversized majority with the opposing group in control. Cracking is still permitted; for example, a group with a 60% systemwide majority could be arranged, in, say, a required five districts, with percentages of 59, 59, 60, 61, and 61. These percentages satisfy symmetry but (probably) render the other group's 39-41 district percentages ineffective minorities.

Perhaps it would be wise to abandon the symmetry focus of equality and accept one of the three other outcomes of interest entertained by our hypothetical cartographer. Two of these, the number of districts in which each group is a majority and the competitiveness of the system, are not really matters of equalizing anything; they are, rather, features related to the electoral system premise. By way of reduction to the essential, there really is not anything to equalize in regard to majorities or competitiveness. It could be said that equal treatment will lead to particular expected outcomes, but even while this is true, the expectations are empirical features that depend on the residential patterns of the groups. So, even though the expected number of majorities and the expected degree of competitiveness are important, indeed more important than symmetry in worldly applications, they are controlled by how the formally adopted districting guidelines are applied on top of the residential patterns.

A third outcome of potential interest to our hypothetical cartographer does address equal electoral prospects, just as with symmetry, but the prospects are more narrowly construed. Backstrom, Robins, and Eller (1978) are concerned with the narrow question of whether each group is expected to receive a majority of seats (although not necessarily the same number of seats) when it has won a bare majority of the votes. They reason that:

> Because our value choice comes down on the side of majority rule . . . [w]e therefore define fair representation as a situation in which the majority party is assured of maintaining numerical supremacy in a majority of districts if its state-wide share—whatever the actual figure—is reduced to a bare majority. (Backstrom, Robins, and Eller, 1978, p. 1135).

They reiterate their majoritarian premise in the modified version of their proposal in this volume; they are "setting majority rule as the primary value" (p. 160, this volume). From this premise Backstrom, Robins, and Eller reason that a districting plan that awards, hypothetically and alternatively, a majority of seat prospects to any party that has a bare majority of votes is unquestionably not a gerrymander; that is, "one need not look at it further" (p. 1138). It is easy to imagine a set of districts that meets the classic notion of a gerrymander, packing one group's voters into one district and spreading the rest of its voters so that they constitute ineffective minorities in the remaining districts (e.g., 97.6%, 49.9%, 49.9%, 49.9%, 34%, 34%, 34%) but satisfy the Backstrom, Robins, and Eller fairness criterion. This narrow construction allows a districting plan to treat the groups quite differently for virtually any given vote percentage. This is a direct consequence of accepting majoritarianism and not equality as the value premise. For that reason the broader construction emphasizing symmetry is preferred to this more narrow construction emphasizing majoritarianism. Of course, majoritarianism is not trivial (*Reynolds v. Sims*, 377 U.S. 533 (1964); *Davis v. Bandemer*, p. 101, n. 9); happily, majoritarianism is an indubitable by-product of symmetry, so nothing is lost.

The symmetry condition can only be used by decision makers, of course, if the expected vote percentages across districts can be anticipated before the lines are chosen. What if one were to adopt a blind-line drawing scheme such as one produced by random selection of various computer programs? That procedure would be legally suspect in some and unrealistic in most contexts.

The random selection of district boundaries amounts to enforced ignorance. As long as the designer is ignorant of the prospective outcomes, whatever happens could not have been intended, as in a lottery in which all prospects are equiprobable. A plan cannot escape culpability for lack of intentional adverse effect, however, when one of the groups is a racial or language minority covered by the Voting Rights Act. Under the 1982 amended version of Section 2 of that Act:

> No voting . . . practice or procedure shall be imposed by any State or political subdivision in *a manner which results in a denial or abridgement* of the right of any citizen of the United States to vote on account of race or color, . . . (U. S. C., 1982, emphasis added).

The results test is an admonishment to mapmakers not to analyze just their consciences for purity of intention. Whatever lines are adopted, they should be analyzed as to the impact they will likely have on racial and language groups.

To prove unconstitutional gerrymandering against other groups, usually referred to as political as distinct from racial gerrymandering, both a discriminatory intent and a discriminatory effect must be shown (*Davis v. Bandemer*). Hence, randomly placed lines may be a defense against "political" gerrymandering. It is doubtful, however, whether politicians whose careers might depend on the placements would allow their future electoral prospects to be randomly affected in this fashion.

The "what" to be equalized is the treatment of votes within a state after those votes are won by contesting groups. The arguments of Schuck (chapter 11) that "the Court would be prescribing the partisan configuration of the legislature" and that *Bandemer* may be "propelling the Court (and us with it) down a path whose destination is proportional representation" are alogical extensions of the equality value in *Bandemer*. As well, Lowenstein's inference that "gerrymandering claims, . . . , call for consideration of the political dynamics of legislative elections" is similarly off the mark. His wondering about extending *Bandemer* to concerns for equalizing groups' campaign funds, press coverage, and attractive candidates suggests that he thinks the equalization of prospects for the treatment of votes after being cast is somehow a prescription by the Court to equalize the ability of groups to attract votes during a campaign.

When discussing "how equal?" one cannot help but take notice of the clamor over the seeming absoluteness of the "one person, one vote" standard. That exacting standard has been equated with "a search for a will-o'-the-wisp" (*Kirkpatrick v. Preisler*, 1969, pp. 538–539, Justice Fortas concurring), a "crusade for the Holy Grail" (Dixon, 1969), and "a single-minded quest" (Baker, 1980–1981, p. 830). The usual criticism is that the "absolutely equal!" answer to the question of "how equal?" is going too far. There exists, it is argued, some reasonable *de minimis* difference when districts approach equal populations, and a concern for other values justifies treating these *de minimis* differences as not worth worrying about. The critics are absolutely right. There are *de minimis* differences. But that is beside the point. First, the search for a numerical standard other than the zero deviation is no less will-o'-the-wispish. Second, the place of other-value justifications is, at least until justified, secondary. And third, the manner of applying the standard is what social scientists refer to as a dominant strategy—one strategy dominates another if it assures a superior outcome in one or more regards and provides at least equivalent outcomes in other relevant regards. These three points, in different forms of expression, are the message of Justice Brennan's reasoning for the majority in *Karcher v. Daggett (I)*, 462 U.S. 725 (1983) (pp. 141, 143–145, and 142–143, 147–149, and 140, 149, respectively, as to the three points). For the malapportionment issue, an apportionment plan that achieves greater population equality and does as well in achieving every other stated goal makes the alternative plans not as equal as is practicable. Or, alternatively stated, the selection of one plan which is dominated by another plan cannot be justified, because there exists a superior outcome—viz., the one that dominates.

So, too, the gerrymandering standard should allow the guidance of being able to say that if and only if one plan is better in regard to both equality and the explicitly adopted formal districting criteria and another is better in some newly introduced and relevant regard need the resolution turn on the degree to which the standard can be relaxed. More pointedly, the function of a standard is to serve as a baseline for making commensurable assessments. For that reason, the standard is absolute. Judicious judgment takes over only when incommensurable baselines are competing. The standard for detecting gerrymanders, therefore, should rest on the two-pronged absolute of equality and the formal districting criteria and should be amenable to the logic of a dominant strategy both within the two-pronged considerations and between these considerations and any others which might be deemed relevant.

A STANDARD

Our proposed standard for judging gerrymandering is this: A gerry-mander exists when (1) the district configurations do not provide, as nearly as is practicable, a symmetrical pattern of the groups percent-ages across districts, or (2) the group percentages are not, as nearly as is practicable, what could be expected to arise from the residential patterns when the formal districting criteria are applied. This verbal statement can best be put into practice by viewing each possible dis-tricting plan as a distribution of group percentages.

To illustrate the usefulness of this distributional conceptualization, we continue with our earlier example. Figure 8.1 portrays each of the ten possible districting arrangements from the hypothetical, simple world of Table 8.1. Each distribution is presented graphically, as a histogram, and numerically. It is apparent on reasonable scrutiny that none of the ten is perfectly symmetrical. That would require one of the districts to have a Blue percentage of 47 with the other two districts equidistant from 47, one above and the other below. In words usually associated with gerrymandering, the absence of perfect symmetry means one group is more or less "packed"; one group has its voters concentrated in a relatively small number of districts compared to the other group. Because differential concentrations, and not concentra-tions *per se*, are the essence of packing, the symmetry indicator is the one of interest. In arrangement B, for example, it is not the *per se* fact that Greens have 80.7% (100-19.3) in one district that gives the Blues majorities in two of three districts, despite having only 47% of the population. It is that the Greens' 80.7% is not balanced by a similarly large (in this case 74.7%, which is the same distance from the mean of 47 as is 19.3) Blue group majority percentage in a district. Were the balance to exist, the third district would have a 47/53, Blue/Green, split, and thus the Greens would be dominant in a majority of districts.

With the possible districting arrangements viewed as distributions, one can ask what is the expected outcome from the explicit districting criteria. This expected outcome can be expressed in the form of two characteristics of the distributions, the mean and the standard devi-ation. With equipopulous districts, the mean is always equal to the systemwide group percentage for one or the other groups—and, of course, it makes no difference which group, Blue or Green. This is obvious inasmuch as each of the ten arrangements in Figure 8.1 has a mean, using the Blue percentage, of 47. The standard deviation describes the general degree of dispersion of the group percentages around the mean. The lower the standard deviation, the closer the

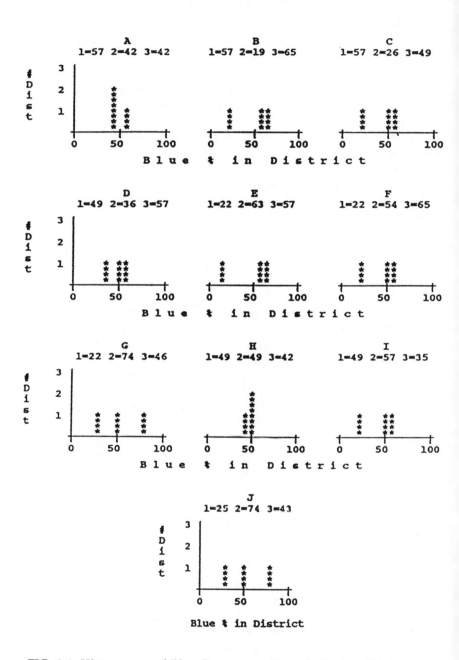

FIG. 8.1. Histograms and Blue Group percentages in the ten district plans
(A through J) from Table 1.

group percentages are to the mean, and vice versa. In terms usually used to describe gerrymandering, a low standard deviation indicates the voting strength of the political minority is "cracked," intentionally or otherwise. In the extreme, a standard deviation of zero would indicate, in our example, that each district has an identical 47/53, Blue/Green, split. If voting patterns are frozen along group lines, this would mean the Blues are large but inefficacious minorities in these districts. Unlike the mean, the standard deviation can vary from one arrangement to another. Of the ten possible arrangements, the dispersion is lowest in H (σ = 3.3) and highest in G (σ = 21.2). Dispersion, therefore, is something to be chosen.[2]

The broad, systematic, and unavoidable significance of this choice arises from the demonstrable fact that, under restricted conditions, most notably that the distribution is symmetrical, the standard deviation controls the way in which group percentages translate into the percentage of district majorities held by the group.[3] Figure 8.2 illustrates the relationship between group percentages and the percentage of districts in which the group constitutes a majority, given standard deviations of 3.3 and 21.2. Both relationships exhibit versions of the often described S-shaped form. Where the group percentage equals 50, the expected percentage of district majorities for the group is 50. This is true regardless of the standard deviation value. Indeed, this is the majoritarian consequence of the symmetry condition. Moving away from a group percentage point equal to 50, the consequence of different standard deviations is dramatic. At a group percentage of 47, for instance, the 21.2 standard deviation leads to an expected majority for the group in 44.4% of the districts, whereas the standard deviation of 3.3 produces an expected majority in only 19.0% of the districts. Even more dramatic, if the group percentage equals 40, the group can expect majorities in 31.8% of the districts when the standard deviation is 21.2, but in only a minuscule 0.7% of the districts when the standard deviation is 3.3. Obviously, by choosing a plan with a low standard deviation, the voting strength of a political minority can be cracked. How can an appropriate value of the standard deviation be selected? Because the district electoral system pays respect to representation founded on geographical locale, the answer depends on the extent to which the cracking is the consequence of group residential patterns. Overlaying the adopted districting criteria on the jurisdiction's residential patterns allows one to say, in the end, that there is an expected distribution of group percentages. In the most straightforward terms, the interplay of residential patterns and districting criteria produces a set (quite likely a very large set) of

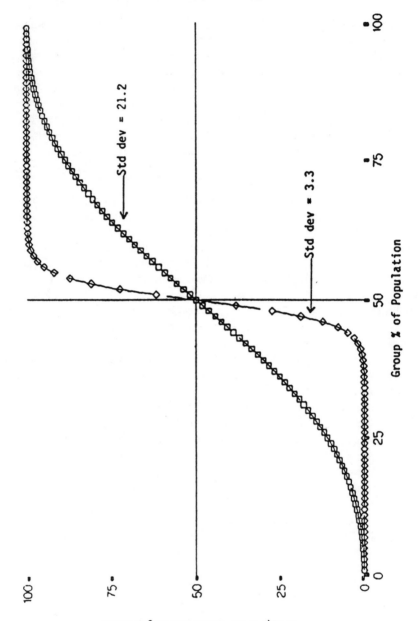

FIG. 8.2. Relationships between group percentage of population and group percentage of district majorities for different standard deviations of group population percentages across districts.

TABLE 8.2. The Group (Blue) District Percentages and Standard
Deviations across Districts

Plan	Blue's Percentages			Standard Deviation
	Dist 1	Dist 2	Dist 3	
A	56.7%	42.0%	42.3%	6.86
B	56.7	19.3	65.0	19.88
C	56.7	35.7	48.7	8.65
D	48.7	35.7	56.7	8.65
E	21.7	62.7	56.7	18.08
F	21.7	54.3	65.0	18.42
G	21.7	73.7	45.7	21.25
H	49.3	49.3	42.3	3.30
I	49.3	56.7	35.0	9.01
J	25.0	73.7	42.3	20.16

possible districts. This set has an average group percentage and an
average standard deviation. The average group percentage is known
in advance; it equals the group's jurisdictionwide percentage (i.e., the
mean). The standard deviation has to be calculated; given the calculation, the benchmark is the precise value of the standard deviation
that the districting criteria are expected to yield, based on residential
patterns.

The average standard deviation in our continuing example is 13.4.
Table 8.2 reveals that the closest arrangement among the ten is I, with
a standard deviation of 9.0. Yet, even if there were an arrangement
with a standard deviation equal to 13.4, it may be an arrangement that
violates the equality value embedded in the symmetry criterion. The
standard for detecting a gerrymander must be one which simultaneously accommodates equality and the formal districting criteria.
The question, therefore, is: In an ideal world, what would the districting arrangement look like with perfect symmetry and a standard
deviation equal to its expected value? The answer is derived from the
often discussed votes to seats translation equation (see, e.g., Theil,
1969; Taagepera, 1973):

$$(S_b/S_g) = (V_b/V_g)^k$$

where S_b and S_g are the respective seat percentages for the Blue and
Green groups, V_b and V_g are those groups' vote percentages, and k is

the power function by which the vote odds ratio translates into the seat odds ratio. This equation has two direct benefits in regard to gerrymandering. First, it always produces a symmetrical translation. Second, under appropriate conditions (see note 1), k is a value that can be derived from the standard deviation (see Kendall and Stuart, 1950; Gudgin and Taylor, 1979, pp. 13–30). That association is:

$$k \approx (40/\text{std dev})$$

where "std dev" is the group percentage (as opposed to proportion) standard deviation. Of course, the votes to seats equation is adaptable to the district electoral context by replacing S_i with D_i, the percentage of districts in which group i is in the majority, and by replacing V_i with G_i, the group i percentage of persons within the jurisdiction.

In our example, the Blue group percentage is 47, and the expected standard deviation is 13.4. Solving first for the value of k, we have

$$k = (40/13.4) = 2.985$$

Then,

$$(D_b/D_g) = (G_b/D_g)^{2.985} = (47/53)^{2.985} = .699.$$

Thus, the ratio of district majorities held by the Blue group to the district majorities held by the Green group is .699. By simple algebra, this ratio readily translates into a percentage of districts in which Blues have a majority, namely,

$$D\% = [.699/(1 + .699)] \times 100 = 41.1.$$

Blues are expected to be a majority in 41.1% of the districts. Given three seats, this works out to 1.23 districts (i.e., .411 × 3). This, then, is our answer to the question. In an ideal world, Blues are expected to have a majority in one of three districts, for this is what a symmetrical distribution with a mean of 47 and a standard deviation of 13.4 would produce.

Obviously, as is the case in our example, the world may not be so kind as to replicate the ideal. The proper rule in that case is to approach the ideal as nearly as is practicable. Or, re-employing our earlier social science expression, the rule is to identify the dominant strategy or strategies. In order and enumerated, the rule is:

1. Accept those arrangements that produce outcomes most consistent with what would occur if the the ideal existed.
2. Among those arrangements in #1, accept the arrangement that is most symmetrical and has a standard deviation most nearly equal to the expected value;
3. If there is not just one single arrangement that dominates all others on both symmetry and dispersion, then exclude any plan that is dominated by another and select any one from among the undominated set.

Table 8.3 puts the rule into practice. For each arrangement (identified in column 1), the number of districts in which the Blues hold a majority (column 2), the symmetry of the arrangement (column 3, where the value reported is the skewness statistic, and zero represents perfect symmetry), and the standard deviation (column 4) are reported. Also, columns 5 and 6 report the rank orderings according to how close each arrangement is to the ideals of skewness = 0 and standard deviation = 13.4 (a lower numerical value [e.g., 1] indicates a plan is superior to one with a higher numerical value on the particular dimension). There are six arrangements with Blue majorities in one district: A, C, D, G, I, and J. This is the set of outcomes most consistent with what would occur if the ideal existed (rule, point #1). There is no single dominant plan, however. Plans A and J are dominated by both C and D, so those two plans are rejected because we undoubtedly could do better. That leaves the set of C, D, G, and I, but the choice among them is indeterminate according to the rule. C and D are equivalent to one another on both skewness and dispersion; C, D, and I are superior to G on dispersion, but G is superior to each of them on skewness. The choice of either C or D or G or I is acceptable, while the choice of any other arrangement is considered gerrymandering.

Lest it be thought that the domination rule could be used to emphasize too strongly one criterion and virtually ignore the other, we take notice of the importance of the constraint supplied by point #1 of the rule. Its purpose and effect are to disallow those arrangements that stray too far from what the *simultaneous* realization of the symmetry and dispersion ideals would bring. This is critical, for in real political terms the standard will not allow one to move so far toward avoiding cracking so as to institute packing, nor can one move so far toward avoiding packing as to institute cracking. In our example, plan E ranks second on dispersion but does so poorly on skewness as to be outside the acceptable range. It is not as if the expected number of

TABLE 8.3. Standard Deviation and Skewness Values and Rank
Orderings Relative to Ideals for Each of Ten Possible Plans

Plan	# of Blue Majority Districts	Numerical Values		Rank Orderings	
		Skewness	Std Dev	Skewness	Std Dev
A	1	.706	6.86	9	7
B	2	−.615	19.88	7	6
C	1	−.282	8.65	2.5	3.5
D	1	−.282	8.65	2.5	3.5
E	2	−.649	18.08	8	2
F	2	−.534	18.42	6	5
G	1	.098	21.25	1	9
H	0	−.707	3.30	10	10
I	1	−.371	9.01	5	1
J	1	.335	20.16	4	8

districts in which the group is a majority is accorded a sort of deference. Rather, that expectation is a number derived from full deference to the simultaneous realization of symmetry and dispersion ideals.

Three final issues need to be addressed. The first is the intent requirement in *Bandemer*. It might be thought that the objective standard described here ignores intent and thereby addresses only half the question. That is not true. Were the court to adopt this sort of standard, the intent question would take care of itself. Where the standard is met, there is no issue because there is no gerrymandering. Where the standard is not met, then as Justice White remarked in *Gaffney*, "the results would be known, and, if not changed, intended" (*Gaffney v. Cummings*, p. 51).

A second issue concerns how the proposed standard relates to the special cases of racial and language minority groups under provisions of the Voting Rights Act as amended in 1982. Because of the lingering effects of discrimination, though a causal nexus need not be shown (U.S. Senate, 1982, p. 29, n. 114), the turnout rates of racial and language minorities are often lower than the turnout rates of others. For these minorities to be considered to have a realistic equal opportunity to hold an electoral majority in a district, some sort of extraordinary population majority, sometimes suggested to be 65%, may be required (e.g., *Ketchum v. Byrne*, 740 F. 2nd 1398 (1984); *United Jewish Organizations v. Carey*, 430 U.S. 144 (1977); Parker, 1984, pp. 108–111; but see Hedges and Carlucci, 1987). When participation rates among minorities are comparatively low, compensation within the proposed standard may be required. Otherwise, point #1 in the rule would knowingly operate to affect adversely these groups' political prospects. The compensation can be accomplished by calculating the expected number of districts where the group holds a population majority, just as in point #1. Given that number and the admonition not to turn known turnout differences against the group, the requisite number of supermajority district for that group can be drawn accordingly. Where other political groups, most likely political parties, are involved, this may require a twice-over application of the rule. The first application would address the racial and language groupings and would result in the drawing of the supermajority districts. That done, the entire standard could then be reapplied to the remaining portions of the jurisdiction with attention now focused on groups other than racial or language minorities.

The final concern relates to the application of the standard to jurisdictions where more than two groups can make legitimate claims. Except in the special case of racial and language groups, where a "twice-over" approach can be used, the application of this standard to three or more political groupings adds an admittedly significant complexity. The procedure we propose is to treat each grouping as a dichotomy on the grounds that if the group can show itself to be a cognizable political group (see below) it is saying by default that it has political interests demonstrable through the ballot box that are in political opposition to all others in the jurisdiction. A jurisdiction with Blues, Greens, *and Yellows* could apply the standard by a multistep set of calculations where the symmetry and dispersion calculations across all possible plans are made for (1) Blues versus others, (2) Greens versus others, and (3) Yellows versus others. An acceptable plan is one that provides the expected number of majority districts to each of the three groups and within that set the plan or plans that are not inferior to any other in regard to the symmetry and dispersion criteria as applied to all three groups. While certainly more complex than the two group case, the application of the standard is still manageable.

REMAINING CONCERNS

There is a simplicity to our proposed standard that makes it appealing in some respects, we suppose, but that could also make it the object of the derisive charge of naiveté. On that critical side, there remain issues that tend toward the gritty, technical details of real-world applications as well as those that reside on the side of grander constitutional values. In anticipation of those arguments, we offer the following observations.

It is easy to imagine that wherever the proposed standard is applied, disputes would arise over what constitutes a cognizable political group? What is the proper database for identifying group membership? What is, in some instances, the desirable/allowable degree of compactness? And whose computer algorithm is to be used?

The notion of a cognizable political group requires supposed members to have a self-identification with political interests of the group as a political group. This would include political parties that are able to field candidates, attract citizens as registrants (where applicable), and attract voters on election day. It would also include a group who can demonstrate it is "sufficiently large and geographically compact to constitute a majority in a single-member district" and who will "be able to show it is politically cohesive" (*Thornburg v. Gingles*, 106 S. Ct. 2752 (1986), pp. 17–18). There are well-developed methods for making such determinations (see, e.g., Engstrom and McDonald, 1985, 1988; Grofman, Migalski, and Noviello, 1985). And those methods can be extended to more than two groups (Engstrom and McDonald, 1987).

The database issue is yet to be well developed. Where census enumerated groups are involved, for example, blacks and Hispanics, the answer is straightforward. Where political parties are the focus, database disputes are likely to be contentious. The most promising possibilities rest with voting statistics as the principal data source. The Backstrom, Robins, and Eller (1978; chapter 6) reliance on low salience elections, what they call a base race, may be a reasonable first step. Its major weakness is that the low salience contest may bias the indicator of group affiliations in favor of the party whose members have a greater tendency to cast ballots in highly visible contests but not to complete the ballot. This worry argues for at least the weighting of the low salience votes by the turnout figures in high salience elections. Indications of group affiliation through party registration records are troublesome. Where they exist, they reflect public declarations and therefore the possibility of intimidation cannot be ignored.

Finally, the use of the Niemi (chapter 7) and Niemi and Wright (chapter 13) seat-vote analysis of the actual legislative elections under scrutiny (see also Browning and King, 1987; Basehart, 1987) is inappropriate. For one thing, as Backstrom, Robins, and Eller argue, and as our notion of clear and precise demands, the post-hoc data cannot fulfill the requirements of a standard to guide decision makers when deciding on the lines. In addition, the choice of lines, in all likelihood, is going to condition the strategies of the candidates and their use of campaign resources. Any analysis attempting to adjust for these side effects of the districting plan, so as to see how the prospects of voting groups were treated before the side effects came into being, would only be trying to re-create what the base race does before the side effects are produced.

Assuming a group can be identified, the compactness criterion (where applicable) employed for the purpose of generating all possible plans, could be pegged to what line-drawers have deemed to be desirable, and/or judged acceptable, in the recent past. There is usually a history to a jurisdiction's compactness, and that provides a benchmark in the form of what has been perceived as needed to accommodate its communities of interest. Both less and more compact districts may be suspicious signs.

It is possible for two or more different computer algorithms to produce sets of "all possible" district plans that differ in important respects (cf. Engstrom and Wildgen, 1977; O'Loughlin, 1982a). It would be most unfortunate if legislators and judges were to be drawn into this sort of quarrel. There are two ways to avoid it, one for the offensive-minded and the other for the defensive-minded. The entire districting process could be opened to the point of inviting the participation of all those who believe they can sustain the claim that they are cognizable political groups. The inclusion of all known plans, generated through whatever algorithm, would then be available to the decision makers *before* the decision is made. While history might suggest it is unrealistic to expect such an open process (*Davis v. Bandemer; Major v. Treen,* 574 F Supp 325 (1983)), it can be argued that openness is in the best interest of those making the decision. Part of the problem arising when districting plans must meet precise mathematical equality is that the original decision makers have an absolute standard to meet with little way of justifying seemingly de minimis differences. When these decisions are challenged in court, the challengers are provided with the leniency of a de minimis standard as set by the deviations in the existing plan. It is at least a risky strategy to move first with no opportunity to countermove after litigation is filed. Hence, for the offensive minded, an open process of choice-counterchoice might actually be appealing. In any case, it is not unthinkable that the Supreme Court would impose some such form of openness (*Davis v. Bandemer,* 1986, p. 133, Justice Powell dissenting). For the defensive minded, it should be possible to avoid the entire issue of computer algorithms and even the "all possible" method. One can use a statistical model to arrive at an expected value of the standard deviation as if all possible plans had been determined (McDonald and Engstrom, 1985).

Even if this standard and its technical underpinnings find acceptance, unresolved constitutional questions remain. The principal concern is how to accommodate other values embedded in the decision. None of these, it appears to us, is foreboding.

We have approached *Bandemer*, to some extent, as if it were the only opinion the Court has ever offered on districting. Consequently, one issue left to the side is where the equal population value fits into the standard. It plays a somewhat technical role in the construction of the all-possible plan formulations. Also, it is an integral part of the calculations in point #1 of the rule. Is this sufficient? Clearly the answer is no. Equipopulous measures must be added to the symmetry and dispersion criteria of the decision rule. Then the preferred plan is to be found within the set that provides the typical number of group district majorities and among those the one or the set that is not dominated on symmetry, dispersion, and equal population criteria.

A more difficult question is what is to be done in circumstances where there is likely to be *direct conflict* between the proposed standard and other political values the Court has found worthy in the past. Most notably, what is to be done when a jurisdiction has decided to provide greater district competitiveness than the average dispersion would allow? In *Gaffney*, the Court agreed to a plan reportedly designed to do just that (*Gaffney v. Cummings*). A desire to respect the political tradition of district electoral systems, with their restriction on voter alignments, conflicts with the promotion of competitiveness beyond the levels consistent with the residential patterns alone. Because neither the district system nor the degree of competitiveness are constitutional values, someone must, or so it would seem, make a value choice. We would point out, however, that it is possible to have both. There is a far simpler way to promote a particular degree of jurisdictionwide competitiveness (the point in *Gaffney*) than through the adjustment of district lines. All one has to do, as Theil (1969) has shown, is select a value of k in the votes to seats translation and apply it to the jurisdictionwide vote. One can keep districts arranged according to our proposed standard and add compensatory seats. The West German system works in this way, with the compensatory seats used to drive the seat distribution toward proportional representation, that is, so k is close to 1 (see Pulzer, 1983;

Kaase, 1984). A desire to grant a seats' bonus to the majority party simply requires choosing a *k* value greater than 1.

Finally, what is to be done about other districting traditions, such as respecting political subdivision boundaries and protecting incumbents? The subdivision boundary protection, where it is a permissable goal, can be accommodated before the calculations of symmetry and dispersion are performed. As for incumbents, if the only way to protect them is by gerrymandering, there does not appear to be much choice (*Major v. Treen*). This is not very soothing, but there may be some available latitude if (1) the undominated set is reasonably large, or (2) if the decision process is open and no cognizable political group promotes a plan that dominates the one selected to protect incumbents, and (3) the effects on racial and language groups are not adverse. Also, respect for the past degree of compactness might help. If all else fails, the incumbent can still run for office and the voters of a new district could decide how much to weigh such qualities as experience and seniority. The alternative is to deny some group of voters an equal opportunity to elect candidates of its choice so that another group can retain its incumbent, which would grant the incumbent some form of antithetical proprietary right to hold public office.

CONCLUSION

In the post-*Bandemer* era, it is possible to take issue with such claims as "there is no ideal standard against which to measure allegedly gerrymandered districting plans" (Jewell, 1968, p. 797), or "no precise mathematical formula for defining gerrymandering is readily available" (Edwards, 1971, p. 893), or "detailed judicial policing of gerrymandering would be a herculean task bordering on the impossible" (Dixon, 1971, p. 32). This possibility exists under the explicit premises of "equality of opportunity" and respect for the political tradition in this country of district electoral systems, as we have adduced them from *Bandemer*. Given those premises, it is possible to state a clear, precise, and manageable standard for detecting gerrymandering. It is a standard that can be used by decision makers when deciding on district lines and which can be enforced by the courts if the need arises.

There will be, to be sure, objections raised to our proposal. That is as it should be. But, lest impossibility theorems become a method for making decisions through nondecisions, one must be careful not to elevate any and all desirable ends to the level of constitutionally protected values. By implication, one must realize that most doubts and most criticisms of the proposed standard will be, in effect, criticisms of a districted electoral system itself.

NOTES

1. Cain (1985a; chapter 5), Baker (chapter 9), and Lowenstein and Steinberg (1985, p. 4) call for a standard, if one is possible, endowed with simplicity. We take this to mean "clear and precise," so that the standard can be followed by anyone desiring to do so.
2. Our use of the word *dispersion*, that refers to the deviation of each district's group percentage from the systemwide average group percentage, is of course quite distinct from Niemi (chapter 7) and Hofeller and Grofman (chapter 14) use of dispersion to refer to the areal scope of a district.
3. The conditions necessary for the standard deviation operating to exert complete control over the translation are not omnipresent. Concisely stated, the residential patterns of group members must be such that the aggregation of individuals into districts produces a normal (bell-shaped) distribution (Gudgin and Taylor, 1979, pp. 13–86). This makes perfect sense to the statistically minded, inasmuch as the normal distribution is completely describable by its mean and standard deviation. Then, in turn, given that the translation function is describable as the cumulative form of the vote distribution across districts (e.g., Niemi and Deegan, 1978), knowing the complete vote distribution is the functional equivalent of knowing the translation.

   The obvious limitation is that not all residential patterns can be expected to lead to a normal distribution. Nevertheless, for the purpose of detailing the logic of the proposed standard, unencumbered by the details of how the normality assumption can be augmented, we assume the conditions leading to normality are approximated. Until the augmentation is detailed, one can keep in mind that, as a general guideline, the more the relevant groups are segregated beyond the "norm" (see, e.g., Gudgin and Taylor, 1979, pp. 40–47, esp. Tables 3.3 and 3.4), the more the power function equation will overstate the majority group's seat proportion.

9

The "Totality of Circumstances" Approach

Gordon E. Baker

Supreme Court decisions in 1983 (*Karcher v. Daggett (I)*, 462 U.S. 725 (1983)) and 1986 (*Davis v. Bandemer*, 106 S. Ct. 2797 (1986)) have focused particular attention on the issue of political gerrymandering, held justiciable by the Court (6-3) in the latter case. Yet Justice Byron White's plurality opinion would confine judicial intervention to the more serious instances of maldistricting as distinguished from the usual, traditional partisan jockeying for political advantage. The Court concluded that a decision holding Indiana's districting invalid on the evidence presented "would invite attack on all or almost all reapportionment statutes" (*Davis v. Bandemer*, p. 2811).

What, then, would comprise the kind of evidence the Court found lacking in Indiana? Justice White suggested several possible indicators that might reveal an electoral scheme designed to thwart the responsiveness of representation to electoral shifts of opinion (*Davis v. Bandemer*, p. 2812; see chapter 2). Since any single measure of possible vote dilution might not be sufficiently conclusive to meet the expectations outlined in *Bandemer*, we should survey several possible indicia of political gerrymandering. In doing so, it might be helpful to adapt a key phrase from the recent history of the Voting Rights Acts. The term *totality of circumstances* became a central feature of the 1982 extension of the Act in an effort to reconcile those emphasizing "intent" and those concerned with "effects" of voting laws and practices (including legislative redistricting) on the representation of racial minorities. The pertinent section reads:

(a) No voting qualification or prerequisite to voting or standard, practice, or procedure shall be imposed or applied by any state or political subdivision.

(b) A violation of subsection (a) is established if, based on the totality of circumstances, it is shown that the political processes leading to nomination or election in the state or political subdivision are not equally open to participation by members of a class of citizens protected by subsection (a) in that its members have less opportunity than other members of the electorate to participate in the political process and elect representatives of their choice. The extent to which members of a protected class have been elected to office in the state or political subdivision is one circumstance which may be considered, provided that nothing in this section establishes a right to have members of a protected class elected in numbers equal to their proportion in the population (Voting Rights Act, 42 U.S.C. 1973 (1982)).

While the situation addressed by the Voting Rights Act under the Fifteenth Amendment is not exactly the same as that of partisan gerrymandering litigation brought under Article I or the Fourteenth Amendment, there are still some striking similarities. In a functional sense, as the late Robert G. Dixon, Jr., pointed out, "racial gerrymandering is simply a particular kind of political gerrymandering" (Dixon, 1971, p. 32). It is worth recalling that *Gomillion v. Lightfoot* (364 U.S. 339), decided in 1960 on Fifteenth Amendment grounds, did not involve population inequalities among districts then prevalent, yet proved to be one of the jurisprudential stepping-stones leading to *Baker v. Carr* (369 U.S. 186 (1962)) in 1962. In both racial and partisan gerrymandering cases, courts may well look for discrimination and disparate impact that, together, yield an equal protection violation.

The totality of circumstances approach would appear to be especially well suited to the majority views in *Bandemer* holding political gerrymandering justiciable. In the firm but cautious plurality opinion, Justice White made it clear that "a mere lack of proportionate results in one election cannot suffice" to prove unconstitutional discrimination, insisting on "more than a showing of possibly transitory effects" (*Davis v. Bandemer*, p. 2814). This view clearly calls for a depth of evidence to support a charge of vote dilution. From recent judicial opinions we can focus on the kinds of circumstances that might be persuasive.

The most thorough discussion of standards that courts might consider in assessing the constitutionality of political gerrymandering is found in Justice John Paul Stevens' concurring opinion in *Karcher (I)*. He wrote: "[I] would consider whether the plan has a significant adverse impact on an identifiable political group, whether the plan has objective indicia of irregularity, and then, whether the State is able to produce convincing evidence that the plan nevertheless serves neutral, legitimate interests of the community as a whole" (p. 751, Justice Stevens concurring). Justice Stevens went on to suggest that an additional showing that a plan "departs dramatically from neutral criteria should suffice to shift the task of justification to the State defendants" (p. 754, Justice Stevens concurring; see Weinstein, 1984). In both the 1983 and 1986 cases, Justices White and Lewis Powell also discussed the kinds of standards appropriate to a finding of political gerrymandering.

From these various opinions, as well as scholarly analyses, we can enumerate eight indicators (some interrelated) that might be considered by courts:

1. DRAMATICALLY IRREGULAR DISTRICT CONTOURS

This has long been the feature of gerrymandering most familiar to the general public. A map of New Jersey's congressional districts was included in *Karcher v. Daggett*, leading Justice Stevens to declare: "A glance at the map . . . shows district configurations well deserving the kind of descriptive adjectives—'uncouth' and 'bizarre'—that have traditionally been used to describe acknowledged gerrymanders" (*Karcher (I)*, p. 762, Justice Stevens concurring). Commentators had referred to one district as "the Swan," another as "the Fishhook." In his dissent from the Bandemer holding three years later, Justice Powell included four maps of the Indiana legislative districts at issue, but virtually none of these appeared to the untrained eye as "uncouth" or "bizarre."

While tortuous shapes of districts are usually a classic sign of boundary manipulation, there are exceptions—for example, districts following irregular terrain. Moreover, it is possible to draw up a partisan gerrymander that is compact, contiguous, and defies many of the usual stereotypes, making judicial determination of constitutionality difficult.

Nevertheless, dramatically contorted districts will likely be prominent in most gerrymander suits, since the absence of territorial restraints ordinarily does produce "bizarre" and tortuous boundaries. The 1982 Democratic gerrymander of California congressional districts in the Los Angeles area (see Map 16.2 in Baker, chapter 16) is an example. Indeed, the California remappings of 1981 and 1982 reveal far more numerous and egregious gerrymanders than were evident in the New Jersey case. Small wonder that California easily won the decennial Elbridge Gerry Memorial Award for Creative Cartography for the second consecutive decade (see Baker, 1986b, pp. 272–273; map of 1981 prize winner also therein depicted).

2. DISREGARD OF COMPACTNESS AND CONTIGUITY

Historically, the most common antigerrymandering standards have been requirements that districts be compact and contiguous—found in many state constitutions and in earlier congressional apportionment statutes over several decades. These guidelines are closely related to checks on irregular districts, since such constituencies, almost by definition, lack compactness (and occasionally, contiguity, as indicated in Map 16.2). There have been attempts to measure compactness mathematically, and at least one campaign to make such a formula a state constitutional requirement.[1] In 1981, Ohio voters considered an initiative ballot measure that would have permitted any person to propose a districting plan by submitting 500 signatures. A commission would compute compactness ratios for each district by dividing its area by the square of its perimeter. These figures would then be summed to produce a compactness ratio for each plan, with the highest-scoring plan going into effect. The measure was rejected.

In *Karcher (I)*, Justice Stevens flirted with the notion of a quantitative measure: "Substantial divergences from a mathematical standard of compactness may be symptoms of illegitimate gerrymandering" (p. 755, Justice Stevens concurring). Stevens conceded that some deviations from compactness may be unavoidable, but wrote "it seems fair to conclude that drastic departures from compactness are a signal that something may be amiss" (p. 758, Justice Stevens concurring). Yet attempts to prove gerrymandering through such quantitative analysis fail to consider the possibility that rectangular or circular shapes may ignore sociopolitical features as well as terrain. A more sensible definition of compactness is the functional one used by California's court-appointed special masters in 1973, which took into account communities of interest, transportation networks, and communication between electors and prospective representatives.

3. IGNORING ESTABLISHED POLITICAL BOUNDARIES

Prior to the one person, one vote rulings, state constitutions frequently guaranteed minimum representation to political subdivisions such as cities and counties, producing widespread variation among district populations. Yet the 1964 decisions did not rule out consideration of local boundaries where possible. In *Reynolds v. Sims* 377 U.S. 533 (1964), Chief Justice Warren noted: "Indiscriminate districting, without any regard for political subdivisions or natural or historical boundary lines, may be little more than an open invitation to partisan gerrymandering" (pp. 578–579). In *Karcher (I)*, Justice Stevens elaborated on this point: "Extensive deviation from established political boundaries is another possible basis for a prima facie showing of gerrymandering" (p. 758, Justice Stevens concurring). He emphasized the stability over time of such boundaries, the development of communities of interest, and the administrative convenience of districts that conform to political boundaries.

4. FRAGMENTING COMMUNITIES OF INTEREST

Preserving the integrity of "communities of interest" is frequently mentioned as an appropriate expectation of redistricting. This objective may sometimes be met at least partially by adhering to political subdivision boundaries, but it merits separate consideration. Some county (and at times, city) boundaries must be broken in order to form districts of approximately equal population. But where they are broken can be critical for any concept of communities of interest. Some "functional" communities can transcend county lines and make more reasonable borders for district boundaries than others. Transportation and communication networks, common social and economic interests, and so forth, can justify such an identity. This standard was successfully used and articulated by California's court-appointed Masters on Reapportionment in 1973 (see chapter 16). The rationale for avoiding the fragmentation of communities of interest has been cogently expressed by Justice Powell as follows: "(a) legislator cannot represent his constituents properly—nor can voters from a fragmented district exercise the ballot intelligently—when a voting district is nothing more than an artificial unit divorced from, and indeed often in conflict with, the various communities established in the State" (*Karcher (I)*, p. 787, Justice Powell dissenting).

5. LEGISLATIVE INTENT

Partisans are often surprisingly frank in discussing the intent of redistricting measures. A case in point is the remark made by the late Rep. Phil Burton, chief architect of the California congressional redistrictings in 1981–1982, who once explained: "The most important thing you do, before anything else, is you get yourself in a position [to] draw lines for [your own] district. Then, you draw them for all your friends before you draw anyone else's" (*California Journal*, 1983, p. 308). In *Karcher (I)*, Justice Stevens called attention to a letter from the Democratic Speaker of the New Jersey General Assembly to Professor Ernest C. Reock, Jr., Director of the Bureau of Governmental Research at Rutgers University, "frankly explaining the importance to the Democrats of taking advantage of their opportunity to control redistricting after the 1980 census" (*Karcher (I)*, p. 763, Justice Stevens concurring). Whether candor will still flourish as courts begin to scrutinize alleged gerrymanders is unclear, though complete silence seems unlikely in a process involving several participants.

However, this standard by itself may not be significant, in view of the plurality position in *Bandemer*. Justice White noted that redistricting ordinarily is intended to have substantial political consequences, asserting that "even if a state legislature redistricts with the specific intention of disadvantaging one political party's election prospects, we do not believe that there has been an unconstitutional discrimination against members of that party unless the redistricting does *in fact* disadvantage it at the polls" (*Davis v. Bandemer*, pp. 2713–2714, emphasis supplied). Hence, intent can be an indicator in conjunction with evidence of discriminatory effects. This linkage underscores the utility of a totality of circumstances approach in determining political gerrymandering.

6. PROCEDURES OF ENACTMENT

Closely related to legislative intent is a procedural standard that takes the political context of a redistricting plan into account. As we have seen, such an inquiry can explain recent redistricting experience in both New Jersey and California. At a minimum, a procedural standard could require public hearings, official explanations of criteria used and justifications for adopted plans, and opportunities for public reaction prior to enactment. Again in *Karcher (I)*, Justice Stevens developed this idea: "If the process for formulating and adopting a plan excluded divergent viewpoints, openly reflected the use of partisan criteria, and provided no explanation of the reasons for selecting one plan over another, it would seem appropriate to conclude that an adversely affected plaintiff group is entitled to have the majority explain its action" (p. 759, Justice Stevens concurring). A procedural standard might well be an attractive one for judges to consider, since fair procedures are fundamental in the American legal system. The mere announcement that courts would expect redistricting acts to follow "fair procedures" might have a valuable deterrent effect by forcing more open and public processes.

7. DISCRIMINATORY PARTISAN IMPACT

More than any other, this standard has triggered legal challenges to legislative redistricting as a gerrymander. A common way of expressing charges of dilution in representation is to compare the proportion of the statewide vote won by a party with the percentage of seats won. In the Indiana case of *Bandemer v. Davis*, Democrats complained of the discrepancy between votes and legislative seats won: in the Indiana house, 51.9% of the statewide vote, but only 43 of the 100 seats; for the state Senate, 53.1% of the vote, but 52% of the seats up for election that year.

While this argument has a commonsense appeal, the fact is that there are hazards in expecting proportional results from a single-member district system of elections. Ordinarily, the party winning a majority of statewide votes will capture a disproportionately larger percentage of seats, since the minority party "wastes" too many votes in winner-take-all constituencies.[2] In *Bandemer*, the Indiana house results suggest a partisan gerrymander, while the Senate results are far from conclusive, especially with only twenty-five contested seats. Indeed, if proportional results are the test, the Senate outcome was virtually on target. In spite of the inherent difficulties in attempting to develop a precise votes/seats measure, it can serve as an impressive indicator of possible vote debasement in more extreme instances—for example, those in which a party captures a clear majority of the statewide two-party vote, but appears relegated to minority status regardless of shifts in public opinion. It is the measure of impact most likely to receive publicity, since it dramatizes—however roughly—the problem of potential minority rule.

Emphasis by the plaintiffs in Bandemer on disproportionate votes-seats results brought various reactions from the three groups on the Supreme Court. Opposing justiciability in political gerrymandering disputes, Justice O'Connor (for herself and two others) insisted that courts would predictably move "toward some form of rough proportional representation for all political groups" (*Davis v. Bandemer*, p. 2817, Justice O'Connor dissenting). Justice Powell's opinion (for himself and Stevens) mentioned the votes-seats disparity as one of several factors in the Indiana case that comprised evidence of discriminatory partisan impact. The Court plurality, however, regarded the lack of proportionate results in a single election as inconclusive. Referring to previous racial multimember district cases, White asserted: "In the statewide political gerrymandering context, these prior cases lead to the analogous conclusion that equal protection violations may be found only where a history (actual or projected) of disproportionate results appears in conjunction with similar indicia" (*Davis v. Bandemer*, p. 2814, Justice White).

There are other, often more conclusive, tests of discriminatory impact. For example, Bernard Grofman would place some reliance on "showing incumbent-centered partisan bias, i.e., a differential treatment of the incumbents of the two major parties" (Grofman, 1983a, 1985a).[3] The Court plurality position in Bandemer would presumably require a substantial degree of differential impact. The view articulated by Justice White accepted some partisan bias as endemic to the political process. Yet, with other indicia, this kind of test could be part of a totality of circumstances that demonstrate a violation of equal protection or due process.[4]

8. MINIMIZING ELECTORAL RESPONSIVENESS

While this indicator overlaps others, especially the previous one (7), it merits a separate status. Indeed, this measure of partisan impact helps distinguish ordinary maldistricting for party advantage from the type the Court plurality in *Bandemer* appeared to suggest as ripe for judicial intervention. It was the potential lack of responsiveness to future electoral shifts that seemed most to concern Justice White and help frame his concept of fairness in representation (see chapter 16). Again, Grofman pinpoints as a standard for judicial notice of political gerrymandering, one "demonstrating that the plan so constrains the probable range of politically competitive seats as to create a near certainty of continued partisan unfairness for the foreseeable future" (Grofman, 1983a, 1985a).

The eight indicators just surveyed are not necessarily exhaustive, but appear to cover the most salient features. Directly or indirectly, all have been noted in opinions by Justices Stevens, Powell, and White in the recent Karcher and Bandemer cases. Some indicia listed are interwoven with others, and one or more of them might not be applicable to a particular districting plan. As we have seen, some categories may be useful only in conjunction with other tests. Hence, the totality of circumstances approach would appear to be an especially appropriate one in judicial determination of challenges to alleged political gerrymandering.

This chapter draws extensively on portions of my article, "Judicial Determination of Political Gerrymandering: A 'Totality of Circumstances' Approach," 3 *Journal of Law and Politics*, Winter, 1986a, pp. 1–19.

NOTES

1. For one attempt to quantify compactness, see E. Reock (1963), pp. 70–74.
2. The literature on the votes/seats "swing ratio" is extensive; see chapter 7.
3. See the revealing table on California's 1982 congressional redistricting in Grofman (1985a, p. 156).
4. For a view advancing due process as a preferable ground in gerrymandering cases, see Baker (1971, p. 142).

10

A Geographer's Perspective

Richard Morrill

Gerrymandering, which is the intentional manipulation of territory toward some desired electoral outcome, is a geographic device to affect the societal distribution of power. It's been done for hundreds of years, and its effects have been measured for as long. Sometimes, it works; sometimes it doesn't. The issue today is whether and how gerrymandering affects the principle of "fair and effective representation." The geographer is interested in territorial behavior—in how and why people organize themselves across the landscape, for example, through administrative subdivisions and electoral districts. Some of the issues that arise in this regard are, first, what are underlying reasons for a territorial basis of representation, and are those bases compromised by an alternative conception of electoral districts as temporary conveniences for the holding of elections? This is the topic of the first and major part of this chapter. Second, what are some of the techniques and measures of gerrymandering? Who does it and does it work? Some aspects of these questions are considered in the context of post 1980 congressional redistricting. Third, is it possible to determine a partisan base, from which the partisan effect of gerrymandering can be estimated? Despite my strong conviction that gerrymandering can and does violate the goal of fair and effective representation, I am not sanguine about such predetermination of effects.[1]

REPRESENTATION AND REDISTRICTING

The purpose of voting is to enable people to express their will with respect to issues of collective choice (Dixon, 1968; Pitkin, 1967). Except for very local governments, the size of territories and of populations preclude direct involvement in most issues of collective governance, so the most critical voting decision is for representation. In the United States there are four fundamental senses of representation (see also Cain, chapter 5).

1. Directly as individuals;
2. Indirectly, in support of a party that expresses a program of governance with which we agree at the time;
3. Indirectly, in support of a representative who shares a sense of belonging to a particular territory and appreciates its interests;
4. Indirectly, in support of a representative who shares a racial or linguistic heritage that may have been historically suppressed.

We could decide all matters by direct plebiscite, but we do not. We could elect all representatives at large by proportional representation, thus meeting the need for representation by party, and probably by race, but we do not. The territorial basis of representation is a fundamental property of our scheme of governance.

The goal of districting, then, is to make possible the meaningful and effective participation of voters in electing individuals who meet these senses of representation—party, place and, if appropriate, race. Voters need to feel that voting is worthwhile, that their vote matters. The argument here is that there can be better and poorer districting. If done poorly, districting can create a sense of disenfranchisement and futility for any of these senses of representation—that one's party is unfairly disenfranchised, that one's territory is unrepresented, that one's racial or linguistic concerns are unaddressed. The consequences of such disillusionment over the long run are reduced voter participation, reduced willingness to support government, and reduced quality of governance. The characteristics of poor quality districting are as follows:

1. Malapportionment;
2. Fragmentation of the territorial base of a party so that it cannot over time win seats in proportion to its popular appeal;
3. Overconcentration of a party's adherents so that its strength is wasted and it cannot win seats in proportion to its popular appeal;
4. Manipulation of territory to unfairly advantage or disadvantage incumbents of particular parties;
5. Fragmentation of the territorial base of a racial or linguistic minority;

6. Overconcentration of a racial or linguistic minority;
7. Unnecessary fragmentation or division of a territory with which people identify—that they view as meaningful, or of districts with which voters traditionally identify;
8. Very high proportions of very safe seats so that voters in general feel that there is no possibility of change;
9. Very high proportions of highly competitive seats, so that representatives are not elected long enough to gain experience or seniority.

Characteristics 2 through 9 are all forms of gerrymandering, with respect to party, race and language, or meaningful territory. Initial pre-election evidence of poor districting can be gleaned from analysis of prior election returns and analysis of maps. Outcome evidence of the effectiveness of gerrymandering can be obtained from who runs or retires, and from turnout, as well as from electoral returns. Despite the "flavor" of *Bandemer*, which seems to suggest a reliance on mainly pre- and post-election evidence of seats versus votes shares (chapters 1 and 11), this is, I hope, a misemphasis or misreading, as the discussion also calls for other supporting evidence, for individual districts as well as for the system as a whole (chapter 3). I do not believe any case for politically suspect gerrymandering will succeed without skillful interweaving of multiple kinds of evidence, the "totality of circumstances" that Baker stresses (chapter 9). The intention here is to discuss a few of these forms of gerrymandering or the criteria aimed at limiting gerrymandering, emphasizing some geographic insights.

Compactness

Geographers, who have a particular concern for territorial measurement, know not to expect too much from a compactness criterion (Gudgin and Taylor, 1979). Compactness is not an end in itself, but rather an operational aid in avoiding discriminatory gerrymandering against parties or territories. Compactness is inherently preferable to irregularity, simply because compact territories tend to have easier communication and greater internal cohesion, because most human settlement is clustered, and because there is a relation between the cost of creating a sense of common identity and irregularity of territory. It is easier for representatives and the represented to develop a mutual identity with the district. But, cleverly executed, compactness could either divide or pack any community of interest—geographic, partisan, or racial. Thus modest departures are not worth worrying about; what is of concern are egregious irregularities that reveal an intention to discriminate. Why is extreme irregularity then suspect? Why else would anyone go to the considerable effort? Logically compactness should be evaluated in conjunction with measures of dilution or packing. For example, a degree of irregularity that brings together multiple concentrations of minorities so as to make representation possible would be evaluated differently from a similar district that was intended to divide that minority or divide a partisan concentration or to put together totally disparate and unrelated kinds of areas (chapter 9).

Measures of compactness are amply discussed elsewhere. I will just observe that as a population geographer I strongly prefer measures based on population, not on boundaries; for example, a measure of variances of the distances of the populations of subareas of the district to the district center; or of the proportions of population inside or outside the district within a polygon enclosing the district (see chapters 3 and 12). It is not necessary to calculate compactness measures for all districts, because what is critical is whether there are extreme districts that reveal the intention to discriminate. These are no mystery to the victims (cf. Baker's "sense of injustice," chapter 9).

Respect for Integrity of Political Units

This criterion is and should be an important one, since local governments are vital, legal, and familiar communities of interest, since in much of the country, counties have been the traditional basis for representation (in state senates, but also as building blocs for congressional districts), and since they often represent a simple barrier to extreme gerrymandering for racial, partisan, or geographic purposes. As such it is a criterion of wider purpose than compactness and deserves higher priority.

Community of Interest

This is probably the least well defined, but the most geographic criterion, in the sense that a major concern of geography is to identify the regional structure of a society, the communities that have evolved over time, the territories with which citizens identify and whose integrity they want to defend. The idea of community of interest of course overlaps with both racial and partisan identity and with political entities. But emphasis here will be on territories within which people share a common sense of identity and value across a range of interests. Communities are revealed through patterns of work, of residence, and of social, religious, and political participation. At the broadest scale there is a strong historic divergence of identity between an urban core (central city), suburbs, and rural small town areas, because they are usually different jurisdictions, because they have different needs and problems, and because they attract people with different values and preferences. At a regional scale, the clearest community of interest, relevant to congressional districts and large legislative districts, is captured by the idea of a small city and its rural hinterland—the area dominated by that city's work opportunities, shopping, and television and newspaper. These are easily identified and have strong common interests, even when they may be racially diverse, or have a close partisan balance. These areas know very well when they have been divided in the process of redistricting.

At a more local level, as within a metropolis, even within a central city, communities of interest are also fairly easily identified, perhaps as a school district, or a named district of a city, often with a post office—in short, a recognized large neighborhood. These tend to be moderately homogeneous in class and partisanship; they also tend to be a sector of a city dominated by a major business district. Most metropolitan areas know these districts and do planning for them. They have community councils and know well when they are divided.

Communities of interest are not conveniently of the precise population of congressional or legislative districts. Obviously, it is impossible to follow the criterion strictly. Also strict adherence, together with compactness, can have the effect of unfairly packing or splitting party concentrations and can thereby increase electoral bias. If one party is more concentrated in metropolitan areas, but is a minority across broad rural small city areas, as is true for the Democrats in much of the north and west, and of the Republicans in much of the south, following the criterion will tend to favor Republicans in the north and west and Democrats in the south (Cain, chapter 5).

This is not a controlling criterion, but is one that deserves evaluation in conjunction with compactness, political unit integrity, and fairness of representation of races and parties. Why does community of interest matter? Because, as stated above, one of the three bases of representation in our culture is territorial—not of arbitrary aggregations of geography for the purpose of conducting elections, but as meaningful entities that have legitimate collective interests arising from the identity of citizens with real places and areas. If districts ignore the neighborhood or community within which most people carry out their daily lives, the representative, even in a strongly partisan district, may be faced with difficult conflicts of interest between people in disparate parts of the district; and citizens in those isolated parts of a district may come to feel that their community is unrepresented, even if their ideology is being represented (Niemi et al., 1990).

The fundamental notion of representation is that the electorate expresses a sense of majority collective will, and that the persons elected do represent that sense of having a common stake. In the American system, representation is indelibly dual—territorial and partisan, with an ancient tradition of representation of named places, to which people are attached. Since it is the people of real places that pay taxes to support national and local activities, it is not unreasonable that they should develop a sense of common interest as to how that money is spent. Remember that it was a profound sense that territorial (that is, cities, prior to 1962) interests were not being fairly represented that led to the entire reapportionment revolution—not mainly a sense of partisan misrepresentation. No matter in how partisan a manner we may vote, the representative also stands for the district. This is the very essence of our federal-territorial system of governance. This legacy is why we do not have proportional representation—and why gerrymandering matters.

District Stability

If it is true that voters of districts develop over time a sense of loyalty and cohesion, then the district, although not an administrative unit, becomes real, as exemplified by district organizations, meetings, newsletters and the like. Then a defensible case can be made for minimizing the number of voters who would have to be shifted to another district, and whose customary allegiance would be disrupted. But this simultaneously has the effect of protecting incumbents and may have the effect of decreasing the number of competitive seats and the responsiveness of the system to swings in voter sentiment (see chapter 11). If the preceding set of districts were very good across most criteria (including proportion of competitive seats) then minimizing change would be desirable, but if the preceding set of districts were unusually bad, then it makes no sense to preserve its imperfections.

Electoral Fairness

Avoidance of discriminatory packing and splitting of partisan concentrations is sometimes unavoidable, simply because of the geographic distribution of party strength, as noted above. The point of this principle is rather that the parties be treated symmetrically or fairly in the redistricting process—that one party is not disproportionately packed or divided (e.g., Niemi, chapters 7 and 8). Whether this occurs is fairly easily measured, either by registration data or from returns of recent preceding elections (chapter 6). Obviously this is exactly what parties do, whether to evaluate districting plans or as a tool to gerrymander effectively. To evaluate its damage to a sense of fair representation is more difficult. Why is this criterion important? Why should parties be entitled to protection? In fact, it is not the parties but the views of voters that are in question (chapters 3 and 11). Voters choose representatives and thereby parties, in order to entrust them with governing. In our winner-take-all system, the voter accepts the reality that the other party may win. But the very idea of fairness, and will of the majority, insists that over the long run, across a set of districts, there be a fair correspondence between the share of votes received and of seats won. Otherwise the frustrated minority voters can only conclude that they are effectively disenfranchised. Disproportionate packing and splitting make the votes of party adherents, even if such allegiance is unstable, unequal, just as it does those of racial minorities. The argument that if parties, why not ethnic groups, the elderly or other interest groups, is of course specious, since it is uniquely parties that are entrusted with governance—the purpose of voting in the first place (chapter 3, p. 36; chapter 6; but see chapter 5, pp. 124–125).

How bad is bad? How blatant and destructive to the other party or to a given area does gerrymandering have to be before fairness tells us it should be invalidated? (chapter 2, p. 23 re: injustice). The presence of electoral bias is not enough, since some disparity of seats and votes may be a consequence of the natural distribution of partisan strength. Rather there needs to be a linked set of indicators: electoral bias (outcome measures), and the presence before elections of an uneven "playing field" or a discriminatory opportunity for election; asymmetry in the distribution of partisan majorities; splitting and packing and/or incumbent discrimination; irregularity and breakup of communities of interest and of political units; a process that excludes the minority party (chapter 5), and lack of competitiveness. Where such a pattern exists, and the result can clearly be demonstrated to be a difference in the number of representatives—from the real expressed sentiment of voters over time—then relief is due. But does it work? (Please see next section.)

Partisan gerrymandering is not always successful, of course, and its effects can be transient, as voter moods swing (Scarrow, 1982; Cain, 1985a). However, this is usually the result when the perpetrators have overreached, were overconfident about a supposed voter realignment and, while packing the other party, riskily tried to maximize the number of seats through devising a large number of seats marginal in their direction. If more adroitly done, in space and in time, gerrymandering can be successful and long-term indeed; otherwise it would not have been so common over the generations, and the subject of all this debate today.

GERRYMANDERING AND THE QUALITY OF CONGRESSIONAL DISTRICTS IN THE 1980s

The motivation for this section was an interest in evaluating the quality of legislative and congressional districting efforts in the 1980s. By quality is meant the degree to which the redistricting meets certain criteria, most of which may be called "antigerrymandering" criteria. Particular attention is paid to the question of whether quality is related to who did the redistricting and how, whether it really makes a difference if the process is partisan or bipartisan or done by legislature, commission or court. Comparison is made on the following criteria:

1. Political fairness: Does the proportion of seats reflect the proportion of votes over time?

1a. Balance of experience and opportunity: Does the set of districts provide for a mix of "safe" and "competitive" seats?

2. Community of interest.

3. Integrity of political units: Are unnecessary splits of counties avoided?

4. Compactness.

Population equality and equality of representation (racial/linguistic fairness) are not discussed here, as all states met these conditions. As this book illustrates, it is difficult to evaluate political fairness, even on the basis of three elections, 1982, 1984, and 1986, since personality, incumbency, and natural concentrations of partisan sentiment are major factors. Bias is measured here simply by the difference in the proportion of seats and votes won, recognizing that some degree of bias may be considered "normal" in traditional one-party states. The proportion of votes and the measure of bias are not based on state totals; rather, each district is treated equally, to adjust for voter turnout and composition. (Lack of such adjustment is a serious problem in the base-line measure; chapter 6.) The descriptive ranking in Table

10.1 is based on the product of the percentage difference and the number of seats this represents. The matter of a balance of safe and competitive seats is complex and related to incumbent protection. Having more competitive seats increases the power of voters, but also leads to high turnover and electoral bias, if one party gets small margins in many seats. There may be virtue in experience. Thus one could argue for a balance of perhaps two-thirds relatively safe seats, giving each party a "saving remnant," and one-third of competitive seats, that permit responsiveness to changing views, and thus electoral fairness to be achieved (Grofman and Scarrow, 1982). The same descriptive terms as before are used for competitiveness; but my sense is that Medium High and Medium Competitiveness (30%–50%) are the more preferred and Low the least preferred, with High and Medium Low as of intermediate desirability. (Table 10.2 lists the number of seats won by less than 60% in 1982, 1984, and 1986. The proportion overall fell from 31% in 1982 to 20% by 1986, as the position of incumbents firmed up.) For community of interest, given the number of districts and the complexity of the concept, it was not practical to attempt any quantitative measure. Instead a descriptive ranking from High to Low was developed, based on a map analysis of districts, and their economic and social profiles, in an effort to estimate the proportion of districts that exhibited an obvious violation of community of interest.

Integrity of political units descriptive rankings were based on the proportion of counties smaller than a congressional district that were divided. Compactness, as argued above, matters to the extent to which there are extreme intentional irregularities. I did not attempt a quantitative measure of districts, but the rankings were based on a combination of the proportion of highly irregular districts and their severity. Since the rankings were substantially identical to those for community of interest, a composite ranking was made (Table 10.1).

The Effect of Who Redistricted.

The 1980 plans are evaluated for any major differences that may be attributed to who did the districting. Redistrictings are classed as shown in Table 10.1. The distinction between "strongly and weakly" partisan is mainly based on intentionality; other than partisan considerations were dominant in the latter type. Utah and Idaho were technically bipartisan, but in effect partisan. The Court group includes Illinois and Michigan, in which the courts accepted essentially partisan plans; the distinction is kept in mind.

TABLE 10.1   QUALITY OF 1980s REDISTRICTING

State	Electoral Fairness	Compactness Community	Integrity of Political Unit	Competition
Strongly Partisan	M	M	M+	ML
California	L	L	ML	L
NewJersey	M H	L	L	L
Massachusetts	L	L	ML	L
Indiana	M H	M	ML	M H
Pennsylvania	H	M L	ML	M L
Oklahoma	M L	M L	MH	M L
Washington	M H	M H	M	L
Texas	M	M H	H-	M L
Maryland	M L	M H	MH	M L
Utah	L	M H	H	M H
Idaho	L,H	M H	H	H
Weakly Partisan	M	M H	H-	ML/M
Alabama	M H	M H	H	M L
Florida	M L	H	M	L
Georgia	M	M	H	L
Kentucky	H	M H	H	L
Nebraska	L	M H	H	M L
New Mexico	M H	M H	H	M L
N. Carolina	L	M H	H	H
Rhode Island	H	M H	?	M
Virginia	M H	H	H	M H
W. Virginia	L	H	H	M
Bipartisan	M H+	M/M H	M+	ML
Arizona	H,M L	ML	L	L
Arkansas	M H	H	H	L
Louisiana	?	M H	M H	L
Nevada	H	H	H	H
New Hampshire	M	M H	M H?	H
New York	H	M L	L	ML
Ohio	M H	M L	M L	L
Oregon	H	H	M	H
Tennessee	M	M L	H	L
Wisconsin	H	M H	M	L
Court	H-/M H	H-	M H/H	M
Colorado	H	M H	M H	M
Kansas	H	H	H	L
Minnesota	M H	H	M	M
Mississippi	M H	H	H	M
Missouri	M L,H	H	H	M H
South Carolina	H	M H	H	M
Court-adopted				
Partisan	M/M H	M/M L	L	M L
Illinois	M	M L	L	M L
Michigan	M H	M	L-	M L
Commission	M/M H	H-	H	M
Hawaii	M H	H	H	L
Iowa	M	H	H	M H
Connecticut	M H	M H	?	H
Montana	H	H	H	M
Maine	L,H	H	H	M
All states	M H	M H	M H-	ML/M

see text for discussion of criteria

221

TABLE 10.2   ELECTORAL BIAS AND COMPETITIVENESS

	1982				1984				1986			
State	% Vote	% Seat	Diff	# Seats	% V	% S	Diff	# Seats	% V	% S	Diff	# Seats
CA	53	64	11 D	5-	51	60	9 D	4-	55	60	5 D	2+
NJ	58	64	6 D	.8	53	57	4 D	.6	55	57	2 D	
MA	71	91	20 D	2+	72	91	19 D	2	84	91	7 D	.8
IN	50	50	0		47	50	3 D		51	60	9 D	.8
PA	54	56	2 D	.6	54	56	2 D	.6	54	52	2 R	.4
OK	63	83	20 D	1	59	83	24 D	1.5	67	67	0	
WA	53	62	9 D	.7	55	62	7 D	.5	60	62	2 D	
TX	70	78	8 D	2	65	67	2 D	.5	65	63	2 R	.5
MD	68	87	19 D	1.6	65	75	10 D	.8	66	75	9 D	.7
UT	29	0	29 R	1	34	0	34 R	1	46	33	13 R	
ID	47	0	47 R	1	41	50	9 D		47	50	3 D	
All Strong Partisan				17-				12-				6
AL	74	71	3 R		76	71	5 R		58	71	13 D	.9
FL	62	68	6 D	1.2	55	63	8 D	1.6	57	63	6 D	1
GA	78	90	12 D	1.3	75	80	5 D	.6	73	80	7 D	.6
KT	63	57	6 R		57	57	0		60	57	3 R	
NB	26	0	26 R	.7	26	0	26 R	.7	36	0	36 R	1
NM	52	33	19 R	.5	41	33	8 R		46	33	13 R	
NC	55	82	27 D	3	53	54	1D		58	73	15 D	1.6
RI	52	50	2 R		50	50	0		43	50	7 D	
VA	47	40	7 R	.7	47	40	7 R	.7	58	50	8 R	.8
WV	64	100	36	1.4	61	100	39 D	1.5	77	100	23 D	.9
All Weak Partisan				9				5				6
AZ	45	40	D		40	20	20 R	1	35	20	15 R	.7
ARK	52	50	2 R		63	75	12 D	1	60	75	15 D	.6
LA	?	75	?		?	75	?		63	63	0	
NV	50	50	0		42	50	8 D		49	50	1 D	
NH	42	50	8 D		32	0	32 R	.6	30	0	30 R	.6
NY	62	59	3 R	1.2	56	56	0		60	59	1 R	
OH	56	48	8 R	1.7	51	52	1 D		51	52	1 D	
OR	57	60	3 D		55	60	5 D		56	60	4 D	
TN	59	67	7 D	.7	54	67	13 D	1	61	67	6 D	.5
WI	53	56	3 D		51	56	5 D		55	56	1 D	
All Bipartisan				4-				3				3-
CO	48	50	2 D		35	33	2 R		44	50	6 D	
KA	47	40	7 R		46	40	6 R		44	50	6 D	
MN	56	62	6 D	.5	55	63	8 D	.6	61	62	1 D	
MS	59	60	1 D		62	60	2 R		61	80	19 D	1
MO	57	67	10 D	1	56	67	11 D	1	59	56	3 R	
SC	56	50	6 R		54	50	4 R		65	67	2 D	
All court				1.5				1.6				1
IL	58	55	3 D	.6	58	59	6 D	1.4	52	59	7 D	1.5
MI	63	67	4 D	.7	58	61	3 D	.6	61	61	0	

TABLE 10.2   (continued)

	1982				1984				1986		
	%	%		#	%	%		#	%	%	#
State	Vote	Seat	Diff	Seats	V	S	Diff	Seats	V	S	Diff Seats
All court partisan				1.3				2			1.5
HA	58	55	3 D		85	100	15 D		58	50	8 R
IA	52	50	2 R		47	33	14 R	.8	48	33	15 R .9
CN	55	67	12 D	1	47	50	3 D		55	50	5 R
MT	54	50	4 R		50	50	0		54	50	4 R
ME	41	0	41 R	1	30	0	30 R	.6	39	50	11 D
All commission				2				1.4			1
ALL STATES				34				25			18

DEGREE OF COMPETITIVE SEATS, 1982-1986

State	Total Seats	Ave % Compe	#'82	#'84	#'86	State	Total Seats	Ave % Comp	#'82	#'84	#'86
CA	45	18	15	5	5	AZ	5	13	1	1	0
NJ	14	17	3	3	1	ARK	4	17	1	1	0
MA	11	12	2	2	0	LA	8	8	0	0	2
IN	10	40	4	4	4	NV	2	83	2	1	2
PA	23	28	8	7	4	NH	2	50	1	1	1
OK	6	22	1	2	1	NY	34	25	8	10	8
WA	8	17	2	1	1	OH	21	19	6	4	2
TX	27	20	4	9	3	OR	5	60	4	4	1
MD	8	25	1	2	3	TN	9	15	1	1	2
UT	3	44	1	1	2	WI	9	7	0	1	1
ID	2	67	2	1	2	All					
All Strong						Bipart	99	23	24	24	19
Partisan	157	22	43	27	25	CO	6	33	2	2	2
AL	7	24	2	2	1	KA	5	13	1	1	0
FL	19	14	5	3	0	MN	8	33	4	2	2
GA	10	10	1	2	0	MS	5	33	2	2	1
KT	7	19	2	1	1	MO	9	44	6	2	4
NB	3	22	1	0	1	SC	6	33	3	0	3
NM	3	22	2	0	0	All					
NC	11	58	5	7	7	Court	39	33	18	9	12
RI	2	33	1	0	1	HA	2	17	0	0	1
VA	10	40	5	4	3	IA	6	44	4	1	3
WV	4	33	2	2	0	CN	6	50	5	3	1
All weak						MT	2	33	1	0	1
Partis	76	27	26	21	14	ME	2	33	1	0	1
IL	22	24	7	4	5	All					
MI	18	22	3	5	4	Comm	18	41	11	4	7
Court						All					
Partis	40	23	10	9	9	States	435	41	132	94	86

The basic question is whether the quality of redistricting, as measured by how well plans meet certain criteria, differs according to agency. As to electoral bias, the hypothesis is that states with partisan districting will have greater bias than states with bipartisan, court, or commission districting, because of self-interest (temptation and opportunity). Bias is not expected to be as great in traditionally one-party states (weakly partisan), because when state legislative control is not at stake, party may be less important than other considerations. No difference in bias is hypothesized between bipartisan, court, or commission plans, although the latter might have bias, to the degree that a highly competitive plan could cause higher bias in our winner-take-all system.

Court and commission plans should be the most competitive, on "good government" grounds; yet some strong partisan plans could be very competitive if the majority were overconfident about its marginal popularity. As to respecting community of interest and as to compactness, the hypothesis is that strongly partisan and bipartisan districting will do least well because party strength and incumbent survival are overriding concerns. Court and commission plans are expected to provide compact looking plans that tend to respect communities, because these criteria are viewed as good criteria for such agencies.

As to integrity of political boundaries, the hypothesis is similarly that strong partisan and bipartisan districting will have little regard to political boundaries, while weak partisan, commission, and especially court districting will.

These expectations will be conditioned by other contexts for districting: The greater the number of districts, the greater the opportunity for manipulation for higher electoral bias, and for irregularity and community breakup. Similarly, a change in representation creates an incentive (for gains in seats) and a feeling of necessity (for losses) for greater electoral bias and for whatever irregularity and breakup of communities and political units that might be necessary. The results will be summarized briefly by who did the districting and then by the four antigerrymandering criteria.

Strongly Partisan Districting

In the 11 states classed strongly partisan it was at least the intention to maximize the interests of the controlling party, and in several states with no hesitation or apology. In part, the zeal was to reduce damage from a reduction in seats or to take advantage of a gain in seats.

Partisan effect: Did it work? For the set of states the partisan gerrymander did appear to raise the party's share of seats above its share of votes, especially in 1982—an average of an 11% "surplus." Strong partisan control does tend to lead to electoral unfairness (but such unfairness is not uncommon in other situations), and these states alone did account for half the number of seats represented by electoral bias in 1982. However, the degree of bias fell over time because of party shifts and because of an increasing share for incumbents.

Competitiveness: Over the three elections, only 22% of races were competitive, the lowest of any set of states. Yet in California, Indiana, Florida, and Pennsylvania, the competitive share was fairly high in 1982. The California plan was more adept at creating competitive but reasonably Democratic districts, while the Republicans in Indiana and Pennsylvania overestimated their 1980 popularity in competitive districts in the 1982 off-year election.

Community of interest: The highly partisan plans followed this criterion, but narrowly as to partisan character, while natural functional areas such as cities and their hinterlands or well known communities of metropolitan areas were often sacrificed.

Political unit integrity: A prime victim of partisan gerrymandering should be the purposeful division of counties and cities, and in this respect several of these efforts are exemplary, especially in California, New Jersey, Indiana, and Pennsylvania.

Compactness: It would be safe to say that the three most extreme examples of gerrymandering in the popular visual sense of blatant irregularity are California, New Jersey, and Massachusetts. Some districts will be classics in textbooks for years to come.

Weakly Partisan Districting

Ten states, mostly traditional southern or border Democratic states, showed only limited partisan manipulation, often because racial or liberal vs. conservative or city-country balance or especially incumbent protection were more important considerations.

Partisan effect: Here we expect either that districting was reasonably "fair" or that one party is so dominant that electoral balance is not really possible. The former seems true in Alabama, Florida, Kentucky, Rhode Island, and Virginia, the latter in Georgia, Nebraska, North Carolina, and West Virginia. Still, in 1982, these states had as high a bias (11% surplus of seats) as the strongly partisan states.

Competitiveness: On average these states had 26% competitive seats over the three elections, falling from one-third in 1982 to under one-fifth by 1986. But there is great variability, from states with very low competition (Florida and Georgia) to very high (North Carolina and Virginia).

Community of interest: Most of this group of states, whether intentional or not, did respect communities of interest rather well—in the sense that districts consist of related rural and urban areas, and showed homogeneity of economic and environmental character.

Integrity of political units: These states did a remarkable job of not cutting county or city boundaries, probably because of the traditional importance and power of counties in these southern states.

Compactness: Without a strong motivation for irregular manipulation, the districts in most of these states are quite regular, in comparison to the more strongly partisan states.

Bipartisan Districting

Another ten states had splits between parties, in the legislatures or between legislature and governor, so that some degree of compromise was required.

Electoral bias: One might expect bipartisan redistricting to be fair, and this is generally borne out, for actually bipartisan situations. Differences between votes and seats are much less on average than for the two partisan groups.

Competitiveness: Incumbent protection appeared to be a prominent feature of plans in this bipartisan group. This set had a low proportion, only 25%, of competitive seats, perhaps reflecting the goal of incumbent protection, and competitiveness has remained low in most of these states.

Community of interest: Is community sacrificed in bipartisan districting? The pattern is mixed, but several states managed to maintain fairly reasonable communities of interest, generally rather traditional district patterns (Arizona, Tennessee, New York, and Ohio did less well than Arkansas, Louisiana, Oregon, and Wisconsin).

Integrity of political units: In general, the southern and western and smaller states (except Arizona, the more partisan case) maintained county integrity, while northern and larger states seemed indifferent.

Compactness: No consistent pattern is apparent. Where regional partisanship was practiced, as in New York and Ohio, irregularity was moderately pronounced, and Tennessee's and Arizona's plans showed more irregularity than those of the remaining states.

Commission Districting

In five states redistricting commission plans were accepted, although only in Hawaii and Montana was this automatic, and little change was required in either state. In Maine and Connecticut, also, little adjustment was necessary.

Electoral fairness: These commission states on average have a higher electoral bias than the court or bipartisan set, and almost as high as the partisan groups. The moderate bias for Connecticut and Maine for 1982, in Iowa and Maine for 1984, and Iowa in 1986 perhaps reflect a too competitive structure of districts. On the other hand, none of the states maintained a consistent bias over all three elections.

Competitiveness: As a group, the commission states have the highest proportion of competitive seats, as expected (41% across the elections), whether or not by intention.

Community of interest, compactness, and integrity of political units: Hawaii, Montana, and Maine have only two seats each, perhaps little choice in design, and reasonably compact districts; counties and towns are respected; and communities of interest are about as meaningful and traditional as possible. Connecticut and Iowa, with six seats each, are the more interesting. While some may ridicule commissions, not to mention use of computers, it seems an inescapable conclusion that it would be hard to improve upon these in the sense of how well they do across the set of criteria—except political fairness. On the other hand, these are small states, without gains or losses of seats; commissions might do less well in large, more complex states.

Court Districting

In the final eight states the courts imposed plans. Court involvement was due to failure of the two parties in a power split to compromise, or due to legal challenges.

Electoral fairness: As expected, results where the courts worked seriously tended to have reasonable electoral fairness, with a balance of safe and swing seats; however, the "hidden partisan" plans in Michigan and Illinois reflected, though modestly, the intended partisan bias. The seats represented by electoral bias amount to only 4% of seats, compared to 11% for partisan districting; and the states with a significant bias changed from election to election.

Competitiveness: The court-drawn plans, except for Kansas and Illinois and Michigan, had a fairly high proportion of competitive seats throughout the period, and at least one seat changed parties in most of the states.

Community of interest: In the more partisan Illinois case, there was not much concern for communities, except political, but there was a fairly careful attention to broad communities in most other cases. In Colorado, Minnesota, and Mississippi, the courts deliberately and effectively brought about a fundamental improvement, with much greater attention to regional identity.

Integrity of political units: Where the courts were directly involved, efforts to maintain county integrity were rather successful. In the de-facto partisan plans in Illinois and Michigan, county integrity was often ignored. Michigan is the extreme case of the 50 states, obviously required by the plan's ludicrous virtue of exact population equality.

Compactness: As with commission plans, when the court accepted the responsibility, they often did an excellent job on this criterion. On the other hand, in Illinois and Michigan, where the courts chose among competing partisan plans, the plans are far more irregular.

Summary by Criterion (see Figures 10.1–10.4)

Electoral bias: Some systematic differences in electoral bias can be discerned, in part depending on who did the redistricting. Of the five commission states, Connecticut, Iowa, and Maine did have a significant bias in one or more elections. The bias may be a consequence of too high a proportion of competitive seats. Of the eight states with court redistricting, only Missouri had a substantial bias in 1982. Electoral bias was not severe in any state with bipartisan redistricting in 1982. But many states with strong or weak partisan districting had moderate to severe electoral bias, often persisting over the three elections. It does make a difference: In 8 of 11 strongly partisan districtings, the efforts were successful in obtaining more seats than "deserved." For the whole country, the total electoral bias amounted to 34 seats in 1982, 25 in 1984, and 18 in 1986, of which 26, 17, and 12 respectively were accounted for by strongly or weakly partisan states.

Competitiveness: Court and commission states do have and maintain higher proportions of more competitive seats (33–41%) while strongly partisan or bipartisan plans had much lower proportions (22–23%), although there is much variability within the groups.

Communities of interest: Greater attention to community was apparent in court, commission, or weakly partisan states, and in most bipartisan plans. Communities were most ignored in some strongly partisan plans, and in the court-accepted Illinois plan.

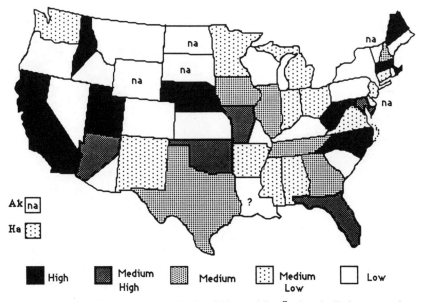

Ranking is based on product of mean electoral bias and the # of seats that represents.
Arizona, Idaho, Maine and Missouri had distinct periods of high or low bias.

FIG. 10.1 Severity of Electoral Bias, 1982–1986

Integrity of political units: Integrity was most sacrificed in several strongly partisan states, in some bipartisan states, and in court/partisan plans. It was most protected in southern and border states generally, and in all weakly partisan states, in commission-drawn plans and in the actual court-drawn plans.

Compactness: Overall, the greatest irregularity occurred in the very large states, under strong partisan districting and under court-accepted partisan plans in large Illinois and in bipartisan New York, Ohio, Arizona, and Tennessee. The most compact plans were in smaller states generally and under weak partisan, court or commission-drawn circumstances.

Summary Evaluation

Overall the strongly partisan set have above-average bias, below-average compactness/community, integrity of political units, and competitiveness. The weakly partisan set has above-average bias also, but above-average compactness/community of interest, and integrity of

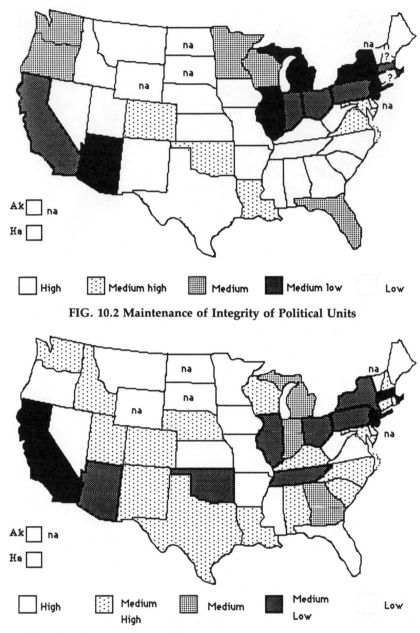

FIG. 10.2 Maintenance of Integrity of Political Units

FIG. 10.3 Compactness and Respect for Communities of Interest Post 1980s Redistricting

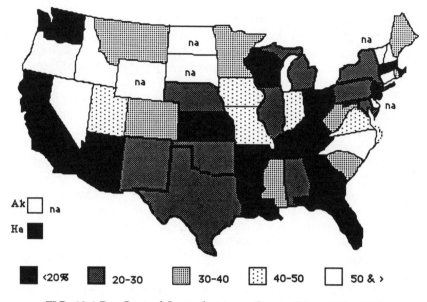

FIG. 10.4 Per Cent of Seats that were Competitive, 1982–1986

political units, and below-average competitiveness. The bipartisan group has slightly below-average bias (but variable), average compactness and community, and below-average competitiveness and integrity of political units. The court plans have below-average bias, and are above-average in compactness/community, integrity of political units, and competitiveness, while the commission plans are slightly above-average in bias, but yet also above-average in compactness, community, integrity of political units, and competitiveness.

Ironically, the "worst" rankings overall appear to be enjoyed by the largest states, that are often leaders in political innovation, whether drawn under partisan, bipartisan, or court circumstances. Of the large states, Florida and Texas fare best over the criteria. Very small states do well under whatever agency, and medium-sized states with the highest rankings included cases of weakly partisan, bipartisan, court, and commission districting. Perhaps the largest states rank lowest, because they had to adjust to more or fewer seats and because many are relatively evenly balanced. Thus each party, when able, might be tempted to employ drastic measures to maintain and enhance their fragile power, whereas this would not be necessary in the less balanced southern and border states. Many of the better plans were not from legislatures: Plans actually drawn by courts and commissions, while hardly perfect, were consistently above average in the rankings, relative to those drawn by legislatures, and of those drawn by legislatures, the best plans were under weak partisan or bipartisan circumstances, where partisan motives were partly submerged into other considerations.

Thus who redistricts does matter, but overall in relatively few states and districts. Not all court or commission plans are consistently "good," nor all strongly partisan plans consistently "bad." Electoral bias, in particular, is not necessarily prevented by a good quality plan with respect to compactness, community of interest, integrity of political units, or one done by court or commission.

Policy implications: The findings do not provide any simple prescription for better redistricting. Although court and commission plans were on average superior to legislative drawn plans, it may be undesirable to rely on courts to undertake a nonjudicial function of districting. Also, it must be admitted that all the commission plans are for smaller states, for which legislative plans tend to be better also.

Districtings that violated one or more of the criteria analyzed were associated with partisan control, large size, loss or gain in seats, and excessive concern with incumbency. The more of these conditions that hold, the greater the temptation, partisan or bipartisan, for manipulative gerrymandering. California should not surprise: It is the state for which all these conditions most held. Combinations of these conditions are and will be inescapable facts of life for many states.

VARIABILITY IN THE PARTISAN BASE

Evaluation of the probable partisan impact of a redistricting scheme is commonly made on the basis of prior election returns; indeed, one measure of gerrymandering is whether a party's "historic" share of the vote is matched by its having a majority in a comparable share of congressional and legislative districts—a logical basic standard of fairness (chapter 6). This section looks briefly at issues in implementing such measures, that attempt to evaluate in advance the "evenness of the playing field" and any persistent discriminatory effect, as the *Bandemer* plurality clearly asks for (chapter 3).

First, reasonably consistent estimates are made of the expected Democratic share of the vote in each state, on the basis of all senatorial and gubernatorial elections between 1980 and 1986, of the 1980 presidential race, of the congressional races, 1980 through 1986, and the composition of the state legislatures, 1980 through 1986 (13–16 races per state). Obviously, it makes a significant difference just what races are included. (Backstrom's claim for the validity of using one partisan race is hard to defend: In most states, the correlations among races are simply not high enough—especially with district races, which is the matter at issue; there may be good behavioral reasons for the political geography of legislative or congressional, partisan propensities to differ from statewide propensities.) The number of races over six years does encompass three critical arenas—legislative, congressional and statewide—and is long enough to capture persistence, including two presidential year and off-year elections for Congress. Second, these results are compared against actual congressional performance via the 1984 and 1986 returns, to try to indicate whether any discrepancies are (a) due to intentional partisan gerrymandering, or (b) the consequence of incumbency, or (c) the result of perhaps unavoidable differences in the natural concentrations of the parties (chapter 11, p. 248). With respect to evaluation, a measure of the variability around the mean Democratic base proves useful: The more the variability, the greater the range of partisan outcomes that may reasonably be expected, and the less valid is the use of a partisan baseline. Table 10.3 presents the mean Democratic vote for statewide races and for Congress, and the mean proportion of the legislatures (both houses) Democratic, a grand average across all types of races, together with the standard error of the mean, a simple measure of the variability of the Democratic share on the various races/measures. The results will not surprise the po-litical observer. On average, despite high variability, one can discern a historic Democratic South; a Democratic base in New York and southern New England, in the urban-industrial Great Lakes/Midwest; and a marginally Democratic Pacific Coast and "northern tier"—some are a shift from historic patterns. The Republican "core" in turn covers most of the mountain states and the great plains, Indiana, and upper New England. The South's "Democraticness" is mainly a function of overwhelming legislative domination, as there is only a marginal Dem-ocratic lead in statewide races. Other areas of Democratic strength are also weakest at the statewide level; while most states with overall Republican majorities also reveal Democratic tendencies on some mea-sures, (see also Figure 10.5).

The Mean Democratic Share and Congressional Results, 1984 and 1986

If one were to believe that the mean Democratic share is behaviorally meaningful, then it is interesting to compare the expected and actual share of congressional seats won. Because of variation in the races defining the average, a range rather than an exact number is appro-

TABLE 10.3   ESTIMATION OF THE DEMOCRATIC PARTISAN VOTE, 1980-1986

State	1980 Pres	1980-1986 Senate			1980-1986 Governors		All States	Congress '80	'82	'84	'86	Aver	Legislatures '80	'82	'84	'86	Ave	GRAND AVER	Error
AL	49	48	63	55	59	54	52	66	74	76	58	68.5	91	92	88	84	89	67.4	4.5
					55														
AK	33	46	28	45	50	52	44	26	29	43	42	35	57	47	50	54	52	43.1	2.7
AZ	32	49+	58	40	65	46	48	47	45	40	35	42	34	37	38	40	37	43.3	2.5
AR	50-	59	57	62	48	64	57	40	52	63	60	54	94	93	90	90	2	65	4.3
					55	63													
CA	41	60	47	51	49	38	47.7	50	53	51	55	52+	59	61	60	57	59	52.3	1.9
CO	36	51	35	51	67	59	50-	46	48	35	44	43	39	39	29	34	35	43.8	2.8
CN	44	57	48	65	53+	59	54+	51+	55	47	55	52+	56	59	40	63	54+	53.8	1.9
DE	49	44		60	29	44	45	38	53	59	66	54	45	60	52	51	52	50	2.8
FL	41	48	62	55	65	46	53-	60	62	55	57	58.5	68	72	68	62	67+	58.6	2.4
GA	58	49	80	51	63	71	62	75	78	75	73	75	88	87	85	84	86	72.6	3.4
HA	51	81	82	69	63	52	66	91	90	85	58	81	74	80	80	79	78	73.9	3.5
ID	28	49+	27	48	51	50+	42	43	47	41	47	44.5	25	31	29	29	29	39	2.7
IL	46	57	51	65	50-	43+	52	50	58	53	52	53+	49	62	55	55	55	53.3	1.6
IN	40	46	46	39	42	47	43	50	50	47	51	49.5	34	41	39	46	40	44.1	1.3
IA	43	46	56	34	47	48	45.7	52	52	47	48	50-	43	59	59	59	55	49.5	1.9
KA	36	36	23	34	54	48	40-	44	47	46	38	44-	42	42	39	41	41	40.8	1.9
KT	49	65	50-	74	59	55	59	63	63	57	60	61-	76	76	74	73	75	63.9	2.5
LA	47	65	50	74	49	62	69	69	75	75	62	70	93	92	89	84	89	75	4.9
ME	48	61		26	61	43	48	27	41	30	39	34	54	62	58	57	58	46.7	3.7
MD	52	34	64	61	62	82	59	64	68	65	66	66	88	88	88	88	88	69.3	4.3
MA	50	61		66	61	69	59	69	71	72	84	74	81	82	79	81	81	70.4	3.1
MI	46	58		52	53	69	56	56	63	58	61	59.5	59	58	51	55	56	56.9	1.6
MN	52	47		42	59	57	51+	49	65	55	61	57.5	57	59	54	65	58	54.8	1.7
MS	49	64		39	61	58	54	60	59	62	61	60.5	95	95	94	94	94	68.5	5.3
MO	46	52	49	47	47	43	47.3	56	57	56	59	59.5	68	66	65	67	66+	55.6	2.3
MT	36	56		57	55	70	55	51	54	50	54	52+	43	53	52	49	49+	52.5	2.3
N B	28	69		52	51	47	49	27	26	26	36	29	-	-	-	-	-	40.2	5.1
N V	30	39	49	53	56	74	50.2	72	50	42	49	53	68	63	48	60	60	53.8	3.4
N H	33	48	41	34	59	33	43	49	42	32	30	38	40	40	26	33	35	39.6	2.2
					48	46													
NJ	43	51		65	50-	30	48	51+	58	53	55	54	54	56	56	44	53-	51.3	2.4
NM	40	54		28	53	47	45	48	52	41	46	47	56	62	56	61	59	49.5	2.6
NY	48.5	49	65	42	52	67	53.8	57.5	62	56	60	59	53	59	57	58	57	56.1	1.8
NC	49	49	48	52	62	45	50.8	58	55	53	58	56	80	85	71	73	77	59.9	3.4
ND	29	29	64	50+	46	55	46	57	72	79	76	71	25	48	42	45	40	51.2	4.6
OH	44	70	57	62	60	61	54	48	56	51	51	51.5	52	60	56	57	56	56.1	1.8
OK	37	45	76	46	62	49	52.5	59.5	63	59	67	62	74	74	69	72	72	60.9	3.3
OR	44	46	33	37	37	53	42	61	57	55	56	57	61	63	58	52	59	50.9	2.6
PA	46	49	41	43	49	51	46.5	45+	54	54	54	52	49	50-	50-	50-	50-	48.1	1.6
RI	56	49		73	74	33	57	56	52	50	50+	50+	83	76	77	79	79	61.1	4.2
					75	40													
					75	33													
SC	49	70	33	64	70	48	55.7	50-	56	54	65	56	87	84	78	75	81	63.3	4.1
SD	34	40	25	52	29	48	38	54	52	57	59	55.5	30	24	23	30	27	39.8	3.6
TN	50-	62		64	40	54	54	51	59	54	61	56	61	63	64	64	63	57.5	2.0
TX	43	59		41	54	47	49	67	70	65	65	67	76	77	68	66	72	61.4	3.3
UT	22	26	41	27	55	44	36	40	29	34	46	37	23	21	19	34	24	33.0	2.9
VT	46	51	48	65	39	55	49.9	0	25	29	4	15	43	44	50	52	47	40.3	4.4
					45	50													
V A	43	49		30	54	55	46	31	47	47	58	46	70	70	70	70	70	53.4	3.9
W A	43	46	73	45	43	53	50.6	51	53	55	60	55	45	54	54	55	52	52.1	2.0
W V	52	69		62	54	47	54.6	58	64	61	77	65	78	88	77	78	80	65.8	3.6
W I	47	49	64	48	57	47	52	52	53	51	55	53-	60	59	54	56	57	53.7	1.4
W Y	31	43		22	63	54	43	31	29	25	31	29	37	39	31	33	35	36.1	3.2

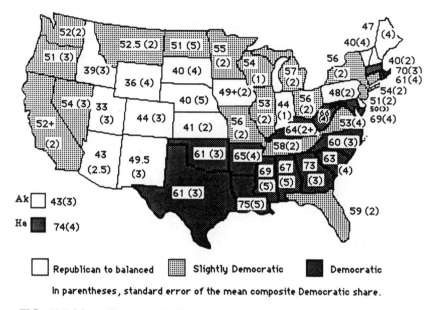

In parentheses, standard error of the mean composite Democratic share.

FIG. 10.5 Mean Democratic Share Across Statewide, Congressional and
Legislative Races 1980–1986

priate (Table 10.4). Calculations are made using the composite index
and also just the congressional vote index. Relative to the composite
vote index, Democrats got more congressional seats than "expected"
in 18 states (23 seats) in 1984, 11 (22 seats) in 1986; Republicans in 11
states and seats in 1984, and 6 in 1986. Taking into account a range of
seats possible because of variability, the net significant cases are 14 to
Democrats in 1984 and 12 in 1986, and 8 to Republicans in 1984 and
5 in 1986. It is likely that intentional partisan gerrymandering played
a role in California, Illinois, Oklahoma, Arizona, and Utah, and perhaps in part in Massachusetts. Traditional partisan concentrations or
long-term incumbency were probably the explanation in Missouri,
Tennessee, Texas, Washington, West Virginia, Iowa, Nebraska, New
Hampshire, and yet other factors in Louisiana and South Carolina
(race?, ideology?) and in Indiana and Pennsylvania, where Republican gerrymanders failed. Considering just the probable gerrymandering cases, the benefits to Democrats were 6-7 seats, to Republicans 2,
with a net to Democrats of 4-5, with 3-4 in California alone.

Partisan Variability and Partisan Regions

Do consistent partisan regions still exist? Can the Democrats or Republicans really count on any states any more? On the simple mea-

TABLE 10.4 EXPECTED AND ACTUAL DEMOCRATIC CONGRESSIONAL SEATS, CONGRESSIONAL AND COMPOSITE BASE

State	% Composite	Expec Seats	% Congre	Exp Seats	1984 Actua	1986	1984 Comp	1986 Discr	1984 Congr	1986 Discr
AL	67.4	4-5	68.5	5	5	5	-	-	-	-
AK	43	0	35	0	0	0	-	-	-	-
AZ	43+	2	42	2	1	1	1 R	1 R	1 R	1 R
AR	65	2-3	54	2	3	3	-	-	1 D	1 D
CA	52+	23-24	52+	23	27	27	4 D	4 D	4 D	4 D
CO	43.8	2-3	43	3	2	3	1 R	-	1 R	-
CN	53.8	3	52+	3	3	3	-	-	-	-
DE	50+	0-1	54	1	1	1	-	-	-	-
FL	58.6	11-12	58.5	11	12	12	1 D	1 D	1 D	1 D
GA	72.6	7-8	75.2	8	8	8	1 D	1 D	-	-
HA	73.9	1-2	81	2	2	1	1 D	-	-	1 R
ID	39	1	44.5	1	1	1	-	-	-	-
IL	53.7	11-12	53	12	13	13	1 D	1 D	1 D	1 D
IN	44.1	4-5	49.5	5	5	6	1 D	2 D	-	1 D
IA	49.5	3	50	3	2	2	1 R	1 R	1 R	1 R
KA	40.8	2	44	2	2	2	-	-	-	-
KT	63.9	4-5	61	4	4	4	-	-	-	-
LA	75	6	70	6	6	5	-	1 R	-	1 R
ME	46.1	1-2	34	1	0	1	1 R	-	1 R	-
MD	69.3	5-6	66	5	6	6	-	-	1 D	1 D
MA	70.4	7-8	74	8	10	10	2 D	2 D	2 D	2 D
MI	56.9	10-11	59.5	11	11	11	1 D	1 D	-	-
MN	54.8	4-5	57.5	5	5	5	1 D	1 D	-	-
MS	68.5	3-4	60.5	3	3	4	-	1 D	-	1 D
MO	55.6	5	59.5	5	6	5	1 D	-	1 D	-
MT	52.5	1	52	1	1	1	-	-	-	-
NB	40	1	29	1	0	0	1 R	1 R	1 R	1 R
NV	53.8	1	53	1	1	1	-	-	-	-
NH	39.6	1	38	1	0	0	1 R	1 R	1 R	1 R
NJ	51.3	7-8	54	8	8	8	1 D	1 D	-	-
NM	49.5	1-2	47	1	1	1	-	-	-	-
NY	56	18-19-20	59	20	19	20	-	1 D	1 R	-
NC	56.9	6-7	56	6	6	8	1 R	1 D	-	2 D
ND	51.2	0-1	71	1	1	1	-	-	-	-
OH	56.1	11-12	51.5	11	11	11	1 R	1 R	-	-
OK	60.9	3-4	62	4	5	4	1 D	-	1 D	-
OR	50.9	2-3	57	3	3	3	-	-	-	-
PA	48.1	11	52	12	13	12	2 D	1 D	1 D	-
RI	61.1	1	50+	1	1	1	-	-	-	-
SC	63.1	4	56	3	3	4	1 R	-	-	1 D
SD	39.8	0-1	55	1	1	1	1 D	1 D	-	-
TN	57.5	5	56	5	6	6	1 D	1 D	1 D	1 D
TX	61.4	16-17	67	18	18	17	1 D	-	-	1 R
UT	33	1	37	1	0	1	1 R	-	1 R	-
VT	40	0	15	0	0	0	-	-	-	
VA	53.4	5-6	46	5	4	5	1 R	-	1 R	-
WA	52.1	4	55	4	5	5	1 D	1 D	1 D	1 D
WV	65.8	2-3	65	3	4	4	1 D	1 D	1 D	1 D
WI	53.7	5	53	5	5	5	-	-	-	-
WY	36	0	29	0	0	0	-	-	-	-

A range of numbers, as 4-5 for Alabama, reflects the standard error around the composite mean (but closer to the underlined value)

sure of the proportion of measures that were consistently for one party or the other, only Hawaii had consistent behavior—to the Democrats on all measures, but even there, a Republican congresswoman was elected in 1986. All the "deep South" states, Democratic on most of the measures, as were Massachusetts, Michigan, and Ohio as well, had one or more Republican statewide victory. The most solidly Republican states again had at least one statewide Democratic victory; Democrats do amazingly well in Congress in Indiana.

A second way to assess the realness of partisan regions is through the variability around the mean Democratic vote. While Democrats have more "significantly" strong states (14 over 55%, taking into account the standard error), than Republicans (5), it is significant that fully 17 states do not have a significant majority for either party, including such large states as California, Illinois, New Jersey, and Pennsylvania.

A third aspect is the degree of variability itself. Variability is low in larger states, and in the Midwest, but is very high in the South—the clash between conservative ideology and Democratic tradition, and in very small states. Clearly, there are few if any states on which either party can truly rely. Inconsistent behavior abounds; half the states blatantly split their rewards between the parties.

The generally significant variability in partisanship across the many races and categories (statewide, congressional, legislative) casts some doubt on the potential of dependence on a measure of the average partisan share as a standard by which to validate prospective congressional (or legislative) districting plans. Clearly, Republicans would generally prefer to use statewide races as a standard, and Democrats, congressional or legislative races. A composite measure would need to be agreed upon by the parties but, especially in closely balanced states, where the majority differs by party between categories, it is difficult to imagine agreement. Measuring the "evenness of the playing field" in this way is important, but this should logically be but one indicator of districting quality or of the presence of discriminatory gerrymandering.

CONCLUSION

Collective decision making in the United States is mainly carried out by voting for representatives in electoral districts. This geographic partitioning of the electorate, in our winner-take-all context, makes gerrymandering of districts a common form of territorial behavior, and raises basic issues of whether representation is "fair and effective." The main argument of this essay is that the very essence of representation in our culture is territorial as well as ideological, and that *meaningfulness* of electoral districts to the voters matters. Electoral districts are not merely passing conveniences for the holding of elections, but entities with which citizens identify. This conception provides a basis for considering multiple criteria for the evaluation of districts with respect to the likelihood of "fair and effective representation"—and in particular supports the use of "antigerrymandering" criteria. It argues that reliance on nongeographic, systemwide statistical averages is useful and indeed necessary, but not sufficient. Examination of the specific districts through which political discrimination is executed is equally vital. If the techniques of gerrymandering can be demonstrated to have a high probability of resulting in a sense of misrepresentation—for example, persistent deficits in the expected numbers of representatives or alienation from the electoral process—then gerrymandering, like malapportionment earlier, must be seen to frustrate the intent of the Constitution.

Gerrymandering obviously works. To suggest otherwise is frivolous and hypocritical. Otherwise it would not be executed with such fervor and care or be defended with such passion. On the other hand, like most human endeavors, it doesn't always worked as hoped. We have reviewed the extent to which state congressional districting after 1980 meets usual criteria for redistricting, and especially whether it makes any difference if the process were controlled by a strongly partisan legislature, a state with split partisan power, or by a commission or the courts. Poorer quality districting was associated with larger, closely balanced states, and with a change in representation. Court and commission-drawn plans really were better, but perhaps the critical need is for legal codification of multiple criteria against which plans can be evaluated, whoever draws them.

Finally the essay briefly examines the utility of establishing a "partisan base" by which to evaluate a state set of districts with respect to electoral fairness. The prospect appears limited, given voter independence and the systematic difference between statewide versus district-based elections.

Representation, and therefore election districts, are basic to the legitimation of government and faith in the political process. Why not do it right? Means as well as ends matter. There is no constitutional or ethical justification for contemptuous manipulation of territory and of voters, or for disregard of the territorial basis for representation for narrow partisan or ideological gains.

NOTES

1. Among the important geographic references are Archer and Shelley (1986), Brunn (1974), Bunge (1966), Gudgin and Taylor (1979), Johnston (1979, 1982a, 1982b), Martis (1982), Merritt (1982), Morrill (1981, 1987), O'Loughlin (1980, 1982b), O'Loughlin and Taylor (1982), Reynolds (1976), Rowley (1975), Schwab (1985), Schwartzberg (1966), Shelley (1982, 1984), Taylor (1985), Taylor and Gudgin (1976), and Taylor and Johnston (1979).

11

Partisan Gerrymandering: A Political Problem Without Judicial Solution[1]

Peter Schuck

Gordon Baker (chapter 2) applauds the Supreme Court's new willingness to adjudicate partisan gerrymandering claims. He believes that judicially manageable standards can be devised. Baker, conceding that courts cannot readily say what a "fair" districting plan is, urges courts to circumvent this problem by only striking down "unfair" plans. Although there is a difference between a court rejecting a plan and drafting its own, that difference is largely irrelevant to the question of what standards it is to apply. Baker's approach simply reformulates that issue; it does not address it. Other proposed standards (e.g., Wells, 1981) are also irrelevant to the problem but for a different reason. Plans must *already* meet these standards when deviations from population equality are challenged in the courts, yet partisan gerrymandering continues. Nelson Polsby (1985) has pointed to an additional problem: Standards like this are also normatively controversial.

I believe that courts attempting to adjudicate partisan gerrymandering claims will find it impossible to vindicate those claims unless they adopt a proportional representation standard. This view may seem odd since all members of the Court in *Bandemer* expressly disavowed proportionality as constitutionally required.

BANDEMER AND PROPORTIONALITY

"The Constitution does not guarantee proportional representation." Saying something, however, does not make it so. There is a dynamic to constitutional adjudication that the Court cannot always control, a dynamic vividly revealed in the steady movement from *Baker v. Carr* (369 U.S. 186 (1962)) to *Bandemer v. Davis* (603 F. Supp. 1479 (1984)).

The links between *Bandemer* and proportionality are straightforward, and are outlined in Justice O'Connor's concurring opinion. Essentially, they amount to this: A court cannot determine whether and to what extent a districting plan "will consistently degrade a . . . group of voters' influence on the political process as a whole"—the plurality's constitutional test—unless the court can compare the group's postgerrymander representation in the legislature to what the group's "true" representation would be under a "fair" plan. But the latter obviously can be determined only by reference to some norm or benchmark. For a political party, that benchmark can only be its performance at the polls.

But how is that performance to be measured in an actual partisan gerrymandering case? Given the need to determine both the substantive justiciability and the remedial tractability of such claims, the court must examine the party's past vote totals and the number of legislative seats that it won with those votes, and must decide whether the putative gerrymanding party's seat/vote ratios are "too" high. This analysis must inevitably rely on some notion of "normal" performance, which necessitates use of a "base race." But a base race, to be a useful construct, must be one in which the effects of issues, candidates' personalities, unusual party effort, and other contingent factors deemed irrelevant to the party's "true" strength are minimal. Judgments about these factors and their effects must be largely subjective and beg questions that lie at the heart of political competition in a democracy.

As a practical matter of judicial administrative feasibility, this sort of analysis would represent not just the beginning but the end of the benchmark inquiry. The reason is that a court will seldom have anything else to go on. It is one thing in a malapportionment case for a political analyst or even a court to attempt to assess the significance of a deviation from population equality by looking to swing ratios and other statistical measures that may be relevant to whether that deviation is justified or tolerable. But it would be far more problematic for a court to use crude, subjective, question-begging measures to decide partisan gerrymandering claims in cases in which population equality has already been achieved. In effect, the court would be prescribing the partisan configuration of the legislature—the most political of tasks—and doing so on the basis of inevitably conflicting, inconclusive expert testimony about the uses and implications of such tests. This is surely a chilling prospect.

A court sensitive to these difficulties would doubtless seek other criteria, but these alternatives would not be better and might even be worse. The court, for example, might choose to focus on the legislative process by which the districting plan was adopted, much as proof of malice in libel cases often looks to the way in which the defendant gathered and analyzed the defamatory material. In *Bandemer* itself, the evidence revealed that the Republican majority in the legislature simply excluded the Democrats from any meaningful participation in the committee process that led to the plan's enactment. It is doubtful, however, whether such egregious tactics are common in the already limited universe of problematic gerrymandering situations. More typically, one supposes, the gerrymandering party would be content simply to rely on its control of the votes needed to pass the bill and, if necessary, to override the governor's veto.

But even if exclusionary tactics are more common than that, it is difficult to discern constitutionally suitable standards for appraising the adequacy of a legislative process. For the validity of a districting law to turn on whether it was preceded by hearings of a certain type, conducted in a certain spirit, and held before committees of a certain composition would surely offend well-established separation of powers principles; and an injunction compelling the legislature to abide by existing procedural rules would be intrusive and unenforceable. Moreover, interventions like these would necessarily require the courts to reconstruct the legislators' reasons for employing the processes that they did. Yet pre-enactment legislative procedures are notoriously informal and diverse, especially in state legislatures. There, the kind of documentation, such as committee reports and floor debates, that courts typically use to divine the legislative purpose of final statutory enactments seldom exists. The effort to infer the legislative motive for using a particular process, as distinguished from construing a statute's legislative purpose, would plunge the court into the deepest of quagmires.

The benchmark problem, then, is extremely vexing. If there is a judicially manageable solution to it, the *Bandemer* decision does not even hint at what that might be: all but two of the Justices failed even to *acknowledge* the existence of this problem.[2]

Once we recognize the striking consensus in *Bandemer* among six Justices as to the centrality of electoral performance in proving a partisan gerrymandering claim, the larger significance of the Court's silence on the methodological issue comes into sharper relief. On the crucial question of how significant proportionality should be in partisan gerrymandering cases, the Court seemed determined to have it both ways. It scrupulously rejected proportionality as the benchmark, yet refused to suggest any other standard that might take its place. By insisting that litigants challenging districting plans as partisan gerrymanders would bear a heavy evidentiary burden while failing to indicate how that burden could be met, the Court simply shoved the problem under the rug.

PROPORTIONALITY AND THE REPRESENTATION OF MINORITIES

There are four senses in which it can be said that a legislator "represents" a minority group or party. First, the legislator may have been the direct choice of a discrete group of voters, selected as its designated candidate and elected through bloc voting. Thus a successful candidate is often said to have been the "unions'," "blacks'," or "women's" candidate. Second, a legislator may possess certain personal attributes—race, ethnicity, or gender, for example—that define, or seem especially salient to, the minority, attributes that are thought to assure the legislator's fidelity to the minority's interest. Third, a legislator, although neither the minority group's designated candidate nor a member of that group, may be impelled to promote the group's interests out of a political need to assemble or maintain a winning electoral coalition. Finally, a legislator may seek to advance the minority's interests for moral, public-regarding, or other nonelectoral reasons, such as the pursuit of future career opportunities.

The standard fair representation argument against partisan gerrymandering emphasizes the first and second of these modes—what Hanna Pitkin (1967) termed the "accountability" and "descriptive" views of representation. This emphasis is grounded in existing law as well as political theory. It finds support in numerous court decisions under the Voting Rights Act, which equate fair representation of a minority with its ability to elect a candidate of its choice, as evidenced (often conclusively, it seems) by the candidate's own membership in that minority group. Proportional representation, as Pitkin shows, particularly reifies the "descriptive" view; it is "the attempt to 'secure a representative assembly reflecting with more or less mathematical exactness the various divisions in the electorate.'" Political accountability is presumed to follow from the formal arrangements under which the representative, elected under proportional representation, must seek reelection. Her descriptive and accountability views merge, then, in a normative conception that is perfectly embodied in a system of proportional representation.

But as we have seen, this conception is not self-evidently correct or desirable. Other, quite different views of representation can also be normatively justified. In particular, the third and fourth notions of representation mentioned earlier emphasize that a legislator may also fairly represent constituents when motivated either by political self-interest or by an altruistic or public-regarding desire to discern and serve their interests. What is more, a legislator may succeed in representing constituents under these other conceptions even though the legislator and the constituents are quite dissimilar—indeed, even though they have little or nothing in common! This "liberal" view of representation, as Pitkin calls it, is also the most common type of representation for Americans, one that reflects our highly diverse, mobile sociopolitical patterns. It presupposes that interests are rooted in individuals, not groups; that individuals' interests are fluid, subjective, multiple, and often conflicting, rather than fixed and determinate; and that even individuals who identify with each other in certain respects (e.g., ethnically or politically) nonetheless conceive of themselves and their interests in distinctive ways that may, and frequently do, cut across these group lines.

In this liberal view, the notion of "wasted" minority votes, so central to the fair representation argument against partisan gerrymandering and to the justification of proportionality, loses most of its descriptive and normative force. Although a minority in a district will usually be unable to elect either its own designated choice or one who mirrors its defining features, that does not imply that minority votes are superfluous or that minority preferences will go unrepresented.

Four problems with the notion of wasted minority votes deserve mention. First, the term "minority," when used in discourse about fair representation, contains an important ambiguity. Although the fair representation argument against partisan gerrymandering is of course vitally concerned about protecting of minority *parties*, it must also—and perhaps more fundamentally—be concerned with representing racial and other minority interests in society *through* parties. One can easily identify a partisan minority simply by counting up the votes that a particular party received and comparing then to the total cast. But one cannot speak so casually about other kinds of minorities in this context, much less about wasting their votes, without making a number of crucial and (as it often turns out) quite arbitrary, question-begging assumptions. These assumptions concern how members of the group in question actually think of themselves in political settings, how uniform and labile their voting patterns and intensity of preferences are, what kinds of political alliances they enter into and on what terms, and many other factors. To treat blacks, for example, as if they were political monoliths is to ignore both the evidence of significant diversity among their members in precisely these respects, and the fact that voting structures can affect, as well as reflect, their political self-definitions.

Second, the analyst who would calculate a minority party's wasted votes in order to judge the adequacy of its representation confronts the same definitional problems noted earlier. The only benchmark against which to measure a party's "true" size is the number of votes cast for its candidates, yet even that index is likely to mislead regardless of how many election cycles are used to calculate the base. A party's fortunes wax and wane over time. In a single election, its success will vary according to the office in question, the attractiveness of particular candidates, coattail effects, salient issues, voter turnout, and many other factors. As one extends the time period backward across a number of elections, these factors interact to make the index less and less relevant for evaluating current party strength and the effect of current conditions and districting configurations.

Third, the system of single-member, first-past-the-post districting weakens minority representation far more than partisan gerrymanders do. Yet that system not only persists but now amounts to a quasi-constitutional *requirement* under the long dominant interpretation of the Voting Rights Act. Partisan gerrymandering, like single-member, first-past-the-post districting, "wastes" minority votes in the interests of creating for the winning party what I have elsewhere called a "victory bonus." In this sense, gerrymandering is similar to patronage, perquisites of office, greater logrolling opportunities, and control of the chairmanship and staff of legislative committees. And like them, it may serve an extremely important social function: promoting effective and responsible governance in a markedly decentralized polity. By consolidating and "defractionalizing" (Douglas Rae's term) American politics, partisan gerrymandering may help to reduce the fragmentation and fluidity that always threaten our political stability and effectiveness.

Finally and perhaps most fundamentally, minority votes are not actually wasted except in the narrow, almost tautological sense in which that term is used by many proponents of proportionality. So long as candidates must compete for electoral pluralities or majorities in a district, simple political expediency dictates that they take into account the preferences and interests of all constituents whose votes they may need some day, including at least some of those who might ordinarily be expected to support their opponents. For some politicians, considerations of political morality and broad, altruistic conceptions of representational trusteeship may fortify these self-regarding incentives. Especially in a system in which two broadly based, weakly organized parties contend for power, a candidate's optimal electoral strategy ordinarily is to appeal not only to his/her own partisans but also to independents and weakly identifying members of the opposition party.

Proportional representation systems create very different incentives. There, the difficulty of obtaining a majority and the organizational pressures of parties encourage candidates to make ideological, regional, or other narrow or parochial appeals to voters. Under such systems, coalition-building tends to occur *after* the election, not before it as in a two-party majoritarian system like ours. Thus, proportional representation does not so much *eliminate* "vote-wasting" as alter its *form and timing*. The votes of the supporters of parties excluded from the governing coalition, then, will be wasted just as minority party members' votes are now wasted.

Indeed, in some important respects, that waste seems more complete under a system of proportional representation. There, politicians have less incentive to cast their nets widely in seeking support because voter allegiances to particular parties, for historical and ideological reasons, tend to be more predictable and fixed. Moreover, the at-large or large multimember district representation usually associated with proportionality tends to weaken candidates' concern for geographically localized claims, on which minority and majority interests often coincide. As to those geographically based issues, at least, proportional representation does not even encourage legislators to promote their minority group constituents' interests when those interests overlap, as they often do, with the neighborhood-specific interests of the majority constituents.

THE CHANGING CONTEXT OF MINORITY REPRESENTATION

It is puzzling that the concern for minority party representation so evident in all of the opinions in *Bandemer*—a concern that animates the argument from fair representation against partisan gerrymandering and in favor of proportionality—has crested at this particular moment in our political history. In some respects, *Bandemer* comes at the least propitious of times for proportionality or indeed for *any* representational standard that attaches a legal significance to party performance at the polls. Understanding why this is so can help to illuminate where the Court went wrong in *Bandemer* and why it matters.

The partisan identification of American voters is probably weaker today than at any time since the founding of mass-based political parties during the Jacksonian era more than 150 years ago. Even this low level of partisan identification, moreover, may diminish further now that President Reagan has retired from the political scene, unless some other strongly partisan figure emerges to occupy his central place in our contemporary politics. If the 1986 elections are indicative, this erosion of party loyalty is already far advanced. The amount of ticket-splitting (a common measure of declining party identification) for offices at all levels of government and in all jurisdictions has risen to unprecedented levels. Although such changes may be cyclical to some degree, few if any political scientists believe that party identification will ever return to its earlier levels.

This fact significantly weakens the argument from fair representation. As we have seen, the structure of that argument, and the norm of proportionality to which it leads, demand some meaningful concept of "true" minority party support that can be used to define deviations from the representational norm. As a practical matter, they also require that such deviations be objectively ascertainable by a court. But if party identification is already weak and growing weaker, and if widespread and increased ticket-splitting means that a party's electoral performance critically depends on the particular office on which one focuses, then the party vote becomes an even more arbitrary and unreliable index of party strength. When measuring true party support is a futile effort to solidify the evanescent, the norm of proportionality becomes a shadowy, manipulable thing.

While party identification is becoming more tenuous, party competition is becoming more robust. There is no contradiction here. Most of the important issues that separated (and in some cases internally divided) the national parties in the past—the New Deal and the role of the federal government, the Vietnam War, civil rights, fiscal policy, labor relations—have dissolved in a consensus, have been blunted and muted, or have disappeared altogether. The shattering of the New Deal coalition and the rising fortunes of the Republican Party in the South and Southwest, especially in presidential election years, have reflected, but also generated, more intense party competition between the parties in many areas of the country. As they vie for support from voters who previously identified strongly with one or the other of them, they further confound efforts to gauge "true" party support on the basis of any particular electoral outcome.

The factors that cause changes in voting behavior between one election and the next are also becoming more salient, making party performance in one election an even less accurate predictor of its future performance. Candidates, by seeking to detach themselves functionally from their parties, have also complicated such predictions. Although the national parties have recently sought, with modest success, to arrest this fragmentation, the important determinants of electoral victory—fund-raising, issue development, campaign management, media activity, and mobilization of voters—are now handled largely by the candidates themselves. With the spread of primaries and the progressive loss of traditional patronage opportunities, party organizations, especially at the state and local levels, have gradually lost influence. Electorally, candidates are increasingly on their own.

External developments further cloud the picture. Party performance, of course, is always influenced to some degree by national issues. But the dramatic political events of recent years—Vietnam, Watergate, the energy crisis, and the severe economic difficulties of the late 1970s and early 1980s—have powerfully affected voter responses, increasing the variation over time in party electoral performances. National developments like these generally exert less influence over the parties' showing at the state and local levels (where districting decisions are made) than local or regional concerns do. Still, such convulsive events further confound efforts to gauge "true" minority party support by resort to historical voting patterns.

A final complication in accurately measuring that support relates to the effects of incumbency. The electoral advantages associated with incumbency today, especially in the House of Representatives on the national level, are already great and probably increasing. The very high reelection rate is said to reflect incumbents' ability to use their perquisites of office (such as free mailings, constituent service, and media coverage) and their superior name recognition and access to campaign funds to discourage primary battles and overwhelm their opponents. Very recently, however, other analysts have refined this view somewhat, observing that the re-election rate in the House has not increased appreciably since the 1950s and that other measures of competition for House seats remain fairly consistent. Although incumbents' vote margins have increased, that has been offset by the volatility of vote swings between elections. According to Gary Jacobson, (1987), this "greater heterogeneity of inter-election vote swings explains how vote margins could increase without making incumbents any safer," and may also explain why "House members have been behaving as if they felt more vulnerable than ever."

For purposes of evaluating the wisdom of a judicial attack on partisan gerrymandering, one need not determine whether the "incumbency effect" (as the phenomenon of high reelection rates is sometimes called) is greater now than it was in the past. The more important fact is that it remains very strong. This has at least two important implications for the use of proportionality or any other methodology that relies on party performance as a criterion for adjudicating the constitutionality of partisan gerrymanders. First, the incumbency effect may dwarf—and in any event is separate from— any electoral advantages that may have been independently conferred by a partisan gerrymander. To put the point another way, unless the court can actually distinguish between that portion of the majority party's seat/vote ratio (or other putative index of gerrymandering activity) that is attributable to the gerrymander and that portion that is instead attributable to the independent advantage that all incumbents (regardless of party) enjoy, it cannot know with confidence whether a gerrymander has really occurred and been effective, much less know how to begin to remedy it.

A second implication is that a post-*Bandemer* judicial attack on partisan gerrymanders may be aimed at the wrong target. It may miss the real possibility that gerrymanders are actually concerned less with partisan advantage than with incumbent protection. As Bruce Cain (1985a, p. 331) has stated,

> [It] seems logical that in an era when party loyalty counts for less and incumbency counts for more, redistricting tactics should include incumbent considerations. Indeed, if recent trends toward independence from the parties continue, redistrictings in the future could come to focus more on [incumbent] displacement issues and less on the partisan makeup of districts.

Thus, a judicial campaign against gerrymandering might also be a largely meaningless sideshow, diverting attention from what should perhaps be the main event.

When all of these factors are taken into account, one is driven to an important but easily overlooked conclusion: Any rule whose application depends on the variable of party performance (however measured) is bound to be highly erratic, perhaps even random, in its effects. No reliable methodology exists that could enable a court or anyone else to isolate the redistricting plan's actual contribution to the electoral outcome. One would need to control for too many unmeasurable factors that powerfully affect party performance. Incumbency effects might easily swamp party and districting effects. Yet *Bandemer's* logic leads to just such a rule. If most contemporary gerrymandering activity is not even directed at party performance, then precious judicial energies that are targeted on partisan gerrymandering—already constrained as that practice is by existing constitutional principles, irreducible political obstacles, and inherent institutional limits—would be tragically misdirected. Moreover, a judicial preoccupation with partisan electoral performance would cast doubt on the legitimacy of election results that may have been influenced only slightly, or not at all, by the gerrymandering effort.

The basic conceptual building blocks of the fair representation argument against partisan gerrymandering—the assumed existence of an identifiable minority party whose "true" strength can be objectively ascertained; the notion that minority votes are "wasted"; and the contention that parties' performances can confidently be ascribed to gerrymandering practices as distinguished from other, potentially more powerful determinants of political outcomes—are highly debatable, if not demonstrably false. These conceptual and administrative dilemmas, moreover, seem insuperable. If the norm of proportionality is applied retrospectively, it presupposes the electoral outcome that "proper" political competition ought to yield, a judgment that no principle can dictate and that no court can legitimately make. If it is implemented prospectively, it would judicially mandate the most fundamental transformation of political processes, structures, and values in our history.

In *Bandemer*, the Court confronted a quintessentially political problem, partisan gerrymandering, for which the courts cannot furnish a satisfactory doctrinal or remedial solution. Indeed, by effectively inviting legal challenges of districting plans despite its disclaimer of that purpose, the Court has created a host of new problems for the lower courts and the electoral process. Court-ordered reform of representational systems based on *Bandemer's* formulation of the problem will either be ineffective or it will be *too* effective. The former would be a cause for regret but not for alarm; the Court's legitimacy will survive and may even prosper from another shootout or standoff with the politicians. The latter, however, would propel the Court (and us with it) down a path whose destination is proportional representation. A change that is so alien to our political institutions should not be taken at the behest of the Court, an institution that—for better *and* for worse—is neither representative nor accountable in any conventional sense.

NOTES

1. This chapter is largely excerpted from a longer paper, "The Thickest Thicket: Partisan Gerrymandering and Judicial Regulation of Politics" that appeared in the *Columbia Law Review*, 87, pp. 1325–84 (November 1987).

2. When the plurality and dissenters *did* divide, it was over an issue that, while methodologically important, was indisputably subsidiary—the question of the number of election cycles over which party performance should be measured. Under that standard, it should be child's play for almost any litigant challenging a districting plan to survive a motion for summary judgment. Applying that standard, it would seem, will almost always require a trial. And until the court reaches a final decision and appeals are exhausted, the legitimacy of elections, and thus of government itself, will remain uncertain. That this is no idle speculation is suggested by the *Richmond* case, *City of Richmond, Va. v. United States*, 422 U.S. 358 (1975), in which the city council remained frozen for seven years while voting rights act litigation continued.

Applications: Indiana

12

Compactness and the 1980s Districts in the Indiana State House: Evidence of Political Gerrymandering?

Richard G. Niemi and John Wilkerson

Ever since the salamander-shaped "Gerry"-mander (1812), bizarre or otherwise noteworthy shapes have been synonymous with partisan gerrymandering. Perhaps as a result, compactness has found its way into the constitution or statutes of fully half of the states (Grofman, 1985a, 177–183). Yet in spite of ancestry and ubiquity that have made it part of the common parlance of legislative districting, compactness has played only a marginal role in judicial decision making. In part this is because until recently partisan gerrymandering was nonjusticiable. But it is also because of an abundance of unrelated definitions of compactness combined with a severe shortage of theoretical and comparative analyses and an almost complete absence of real-world calculations.

In this paper, we analyze the 1980s House districting plan in Indiana using multiple quantitative measures. We find that the 1980s plan is less compact than the plan it replaced; multimember districts are generally less compact than single-member districts; and the "worst-case" districts noted by the Indiana District Court are especially ill-compact. In addition, as shown in Niemi and Wright (chapter 13), the least compact districts contributed heavily to Republican victories. Thus, insofar as compactness is relevant, the findings strengthen the argument that the 1980s plan was a political gerrymander.

COMPACTNESS AS A FACTOR IN
PARTISAN GERRYMANDERING

Though unusual shapes have been a hallmark of partisan gerrymandering from the start, compactness and the closely related concepts of
communities of interest and use of existing political boundaries have
thus far played a minor role in court involvement in political districting. In the 1960s equal population and urban-rural malapportionment
were the key issues. In the 1970s and into the 1980s, racial fairness
was the watchword, with at-large districts, nonretrogression, the 65%
rule, anti-single-shot provisions, and other such questions being considered by the courts. Compactness and related concepts had relatively little to do with these matters.

Factors such as compactness were mentioned, of course, in a number of contexts (as in *Connor v. Finch*, 431 US 407, pp. 422–425), where
it was charged that irregularly shaped districts diluted the voting
strength of blacks. One could even interpret a concern over gerrymandering as a natural extension of the equal population cases; compactness and similar considerations were mentioned as early as *Reynolds v. Sims* (377 US 533 (1964), pp. 578–579) as possible justifications
for deviations from exact equality. Until recently, however, compactness was never the primary consideration. With the Supreme Court's
decision in *Karcher v. Daggett I* (103 S. Ct. 2653 (1983)) and now in
Davis v. Bandemer (106 S. Ct. 2797 (1986)), this may be changing. In
Karcher the issue was still phrased as one of population equality. Yet
Justices Stevens (concurring) and Powell (dissenting) went out of
their way to write opinions castigating the New Jersey plan for its
"wanton" disregard of county boundaries (*Karcher I*, p. 2676) and its
"contorted" districts (p. 2690). Justice White (dissenting, joined by
Chief Justice Burger, Justices Powell and Rehnquist), though saying
less about New Jersey per se, also invited a case involving alleged
gerrymandering. In the process he mentioned compactness and respect for political subdivisions.

Not surprisingly, this invitation was soon taken up by Indiana
Democrats, who charged that the 1980s districting plan was a political
gerrymander, leading initially to the district court decision in *Bandemer
v. Davis* (603 F. Supp. 1479 (1984)). The district court, relying heavily
on Justice Stevens' opinion in *Karcher*, made shape and related characteristics a key factor in its decision. In addition to summary statements about egregious distortions,[1] the majority opinion cited more
than a half dozen specific districts as especially unreasonable in their
shape or in the way they crossed community and county boundaries.

In the Supreme Court, Justice Powell (concurring in part and dissenting in part, joined by Justice Stevens) echoed the theme of compactness and respect for political and community lines. He relied mostly on the district court's analysis but went further by pointing out similar characteristics in some of the state Senate districts. A plurality, however, assigned a secondary role to district shape. Justice White (joined by Justices Brennan, Marshall, and Blackmun) argued that such factors were relevant only if election results (real or projected) showed an expectation of sustained disadvantage to the minority party (*Davis v. Bandemer*, pp. 2814–2815). Then factors such as compactness could be part of an equal protection claim because they speak to intent and because "evidence of valid and invalid configuration would be relevant to whether the districting plan met legitimate state interests" (p. 2815).

Thus, as things stand now, compactness and related factors will play a subsidiary role in gerrymandering claims, as no doubt they should (Cain, 1984, Chapter 3; Niemi et al., 1990). Nonetheless, once a showing of electoral disadvantage is made, these features will become important. For this reason, as well as the possibility of changes in emphasis as the Court confronts future cases, it is important to understand the concept of compactness and its various operationalizations.

COMPACTNESS IN INDIANA

To assess systematically the compactness of Indiana's state House districts, we will use two of the most common quantitative measures. The first is from a class of "dispersion measures," so-called because they assess the degree to which the area of the district is "bunched together" or "spread out." Though sounding complex—the ratio of the district area to the area of the circle with diameter equal to the district's longest axis—the "longest-axis circle" measure is simple both conceptually and operationally. In addition, it is usually identical to the ratio of the district area to the area of the smallest circumscribing circle, which is used by Hofeller and Grofman to describe California's districts (chapter 14); when the measures are not equal, the one we use is considerably simpler to compute.[2] The second measure is a "perimeter measure," which assesses the degree to which district boundaries weave and twist. Area/perimeter is basically the area of the district divided by the square of the perimeter.[3]

Like most measures of compactness, the ones we use here are invariant to size. Both vary between zero and one, assigning zero to the least compact and one to the most compact district. For both measures, a circle is perfectly compact, and long, narrow districts have compactness values approaching zero.[4] However, except in ideal circumstances the two measures will assign different scores to individual districts.

The two measures are likely to order a set of districts (i.e., with respect to their compactness) in roughly similar though not identical ways. They may or may not give the same ordering to alternative districting plans. That, in fact, is one of the major considerations here: Is the 1980s districting plan in Indiana ill-compact when judged by multiple measures of compactness? Because no single measure of compactness is perfect inasmuch as they all measure different aspects of the concept (Niemi et al., 1990), consistency is important. If both measures point to a particular plan or particular districts as noncompact, the evidence is much stronger than if a plan is more compact by one definition and less compact by another.

In Table 12.1 we show the two compactness values for all 77 districts under the 1980s Indiana districting plan.[5] Summary scores are shown at the bottom of the table. In this instance the averages for the two measures are identical. As noted, however, the two scores differ across districts. The correlation between them is .66 (Pearson r) using the actual scores and .67 (Spearman rho) using the district rankings. For both measures, but especially the dispersion measure, the range is sharply truncated at the top.

Significantly, the measures yield consistent conclusions about the overall 1980s districting plan and parts of it. It is clear, first of all, that the 1980s plan is less compact than the 1970s plan (Table 12.2). This is so despite the fact that the most compact individual districts are found in the 1980s. The differences between the 1970s and 1980s averages are not large. How meaningful such a difference is will perhaps be apparent after more computations of this sort are available. It should be noted, however, that not all district lines would need to be manipulated to have an effective gerrymander. An average decline of .04–.05 over 77 districts may in fact be quite substantial (especially when the overall range is .4 or .5 as here rather than the theoretical maximum of 1.0).

Analysis of specific parts of the plan gives an indication of why the 1980s districts are less compact overall. The district court, and Justice Powell in his dissenting opinion, cited the multimember districts as especially discriminatory in that "they were intentionally employed to minimize Democratic voting power" (*Davis v. Bandemer*, p. 2837).

TABLE 12.1. Compactness of 1980s Indiana House Districts

District	"Longest-Axis Circle" Area/[π(Longest axis/2)^2]	"Area/Perimeter" 4πArea/Perimeter^2
1	.52	.64
2	.58	.51
3	.32	.39
4	.42	.31
5	.46	.44
6	.53	.41
7	.53	.68
8	.24	.33
9	.43	.45
10	.54	.47
11	.16	.31
12	.20	.30
13	.33	.44
14	.32	.47
15	.42	.51
16	.40	.32
17	.43	.32
18	.48	.45
19	.55	.52
20	.26	.27
21	.41	.51
22	.24	.32
23	.29	.31
24	.49	.46
25	.44	.28
26	.23	.34
27	.49	.67
28	.29	.31
29	.62	.37
30	.50	.61
31	.51	.47
32	.42	.47
33	.41	.41
34	.52	.73
35	.56	.56
36	.37	.31
37	.57	.62
38	.39	.42
39	.30	.31
40	.36	.27
41	.37	.40
42	.20	.21

(continued)

TABLE 12.1. (*Continued*)

District	"Longest-Axis Circle" Area/[π(Longest axis/2)²]	"Area/Perimeter" 4πArea/Perimeter²
43	.30	.44
44	.40	.44
45	.22	.18
46	.29	.26
47	.52	.29
48	.30	.24
49	.38	.30
50	.31	.36
51	.40	.37
52	.59	.44
53	.36	.28
54	.56	.55
55	.43	.36
56	.50	.61
57	.47	.35
58	.44	.54
59	.52	.40
60	.47	.45
61	.41	.58
62	.33	.25
63	.46	.31
64	.30	.23
65	.37	.41
66	.28	.22
67	.44	.36
68	.37	.38
69	.47	.30
70	.27	.23
71	.48	.72
72	.66	.66
73	.23	.18
74	.28	.24
75	.31	.38
76	.51	.29
77	.41	.51
All districts		
Mean	.40	.40
Standard Deviation	.11	.13
Minimum-maximum	.16–.66	.18–.73

Averages are calculated before rounding.

The Marion County districts were "particularly suspect with respect to compactness" (*Bandemer v. Davis*, p. 1487).

The multimember districts are indeed less compact if one compares them with the 1970s multimember districts, though they have about the same degree of compactness as the 1980s single-member districts (Table 12.3). The 1980s Marion County districts, though not highly dispersed, have considerably longer perimeters, given their area, than any other set of districts.

The district court also cited a set of 10 "worst-case" districts "whose irrational shapes," according to Justice Powell, "called out for justification" (*Davis v. Bandemer*, p. 2834).[6] While these districts were not chosen on the basis of shape alone—"communities of interest" were mentioned as well—we would expect them to be less compact than other districts. Indeed they are (Table 12.4). By both dispersion and perimeter measures, the worst case districts are far and away the least compact of the sets of districts examined.

Not surprisingly, there is a range of compactness scores for each of the groups of districts that we have discussed. It is appropriate, then, to turn the question around in the sense of looking at the least compact districts according to the quantitative measures and seeing whether these include the multimember and worst-case districts. We should ask, in other words, if we began with the quantitative measures rather than with the court's analysis, which districts would we cite as ill-compact?

Examining the top and bottom quartiles of the 1980s districts yields the results in Table 12.5. Obviously there are districts not cited by the court that are ill-compact and multimember districts cited by the court that are, by these quantitative measures, relatively nicely shaped. This is not really surprising; the district court noted both that it was not providing an exhaustive list of the poorly compact districts (*Bandemer v. Davis*, p. 1494) and that its list of notably bad districts was not based on geography alone. Nevertheless, there are cautionary notes in these distributions about careless use of or over-reliance on quantitative compactness scores.

Quantitative measures fail to distinguish between naturally and intentionally noncompact districts. For example, the districts that are identified as least compact by the perimeter measure (and are two of the four least compact by the dispersion score) trace natural features (rivers) for a substantial portion of their boundaries. At least portions of their meandering borders are of no particular political consequence. Even noncompact districts that follow manmade features

TABLE 12.2. Average Compactness of 1980s
and 1970s Indiana House Districts

	"Longest-Axis Circle"	"Area-Perimeter"
1980s Districts		
Mean	.40	.40
Standard deviation	.11	.13
Minimum-maximum	.16–.66	.18–.73
1970s Districts		
Mean	.45	.44
Standard deviation	.11	.13
Minimum-maximum	.20–.62	.19–.70

TABLE 12.3. Compactness of 1980s
and 1970s Multimember Districts

	"Longest-Axis Circle"	"Area-Perimeter"
1980s Single-Member Districts $n = 61$		
Mean	.41	.40
Standard deviation	.11	.14
Minimum-maximum	.20–.66	.18–.73
1980s Multimember Districts $n = 16^*$		
Mean	.39	.41
Standard deviation	.13	.11
Minimum-maximum	.16–.59	.24–.68
1970s Multimember Districts $n = 20$		
Mean	.43	.48
Standard deviation	.11	.13
Minimum-maximum	.26–.60	.27–.70
1970s Marion County Districts $n = 5$		
Mean	.40	.34
Standard deviation	.11	.07
Minimum-maximum	.30–.59	.24–.44

*Includes the Marion County districts shown separately below.

**TABLE 12.4. Compactness of 1980s
"Worst-Case" Districts**

	"Longest-Axis Circle"	"Area-Perimeter"
1980s Worst Case Districts n = 10		
Mean	.29	.24
Standard deviation	.06	.04
Minimum-maximum	.22–.44	.18–.32

TABLE 12.5. Quantitative Compactness Compared to Court-Cited Districts

	"Worst-Case" Districts		Multimember Districts	
	Dispersion	Perimeter	Dispersion	Perimeter
19 (25%) Least Compact Districts	9	9	4	4
19 (25%) Most Compact Districts	0	0	5	3

Note: Results show the number of worst-case districts (out of 10) and multimember districts (out of 16) judged to be least and most compact according to the longest-axis circle and area/perimeter measures.

may not be gerrymandered (e.g., they may follow county boundaries that for historical reasons twist and turn). Conversely, districts whose shapes do not immediately call them to attention may be gerrymandered because of the specific (relatively regularly shaped) areas that they combine.

The results in Table 12.5 add to our theoretical understanding that compactness alone—even if one were to adopt Justice Powell's stance rather than that of the plurality—is not a foolproof guide to the presence of a gerrymandered plan or to the identification of gerrymandered districts. Moreover, there is presently too little solid empirical evidence about compactness for us easily to judge the significance of the results presented here. Nonetheless, the consistency of results from the two measures (i.e., relative agreement between the district court and the quantitative measures that some of the multimember districts and certain other identifiable districts are very ill-compact) plus evidence that the noncompact districts contributed to Democratic losses (chapter 13), are at least sufficient to raise serious questions about the legitimacy of the state's interest in drawing the 1980s district boundaries. Our findings are not proof of, but they are consistent with, the presence of a political gerrymander in Indiana in the 1980s.

CONCLUSION

If the future treatment of political gerrymandering by the courts is relatively unclear, the place of compactness in identifying gerrymanders is especially cloudy. If one judges simply by the opinion of the plurality in *Bandemer*, compactness will play a minimal role. But with a lineage going back to the original gerrymander, inclusion in many state constitutions, and a greatly expanded technical ability to calculate proposed measures, compactness may become a more significant, if secondary, consideration in future cases. Whether quantitative measures will be of much use is more problematic still. The analysis here reveals agreement of multiple measures in an important case; yet it also highlights some of the technical problems associated with quantitative measures, such as their failure to account properly for natural geographical features.

Our best guess is that if quantitative measures have a role to play, it is in alerting analysts to districts or to entire plans that appear to be substandard with regard to shape. More detailed analyses by individuals familiar with the areas in question can then be directed specifically at those plans. With their considerable variety, quantitative scores may also play a part in pinpointing the specific features of districts, such as their perimeters, that are considered poorly drawn. In these roles, newly understood quantitative measures may in fact make real contributions to the identification of and prevention of gerrymanders.

*Acknowledgments.*This research was supported by National Science Foundation Grant No. SES-8421050.

NOTES

1. "The lack of compactness in the present plan is clearly supportive of the plaintiffs' argument that partisan considerations are unconstitutionally reflected in the redistricting lines. . . . Repeated examples exist of bizarre district configurations, drawn with no recognition or adherence to political subdivisions such as municipalities and counties" (*Bandemer v. Davis*, p. 1493).
2. By our measure, dispersion $= A/\pi r^2$, where $A =$ the area of the district,

$r = L/2$, and L = the district's longest axis. (The longest axis is the greatest distance between two points in the district, which may be on a line that goes outside the district itself.)

3. Formally, area/perimeter = 4π(area)/perimeter^2. The adjustments are so that the measure varies between zero and one, with one being the compactness of a circle.

4. Maximum: The area of a circle with radius r is πr^2. The longest axis is $2r$ (the diameter of the circle), so the area of the longest-axis circle also equals πr^2. The perimeter of a circle equals $2\pi r$; therefore both numerator and denominator of the area/perimeter measure equal $4\pi^2 r^2$. Minimum: For a given area, if one "stretches out" the district so it has almost no "width," it will have virtually zero area (the numerator of both measures) and yet have positive longest axis and perimeter (the denominator); therefore both measures will be zero.

5. We traced the boundaries of individual districts onto transparencies, digitized them using an optical image scanner, and used a computer to calculate compactness measures. Although the accuracy seems adequate for our initial work, we hope to improve it, especially by increasing the size and therefore the detail of the maps that we can work with.

6. Districts 20, 22, 25, 45, 46, 48, 62, 66, 70, 73, electing 14 representatives (20 and 48 are three-member districts).

13

Majority-Win Percentages: An Approach to the Votes-Seats Relationship in Light of *Davis v. Bandemer*

Richard Niemi and Stephen G. Wright

Initial reactions to the Supreme Court's ruling in *Davis v. Bandemer* (106 S. Ct. 2797 (1986)) suggested tortured logic and indecision. Witness, for example, the Toles' cartoon, which showed a snakelike sentence proclaiming that "gerrymandering is unconstitutional, in some cases, even when districts meet one-person one-vote requirements," and so on for nearly a dozen more clauses (*Buffalo News*, July 6, 1986). In fact, the decision and accompanying arguments may be less convoluted than they first appeared to be. As Justice White noted (*Davis v. Bandemer*, p. 2805), the 1962 case of *Baker v. Carr* only determined justiciability and certainly did not settle all the questions of how to measure population equality and what deviations from exact equality were permissible. When we consider the greater complexity of the gerrymandering issue, it is not surprising that much was left undecided by the *Bandemer* ruling. Moreover, there are strong clues in the plurality opinion as to what is needed to demonstrate an impermissible gerrymander.

In this paper we draw on the plurality opinion written by Justice White to suggest the kind of work needed to show (an expectation of) the "continued frustration of the will of a majority of the voters" (*Davis v. Bandemer*, p. 2811). Our approach is analogous to what in the political science literature has been called swing ratio analysis, but it is designed specifically to address major points made by the plurality.

The analysis inevitably deals with what might have been. While no analysis that deals with hypotheticals is absolutely conclusive, the results strengthen the argument that the 1980s districting in Indiana was a political gerrymander and that the minority party suffered a long-term handicap.

THE PLURALITY OPINION: FAIRNESS IN THE EXPECTED VOTES-SEATS RELATIONSHIP

The plurality opinion in *Davis v. Bandemer* emphasized that a "threshold" showing of discriminatory vote dilution was required. The plurality explicitly rejected the reliance of Justices Powell and Stevens on factors not tied directly to the votes-seats relationship: Even though factors such as district shape suggest an intention to discriminate, a finding of unconstitutional discrimination requires that "the redistricting does in fact disadvantage it [the minority party] at the polls" (pp. 2813–2814).

The relationship between votes and seats is thus of paramount importance. But the plurality rejected the notion that disproportionate results from a single election are sufficient to find a constitutional violation. Establishing unconstitutional gerrymandering requires evidence of the "continued frustration of the will of the majority" (p. 2811); "[r]elying on a single election to prove unconstitutional discrimination is unsatisfactory" (p. 2812).

A third point follows by inference. Since the interest of the plaintiff is generally in overturning a districting plan before any elections are held under the challenged plan—or perhaps after a single election—some sort of projected results are almost certainly necessary in identifying a gerrymander.[1] Recent past elections may also be relevant, as we shall see, but because they are based on a different districting plan, they are necessarily of limited value.

Finally, while the plurality emphasized the importance of demonstrating statewide discrimination, they also noted that analysis of particular districts may be useful. Specifically, "[i]t could be, were the necessary threshold effect to be shown, that multimember districts could be demonstrated to be suspect on the ground that they are particularly useful in attaining impermissibly discriminatory ends" (p. 2812). We shall in fact examine the multimember districts as well as a set of "worst-case" districts after examining the overall results in the next section.

TABLE 13.1. Democratic Percentage of Two-Party Vote and Seats Won,
Indiana State House and Senate Elections, 1970–1988

	House			Senate		
Year	Votes	Seats	Difference	Votes	Seats	Difference
1970	50.0%	46.0%	−4.0	51.9%	56.0%	+4.1
1972	45.2	27.0	−18.2	41.5	23.1	−18.4
1974	53.9	56.0	+2.1	56.6	68.0	+11.4
1976	51.7	48.0	−3.7	50.0	48.0	−2.0
1978	50.2	46.0	−4.2	49.5	40.0	−9.5
1980	46.8	37.0	−9.8	43.6	20.0	−23.6
1982	51.6	43.0	−8.6	53.1	52.0	−1.1
1984	44.0	39.0	−6.0	42.3	28.0	−14.3
1986	50.9	48.0	−2.9	54.3	52.0	−2.3
1988	49.6	50.0	+0.4	44.6	44.0	−2.6

Source: Calculated by authors from State of Indiana, 1970–1988 Election Reports.

INDIANA IN 1982: CONTINUED FRUSTRATION OF THE WILL OF THE MAJORITY?

Given the plurality's emphasis on the inability to identify a gerrymander from a single election, an obvious first step is to compare the
1982 election results with outcomes from previous years. Table 13.1
shows the Democratic percentages of votes and seats in the last ten
elections, held under three different districting plans.[2] We show results for both houses, but we shall defer discussion of the Senate until
later. It should be pointed out that in 1971, as in 1981, the Republicans
controlled both houses of the legislature and the governorship. The
districting plan utilized in 1970 was created in 1965 under Democratic
control of both the governorship and the state legislature.[3]

Note that in four of the five House elections in which the Democrats earned a majority of the votes, they won a minority of the seats.[4]
In addition, in 1970 a change of less than one-tenth of 1% of the votes
would again have given the Democrats a majority of the votes, and
such a small change—even if concentrated entirely in districts that
the Democrats just barely lost—could not have given them a majority
of seats. Thus there is reason to suspect that the 1982 result is not an
isolated case but part of a pattern of results in which the Democrats,
when chosen by a majority of voters, do not win control of the House.

Still, the Democrats did win a majority of the seats in the House in one year (1974), and they came very close in other years. In 1976, for example, three more seats would have given them a majority, and the Democratic candidates in districts 60, 25, and 6 lost by only .5%, .7%, and 1.4% of the vote, respectively. In 1986—though this result was not available to the District Court or the Supreme Court at the time of their deliberations—the Democrats almost won a majority of the seats, with just over 50% of the statewide vote. Thus one must ask, is there anything special about the 1982 result, along with the historical data just presented, that would suggest unconstitutional discrimination? The larger-than-average discrepancy between votes and seats in 1982 suggests that there might be, but what would that evidence be?

One way to approach this question is posed by the *Bandemer* plurality. Justice White wrote that "the District Court did not ask by what percentage the statewide Democratic vote would have had to increase to control either the House or the Senate" (p. 2812). In fact, the state argued, "without a persuasive response," according to White, that "had the Democratic candidates received an additional few percentage points of the votes cast statewide, they would have obtained a majority of the seats in both houses" (p. 2812). But the 1982 results, if combined with statewide voting statistics from the 1970s, suggest that the Democrats would have had a remarkably difficult time winning a majority in the House.

Consider the 1982 results. The Democrats won 43 of the 100 House seats, so they needed 8 more seats to have a majority. The most likely seats for them to have won are, of course, those in which they already received relatively close to 50% of the votes. For example, the Democratic candidate in district 22 won 48.5% of the vote, so with just over 1.6% more of the vote, he would have won; with just over 1.9% more of the vote, one of the Democrats in district 31 would have won, and so on.

Now for these candidates to have won a greater percentage of the vote, it is not a logical necessity for the Democratic vote elsewhere in the state to have been greater. If the Democratic (Republican) candidate in district 22 had had a bit more (less) attractive personality, if the Democrat (Republican) had campaigned a little harder (less hard), if more of the district's Democrats (fewer Republicans) had gone to the polls, and so on, the Democrat would have won even if the vote remained the same outside that district. It seems fair to presume, however, that each party nominated the best candidate it could, that both candidates campaigned as effectively as they were able, and that there were no factors that systematically reduced Democratic or in-

TABLE 13.2. Projected Democratic Percentage of Two-Party Vote Needed to Win A Majority of Seats, Indiana State House and Senate, 1970–1986

Year	House	Senate
1970	51.6%	50.6%
1972	51.8	54.0
1974	53.5	51.2
1976	53.2	51.0
1978	53.4	52.0
1980	53.7	49.8
1982	56.4	52.0
1984	54.1	56.1
1986	55.2	53.4
1988	50.3	53.0

creased Republican turnout in this particular district in this specific election.

It seems particularly fair to assume that the parties made their best efforts in these districts because they are, by definition, among the most competitive in the state, so the parties had the greatest incentive to do well. In addition, the election result depends on the actions of both parties. The Democrats might have won the close seats if they had better targeted their efforts. But this conclusion is a post-hoc judgment about which districts should have been targeted; there were districts that the Democrats barely won, and probably districts where the election looked as if it would be closer than it was, and these were also excellent districts to target. Moreover, had the Democrats targeted the districts that they barely lost, Republicans might have targeted these districts as well.

A reasonable assumption, therefore, is that for Democratic candidates to have won in these close districts, the Democrats would have had to win proportionately more votes statewide. That is, for the Democrat in district 22 to have won 1.6% more of the vote in his district, the Democrats would have had to win 1.6% more of the vote statewide, and so on. Using this approach, one can calculate "majority-win percentages": the percentage of the statewide Democratic vote required for the Democrats to control the House. Such a calculation for each of the past ten elections is shown in Table 13.2.

Note first that the percentage of the vote required for a Democratic House majority was greater in 1982 than for any other year shown. But the most important datum is that for the Democrats to control the

House in 1982, they would have had to win more votes than they had won in any of the prior six elections, including the Democratic high point of 1974. Indiana has long been regarded as a swing state, as both the District Court (*Bandemer v. Davis*, p. 1485) and Supreme Court (p. 2812) noted. And indeed, at its lowest point (1984), the Democrats received over 43% of the statewide vote for House candidates. Yet they never won more than the 53.9% garnered in 1974, and under the current districting plan, estimates based on 1982 results indicate that they would have needed nearly 57% of the vote to gain a majority of the seats. After the fact, we can also see that the Democrats would have had to win more votes in 1984 and in 1986 than they had won at any time from 1970 to 1980 if they were to win a majority of seats.

Of course, elections are somewhat unpredictable, as the various estimates in Table 13.2 remind us. As a consequence of this inherent unpredictability, one cannot say with certainty that the districting plan in force renders the Democrats a long-term minority party (cf. 1988). Yet we also know that there is a great deal of regularity in voting behavior. The very fact that the Indiana House Democratic vote has not been higher than 54% nor lower than 44% since 1970 is evidence of that.

Given this regularity and the need to make a decision about the likely consequences of a districting plan, the fact that Indiana voters in 1982 again gave a majority of their votes to the Democrats, together with the fact that they would have had to give a larger-than-ever proportion of their votes to the Democrats in order for them to obtain a majority of the House seats, strongly suggest that the districting plan enacted by the Republicans in 1981 is in fact evidence of "continued frustration of the will of the majority."

One might look at the 1970s and 1980s districting in another way. Figure 13.1 shows the Republican vote percentages in each of the House districts they won in 1980 and 1982. It shows, first, that winning percentages were less likely to cluster very close to 50% in 1982. This is, of course, an alternative demonstration of why the Democrats would have had to gain over 5% more of the statewide vote in order to capture a majority of the seats. But it also makes two points about the possible aims of the Republicans in designing the 1981 plan. In comparison with 1980, the Republicans may have set out to protect marginal Republican seats; in any event, the plan had this effect, giving the winners in the least Republican seats a cushion they did not have in 1980.[5] But there is also some suggestion that the Republicans were not unmindful of the goal of winning seats efficiently. The modal winning percentage moves toward the left in 1982 even though

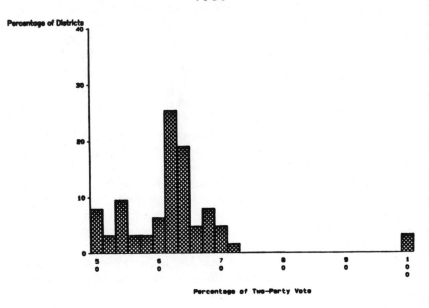

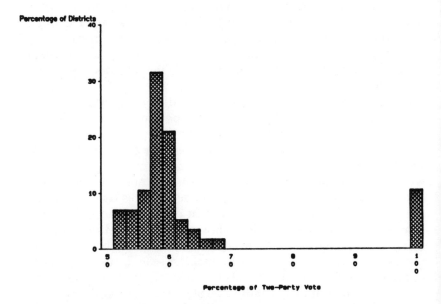

FIG. 13.1. Republican Winning Percentages, Indiana State House, 1980 and 1982

the number of uncontested seats goes up. This perspective on the 1982 election thus supports the contention that the districting plan of 1981 has the look of a very well-designed gerrymander.

MULTIMEMBER AND "WORST-CASE" DISTRICTS

As noted earlier, the plurality opinion suggested that some kinds of districts might be especially likely to account for the differences between winning proportions of votes and seats. To explore this possibility—always with an eye toward post-1982 effects—we can do an almost identical analysis of the votes-seats relationship in sets of districts identified as particularly problematic. Of course, in analyzing subsets of the legislature, it is less reasonable to expect that the party winning a majority of the votes will always win a majority of the seats. For example, in a set of three districts, one party may win one district by a wide margin and lose the other two with just under 50% of the votes, thereby winning a solid majority of the votes but only one out of three seats. Moreover, for this sort of analysis to make sense, the districts must not be chosen initially on the basis of the electoral strength of the parties; it would be tautological to select a set of districts, all of which were heavily Republican, and then conclude that it would take a very large shift in votes for these districts to swing to the Democrats. In Indiana two sets of districts are appropriate for consideration: multimember districts and those districts identified by the district court as especially ill-compact or otherwise badly drawn.

Consider first the multimember districts. Justice White, echoing the district court, cited the fact that in Marion and Allen counties, the Democratic candidates won 46.3% of the votes and only 14.3% of the seats (3 of 21). While such a large votes-seats discrepancy is "startling" (p. 2836) and might appear to speak for itself (*Bandemer v. Davis*, p. 1489), it should be noted that in the multimember districts as a whole, the Democrats won 38% of the seats (compared to 53.3% of the votes). Moreover, because of the nature of multimember districts, it is possible that the Democrats would have gained a large number of seats had they won just 1% or 2% more of the votes in each district.[6]

What we need to consider, then, is the number of seats the Democrats might have captured if they had won somewhat more of the vote. Using the same assumptions as in the previous section, this is easily derived from the distribution of winning margins of the 39 House members elected from multimember districts. The first column of Table 13.3 shows that if the Democrats had won 5% more of the vote in each district, they would have picked up only one additional

TABLE 13.3. Democratic Vote Percentages in Multimember and "Worst-Case" Districts, Indiana State House and Senate, 1982

Democratic Percentage of Two-Party Vote	Number of Seats in Multimember Districts (House only)	Number of Seats in "Worst-Case" Districts	
		House	Senate
60–100	11	5	2 (1984)
55–59.9	2	0	0
50–54.9	2	1	0
45–49.9	1	1	0
44–44.9	2	2	0
43–43.9	1	0	0
42–42.9	2	0	0
41–41.9	9	1	1 (1982)
40–40.9	3	1	0
Below 40	6	3	5 (1,1982;4,1984)
Total	39	14	8

seat. Indeed, they would not have gained a substantial number of these seats until they had won over 8% more votes than in 1982. Since their historical high between 1970 and 1980 was less than 2.5% more than they won in 1982 (Table 13.1), it is indeed likely on the basis of the 1982 results that the multimember districts would contribute significantly to future discrepancies between the Democratic proportion of votes and seats. Insofar as one could project that the Democrats would be frustrated should they win a majority of votes, one can point especially to the results in the multimember districts.

A second set of districts to examine are those identified by the district court as especially strong examples of "bizarre" or "irrational" map-making (pp. 1487, 1493–1494).[7] Since these districts were identified on the basis of their shapes and their lack of recognition of traditional political boundaries, and not on the basis of their voting records (though the district court was well aware of probable partisan reasons for drawing these lines), it makes sense to examine them as a bloc to see how the Democrats would have fared had they won more votes than they did in 1982. The votes in these districts are listed in Table 13.3.

Compared to the multimember districts, these "worst case" districts were not quite so unfavorable to the Democrats' hypothetical future prospects. With slightly over a 5% gain, for example, the Democrats would have picked up 3 of the 14 seats in worst-case districts (compared to 3 out of 39 in the multimember districts). Still, as noted, a 5% gain over 1982 would require a larger vote for the Democrats than they had won in over a decade. The evidence from 1982, therefore, suggests that the most egregiously misshapen districts would also contribute to continued frustration of the will of the majority.

THE SENATE

Most of the discussion in *Davis v. Bandemer* concerns the disproportionate votes-seats result in the 1982 House election. Relatively little has been said about the state Senate election in the same year, presumably because the relationship between seats and votes was almost exactly proportional: Democrats won 52% of the seats (13 of 25 up for election) with 53.1% of the votes. Assuming uniform changes across districts, Table 13.2 shows that the Democrats could have won this number of seats (which is a bare majority of those up for election) with 52% of the votes. This "majority win percentage" is in line with similar estimates from the 1970s and is within the range of votes that Democrats had won in the 1970s as well as in 1982.

Despite these near-proportionate results, there is reason to suspect that the 1982 Senate election camouflaged a gerrymander of these district lines as well as those of the House. Justice Powell noted the Democrats' contention that "most of the Senate seats won by Democrats in 1982 were 'safe' Democratic seats" (*Davis v. Bandemer*, p. 2837) and that in 1984 the Democrats won 42.3% of the votes and only 28% of the seats. He also noted that irregularly shaped and cross-county districts characterized Senate as well as House districts (p. 2833, n. 16 and p. 2837, n. 24).

With the benefit of hindsight, we can see that there may be some truth to this suggestion. As noted, the Democrats won considerably fewer seats than votes in 1984. In fact, using the same assumptions as above, they would have had to win over 56% of the votes to win a majority of the seats up for election. If one were simply to combine the 1982 and 1984 results, it would suggest that the Democrats would have had to win 53.2% of the two-year vote to win a majority of the Senate seats, a percentage achieved only in the Democratic landslide year of 1974 and the 1986 midterm election and surely never achieved two elections in a row.[8]

Courts, of course, would normally not have the benefit of a second election, so they typically would not be able to consider an election in all Senate seats. (Over half of the upper houses nationwide have staggered terms.) Thus, if one wished in 1982 to have an estimate of votes-seats relationship for the entire upper house, some sort of hypothetical results would have to be used. If election districts for the two houses were nested, we could use lower house results, combining the multiple house districts that make up a single Senate district. Alternatively, if the results of some other election were compiled by Senate districts, those results could be used. Unfortunately, in Indiana the House and Senate districts are not nested, and no other election results are recorded by Senate district. Thus, it would be a major task to construct hypothetical 1982 results for the Senate seats that were not up for reelection, and we have not undertaken that chore. Assuming, however, that such a construction would approximate the actual outcome in 1984, the analysis above lends support to the conclusion based on the House results that the 1980s redistricting would continually frustrate the majority if more than half of the Indiana voters were to support the Democrats in two successive elections.

With respect to "worst-case" districts in the Senate, only two districts identified by Justice Powell (p. 2837) as having bizarre shapes held elections in 1982, so no conclusion can be drawn from that year alone. In 1984 six more such districts held elections. The number is still small, but the distribution of Democratic vote percentages (Table 13.3) supports the conclusion based on the House elections that these districts would continue to be a source of votes-seats discrepancies.

CONCLUSION

Our analysis should not be interpreted as a partisan brief for the Democrats in Indiana. We did not set out to show that a gerrymander existed but rather to see how the votes-seats relationship could be examined for more conclusive evidence of the sort called for in the plurality opinion. The results might well have shown majority-win percentages within the normal range of recent votes. In that case we would have interpreted the findings as failing to show the continued frustration of the will of the majority in spite of the disproportionate 1982 results. As it is, results based on the information available to the courts immediately after the 1982 election are consistent with the conclusion that the districting in the Indiana House represented a political gerrymander. Moreover, there is suggestive evidence that the same may have been true of the Senate even though the seat-votes proportions in the 1982 election could hardly have been more similar.

The important point on which to conclude, however, is not regarding Indiana in the 1980s but whether the procedures outlined here could lead to a simple standard for determining the existence of an unconstitutional gerrymander. In a trivial sense the answer is obviously no; if courts were to adopt the approach outlined here, it would surely not end all controversy. One might argue, for example, about the assumption of uniform statewide changes in calculating majority-win percentages; and there is the question we raised earlier about the appropriate period of comparison. There are also multiple ways of calculating majority-win percentages. Instead of using the results of the 1982 election, one might use votes from 1980, calculating the number of seats that would have gone to a given party assuming the new district boundaries. Or one might use voter registration figures or some strongly partisan vote (as suggested, for example, by Backstrom, Robins, and Eller, 1978, pp. 1131–1139; chapter 6) to estimate the partisanship of each district. These alternative calculations might be justified on the grounds that they can be made before any elections are held and that they utilize the very information available to legislators during the districting process.

Despite these unresolved points, the matter is no different in many respects from that of population equality. Even now, more than two decades after the principle was enunciated, there is controversy over exactly how to apply the one-person, one-vote requirement. Whether a given deviation from exact equality is permissible depends not only on the mathematical count but on the strength of the case that can be made for the deviations. If a strong case can be made, deviations 5% or more above the nominal maximum of 10% deviation may be permissible in state legislative cases (*Mahan v. Howell*, 410 U.S. 315 (1973)), but weak to nonexistent justification is insufficient to permit even a 1% deviation from the 0% standard used in congressional cases (*Karcher v. Daggett I*, 103 S. Ct. 2653 (1983)).

Similar reasoning will surely apply in gerrymandering cases. If alternative procedures for calculating majority-win percentages yield consistent results, the case for or against a gerrymander ruling is that much stronger. If using three or four or five past elections all point to the same conclusion, there is that much more reason to believe it. If the majority-win percentage for a given party is well above the highest recent vote for that party, the case is much stronger than if the percentage is just barely above the highest recent vote.

In the end, it is unlikely that the question of political gerrymandering will ever surrender to quantification to the extent that the equal population requirement does. Nonetheless, to the degree that the present analysis is persuasive, it disputes Justice O'Connor's contention that there is no "judicially manageable standard for adjudicating political gerrymandering claims" (*Davis v. Bandemer*, p. 2822). Certainly there are no agreed-upon standards as yet. It is much less clear that such standards are inherently unreachable.

Acknowledgments. This research was supported by National Science Foundation Grant No. SES-8421050.

NOTES

1. Justice White clearly recognizes this point. See p. 2814, note 17.
2. So that votes in multimember districts are weighted appropriately, we divided the party vote total in each multimember district by the number of that party's candidates.
3. Exactly how many previous elections are relevant is rather arbitrary, and in a court test, some of the dispute would no doubt center on justifications for the choice made. One justification here is that by including 1970 we find a fourth instance in which the Democrats won a majority of the vote. In addition, the 1970 election was the one that chose the legislature that created the districting plan in effect throughout the rest of the 1970s. Finally, we note that, despite the fact that the redistricting plan in use at the time of the 1970 election was drawn by Democrats, by 1970 the plan had the support of the Republican governor against suits brought by Democrats challenging the constitutionality of this plan (Hardy et al., 1982, pp. 112–114).
4. That the Democrats typically won fewer seats than votes when they won a *minority* of the vote is no surprise. One could, of course, question the magnitude of the votes/seats discrepancy in those instances, but in nonproportional representation systems a party winning a majority of the votes almost always wins a larger proportion of the seats (Rae, 1971; Tufte, 1973).
5. The districting plan could not assure all Republican incumbents of reelection: five Republican incumbents lost in 1982, all but one receiving more than 47% of the vote. Thus, despite partisan intentions—"We wanted to save as many incumbent Republicans as possible" (*Bandemer v. Davis*, 603 F. Supp. at 1484)—election results remain somewhat unpredictable.
6. The only thorough analysis of the partisan effects of multimember districts found no systematic underrepresentation of the statewide minority party (Niemi, Hill, and Grofman, 1985). Often the minority party actually benefited from pockets of strength in which it won all of the area's legislators because of multimember districts.
7. For the House, we utilize the districts explicitly cited by the District Court. For more discussion of these districts, see Niemi and Wilkerson (chap. 12).
8. This calculation measures the changes in the Democratic vote necessary to win a majority of the 50 senate seats up for election in 1982 and 1984 combined, assuming, as earlier, uniform changes across districts. Democrats won 20 of the 50 seats in the 1982–1984 period with 47.2% of the two-party vote. To win a majority of seats would have required an increase of six percentage points in the Democratic vote in each district, or 53.2% of the overall vote.

Applications: California

14

Comparing the Compactness of California Congressional Districts Under Three Different Plans: 1980, 1982, and 1984

Thomas Hofeller and Bernard Grofman

Gerrymandering is the drawing of boundaries of districts, so as to advantage candidates of one political or racial group at the expense of another. While ill-compactness has often been proposed as the hallmark of a gerrymander, we believe that it is better seen as a potential indicator of gerrymandering. In our view, analysis of ill-compactness must be coupled with an analysis of the political (racial) consequences of boundary manipulations if it is to be relevant to a determination of probable partisan (racial) gerrymandering (Grofman, 1983a; Niemi et al., 1990).

Gerrymandering is based on the wasting or weakening of the votes of what is usually the minority political party or racial interest group. This is accomplished by packing minority voting strength in a limited number of districts, and/or by fracturing smaller areas of concentrations of minority voting strength and submerging them in districts with just enough majority voting strength to render them ineffective. Usually both of these methods of dilution are present in gerrymanders involving large numbers of districts. The gerrymander does not require the construction of irregularly shaped districts in all situations. There are many instances, particularly in racial gerrymandering, when very compact districts can, if cleverly drawn, result in plans that are dilutive of minority voting strength.

While irregular boundaries can result from an attempt to follow neutral criteria, it is unlikely that a plan with a significant number of irregularly shaped districts does not have some of its irregularities due to gerrymandering. The combination of ill-compactness and other evidence of gerrymandering intent, when combined with indicia of gerrymandering effects, should shift the burden of proof to those drafting (or defending) a plan to explain why districts are not compact. (Cf. the view of Justice Stevens in *Karcher v. Daggett (I)*, 462 U.S. 725 (1983).)

We look at the compactness of three congressional plans for a single state, the state of California: the Masters' Plan, adopted in 1973 and used for the 94th through the 97th Congress (43 seats); the plan adopted in 1981 (commonly known as Burton I in honor of the late Congressman Philip Burton who was its chief drafter) and used for only one election (1982, the 98th Congress), because it was subsequently rejected by voter referendum (45 seats); and the plan adopted in 1982 (commonly known as Burton II), which was used in the 1984 and 1986 elections (the 99th and 100th Congress) and will be used for the rest of the decade absent court intervention, also a 45-seat plan.

A necessary starting point is the specification of compactness scores so as to identify ill-compact districts or ill-compact plans. There are three key issues involving compactness. First, how is the term to be defined? Second, how can we best measure compactness? Third, are judgments of compactness to be made about individual districts or about plans (or large geographic areas) as a whole?

DEFINING AND MEASURING COMPACTNESS

Webster defines the adjective compact as "occupying a small volume by reason of efficient use of space" or "having parts or units closely packed or joined." This definition is a useful starting point in terms of redistricting. The ideal shape, in terms of these definitions, would be a circle. A circle is the geometric figure that is the most compact, that is, having the largest area possible within the shortest boundary (perimeter).[1]

There are two conceptually distinct ways in which a district can fail to make efficient use of space; one is by having an area that is unduly "spread out"; the other is by having a perimeter that is large relative to the minimum perimeter needed to contain the same area. We refer to measures of these two distinct aspects of ill compactness as *dispersion measures* and *perimeter measures*, respectively (Niemi et al., 1990). Perimeter measures penalize for irregularities in the shape of boundaries, for example, sawtooth edges. Dispersion measures are not affected by irregular boundaries unless the irregularities have substantial effects on how large an area is contained in the district.

We will make use of one standard dispersion measure of compactness, the ratio of the district area to the area of the smallest circle that contains (circumscribes) the district;[2] and one standard perimeter measure of compactness, the ratio of the district area to the area of the circle whose circumference is identical to the district perimeter.[3] We will refer to the first of these measures as the *circumscribing circle measure*, and the second as the *perimeter circle* measure.

As noted by Niemi and Wilkerson (chapter 12), the circumscribing circle and perimeter circle measures are each invariant with respect to the units (e.g., miles, kilometers) in which district boundary is being measured. Both vary between zero and one, assigning zero to the least compact and one to the most compact district. For both measures a circle is perfectly compact. However, except for extreme cases, the two measures will usually assign different scores to a given district; although both measures are likely, in practice, to be similar in the way they rank order districts as to compactness (see further discussion of this point in Niemi et al., 1990). The circumscribing circle model, unlike the perimeter circle model,[4] does not require extreme accuracy in entering the perimeter of the districts into the computer.[5]

We will also make use of a third measure of compactness, one based on population dispersion rather than a real dispersion or perimeter irregularities. Population dispersion measures form an important third type of compactness measures. What measures of this type penalize for are excessive extrusions and indentations that actually reach out for or are drawn to exclude significant centers of population.

The *population polygon* measure of population compactness calculates the ratio between the population of each district and the population of the area inside the polygon with the shortest possible perimeter length that completely surrounds the district.[6] This method takes into account both extrusions and intrusions. The real advantage of this measure, however, is that it only punishes for irregular shapes that bypass voters—not geographic areas that may contain few people (see, however, discussion of this method in Niemi et al., 1990).[7]

It is the fracturing or packing of voters that comprises the fundamental element of the gerrymander. Any model that does not take into account the distribution of population may miss gerrymandering even in many cases in which visual examination would clearly indicate its presence. Consider an example in which portions of one or more geographically large but sparsely populated rural counties are combined with a portion of densely populated city. There could be an extremely intricate gerrymander present in the geographically small (but highly populous) urban portion of the district; yet, because the portion of the district affected by this gerrymander is extremely small in comparison to either the total geographic area of the district or the total perimeter length of the district, neither the circumscribing circle model nor the perimeter circle model might indicate any aberration.

Each of the three measures described above has limitations, and we urge that none be used in mechanical fashion to reject districts (or plans) that lie below some preset threshold. For example, the perimeter measure of compactness penalizes for irregular boundary lines that may result due to natural features such as winding coastlines, rivers, ridge lines of mountain ranges, or governmental boundaries of political subunits such as cities or counties. Such factors might provide the basis for rebuttal to claims of ill-compactness. Also, what is on average possible for a plan as a whole may vary from jurisdiction to jurisdiction. We believe it useful to compare alternative plans for the same jurisdiction to see what overall level of compactness is feasible. That is why we are comparing three different plans for California.

DATA ANALYSIS

The application of the perimeter-circle model produced values that were generally in the .3% to .5% range, with only one district above .6% out of the 212 districts analyzed. The application of the circumscribing-circle model produced values that were generally in the .3% to .5% range, with no district above .6% out of the 212 districts analyzed. The application of the population polygon model produced values that were generally in the .5% to .8% range, with districts running from a high of .96 to a low of .26. See Table 14.1.

Now we turn to a comparison of plans. Looking at the perimeter circle measure, the range of scores in the Masters' Plan was .15 to .72 with a mean of .38 and a standard deviation of .11. In contrast, in Burton I the range was .05 to .40, the mean was .19, and the standard deviation was .09; for Burton II the range was .06 to .39, the mean was .20, and the standard deviation was .09. Thus, it is apparent that, in terms of the perimeter circle measure, the Masters' Plan was far more compact than either of the other two plans, but that there was little to choose between Burton I and Burton II.

Looking at the circumscribing circle measure, the range of scores in the Masters' Plan was .13 to .60 with a mean of .40 and a standard

TABLE 14.1. Comparison of Measures of Compactness for
California Congressional Plans 1974–1986

District Plan	Perimeter Circle			Circumscribing Circle			Population Polygon		
	94 Masters'	98 Burton I	100 Burton II	94 Masters'	98 Burton I	100 Burton II	94 Masters'	98 Burton I	100 Burton II
CD01	.57	.17	.17	.59	.22	.17	.84	.66	.83
CD02	.23	.17	.29	.18	.36	.39	.96	.72	.77
CD03	.53	.36	.39	.55	.53	.54	.87	.86	.88
CD04	.30	.21	.22	.39	.43	.42	.40	.45	.44
CD05	.34	.40	.39	.37	.51	.34	.87	.87	.73
CD06	.49	.17	.26	.49	.30	.43	.55	.32	.61
CD07	.30	.24	.30	.38	.34	.36	.67	.67	.66
CD08	.30	.11	.16	.55	.22	.30	.86	.66	.69
CD09	.29	.19	.24	.30	.29	.28	.61	.59	.57
CD10	.25	.21	.30	.30	.32	.40	.86	.74	.80
CD11	.42	.17	.24	.43	.40	.41	.85	.83	.93
CD12	.44	.10	.14	.55	.26	.32	.78	.28	.30
CD13	.33	.13	.17	.45	.35	.36	.51	.67	.70
CD14	.33	.21	.21	.35	.34	.24	.55	.26	.33
CD15	.41	.21	.23	.49	.50	.41	.51	.52	.52
CD16	.35	.24	.19	.27	.27	.25	.78	.83	.81
CD17	.37	.20	.29	.42	.53	.52	.89	.56	.53
CD18	.32	.11	.13	.45	.27	.30	.66	.45	.45
CD19	.35	.27	.27	.38	.34	.34	.59	.79	.81
CD20	.37	.14	.17	.56	.28	.28	.67	.59	.40
CD21	.42	.10	.10	.33	.30	.37	.80	.42	.33
CD22	.38	.11	.14	.39	.26	.41	.59	.35	.47
CD23	.50	.10	.07	.48	.40	.19	.83	.68	.60
CD24	.52	.26	.29	.46	.42	.40	.84	.76	.78
CD25	.49	.16	.19	.40	.26	.29	.83	.71	.67
CD26	.29	.05	.09	.33	.36	.44	.51	.57	.61
CD27	.15	.06	.06	.13	.15	.13	.50	.46	.52
CD28	.38	.17	.24	.35	.37	.38	.84	.67	.74
CD29	.58	.22	.19	.52	.36	.31	.80	.74	.69
CD30	.30	.09	.11	.38	.21	.20	.76	.54	.54
CD31	.32	.18	.16	.29	.40	.38	.78	.64	.65
CD32	.39	.08	.08	.46	.18	.24	.69	.64	.56
CD33	.25	.13	.17	.21	.39	.38	.52	.27	.37
CD34	.35	.09	.10	.34	.28	.31	.75	.66	.62
CD35	.45	.33	.38	.51	.33	.48	.92	.34	.34
CD36	.48	.09	.11	.46	.34	.35	.85	.79	.74
CD37	.72	.37	.38	.60	.26	.26	.79	.71	.77
CD38	.29	.17	.09	.29	.37	.25	.74	.71	.64
CD39	.52	.36	.27	.52	.57	.50	.88	.87	.81
CD40	.39	.21	.24	.35	.49	.47	.70	.59	.64

(continued)

TABLE 14.1. (*Continued*)

District Plan	Perimeter Circle			Circumscribing Circle			Population Polygon		
	94 Masters'	98 Burton I	100 Burton II	94 Masters'	98 Burton I	100 Burton II	94 Masters'	98 Burton I	100 Burton II
CD41	.31	.15	.18	.34	.42	.38	.55	.68	.66
CD42	.34	.10	.08	.46	.23	.22	.81	.50	.38
CD43	.37	.29	.29	.32	.37	.35	.44	.86	.89
CD44		.12	.12		.33	.37		.68	.77
CD45		.31	.33		.36	.37		.42	.36
Average	.38	.16	.20	.40	.34	.34	.72	.61	.62
Stan. Dev.	.11	.09	.09	.11	.10	.09	.15	.17	.17

deviation of .11. In contrast, in Burton I the range was .15 to .57, the mean was .34, and the standard deviation was .10; for Burton II the range was .13 to .54, the mean was .34, and the standard deviation was .09. Thus, it is apparent, in terms of the circumscribing circle measure, that the Masters' Plan was more compact than either of the other two plans, but that again there was little to choose between Burton I and Burton II.

Looking at the population polygon measure, the range of scores in the Masters' Plan was .44 to .96 with a mean of .72 and a standard deviation of .15. In contrast in Burton I, the range was .26 to .87, the mean was .61, and the standard deviation was .17; for Burton II the range was .30 to .89, the mean was .62, and the standard deviation was .17. Thus, it is again apparent that, in terms of the population polygon measure, the Masters' Plan was more compact than either of the other two plans, but there was little to choose between Burton I and Burton II.

Hence, whichever compactness measure we choose, the Masters' Plan is more compact than either Burton I or Burton II.[8] Grofman (1983a) has shown that a number of the ill-compact aspects of these two plans are directly related to attempts to achieve partisan advantage through concentration or dispersal gerrymandering techniques.

Acknowledgments. This research was supported in part by NSF Grant #SES 85-06376, Political Science Program, to the second-named author. Data are courtesy of the Republican National Committee. We are indebted to Wilma Laws and the staff of the Word Processing Center, School of Social Sciences

UCI, for manuscript and table preparation, and to Marc Whitman, Dee Pak Brar, and Mark Acton for research assistance.

NOTES

1. Of course, an area cannot be packed with contiguous circles. Nonetheless most measures based on other geometric figures such as squares or hexagons can in general be treated simply as mathematical transformations of measures based on circles (Manninen, 1973; Niemi et al., 1990).
2. This measure is identified as "Dispersion 2" in Niemi et al. (1988). It is almost always identical to the "longest axis" measure used by Niemi and Wilkerson (chapter 12). See Niemi et al. (1990) or Manninen (1973) for details of possible differences between the two measures. In the political science literature this measure is often called the Reock measure, although Reock (1963) was not in fact the first to propose it.
3. This measure is what Niemi and Wilkerson (chapter 12) and Niemi et al. (1990) refer to as "Perimeter 2." The area of a circle with circumference equal to the perimeter, P, of the district is found by solving $R = 2\pi r$ in terms of r, the radius of the desired circle, and then substituting that value in the formula for the area of a circle, Πr^2. Doing so we obtain $p^2/4\Pi$. Dividing the area of the figure, A, by that fraction, we obtain the formula $4\Pi A/p^2$.
4. Data used are "digitized" district boundaries expressed in terms of very small line segments. A digitizer is a piece of computer graphics input hardware that registers "x" and "y" coordinates into the computer each time the end of a straight-line segment is passed in order around the district's boundary. Using this methodology, we must be sure that the computer properly "closes" the polygon that represents the outside perimeter of the district, and that the program is fed the "x" and "y" coordinates in correct order around the polygon. There are various other technical issues. For example, when "digitizing" district boundaries, extreme care must be used to enter in all the details of the perimeter of each district. There is a real possibility that use of maps of different scales will mask details in "rural" districts, since urban districts are shown in more detail on a smaller scale map. This, in turn, will result in better ratios for the rural districts in comparison to the urban districts, which are usually drawn on much more detailed maps. What non-attention to this technical requirement amounts to is unintentional and inconsistent line-smoothing. Of course, in comparing plans, if rural and urban districts are treated similarly in calculating values for each of several different plans the bias imposed is apt to be minimal to nonexistent.
5. The circumscribing circle measure requires a somewhat complex algorithm to calculate if the circle using the longest axis of the district as diameter is not large enough to circumscribe the district. The first step in this process is to determine which two points on the perimeter are the greatest distance away from one another. This requires calculating a pairwise distance matrix. A circle is then computed that has its center midway between the two maximally distant points and a radius equal to half the distance between those points. After the first circle has been calculated, each point on the district perimeter is tested to see if any point is

outside the circumference of the circle. If not, then the first circle is the correct circumscribing circle. If one or more points are outside, the point furthest outside is used with the two original points to calculate a new circle center. The three new points then form a triangle. A new circle center is determined which is the point equidistant from the three points of the triangle. A new circle is calculated and all the points on the perimeter of the district are again tested to see if all are inside or tangent to the circle. This process is then repeated as often as needed.

Calculations of the circumscribing circle measure using data of different standards of precision should, nonetheless, generally be comparable. Moreover, a very good approximation to the circumscribing circle can often be determined visually, as can the length of a district's longest axis.

6. If the shape of the district were to be cut out of a sheet of wood, and a rubber band were to be stretched around the sides of the cut-out shape, roughly speaking, the rubber band would form the smallest possible polygon in terms of total length. This model is not without some problems in terms of its practical applications. Considerably more data are required to run the model than for either the perimeter circle or circumscribing circle model. Not only must the boundaries of the districts be accurately entered into the computer, but the model also requires that populations within small units of census geography (e.g., enumeration districts or census blocks) be specified. However, population centroid data may be substituted for exact boundaries, and this considerably simplifies the computational problems.

7. One distinct advantage of this model is that it can realistically give rise to values at or near 1.0. For example, a straight line bisecting any state will produce two districts with 1.00 values (areas outside state lines are not counted for population purposes). If either of those two districts is bisected by another straight line, the compactness value for each of the districts will still be 1.00.

8. Comparing alternative plans helps to judge whether deviations from compactness are in fact mandated by geographic necessity, as defendants of a plan sometimes claim. Sometimes, however, detailed inspection of specific districts and their possible justifications is also called for. For example, in California, cities such as Fresno and San Jose have extremely irregular boundaries. Thus, following city boundaries may decrease compactness. Burton II, however, has districts that divide these cities. If irregular city boundaries were the primary reason for irregular district boundaries in metropolitan areas in Burton II, then the portions of the perimeters of the districts that run through the interior of these cities and through unincorporated areas should be relatively smooth; this is simply not the case.

15

Determining the Predictability of Partisan Voting Patterns in California Elections, 1978–1984

Samuel Kernell and Bernard Grofman

Gerrymandering is intended to have the effect of creating unequal opportunities for racial or political groups to elect candidates of choice.[1] For example, Morrill (chapter 10) defines gerrymandering as "the intentional manipulation of territory toward some desired electoral outcome," while McDonald and Engstrom (chapter 8) define it as "the drawing of electoral districts so as to assign unequal voting weights to cognizable political groups." These definitions highlight two key aspects of the gerrymandering issue: the need to identify relevant cognizable groups and the need to identify the probable consequences for these groups of particular manipulations of district boundaries.

In this paper we shall focus on one important type of political group, the political party, and confine ourselves to one state, California. Moreover, we shall look only at the major parties in California, Democrats and Republicans. Before we can decide if there are manageable standards to detect and control partisan gerrymandering, we believe it is important to determine if the concept of partisan voting strength can be meaningfully defined for the units of political geography (ranging in size from census blocks or census tracts to whole cities or counties) that are the building blocks of state legislative or congressional districts. If this cannot be done, then the search for a measure of gerrymandering may be futile (see however, Wells, 1981; chapters 13 and 16, this volume, for other points of view).

It has been argued that the concept of partisan voting strength is inherently nebulous because in a given year some voters may vote for candidates of different parties for different offices, and, over time, relatively few voters vote a straight-ticket in *all* elections (see chapter 11). This issue was confronted by the Supreme Court in *Davis v. Bandemer*. There, Justice White, speaking for the plurality, refused to rule out political parties as cognizable groups that could be protected under the Fourteenth Amendment: "That the characteristics of the complaining group are not immutable or that the group has not been subject to the same historical stigma may be relevant to the manner in which a case is adjudicated but these differences do not justify a refusal to entertain the case" (106 S. Ct. 2797, p. 2806 (1986)).

In our view, the question is simply whether or not (voters in) different areas of the state demonstrably differ in their relative propensities to support candidates of a given party. If so, then those who draw district lines can make sensible predictions about the likely political consequences of alternative districting plans—taking into account, of course, such additional relevant facts as the presence or absence of an incumbent of a given party. It is not necessary to wait until hindsight has established whether politicians were in fact able to predict perfectly the electoral tides of an entire decade. The issue is whether or not the plan is intended to treat the two parties unequally, and whether, based on existing vote patterns, it could reasonably be expected to "consistently degrade a voter's or a group of voters' influence on the political process as a whole" (*Bandemer*, p. 2810 (1986)).

When political consultants advise legislatures on redistricting they customarily provide legislators with evaluations of the political and demographic characteristics of the new districts as compared to the old. Often, this involves generating "hypothetical" outcomes of previous election contests in the new district boundaries. For example, Bruce Cain when serving as a reapportionment consultant to the California Assembly in the 1980s provided information of this type to its members (Cain, 1984). Such information would not be provided if the previous electoral history of the geography that goes to make up the new districts were not thought to be informative about its probable future voting behavior.

This commonsense view of how previous election returns can be used to support inferences about future electoral behavior has been endorsed by the Supreme Court:

> The political profile of a state, its party registration and voting records are available precinct by precinct, ward by ward. These subdivisions may not be identical with census tracts, but, when overlaid on a census map, it

requires no special genius to recognize the political consequences of drawing a district line along one street rather than another. It is not only obvious, but absolutely unavoidable, that the location and shape of districts may well determine the political complexion of the area . . . They can well determine what district will be predominantly Democratic or predominantly Republican, or make a close race likely. (*Gaffney v. Cummings*, 412 U.S. 735, pp. 735–753 (1973))

In this brief note we make use of electoral data for California statewide elections and for elections to the U.S. Congress, and State Assembly in 1978, 1980, 1982, and 1984, aggregated to the census tract level. We look at the extent to which there are geographic patterns in the nature of Republican voting support at the census tract level. There are 5052 whole census tracts in the state. For one election in 1982 we have an *N* of only 4801 and for one election in 1984 we have an *N* of 4929 because of missing data. In all elections we look at Republican share of the two-party vote, and at Republican registration as a share of all registration.

In addition to State Assembly and State Senate and U.S. congressional races, in 1978 there were contests for governor, lieutenant governor, secretary of state, controller, attorney general, and treasurer; in 1980 there were contests for U.S. Senate and president; in 1982 there were contests for governor and lieutenant governor, U.S. Senate, secretary of state, and attorney general; and in 1984 there was a presidential race but no statewide contests. We include data on all these elections except for State Senate contests. Because of problems in matching electoral and census boundaries for the Senate staggered elections held under different redistricting plans, we had to omit those elections from our analyses. We show in Tables 15.1 through 15.4 correlation matrices for all statewide contests from 1978 to 1984 except those for the State Senate.

In each year the correlations range from a low of roughly .7 to values above 95. All correlations are statistically significant at least at the .0001 level. The implication is clear. In California, in any given year the greater the Republican vote for any given office in some census tract, the more likely on average is that census tract to provide a high vote (relative to other census tracts) to Republican candidates for other offices. Of course, even census tracts that generally give very high votes to Republican candidates need not do so in every instance—other factors, such as incumbency, will be relevant. Also, even though the most Republican-leaning tracts can be identified, in some contests even these census tracts will not always deliver majorities to Republican candidates although they will be more pro-Repub-

TABLE 15.1. Election Matrix of California Correlations 1978

	Rep. Reg.	Assembly	Congress	Gov.	Dem. Vote Lt. Gov.	Sec'y. State	Comptroller	Treasurer	Att'y. Gen
Rep. Reg.	1.00	.68	.80	.92	−.74	.94	.97	.96	.88
Assembly	.68	1.00	.65	.68	−.53	.68	.67	.69	.68
Congress	.80	.65	1.00	.77	−.60	.79	.79	.80	.75
Governor	.92	.68	.77	1.00	−.76	.93	.92	.92	.94
Dem. Vote Lt. Governor	−.74	−.53	−.60	−.76	1.00	−.73	−.74	−.74	−.75
Sec'y. State	.94	.68	.79	.93	−.73	1.00	.97	.94	.91
Comptroller	.97	.67	.79	.92	−.74	.97	1.00	.97	.89
Treasurer	.96	.69	.80	.92	−.74	.94	.97	1.00	.89
Att'ny. General	.88	.68	.75	.94	−.75	.91	.89	.89	1.00

TABLE 15.2. Matrix of California Election Correlations 1980

	Rep. Reg.	Assembly	Congress	President	U.S. Senate
Rep. Reg.	1.00	.74	.79	.91	.89
Assembly	.74	1.00	.67	.74	.70
Congress	.79	.67	1.00	.80	.78
President	.91	.74	.80	1.00	.96
U.S. Senate	.89	.70	.78	.96	1.00

TABLE 15.3. Matrix of California Election Correlations 1982

	Rep. Reg.	Gov.	U.S. Senate	Lt. Gov.	Att'ny. Gen.	Sec'y. State	Congress	Assembly
Rep. Reg.	1.00	.89	.93	.94	.93	.90	.85	.79
Gov.	.89	1.00	.98	.96	.95	.91	.81	.73
U.S. Senate	.93	.98	1.00	.98	.97	.94	.84	.77
Lt. Gov.	.94	.96	.98	1.00	.96	.93	.83	.78
Att'ny. Gen.	.93	.95	.97	.96	1.00	.91	.82	.76
Sec'y. State	.90	.91	.94	.93	.91	1.00	.84	.77
Congress	.85	.81	.84	.83	.82	.84	1.00	.74
Assembly	.79	.73	.77	.78.	.76	.77	.74	1.00

TABLE 15.4. Matrix of California Election Correlation 1984

	Rep. Reg.	Assembly	U.S Congress	President
Rep. Reg.	1.00	.72	.83	.91
Assembly	.72	1.00	.77	.73
U.S. Congress	.83	.77	1.00	.84
President	.91	.73	.84	1.00

lican, on average, than other census tracts. Nonetheless, Tables 15.1 through 15.4 demonstrate rather conclusively that, at least in any given election year, we can identify areas of greater or lesser Republican voting strength at the census tract level. These levels of consistency in voting are directly comparable to those observed for racial polarization (see, e.g., *Gingles v. Edmisten*, 590 F. Supp. 345, p. 368 n. 30 (1984)).

Now we look to see whether census tracts exhibit consistency in their Republican leanings over time. If so, then the claim that previous election results can be used to predict election tendencies in future elections is further supported.

Table 15.5 shows interyear correlations of Republican share of the two-party voter for five levels of office, State Assembly, governor, secretary of state, attorney general, and Congress, at the census tract level. While correlations for a given office across election years do not average quite as high as correlations between different levels of office within a single year, they are still remarkably high—in the .5 to .8 range. All the correlations are statistically significant at least at the .001 level. Indeed, (bivariate) correlations that high are quite rare within the social sciences (*Gingles v. Edmisten*, 590 F. Supp. 345, p. 368 n. 30 (1984)). The highest correlations occur for the statewide offices. For other offices the highest correlations, as expected, in general occur between years in which the districting plans have not been changed. Differences between plans make it more likely that census geography with a Democratic incumbent in one year may have a Republican incumbent in another year and vice versa. Such incumbency effects will usually reduce the magnitude of the bivariate correlations.

However, if we were to make use of multivariate models, we could significantly improve our ability to ascertain the probable political leanings of any given piece of census geography. Voting in any given election has both long-run and short-run components. The long-run component can often better be estimated by some composite of elec-

TABLE 15.5. Matrix of Interyear Correlations for California Elections
1978–1984

| | | State Assembly | | | |
		78	80	82	84
Assembly	78	1.00	.70	.52	.61
Assembly	80	.70	1.00	.64	.58
Assembly	82	.52	.64	1.00	.66
Assembly	84	.67	.58	.66	1.00

| | | Governor | |
		78	82
Governor	78	1.00	.82
Governor	82	.82	1.00

| | | Secretary of State | |
		78	82
Sec'y. State	78	1.00	.86
Sec'y. State	82	.86	1.00

| | | Attorney General | |
		78	82
Attn'y. Gen.	78	1.00	.76
Attn'y. Gen.	82	.76	1.00

| | | U.S. Congress | | | |
		78	80	82	84
Congress	78	1.00	.84	.68	.74
Congress	80	.84	1.00	.77	.81
Congress	82	.68	.77	1.00	.81
Congress	84	.74	.81	.81	1.00

tion outcomes than by any single election, even a previous one for that same office. In addition to registration data for the two major parties,[2] two key short-run factors, are the presence or absence of an incumbent and the party affiliation of that incumbent (Cain, 1985a). Also, in California there are two minor parties whose registration figures are potentially informative of a given area's political leanings (Cain, 1985a). Finally, demographic variables such as racial and income data may also be informative about both partisan leanings and probable rates of turnout in different types of contests. The issues of multivariate prediction equations must be left to subsequent research. Here, our task has simply been to demonstrate that the idea of partisan leanings can be operationalized at the census tract level.

Acknowledgments. We are indebted to Thomas Hofeller and Mark Acton of the Republican National Committee Computer Services Division for making available to us the data used in this analysis. Opinions expressed are solely those of the authors. We are indebted to Wilma Laws and the staff of the Word Processing Center, School of Social Sciences UCI, for typing and table preparation and to Thomas Weko for research assistance.

NOTES

1. Clearly "equal opportunity to elect candidates of choice" does not translate as "identical outcomes." The ability of a cognizable political group to elect candidates of its choice obviously will be a function of its size and (in a system that makes use of districts) of its geographic dispersion. Regardless of districting plan, some groups may be too small or too dispersed to have any realistic opportunity to elect candidates of choice.
2. In California, Republican registration is highly correlated with Republican voting strength, but Republican voting strength in a district will, in general, considerably exceed the Republican share of party registration. For example, in 1978 over 70% of all census tracts had a majority of registered Democrats. The same was true in 1984. If Republican registration equaled Republican voting strength, Republicans would never be elected to statewide office in California. Of course, in reality the state is generally competitive at the statewide level and has repeatedly elected Republican governors and U.S. senators in the 1980s. In California, if we regress Republican vote share for some given office on Republican registration, the slope of the bivariate regression will in general be greater than one. This is not surprising. As Jewell and Olson (1986, p. 43) note,

   Party registration figures for a state are a poor measure of existing or potential competition or of the strength of the respective parties, even though politicians and journalists frequently refer to these figures as if they were meaningful indicators.

16

Lessons from the 1973 California Masters' Plan

Gordon E. Baker

From 1974 through 1980, legislative and congressional elections in California were held in districts drawn, not by the legislature or a commission, but by court-appointed Masters. From the perspective of approximately a decade later it is now possible to examine this unique undertaking. What lessons can we learn from the experience? To what extent did the actual results validate the objectives set forth in 1973 by a three-man, nonelected agency unfamiliar with the intricacies of legislative apportionment, as well as the political world? And, finally, does the experience help define the meaning of "fair and effective representation for all citizens" as articulated by the United States Supreme Court from *Reynolds v. Sims* (377 U.S. 533 (1964)) through *Davis v. Bandemer* (106 S. Ct. 2797 (1986)).

The circumstances responsible for this episode emerged from the intense political conflict in California that followed the 1970 census. The state legislature, controlled by Democrats, passed several reapportionment measures that were vetoed by the Republican governor on gerrymandering grounds. With no valid redistricting laws in effect, the State Supreme Court retained existing legislative districts for the 1972 election only. Such an expedient was not possible for the congressional delegation, since California had gained five seats. Consequently, the district lines drawn by the legislature but vetoed by the governor were implemented by court order for the 1972 election only. When the impasse between legislature and governor continued into 1973, the high court appointed three retired judges to serve as Special Masters to fashion new district lines for the court's approval. The presiding Master was Martin J. Coughlin, a former State Court of

Appeal justice; the other two Masters were retired Superior Court judges Harold F. Collins and Alvin E. Weinberger. All three had retired within approximately the previous two years. *California Journal* identified Coughlin as a Republican, the other two as Democrats (*California Journal*, 1973, p. 334).

The Masters held four well-publicized hearings in diverse areas of the state, consulted expert opinion and literature as well as judicial precedent, and developed criteria later adopted as part of the court record. These standards were:

1. As required by the Federal Constitution, the districts in each plan should be numerically equal in population as nearly as practicable, with strict equality in the case of congressional districts . . . and reasonable equality in the case of state legislative districts . . .

2. The territory included within a district should be contiguous and compact, taking into account the availability and facilities of transportation and communication between the people in a proposed district, between the people and candidates in the district, and between the people and their elected representatives.

3. Counties and cities within a proposed district should be maintained intact, insofar as practicable . . .

4. The integrity of California's basic geographical regions (coastal, mountain, desert, central valley and intermediate valley regions) should be preserved insofar as practicable.

5. The social and economic interests common to the population of an area which are probable subjects of legislative action, generally termed a "community of interests" . . . should be considered in determining whether the area should be included within or excluded from a proposed district in order that all of the citizens of the district might be represented reasonably, fairly and effectively. Examples of such interests, among others, are those common to an urban area, a rural area, an industrial area or an agricultural area, and those common to areas in which the people share similar living standards, use the same transportation facilities, have similar work opportunities, or have access to the same media of communication relevant to the election process . . .

6. State senatorial districts should be formed by combining adjacent assembly districts, and, to the degree practicable, assembly district boundaries should be used as congressional district boundaries (*Legislature of California v. Reinecke*, 110 Cal. Rptr. 718 (1973), pp. 727–728).[1]

The formal criteria outlined in the first five points above comprise either application of judicial precedent or refinement of certain traditional and constitutional standards. The public hearings had revealed widespread concern over the contorted boundaries that characterized the recent legislatively drawn plans. The Masters' Report drew this justification for adhering as closely as possible to such spatial standards:

> Many presentations were made urging adherence to the criteria of maintaining the integrity of counties and cities, and deploring needless division thereof in the formation of districts. It is clear that in many situations county and city boundaries define political, economic and social boundaries of population groups. Furthermore, organizations with legitimate political concerns are constituted along local political subdivision lines. Therefore, unnecessary division of counties and cities in reapportionment districting should be avoided . . . (Special Masters' Report, *Legislature of California v. Reinecke*, p. 728)

In applying these criteria, the Masters sought to take into account the potential political implications of creating new constituencies, as well as achieving a goal of fairness to those most affected by the results. During the early stages (June 1973) of their operations, the Masters were clearly influenced by three key decisions of the United States Supreme Court, especially *Gaffney v. Cummings* (412 U.S. 735 (1973)). From the Court's opinion there, two generalizations appeared noteworthy. One was that districting without regard for political impact "may produce, whether intended or not, the most grossly gerrymandered results" (quoted in Special Masters' Report, *Legislature of California v. Reinecke*, pp. 749–750).[2] The other was that "It is also true that political fairness is an appropriate goal of reapportionment . . . and that there are legitimate interests to be served by allowing incumbents and their constituents to maintain existing relationships and in affording incumbents fair opportunities to seek reelection" (p. 750). The Masters were satisfied that the proposed and recommended plans are neither politically unfair nor unfair to incumbents, but may result in fewer "safe seats" and more "competitive seats" (p. 750).

In conclusion, the Masters' Report drew on literature in political science as well as judicial opinions, placing its efforts and goals in a broad conceptual framework rarely found in comparable committee reports or public documents:

> Ideal districting should accommodate shifting political trends, allowing electoral majorities to be represented by legislative majorities. The central rationale of two-party politics is that it offers voters alternative choices of candidates and programs. According to democratic theory, parties should contest for public support through electoral mechanisms that translate predominant public opinion into public policy. This involves the ability of popularly elected majorities to govern, while insuring the representation

of the minority party, temporarily out of power, as a check on a usually transitory majority party . . . (Special Masters' Report, *Legislature of California v. Reinecke*, p. 750)

After the Masters' Report was made public, an opportunity for reactions from those areas and individuals affected most directly brought forth a number of communications. A substantial memorandum drafted by the Counsel for the Masters (Paul McKaskle, Professor of Law, University of San Francisco) carefully explained reasons for the proposed plans. This entailed a discussion of the kinds of tradeoffs involved in any redistricting, with an explanation of the choices—seldom easy—that must be made, even by those committed to maximizing the ideal of political fairness. None of the objections filed appeared to charge gerrymandering or political favoritism.

The Masters made their report public on August 31, 1973, the deadline that had been stipulated at the time of their appointment on May 1. After a period that allowed those affected to file *amici curiae* briefs or communications objecting to or supporting the proposed plans, the state Supreme Court, on November 28, issued its unanimous decision in a brief decree that attached the Masters' recommendations and implemented the new constituency boundaries. The only change made by the high court was the reversal of numbers for two pairs of Senate districts, permitting three incumbents to retain their regular phasing (since the upper house has staggered four-year terms, with only even-numbered seats scheduled for election in 1974, the other half not until 1976). On the recommendation of the Masters, the court also waived the one-year district residence requirement for candidates, who now had until January 28, 1974, to declare their intention to run.

In maintaining the state constitutional requirement that only half the Senate be chosen in each election, the court surprised some who felt that the impact on voters and candidates would be inequitable. In 1966, because of the massive shifts from an area-based chamber to one reflecting one person, one vote, all 40 Senate seats were contested, half for two-year terms, the remainder for four. While the 1973 redistricting was less disruptive, it was still more so than would ordinarily be the case. *California Journal* summarized the problem as follows:

> As a result of this ruling, California will have three categories of citizens so far as Senate representation is concerned:
>
> The first group will be those who voted for a Senator in 1972 and will do so again in 1974. They will be represented by two Senators for two years following redistricting.

The second group consists of those who voted for a Senator in 1970 and will do so again in 1974. They will be represented by one Senator, regardless of reapportionment.

The third group selected a senator in 1970 but will not do so again until 1976. For two years, they will not be represented by any Senator in whose election they could participate. (*California Journal*, 1974, p. 17)

While a compelling logical case could be made that equal protection required the election of all 40 senators in 1974, the court understandably was reluctant to upset incumbents—as well as tradition and state constitutional provisions—more than would already be the case. Pointing out that such inequalities are an inevitable by-product of staggered terms, Chief Justice Donald Wright gave the following justification for maintaining the alternating schedule of elections:

The resulting inequality among electors is limited to the two-year period following reapportionment and results in even less temporary disenfranchisement than may be imposed on residents who move into a senate district or who become of voting age shortly after an election has taken place. We conclude that adherence to staggered terms following reapportionment involved no invidious discriminations. (*Legislature of California v. Reinecke*, p. 724)

This dilemma reflects an inherent conflict in public philosophies. Staggered senate terms promote stability, continuity, and checks, while the concept of one person, one vote emphasizes ready responsiveness to public opinion. Although not mutually incompatible, these two mechanisms embody basic tensions typically resolved only by temporarily deferring representative equality for a portion of the state's electorate. Yet another query is posed by the situation. It calls further into question the obsession of some courts and judges nationally with precise population equality as the goal of reapportionment. Why aim for an elusive and illusory minuscule population deviation when far greater disparities are accepted for an additional two (or in this case, four) years?

RESULTS: 1974–1980

In assessing the results of the 1973 Masters' Plan, we should first focus on the criteria they set forth and the extent to which these were implemented. Second, we should attempt a preliminary evaluation of how successfully the announced goal of "political fairness" was achieved.

Population Equality

The masters followed a stricter standard regarding congressional districts, in accordance with federal judicial interpretation. For the California legislature, the Masters determined that districts should fall within 1% of ideal population equality except in unusual cases, but in no event should a deviation exceed 2%. Although greater percentage flexibility (approaching a 10% plus-to-minus range) was permitted by the U.S. Supreme Court in June 1973 (*White v. Regester*, 412 U.S. 755 (1973)), the Masters opted for a tighter deviation range because of the large population of legislative districts in California, meaning that even smaller percentages involve greater absolute numbers of voters.

The results carried through the proposed guidelines very well. At the state legislative level, only four of the proposed 80 Assembly districts exceeded a 1% deviation, and all of these were within the 2% margin. Similarly affected were only two state Senate districts. The congressional plan submitted adhered to the more stringent standard, with all districts falling within a range of 0.45% variance and no district deviating by as much as even one-fourth of 1%. The Report noted: "Owing to the nature of U.S. Census Bureau data, it would be extremely difficult to reduce these deviations" (*Legislature of California v. Reinecke*, p. 746).

Communities of Interest

Five of the six criteria listed above can be grouped under the general rubric of "communities of interest." (The exception is population equality, which can work in an opposite direction.) The term *community of interest* is specifically mentioned in the social and economic context, broadly defined to include transportation facilities and communications media relevant to the political process. This functional designation is augmented by various spatial criteria: contiguity, compactness, integrity of geographical regions and of counties and cities to the extent feasible. Such considerations have as their goal the enhancement of political communities. One reason that grotesquely contorted districts arouse considerable public outcry, evident at hearings held by the Masters, is the violation of natural communities of interest.

A good example of the above point is the contrast between the congressional districts for the Los Angeles area drawn by the Masters in 1973 with the subsequent Democratic gerrymander of 1982 (see Maps 16.1 and 16.2). The shaded areas in Map 16.2 illustrate extremes in discriminatory cartography, with one district lacking contiguity as well as compactness. Map 16.1 which shows comparable districts drawn by the Masters less than a decade earlier, indicates that such boundary manipulation was not required by geographical constraint. These 1973 districts are not only substantially compact, but were justified by such criteria as city and county boundaries, transportation networks, and socioeconomic communities of interest. They were presented in public with an opportunity for response from interested groups and parties before final approval. By contrast, the 1982 boundaries were hurriedly devised by a newly elected legislature shortly before a Democratic governor was to be succeeded by a Republican. There were no public hearings or any official public explanations of districts.

Moreover, for the state of California generally, the Masters' Plan implemented its spatial criteria with remarkable fidelity. Only 4 of the 43 counties with under 250,000 population were divided, while only 11 cities of less than 250,000 inhabitants were not kept intact (and in most of these the bulk of the population was located in one district) (*Legislature of California v. Reinecke*, p. 753). In such instances the Report explained the reasons for the few exceptions to its goal of attempting to preserve the integrity of local subdivision boundaries.

While such formal antigerrymandering standards have traditionally been regarded as neutral guidelines, they have been boldly challenged by two advocates of partisan redistricting. Daniel Lowenstein and Jonathan Steinberg recently condemned the standard of compactness as a "Republican Trojan horse," insisting that criteria such as communities of interest and following county and city boundaries are similarly flawed (Lowenstein and Steinberg, 1985, pp. 27, 34).[3] These conclusions are not based on any concrete evidence but rather on abstract theorizing based on partisan population distribution, especially in urban areas. It is curious that these writers have ignored the experience in their own state of California, notably the elections of 1974 through 1980 held under the Masters' court-ordered districts. The elaborate formal standards noted above should have produced, under the Lowenstein-Steinberg hypothesis, the most thoroughgoing Republican gerrymander imaginable. Instead, overwhelming Democratic majorities were elected in both state legislative houses and the congressional delegation in 1974 and 1976, reflecting unusually strong Democratic voting majorities. Indeed, some Republicans and journalistic observers began to suspect that the plans, perhaps inadvertently, manifested a Democratic bias. But significant Republican gains at the ballot box in 1978 and 1980 resulted in substantial loss of

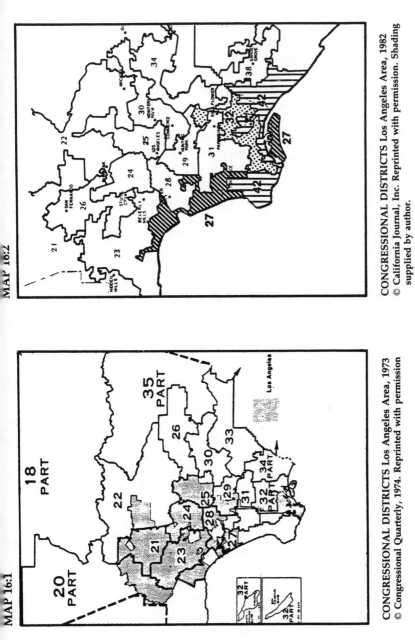

MAP 16:1

MAP 16:2

CONGRESSIONAL DISTRICTS Los Angeles Area, 1973
© Congressional Quarterly, 1974. Reprinted with permission

CONGRESSIONAL DISTRICTS Los Angeles Area, 1982
© California Journal, Inc. Reprinted with permission. Shading supplied by author.

Democratic seats, indicating that the plans were readily adaptable to shifts in electoral preference.

The remaining spatial criterion—comprising state Senate districts from pairs of adjacent Assembly districts—also reflected a concern for communities of interest, among other values. Since there are 80 districts in the lower house and 40 in the upper chamber, such a linkage (termed *nesting* by the U.S. Supreme Court) (*Davis v. Bandemer*, 106 S. Ct. 2797 (1986), p. 2801), seems logical. For one thing, this serves as a partial deterrent to gerrymandering, since it would be difficult to manipulate two coordinate sets of boundaries simultaneously to achieve partisan or personal goals. Hence, such a procedure is anathema to legislators, who would never voluntarily implement such a scheme, because it markedly reduces their discretion. The Masters' Report gave this justification: "The resulting legislative districts will be more comprehensible to the electorate and the task of administering elections would be considerably simplified, thus saving money and insuring greater accuracy" (*Legislature of California v. Reinecke*, p. 728). The various advantages of this feature would be advanced by the use of Assembly district boundaries, to the extent feasible, in forming congressional districts. Since there were 43 of the latter and 80 of the former, total congruence would be impossible, but the Masters were able to use such common boundaries in a substantial number of cases.

There are obvious impediments to maximizing communities of interest in a state as large and diverse and as populous as California. Moreover, the state legislature is small, with resulting legislative districts more populous by far than in any other state. Together with a fairly close range of population equality sought, the result is that some communities cannot be kept intact, while others must be combined in forming districts. In spite of this, the Masters achieved their goal to a remarkable degree, while making some substantive contributions to defining communities of interest in functional terms.

Political Fairness

As indicated earlier, this goal included several facets: avoiding even unintentional gerrymandering by taking into account likely political impact of boundaries; allowing incumbents a fair opportunity to seek reelection; and, an even-handed treatment of political parties, with somewhat more competitive seats that could reflect shifts in public opinion. The Masters also acknowledged that the components of fairness would at times be in unavoidable conflict.

From the standpoint of subsequent electoral experience, the redistricting plans drawn by the Masters in 1973 reflected shifts in voter support over the period of 1974 through 1980. In 1974, Democrats captured 28 congressional seats, the Republicans only 15. This disparity did not result from constituency boundaries as much as a strong Democratic tide that year. The *California Journal* noted: "Considering the depth of the nationwide Democratic sweep, Republicans probably did well to retain 15 congressional seats in California's 43-member delegation" (*California Journal*, 1974, p. 409). Although the Democratic Party's share of seats was 65%, this reflected a statewide total of 59.89% of the two-party congressional vote. While there are hazards in applying "swing-ratio" formulae precisely to such a situation, it is clear that this particular votes-seats yield is modest indeed. Any system of single-member districts will ordinarily produce a disproportionately larger percentage of seats for the party winning a majority of the total two-party vote in a state. Moreover, the 1973 plan's adaptability to electoral change is demonstrated by the substantial gains made by Republicans in 1978 and 1980, by the latter year reducing the Democratic congressional margin to 22-21. During the 1974–1980 period, a total of 9 of 43 congressional districts changed party hands.

State legislative districts also shifted over the same period, though not as impressively as at the congressional level. In the strong Democratic tide of 1974, that party took a commanding lead in the Assembly of 55 to 25, reduced to 48-32 by the 1980 election. Another measure of sensitivity to electoral trends is the number of districts (of the total of 80) that changed party representation, in either direction, in the four-election period of 1974 through 1980—a total of 21. This contrasts with 15 during the preceding comparable period of four elections under the legislatively drawn 1965 districting. Less reflective of change was the state Senate, whose staggered terms make the tracing of trends difficult. Before the election of 1974, Democrats held a 22-16 lead, with two vacancies. This became 25-15 after that election, 26-14 after 1978, then a stable 23-17 split after 1978 and 1980. This displays the kind of stability for which the upper chamber was designed, with a somewhat conservative reputation, regardless of party control.

Impact on Incumbents

The Masters' aim of allowing incumbents a fair opportunity to stand for reelection was one that inevitably would conflict with the spatial criteria that produced significantly different district patterns than known previously or that had been proposed during the 1971–1973 political impasse. For example, adhering to geographic guidelines made it virtually impossible to avoid placing more than one incumbent in the same district (usually the most extreme form of disadvantage). Yet even this appears to have been minimized, without disparate partisan treatment of incumbents evident. Citing the Masters' expressed anticipation on making their plans public, that they would probably result in fewer "safe" seats and more competitive ones, the *California Journal* commented: "An analysis of the plan, however, indicates that only about 10 incumbents out of 163 will lose their seats as a direct result of it and that only a few more seats than usual will be up for grabs" (*California Journal*, 1973, p. 334).

The *California Journal* estimate may have been a bit conservative, though not by a great deal. For congressional constituencies, two pairs of incumbents (one set from each party) were put in the same district: two Democrats in Los Angeles (Chet Holifield and George Danielson) and two Republicans further south (Victor Veysey and Clair Burgener). Holifield, dean of the delegation, retired, while Danielson and Burgener won. Since there is no residency requirement for Congress, Veysey ran in a nearby open (no incumbent) district, but lost in a close election. One other Republican incumbent, Bob Mathias, lost a close race. Yet both of these two districts reverted to the GOP column by 1980. In the Assembly, five incumbents—two Democrats and three Republicans—lost in 1974. The state Senate situation was complicated by the numbering of districts and staggered elections. As noted earlier, the state high court made a numbering change in two pairs of Senate districts to bring three incumbents into logical phasing. A few other Senate incumbents found themselves with no logical district in which to file, or would have to sit out two years, or else move to an open district.

Minority Representation

The Masters were clearly aware of the impact of district boundaries on the electoral prospects of racial and ethnic minorities. In explaining why they could not accept the various legislative plans submitted to them, the Masters noted a number of objections to the Senate plan, which had broader political support than the others. They added: "There is also evidence that the Senate plan dilutes the voting strength of blacks and persons of Spanish-surname by dividing homogeneous ethnic groups into a number of districts or by 'packing' too many members of an ethnic group into a single district" (*Legislature of California v. Reinecke*, p. 730). On some occasions, the Report's description of proposed legislative districts mentions the relationship to a partic-

**TABLE 16.1. Black and Hispanic Representation,
California Elections, 1970–82**

	1970	1972	1974	1976	1978	1980	1982
Blacks							
Congress	1	2	3	3	3	4	4
Senate	1	1	2	2	2	2	2
Assembly	5	6	6	6	6	6	6
Hispanics							
Congress	1	1	1	1	1	1	3
Senate	0	0	2	2	3	3	3
Assembly	2	5	4	4	3	4	4

Note: Assembly and Senate districts identical for 1970 and 1972. Congressional districts were differently constituted, with 38 in the delegation, 1962–70; 43 in 1972; 45 in 1982.

ular minority community. When the Masters' Plan was announced, representatives of black and Hispanic political groups expressed satisfaction.

Representation of California's two major minority communities is revealed in the electoral outcomes from 1970 through 1982, shown in Table 16.1. The four elections held under the Masters' Plan (1974–1980) can be examined in the context of the two preceding contests held under previous redistrictings, and the election immediately following the 1981 redistricting.

The data in Table 16.1 suggest that the constituencies drawn by the Masters permitted a modest increase in minority representation. In particular, the results do not bear out complaints of disadvantage voiced later by a few Hispanic spokesmen.[4] Even the Democratic redistricting of 1981, more avowedly concerned to maximize such minority strength, triggered no dramatic changes. The only significant increase was in the Hispanic proportion of the expanding congressional delegation, moving from one to three seats (one of which had been left open by an Anglo incumbent appointed to a judgeship). Growth in Hispanic representation has been slowed by several factors: a relatively high noncitizen percentage of persons counted by the Census; lower registration totals and voter turnouts; and a greater dispersion geographically than is the case with other minority groups.

SUBSEQUENT INFLUENCES

The 1973 California Masters' Plan was in effect for only eight years, to be replaced—ironically—by redistrictings that approximated, as nearly as one could imagine, a diametrically opposed set of assumptions, criteria, and goals. Yet the work of the Masters stands as a reference point—a base line—by which to compare alternative reapportionment measures. Moreover, some of the ideas set forth in 1973 appear to have had a subsequent influence that may not be as dormant as the 163 districts then created. Three later episodes are worth noting:

1980: New Constitutional Language

While the Masters had attempted to adapt the spirit of the state constitution of 1879 setting forth the principle of one man, one vote plus geographic restrictions on gerrymandering, the constitutional language had undergone a major modification (the so-called "federal plan" of legislative representation added in 1926). In turn, this, plus some significant geographic restrictions on district formation, had been rendered inapplicable by the U.S. Supreme Court's key reapportionment decisions of the 1960s. As a result, revised wording seemed in order and in 1980 the legislature proposed section XXI to replace previous provisions. In addition to calling for contiguous, single-member districts "reasonably equal" in population, the section included this proviso: "(e) The geographical integrity of any city, county, or city and county, or of any geographical region shall be respected to the extent possible without violating the requirements of any other subdivision of this section" (California Ballot Pamphlet, 1980, p. 22).

Broadly viewed, this section seemed to build on the foundations laid by the Masters in 1973. It was offered to the electorate for ratification as Proposition 6 and presented as an antigerrymandering safeguard. In the official state pamphlet sent to all voters, the argument favoring the proposed revision made this point: "From past experience, we know what could happen with next year's reapportionment. Without the restrictions in Proposition 6 California could end up with districts that are confusing, unfair and unrepresentative. Proposition 6 will block forces in the Legislature from gaining unfair dominance by one political party or insuring reelection for particular incumbents" (California Ballot Pamphlet, 1980, p. 22).

This measure easily won voter approval, but its bold claim of preventing serious boundary manipulation was belied by the Democratic gerrymanders of 1981 and 1982. Why did not those adversely affected seek Article XXI's protection? The answer may be due to Republican reluctance to see the new language defined out of existence by a highly partisan Democratic majority on the state Supreme Court (see

Assembly of the State of California et al. v. George Deukmejian, Attorney General et. al., Sup. 180 Cal. Rptr. 297 (1982)),[5] then chaired by Rose Bird, ultimately refused reconfirmation by an overwhelming vote in the election of 1986. Whether Article XXI will now be invoked under new circumstances remains to be seen.

1982: Proposition 14

A few years prior to the 1980 census, the reform group Common Cause had been contemplating a constitutional amendment that would transfer the redistricting function. When the electorate in June 1982 overwhelmingly rejected Democratic redistricting statutes in referenda sponsored by the Republican Party, the time seemed ripe for a new approach. Common Cause joined forces with the Republicans, who contributed modest sums to help qualify an initiative constitutional amendment, Proposition 14, for the November 1982 election. The measure would vest the redistricting function in a bipartisan commission chosen by an appellate court panel of justices and political party representatives. The influence of the 1973 Masters' experience can be seen in the following extracts from the ballot statement of the Legislative Analyst:

> The Plans would have to conform to certain objectives and standards, some of which are as follows:
>   1. Each districting plan shall provide fair representation for all citizens, including racial, ethnic, and language minorities, and political parties.
>   2. . . . each Senate district shall be composed of two Assembly districts.
>   3. The population of state legislative districts shall be within 1% of the average district population, but can vary by up to 2% to accomplish the objectives and standards specified in this measure. Congressional districts shall be as nearly equal in population as practicable.
>   4. . . .
>   5. . . .
>   6. To the extent practicable, districts:
>   Shall be geographically compact,
>   Shall not cross any common county boundary more than once,
>   Shall be comprised of whole census tracts, and
>   Shall minimize the division of cities, counties, and geographical regions
> (California Ballot Pamphlet, 1982, pp. 54–55).

The measure further provided that, in the event that no valid apportionment plans were approved by the commission, the State Supreme Court would adopt a plan or plans "in accordance with the objectives and standards set forth in this measure" (California Ballot Pamphlet, 1982, p. 55).

1984: Proposition 39

Frustrated by the survival of the Democratic gerrymanders of 1981 and 1982, Republican Governor George Deukmejian sponsored another constitutional initiative, with more than sufficient signatures to qualify it for the 1984 general election ballot. This measure would transfer the responsibility for reapportionment from the state legislature to a special commission composed of eight voting members plus two nonvoting members (one each appointed by the governor and the top official of the largest opposing political party). The voting members would be drawn from a pool of retired or voluntarily resigned appellate court justices (or, if necessary, lower court judges). The state Judicial Council would prepare two lists, each comprised of judges initially appointed by governors of the two major political parties. Four from each list would be drawn by lot by the president of the University of California (a curious degree of expertise for a mechanical chore that could more easily be performed by the spin of a lottery wheel!). The procedure would go into effect for the 1986 elections, and thereafter following each decennial census. Plans drawn by this commission would be subject to referendum and to judicial review under state or federal law.

Apparent influences of the 1973 Masters' Plan can be seen not only in the reliance on retired judges as line-drawers, but in Proposition 39's guidelines for districts. The legislative analyst provided the following summary:

Objectives and Standards Governing Reapportionment Plans. The commission would be required by the measure to solicit public comments and hold public hearings prior to adopting final reapportionment plans. In addition, the measure requires that the commission's reapportionment plans promote certain objectives and conform with certain standards. Among the more important of these objectives and standards are those that require the plans to:

Promote competition for elective office,

Provide that each State Senate district shall be composed of two adjacent Assembly districts . . .

Assure that districts shall be comprised of whole census units, and

Provide that districts shall be geographically compact, shall be composed of contiguous territories, and shall not cross any common county boundary more than once. (California Ballot Pamphlet, 1984, p. 55)

In contrast to the relative quiet that had characterized the campaign over Proposition 14 in 1982, Proposition 39 two years later engendered an intense and financially costly battle. Democratic opponents recruited Hollywood talent to produce a number of television spots shown at saturation levels, denouncing the dangers of dragging judges (even retired ones) into the seamy political thicket. In contrast, the Republican advertising campaign was "too little and too late" to be effective. The *California Journal* remarked on "Deukmejian's late start and lackluster campaign" (*California Journal*, 1984, p. 482). Also puzzling is the lack of commentary by the press, and especially by proponents of the measure, concerning the success of retired judges using comparable guidelines in 1973. In November 1984, Proposition 39 lost by an approximate margin of 45% to 55%, close to the proportion by which Proposition 14 had lost two years earlier.

Does It Really Matter, Anyway?

Close observers of the reapportionment process in California have questioned whether partisan gerrymandering has a long-range impact, noting the erosion of party majorities over a given decade. For example, Tony Quinn, veteran Republican reapportionment staff expert, surveyed the 1974 election results in the context of earlier redistrictings:

> What all this suggests is that gerrymandering not only distorts the state's representation but also doesn't work. In 1951, Republican map-makers opened the door to gerrymandered legislating by drawing a plan that so masterfully disenfranchised Democrats that the 1952 election produced 56 Republican assemblymen. By the time the Democratic tide of 1958 rolled over California, however, the GOP was down to 34 seats. In the 1962 election, the reapportionment experts of Speaker Jesse Unruh helped the Democrats win a majority just short of two-thirds. Yet, within six years that majority had collapsed and the Republicans held a majority in the Assembly.
>
> Now, after all the partisan politicking that resulted in legislative failure to reapportion the state, the court's nongerrymandered districts yielded a Democratic majority beyond the party's dreams. And so the great and futile political power struggle to draw new district lines dissolved, as the 1974 elections proved, into much ado about nothing. (*California Journal*, 1975, p. 9)

A similar refrain has been sounded by political scientist Leroy Hardy, longtime consultant to Democrats on the state's congressional delegation. Hardy insists that "redistricting, no matter how good, or bad, is limited in duration. With time control, correction takes its natural course (Hardy, 1986, p. 9)."[6] Indeed, the raw data appear to validate at the congressional level the same conclusion reached by Quinn. Consider the following scenario.

The Republican congressional redistricting of 1951 shifted the delegation's margin from R13-D10 to R19-D11. After the 1960 elections, this had shifted to a split of 16 Democrats to 14 Republicans. The Democratic remapping of 1961 produced a delegation of 25 Democrats, 13 Republicans. After the 1970 election, the partisan advantage had shrunk to 20 Democrats, 18 Republicans. These developments might support Hardy's conclusion that partisan boundary manipulation is not durable, so why be concerned if a relatively short passage of time changes the best laid plans of political cartographers? Yet such a conclusion must be substantially modified after the indicators of change are analyzed further.

The strong Republican margin of votes (54% statewide) for congressional candidates in 1952, plus the new district lines, produced a commanding margin in the delegation (19-11). By 1954, the statewide congressional vote had ebbed to 48.5%, but the delegation margin remained the same, probably reflecting, at least in part, favorable boundary lines. Only a combination of Democratic organization and voting power was able to cause a breakthrough, and then only a partial one. In fact, most of the Democratic gains occurred in nonmetropolitan areas where districts had been subject to little, if any, gerrymandering. Of 12 seats allotted to Los Angeles County in 1951, 8 were designed as safe Republican districts, and the GOP lost only one of these[7] in a decade characterized by enormous population mobility, internal party strife, and a greatly strengthened Democratic opposition.

In 1961 the situation was reversed. Democrats held both houses of the state legislature in addition to the governor's office. The opportunity to regerrymander congressional districts was sweetened by California's acquisition of 8 new seats, the greatest absolute gain of any state. The new district maps revealed some definite advantages for the Democrats. For one thing, Republican districts were generally more populous, averaging 103.8% of the norm, while Democratic seats averaged 98%. In the 1962 elections, the Democrats gained 9 seats, while the Republicans lost 1. With 52% of the statewide popular vote, Democrats captured nearly 66% of the state delegation. As in 1951, Los Angeles County offered the greatest opportunity for gerrymandering, since state constitutional provisions limited discretion in nonmetropolitan areas. Of the 15 new districts in Los Angeles County, the 1962 elections yielded 11 Democratic winners and only 4 Republicans.

By the end of the decade, 8 of California's congressional districts drawn in 1961 had changed partisan hands, with Democrats losing (and Republicans gaining) a net of 5 seats. This transformation included more changes in Los Angeles County than in the previous decade, with 3 of the Democrats' 11 districts being captured by Republicans. But it must be noted that 2 of these became "open" districts due to either the death or voluntary retirement of Democratic incumbents. Two districts outside of Los Angeles County also had become "open" for similar reasons. Boundary manipulation in 1961, as in 1951, had not necessarily failed, though it had been moderated to some degree by other variables.

This survey demonstrates that congressional redistricting in 1951 and 1961 had been conditioned by several factors. State constitutional provisions designed to limit gerrymandering provided that in forming congressional districts no county could be divided unless its population entitled it to one or more; also, in populous counties, congressional districts had to be composed of compact, contiguous Assembly districts (which, in turn, had to meet comparable boundary restrictions). Hence, boundary manipulation by both Republicans and Democrats was confined in nature and extent. Moreover, at the time of a redistricting, the majority party attempted to gain the lion's share of newly allotted seats, without placing opposition incumbents in dire jeopardy. This contrasts with the 1981 congressional redistricting, which placed six Republicans in three districts, thus necessarily eliminating at least three from the delegation.

When state constitutional restrictions on district boundaries were voided in the wake of the one person, one vote rulings, another constraint on gerrymandering fortuitously occurred—a partisan split between governor and legislature, encouraging some bipartisan compromise in 1971. By 1981, none of the former constraints was present. Moreover, computer technology made partisan gerrymandering a more precise and sophisticated process than in the past. The results clearly stand in marked contrast with the earlier redistrictings outlined above. Routine or ordinary gerrymandering of the past had been replaced by a new form of discriminatory vote dilution, a "hardening" of the electoral arteries.

CONCLUSION

The evidence presented supports the conclusion that the legislative and congressional redistricting designed by the Special Masters in 1973 met the ideal of "fair and effective representation for all citizens" for the 1974–1980 period. The criteria initially devised comprised logical guidelines for district formation. The statewide electoral results indicate that such standards can work in the real world of politics, while also accommodating shifts in voter sentiment.

Such a positive appraisal does not imply that the plans were equally "fair" to all incumbents and potential candidates for office. Such a utopian result would be impossible to achieve with the best of intentions. Perhaps sensing this, the Masters' report cautiously claimed only that the districts were not politically "unfair."

Achieving this result may well have been facilitated by the criteria set forth (functional compactness, communities of interest, etc.), but would scarcely be assured automatically by them. That is, a variety of districting arrangements would have been possible under the 1973 guidelines. Choices had to be made, and the Masters clearly accepted the responsibility of taking political effects into account. Some might object that retired judges, however fair-minded, are not necessarily well equipped to make judgments that have inherent political implications. This may explain provisions in the initiative measures of 1982 and 1984 calling for some involvement of political personages in proposed reapportionment commissions.

As for future prospects, it seems unlikely that the status quo regarding legislative representation in California will go unchallenged. Judicial appeals comprise one prospective avenue. As indicated earlier, Article XXI was added to the California Constitution in 1980 as a restraint on gerrymandering and has not yet been invoked. The U.S. Supreme Court's 1986 decision in *Davis v. Bandemer* holding political gerrymandering justiciable has drawn attention to California as the logical site for the next round in federal courts.

Another initiative campaign to remove the responsibility for redistricting from the legislature remains a live possibility, in spite of the unsuccessful results in 1982 and 1984. Any future measure might well profit from the lessons of these earlier failures. Recurring problems with proposed redistricting commissions include keeping the measure simple and comprehensible to the average voter and creating an agency that is both neutral and wise in political acumen. Efforts to insure a "fair" process typically result in a plethora of details to anticipate a variety of contingencies. Moreover, attempts to create a "representative" or "balanced" commission can result in rather large agencies for effective functioning, while the nagging questions remain as to how its members should be chosen.

These difficulties might be circumvented by directing reform efforts in a different direction entirely: by retaining legislative authority to redistrict, but with additional safeguards to restrain existing conflicts of interest. Such a proposal was recently put forth by Robert Monagan, a former Speaker of the Assembly, as follows:

> My suggestion is that we leave reapportionment in the hands of the Legislature but with a major change. We should have the same number of senators as we have members of Congress, currently 45, and twice that number of Assembly members—90. The Legislature then would create common Congressional and Senate districts and simply divide them to create Assembly districts.
>
> This change would substantially increase the odds against having lawmakers redraw district boundaries only to protect themselves. With so many persons interested in each district's boundaries, their interests would tend to cancel each other out. As a result, other reapportionment provisions, such as requirements to observe existing city and county boundaries, would come to the fore . . .
>
> Naturally, if the Legislature fails to reapportion itself and the Congressional districts during the session following the federal census, then the California Supreme Court would do the job through the appointment of a special master or similar process, using the same rules as those required of the Legislature. (*California Journal*, 1985, p. 83).[8]

This idea merits serious consideration, perhaps with an added safeguard of requiring a two-thirds vote in each house (in addition to the governor's signature, as at present) for a valid redistricting plan. Such an arrangement would embody the spirit of James Madison's familiar aphorism: "Ambition must be made to counteract ambition. The interest of the man must be connected with the constitutional rights of the place" (*The Federalist*, No. 51). A system of checks and balances— Madison's "policy of supplying, by opposite and rival interests, the defect of better motives—"seems peculiarly suitable to the process of creating constituencies, even though that was not the specific object of Madison's concern.

The Monagan proposal would have the further advantage of modestly increasing the representative character of the legislature by stemming the escalating population totals of districts. California has, by far, the nation's smallest legislature in relation to both population and territory. In Monagan's words, the reduced sizes of constituencies "could make legislators a bit more responsive. . . . In addition, the change would allow voters to identify their representative more easily and would open some new districts for non-incumbents" (Monagan, 1985).

While such a reform would have the advantages of simplicity and of assuring a buffered form of political responsibility for reapportionment, legislative resistance would be substantial since incumbents would be less insulated from potential competition. Members of Congress, especially, would feel threatened by a system that, each two years, could offer a "free ride" to half of the state senators from identical areas. Moreover, such "nesting" of constitutencies is anathema to legislators who would chafe at the mutual restraints imposed. For these reasons, such a measure would necessitate a constitutional initiative ballot measure. Yet its relative simplicity, along with the prospect of a more representative legislature in both size and composition, could be attractive to the electorate.

Whatever the future course of resolving California's reapportionment problem, the lessons of the 1973 Masters' Plan are not likely to be forgotten. While such a court-ordered remedy must be regarded as an exceptional act, its prospective use should not entirely be discounted in the event that regular procedures fail. If that ever occurs, the experience of 1973–1980 gives us ground for considerable hope and confidence.

NOTES

1. Report and Recommendations of Special Masters on Reapportionment, August 31, 1973, in *Legislature of California v. Reinecke*. The California legislature consists of a 40-member Senate and an 80-member Assembly. At the time of this report, there were 43 congressional districts.
2. Quoting *Gaffney v. Cummings*, 93 S. Ct. 2321, 2331, 2332 (1973).
3. The authors have worked extensively for California's Democratic congressional delegation in litigation involving redistricting.
4. See references to two such complaints in 1981 in Cain (1985c, p. 563).
5. This case involved a challenge by Democratic legislators to Republican-sponsored referendum petitions on the 1981 redistricting acts. The three referendum measures qualified for the ballot, thus holding the statutes in abeyance until the next election (June 1982), when all were defeated by decisive margins. Yet the previous January, the state Supreme Court, in a four-to-three decision (Chief Justice Bird writing for the majority) mandated the use for 1982 of the challenged Assembly and Senate districts, instead of retaining existing constituencies, thus ignoring the Court's own precedent of a decade earlier (*Legislature of California v. Reinecke*, Sup. 99 Cal. Rptr. 481 (1972)). As a result, the 1982 election gave a bonus of several seats to the Democrats and conditioned the process in late 1982 of redrawing district lines to replace the invalidated constituencies.
6. Hardy predicted that the Democrats' "adolescent games of the 1981–82 session will run their course in the 1986 election" (p. 28). Yet, the congressional delegation remained identical in party split after that election, in spite of three open seats.
7. Republicans lost one of their eight by a scant margin in the Democratic landslide of 1958, but regained that district in 1960, when they lost a

different district. Thus the GOP total in Los Angeles County did not fall below seven.

8. Nearly two decades earlier, Hinderaker (1966) had proposed a similar "nesting" of districts.

References/Author Index

Numbers in parentheses following each reference indicate the page or pages on which the work is cited. Below is an alphabetical listing of coauthors cited in references, followed by the name of the senior author under whose name a complete entry will be found. Many of these coauthors' names will also be found listed as senior authors for other works.

At the end of the References section there is a separate listing of court cases, each followed by the page number(s) in parentheses where the case was cited.

318

References

Alfange, Dean Jr. (1986). Gerrymandering and the Constitution: Into the thorns of the thicket at last. *Supreme Court Review* 175. (49, 57, 64, 71, 83, 85, 90, 106)

Anderson, Jon M. (1989). Politics and purpose: Hide and seek in the gerrymandering thicket after *Davis v. Bandemer. University of Pennsylvania Law Review.* (64)

Archer, J. Clark, and Fred Shelley (1986). *American Electoral Mosaics.* Washington: Association of American Geographers. (239)

Auerbach, Carl A. (1964). The reapportionment cases: One person, one vote—one vote, one value. *Supreme Court Review,*1. (64)

Auerbach, Carl A. (1971). Commentary. In Nelson Polsby (ed.), *Reapportionment in the 1970s.* Berkeley: University of California Press. (104)

Backstrom, Charles, Leonard Robins, and Scott Eller (1978). Issues in gerrymandering: An exploratory measure of partisan gerrymandering applied to Minnesota. *Minnesota Law Review* 62: 1121–1159. (5, 8, 44, 45, 56, 59, 61, 98, 154, 162, 164, 167, 168, 180, 186, 198, 277)

Baker, Gordon E. (1968). New district criteria. *National Civic Review* 55: 293. (15, 114)

Baker, Gordon E. (1971). Gerrymandering: Privileged sanctuary or next judicial target? In Polsby, *Reapportionment in the 1970s.* (211)

Baker, Gordon E. (1980–81). An historical tour through the political thicket: Tracing the steps of the late Robert G. Dixon, Jr. *Policy Studies Journal* 9: 825–838. (188)

Baker, Gordon E. (1986a). Judicial determination of political gerrymandering: A "totality of circumstances" approach. *Journal of Law & Politics* 3: 1. (40, 53, 114, 211)

Baker, Gordon E. (1986b). Whatever happened to the reapportionment revolution in the United States? In Bernard Grofman and Arend Lijphart (eds.), *Electoral Laws and their Political Consequences.* New York: Agathon Press. (3, 206)

Balitzer, Alfred (1979). *The Commission Experience.* Claremont: Rose Institute of State and Local Government (October). (124)

Barnes, G. P. (1985). The general review of parliamentary constituencies in England. *Electoral Studies* 4(2): 179–181, and in J. C. Courtney (ed.), Theories masquerading as principles: Canadian electoral boundary commissions and the Australian model. *The Canadian House of Commons: Essays in Honour of Norman Ward.* University of Calgary Press. (140)

Basehart, H. (1987). The seats/votes relationship and the identification of partisan gerrymandering. *American Politics Quarterly* 15: 484–498. (198)

319

Bickel, Alexander M. (1962). The durability of *Colegrove v. Green. Yale Law Journal* 72: 39. (105)
Bickel, Alexander M. (1971). The Supreme Court and reapportionment. In Polsby, *Reapportionment in the 1970s*. (105)
Bickel, Alexander M. (1978). *The Supreme Court and the Idea of Progress* (originally published in 1970). New York: Harper & Row. (107)
Bicker, William E. (1971). The effects of malapportionment in the states—a mistrial. In Polsby, *Reapportionment in the 1970s*. (104)
Blasi, Vincent (1979). *Bakke* as precedent: Does Mr. Justice Powell have a theory? *California Law Review* 67: 21. (104)
Blasi, Vincent (1985). The pathological perspective and the First Amendment. *Columbia Law Review* 85: 449. (110)
Born, Richard (1985). Partisan intentions and Election Day realities in the congressional redistricting process. *American Political Science Review* 79: 305–319. (53)
Brace, Kimball, Bernard Grofman, Lisa Handley, and Richard Niemi (1988). What's special about 65%: The mathematics of minority voting equality. *Law and Policy* 10(1): 43–62. (61)
Brischetto, Robert, and Bernard Grofman (1980). The Voting Rights Act and minority representation in Texas cities. Unpublished manuscript. (p)
Browning, Robert X., and Gary King (1987). Seats, votes, and gerrymandering: Estimating representation and bias in state legislative redistricting. *Law and Policy* 9(3): 305–322. (44, 198)
Brunn, Stanley (1974). *Geography and Politics in America*. New York: Harper & Row. (239)
Bunge, William (1966). Gerrymandering, geography and grouping. *Geographical Review* 56: 256–262. (239)
Bureau of Census, Conference on Census Undercount: Proceedings of the 1980 conference (1980). Washington, D.C., Esp. Nathan Keyfitz, Facing the fact of census incompleteness, 27–36. (25)
Butler D. E. (1963). *The Electoral System in Britain Since 1918*. Oxford: Oxford University Press. (140)
Cahn, Edmond N. (1949). *The Sense of Injustice*. New York: New York University Press. (23)
Cain, Bruce E. (1984). *The Reapportionment Puzzle*. Berkeley: University of California Press. (112, 117, 138, 139, 167, 179, 257, 290)
Cain, Bruce E. (1985a). Assessing the partisan effects of redistricting. *American Political Science Review* 79(2): 320–333. (30, 46, 47, 52, 53, 128, 202, 219, 249, 294)
Cain, Bruce E. (1985b). Simple vs. complex criteria for partisan gerrymandering: A comment on Niemi and Grofman, *UCLA Law Review* 33: 213–226. (4, 8, 127, 141, 176, 177, 179)
Cain, Bruce E. (1985c). Excerpts from declaration in *Badham v. Eu. PS* 18 (Summer): 561–567. (316)
Cain, Bruce E., and Janet Campagna (1987). Predicting partisan redistricting disputes. *Legislative Studies Quarterly* 12: 265–274. (125)
Cain, Bruce E., John A. Ferejohn, and Morris Fiorina (1987). *The Personal Vote*. Cambridge: Harvard University Press. (112, 142)
California Ballot Pamphlet (1980). For primary election of June 3. Sacramento: Office of Secretary of State. (308)

California Ballot Pamphlet (1982). For general election of November 2. Sacramento: Office of Secretary of State. (309)

California Ballot Pamphlet (1984). For general election of November 6. Sacramento: Office of Secretary of State. (310)

California Journal (1973). Vol. 4 (October). (297, 306)

California Journal (1974). Vol. 5 (January). (300, 305, 311)

California Journal (1975). Vol. 6 (March). (311)

California Journal (1983). Vol. 14 (August). (208)

California Journal (1984). Vol. 15 (December). (311)

California Journal (1985). Vol. 16 (February). (315)

Campbell, A., P. Converse, W. Miller and D. Stokes (1966). *Elections and the Political Order.* New York: Wiley, 9–39, n. 21. (167, 168)

Campbell, J., J. Alford, and K. Henry (1984). Television markets and congressional elections. *Legislative Studies Quarterly* 9: 665. (167)

Casper, Gerhard (1973). Apportionment and the right to vote: Standards of judicial scrutiny. *Supreme Court Review* 1. (110)

Common Cause (1977). Toward a system of "Fair and Effective Representation." Washington, DC: Common Cause. (142)

Congressional Quarterly Service (1969). *Congress and the Nation, 1965-1968.* Washington, DC: Congressional Quarterly Inc., 423–434. (150)

Cortner, Richard C. (1970). *The Apportionment Cases.* Knoxville: University of Tennessee Press. (65, 106)

Cox, Archibald (1968). *The Warren Court.* Cambridge: Harvard University Press. (106)

Cox, Archibald (1976). *The Role of the Supreme Court in American Government.* New York: Oxford University Press. (106)

Cranor, John, Gary Crawley, and Raymond Scheele (1986). The anatomy of a gerrymander. Unpublished manuscript. (167)

Crotty, W. (1984). *American Parties in Decline.* Boston: Little Brown. (147)

Crouch, Thomas H. (1987). Political gerrymandering: Judicial scrutiny under the equal protection clause. *Hamline Law Review.* 10: 313. (64, 66)

Dahl, Robert (1956). *A Preface to Democratic Theory.* Chicago: University of Chicago Press. (142)

Dixon, Robert G. (1963). Apportionment standards and judicial power. *Notre Dame Lawyer* 38: 367. (114)

Dixon, Robert G. (1964). Reapportionment and Congress: Constitutional struggle for fair representation. *Michigan Law Review* 63: 209. (64)

Dixon, Robert G. (1968). *Democratic Representation: Reapportionment in Law and Politics.* New York: Oxford University Press, p. 493. (106, 170, 212)

Dixon, Robert G. (1969). The Warren Court crusade for the Holy Grail of "one man, one vote." *The Supreme Court Review.* Chicago: University of Chicago Press. (188)

Dixon, Robert G. (1971). The court, the people and one man, one vote. In Polsby, *Reapportionment in the 1970s.* pp. 7–45. (19, 53, 184, 201, 204)

Dixon, Robert G. (1980–81). Fair criteria and procedures for establishing legislative districts. *Policy Studies Journal* 9(3): 839–850. (15, 182)

Downs, Anthony (1957). *An Economic Theory of Democracy.* New York: Harper & Row. (142)

Edsall, Thomas B. (1986). The winners in the High Court's gerrymandering ruling: Lawyers. *Washington Post* (July 14). (3)

Edwards, J.M. (1971). The gerrymander and "one man, one vote." *New York University Law Review* 46: 879–899. (201)

Emerson, Thomas I. (1962). Malapportionment and judicial power. *Yale Law Journal* 72: 64. (105)

Engstrom, Richard L. (1977). The Supreme Court and equipopulous gerrymandering: A remaining obstacle in the quest for fair and effective representation. *Arizona State Law Journal* 2: 277–319. (3)

Engstrom, Richard L. (1981). Post-census representational districting: The Supreme Court, "one person, one vote," and the gerrymandering issue. *Southern University Law Review* 7: 173–226. (183)

Engstrom, Richard L., and M. D. McDonald (1985). Quantitative evidence in vote dilution litigation: Political participation and polarized voting. *The Urban Lawyer* 17: 369–377. (198)

Engstrom, Richard L., and M. D. McDonald (1987). Quantitative evidence in vote dilution litigation, Part II: Minority coalitions and multivariate analysis. *The Urban Lawyer* 19: 65–75. (198)

Engstrom, Richard L., and M. D. McDonald, (1988). Definitions, measurements, and statistics: Weeding Wildgen's thicket. *The Urban Lawyer* 20: 175–191. (198)

Engstrom, Richard L., and John K. Wildgen (1977). Pruning thorns from the thicket: An empirical test of the existence of racial gerrymandering. *Legislative Studies Quarterly* 2: 465–479. (61, 171, 199)

Erikson, R. S. (1972). Malapportionment, gerrymandering, and party fortunes in congressional elections. *American Political Science Review* 66: 1234–1245. (179, 185)

The Federalist Papers (1986). New York: New American Library. (142, 315)

Fenno, R. (1978). *Home Style: House Members in Their Districts*. Boston: Little Brown, 113. (147)

Finkel, Steven, and Howard A. Scarrow (1985). Party identification and party enrollment: The difference and the consequence. *Journal of Politics* 47: 620–642. (46)

Glazer, Amihai, Bernard Grofman, and Marc Robbins (1987). Partisan and incumbency effects of 1970s congressional redistricting. *American Journal of Political Science* 30(3): 680–701. (44)

Gottlieb, Stephen E. (1987). The effort to fashion a test for gerrymandering. Presented at the Annual Meeting of the American Political Science Association, Chicago, September 3–6. (141)

Grofman, Bernard (1981). Fair and equal representation. *Ethics* 91: 477–485. (184)

Grofman, Bernard (1982). For single-member districts, random is not equal. In Grofman et al., *Representation and Redistricting Issues*. pp. 55–58. (47, 52, 56)

Grofman, Bernard (1983a). First declaration in *Badham v. Eu*. (N.D. California, No. C–83–1126, dismissed April 21, 1988), certiorari denied for want of jurisdiction by the U.S. Supreme Court, October 1988. (44, 56, 117, 210, 281, 286)

Grofman, Bernard (1983b). Measures of bias and proportionality in seats-votes relationships. *Political Methodology* 9: 295–327. (6, 44)

Grofman, Bernard (1984). Second declaration in *Badham v. Eu.* (N.D. California, No. C–83–1126, dismissed April 21, 1988), certiorari denied for want of jurisdiction by the U.S. Supreme Court, October 1988. (47)

Grofman, Bernard (1985a). Criteria for districting: A social science perspective. *UCLA Law Review* 33(1): 77–184. (p, 6, 46, 47, 51, 59, 81, 97, 141, 182, 183, 185, 210, 211, 255)

Grofman, Bernard (1985b). Declarations in *Badham v. Eu.* (excerpts), *PS* 18(3): 544–549, 573–574. (6, 47, 52, 53, 141)

Grofman, Bernard (1989a). One person, one vote: The legacy of *Baker v. Carr*. Prepared for the Twentieth Century Fund Conference on the Legacy of *Baker v. Carr*. (p)

Grofman, Bernard (1989b). The fight to define racially polarized voting. Unpublished manuscript, School of Social Sciences, University of California, Irvine. (p)

Grofman, Bernard, Arend Lijphart, Robert McKay, and Howard Scarrow, eds. (1982). *Representation and Redistricting Issues*. Lexington, MA: Lexington Books.

Grofman, Bernard, Michael Migalski, and Nicholas Noviello (1985). The "totality of circumstances" test in section 2 of the Voting Rights Act: A social science perspective. *Law and Policy* 7(2): 209–223. (p, 50, 198)

Grofman, Bernard, Michael Migalski, and Nicholas Noviello (1986). Effects of multimember districts on black representation in state legislatures. *Review of Black Political Economy* 14(4): 65–78. (56)

Grofman, Bernard, and Howard Scarrow (1982). Current issues in reapportionment. *Law and Policy Quarterly* 4(4): 435–474. (185, 220)

Grofman, Bernard, and Donald Wittman, eds. (1989). *The Federalist Papers in Contemporary Perspective: The New Institutionalism and the Old*. New York: Agathon Press. (142)

Gudgin, G., and P. Taylor (1979). *Seats, Votes and the Spatial Organization of Elections*. London: Pion. (194, 202, 214, 239)

Hacker, A. (rev. ed., 1964). *Congressional Districting: The Issue of Equal Representation*, Washington, DC: The Brookings Institution, p. 72. (167, 182)

Hardy, Leroy C. (1986). The conception and birth of gerrymanders and their offspring. Presented at the Annual Meeting of the American Political Science Association, August 28. (311)

Hedges, R., and C. P. Carlucci (1987). Implementation of the Voting Rights Act: The case of New York. *Western Political Quarterly* 40: 107–120. (197)

Henderson, Gordon R. (1982). Testimony, afternoon session, September 8, 1982, trial transcript, at 63, *Rhode Island Republican Party v. Friedemann*, 82: 1727 (R.I. Super. Ct.) (original name of *Holmes v. Burns*). (183)

Hess, Michael (1987). Beyond justiciability: Political gerrymandering after *Davis v. Bandemer. Campbell Law Review* 9 (Spring): 207–254. (49, 64)

Hinderaker, Ivan (1966). Politics of reapportionment. In Eugene P. Dvorin, and Arthur J. Misner (eds.), *California Politics and Policies*. Palo Alto, CA: Addison-Wesley. (317)

Holcombe, Donna R. (1987). Political gerrymandering: Entangled in the political thicket. *Stetson Law Review* 16: 777. (64)

Horn, David L., Victor Goedicke, Charles R. Hampton, Ellsworth Holden, John W. Lawrence, Anthony J. Vandenberg, and Benson A. Wolman (1988). An Ohio response to "What's next in gerrymandering?" A review essay. Prepared for the Panel on Gerrymandering, Annual Meeting of the American Political Science Association, September 4. (6)

Jacobson, Gary (1987). The marginals never vanished: Incumbency and competition in elections to the U.S. House of Representatives. *American Journal of Political Science* 81: 31. (248)

Jewell, Malcolm E. (1968). Local systems of representation: Political consequences and judicial choices. *George Washington Law Review* 36: 790–821. (201)

Jewell, Malcolm E., and David M. Olson (1986). *Political Parties and Elections in American States*, 3rd ed. Chicago: Dorsey Press. (295)

Johnston, Ronald J. (1979). *Politics, Elections and Spatial Systems*. New York: Oxford. (239)

Johnston, Ronald J. (1982a). The changing geography of votes in the U.S. 1946–1980. *Transactions, Institute of British Geography* 7: 187–204. (239)

Johnston, Ronald J. (1982b). Redistricting by independent commission. *Annals, Association of American Geographers* 72: 457–470. (239)

Kaase, M. (1984). Personalized proportional representation: The "model" of the West German electoral system. In A. Lijphart and B. Grofman (eds.), *Choosing an Electoral System*. New York: Praeger. (201)

Kelly, Alfred H. (1965). Clio and the court: An illicit love affair. *Supreme Court Review* 119. (106)

Kendall, M. G., and A. Stuart (1950). The law of cubic proportions in election results. *British Journal of Sociology* 1: 183–196. (194)

King, Gary, and Robert Browning (1987). Democratic representation and partisan bias in congressional elections. *American Political Science Review* 81(4): 1251–1273. (44, 169)

Kurland, Philip B. (1964). Foreword: Equal in origin and equal in title to the legislative and executive branches of the government. *Harvard Law Review* 78: 143. (69)

Kurland, Philip B. (1970). *Politics, the Constitution, and the Warren Court*. Chicago: University of Chicago Press. (65)

Laswell, Harold (1951). *Who Gets What, When and How*. Westport, CT: Greenwood Press. (118)

Levinson, Sanford (1985). Gerrymandering and the brooding omnipresence of proportional representation: Why won't it go away? *UCLA Law Review* 33(1): 1–75. (4, 56)

Lewis, Anthony (1978). Foreword. In Alexander Bickel, *The Supreme Court and the Idea of Progress*. New York: Harper & Row. (104)

Lijphart, Arend (1976). *The Politics of Accommodation*. Berkeley: University of California Press. (142)

Lijphart, Arend, and Bernard Grofman, eds. (1984). *Choosing an Electoral System: Issues and Alternatives*. New York: Praeger. (142)

Lowenstein, Daniel (1986). Congressional reapportionment and the party system. Paper delivered at the meeting of the American Political Science Association, Washington, DC, August 19. (169)

Lowenstein, Daniel H., and Jonathan Steinberg (1985). The quest for legislative districting in the public interest: Elusive or illusory? *UCLA Law Review* 33: 1–75. (4, 8, 63, 93, 97, 107, 108, 109, 111, 112, 113, 114, 117, 139, 163, 164, 179, 202, 302)

Lyons, W.E., and Malcolm E. Jewell (1986). Redrawing council districts in American cities. *State and Local Government Review* 18: 71–81. (183)

Mann, Thomas E. (1987). Is the House of Representatives unresponsive to political change? In A. James Reichley (ed.), *Elections American Style*. Washington, DC: Brookings. (6, 31, 191)

Manninen, Diane L. (1973). The role of compactness in the process of redistricting. Unpublished Masters Thesis. Department of Geography, University of Washington, Seattle. (287)

Martis, Kenneth (1982). *The Historical Atlas of U.S. Congressional Districts*. New York: Free Press. (239)

Maveety, Nancy (1987). The Burger court and group access to the political processes. Presented at the Annual Meeting of the American Political Science Association, Chicago, September 3–6. (141)

Mayhew, D. R. (1974). The case of the vanishing marginals. *Polity* 6: 298. (147, 183)

McCloskey, Robert G. (1962). Foreword: The reapportionment case. *Harvard Law Review* 76: 54. (64, 65, 105)

McDonald, Michael D., and Richard L. Engstrom (1985). Council size and the election of blacks: Clarifying an apparent inconsistency between theory and data. Presented at the 13th World Congress of the International Political Science Association in Paris, France. (200)

McKay, Robert B. (1968). Reapportionment: Success story of the Warren Court. *Michigan Law Review* 67: 223. (65, 104)

McRobie, A. (n.d.). Reflections on reapportionment: New Zealand and California. Unpublished manuscript. (140)

Merritt, Anna (1982). *Redistricting: An Exercise in Prophecy*. University of Illinois, Institute of Government and Public Affairs. (239)

Mill, J. S. (1975). Considerations on representative government. In *Three Essays*. Oxford: Oxford University Press. (134)

Minisymposium: Political gerrymandering: *Badham v. Eu*, political science goes to court. (1985) *PS* (Summer). (9)

Monagan, Robert (1985). In *California Journal* Vol. 16 (February): 83. (315)

Morrill, Richard (1981). *Political Redistricting and Geographic Theory*. Washington DC: Association of American Geographers. (239)

Morrill, Richard (1987). Redistricting, region and representation. *Political Geography Quarterly* 6: 241–260. (183, 289)

Neal, Phil C. (1962). Baker v. Carr: Politics in search of law. *Supreme Court Review* 252. (105, 114)

Nelson, William (1980). *On Justifying Democracy*. London: Routledge & Kegan Paul. (134, 142)

Nicholson, Marlene Arnold (1974). Campaign financing and equal protection. *Stanford Law Review* 26: 815. (77)

Niemi, Richard G. (1982). The effects of districting on trade-offs among party competition, electoral responsiveness, and seats-votes relationships. In Grofman et al., *Representation and Redistricting Issues*. (56, 176)

Niemi, Richard G. (1985). The relationship between votes and seats: The ultimate questions in political gerrymandering. *UCLA Law Review*, 33: 185–212. (141, 171, 175, 177, 179)

Niemi, Richard, and John Deegan, Jr. (1978). A theory of political districting.

American Political Science Review 72(4): 1304–1323. (6, 44, 47, 176, 179, 185, 202)

Niemi, Richard, and Patrick Fett (1986). The swing ratio: An explanation and assessment. *Legislative Studies Quarterly*, 11(1): 75–90. (44, 172, 175)

Niemi, Richard, Bernard Grofman, Carl Carlucci, and Thomas Hofeller (1990). Measuring the compactness and the role of a compactness standard in a test for partisan gerrymandering. *Journal of Politics*, forthcoming. (217, 257, 258, 281, 282, 283, 287)

Niemi, Richard G., Jeffrey Hill, and Bernard N. Grofman (1985). The impact of multimember district elections on party representation in state legislatures. *Legislative Studies Quarterly* 10: 441–455. (56)

Note (1986). The Supreme Court, 1985 term. *Harvard Law Review* 100. (47, 66, 85, 91)

O'Loughlin, John (1976). Malapportionment and gerrymandering in the ghetto. In Adams, *Urban Policy-Making and Metropolitan Dynamics* pp. 539–565. (61)

O'Loughlin, John (1980). District size and party electoral strength. *Environment and Planning* A12: 247–262. (239)

O'Loughlin, John (1982a). Racial gerrymandering: Its potential impact on black politics in the 1980s. In M. G. Preston, L. J. Henderson, Jr., and P. Puryear (eds.), *The New Black Politics*. New York: Longman. (61, 179, 199)

O'Loughlin, John (1982b). The identification and evaluation of racial gerrymandering. *Annals of the Association of American Geographers* 72: 165–184. (61, 239)

O'Loughlin, John, and A. M. Taylor (1982). Choices in redistricting and electoral outcomes: The case of Mobile, Alabama. *Political Geography Quarterly* 1: 317–340. (239)

Owen, Guillermo and Bernard Grofman (1987). Optimal partisan gerrymandering. *Political Geography Quarterly* 7: 5–22. (6, 40, 52)

Padover, Saul (1956). *A Jefferson Profile: As Revealed in His Letters*. New York: J. Day, p. 327. (25)

Parker, F. R. (1984). Racial gerrymandering and legislative reapportionment. In C. Davidson (ed.), *Minority Vote Dilution*. Washington, DC: Howard University Press. (196)

Pateman, Carole (1970). *Participation and Democratic Theory*. Cambridge: Cambridge University Press. (142)

Pitkin, Hanna Fenichel (1967). *The Concept of Representation*. Berkeley: University of California Press. (73, 135, 212, 243)

Pollak, Louis H. (1962). Judicial power and the "politics of the people." *Yale Law Journal* 72: 81. (105)

Polsby, Nelson W., ed. (1971). *Reapportionment in the 1970s*. Berkeley: University of California Press. (104)

Polsby, Nelson W. (1985). Declaration of Nelson W. Polsby in *Badham v. Eu*. PS 18: 568–572. (179, 240)

Pulzer, P. (1983). Germany. In V. Bogdanor and D. Butler (eds.), *Democracy and Elections*. Cambridge: Cambridge University Press. (200)

Rae, Douglas W. (1971a). *The Political Consequences of Electoral Laws*, 2nd ed. New Haven: Yale University Press.

Rae, Douglas W. (1971b). Reapportionment and political democracy. In Polsby, *Reapportionment in the 1970s*. (77)

Rae, Douglas W., D. Yates, J. Hochschild, J. Monroe, and C. Fessler (1981). *Equalities*. Cambridge: Harvard University Press. (183, 185)

Reynolds, David (1976). Progress toward achieving an effective and responsive spatial-political system. In John Adams (ed.), *Urban Policy Making and Metropolitan Dynamics*. Cambridge: Ballinger, pp. 453–536. (239)

Riker, Williams, and Peter Ordeshook (1973). *An Introduction to Positive Political Theory*. Englewood Cliffs: Prentice-Hall. (133, 142)

Roeck, E. Jr. (1963). Measuring compactness as a requirement of legislative apportionment. *Midwest Journal of Political Science* 5: 70. (167, 211, 287)

Rowley, G. (1975). Electoral change and reapportionment—Prescriptive ideals and realities. *Tijd. V. Econ en Soc. Geogr.* 66: 108–120. (239)

Sabato, Larry J. (1988). *The Party's Just Begun: Shaping Political Parties for America's Future*. Glenview, IL: Scott, Foresman. (102)

Scarrow, Howard (1982). Partisan gerrymandering—invidious or benevolent? *Gaffney v. Cummings* and its aftermath. *Journal of Politics* 44: 810–821. (44, 52, 161, 219)

Schuck, Peter H. (1987). The thickest thicket: Partisan gerrymandering and judicial regulation of politics. *Columbia Law Review* 87: 1325. (p, 4, 46, 103, 104)

Schwab, L. (1985). The impact of the 1980 reapportionment in the U.S. *Political Geography Quarterly* 4: 141–158. (239)

Schwartzberg, J. (1966). Reapportionment, gerrymandering and the notion of compactness. *Minnesota Law Review*, 50: 443–457. (239)

Shapiro, Martin (1985). Gerrymandering, unfairness, and the Supreme Court. *UCLA Law Review* 33: 227. (108, 109, 141)

Shelley, Fred (1982). A constitutional choice approach to electoral district boundary delineation. *Political Geography Quarterly* 1: 341–350. (239)

Shelley, Fred (1984). Spatial effects on voting power in representative democracies. *Environment and Planning* A16: 401–405. (239)

Sickels, R.J. (1966). Dragons, bacon strips, and dumbbells: Who's afraid of reapportionment. *Yale Law Journal* 75: 1300–1308. (40)

Still, J. W. (1981). Political equality and election systems. *Ethics* 91: 375–394. (184)

The Supreme Court—leading cases. (1986). *Harvard Law Review* 100: 153–163. (167)

Taagepera, Rein (1972). The size of national assemblies. *Social Science Research* 1.

Taagepera, Rein (1973). Seats and votes: A generalization of the cube law of elections. *Social Science Research* 2: 257–275. (193)

Taagepera, Rein (1986). Reformulating the cube law for proportional representation elections. *American Political Science Review* 80(2): 489–504. (6, 44)

Taylor, Peter (1985). *Political Geography: World-Economy, Nation-State, and Locality*. New York: Longman. (239)

Taylor, Peter, and G. Gudgin (1976). The statistical basis for decision making in electoral districting. *Environment and Planning* A8: 43–48. (239)

Taylor, Peter and R. Johnston (1979). *The Geography of Elections*. London: Croom. (239)

Theil, H. (1969). The desire for political entropy. *American Political Science Review* 63: 521–525. (193, 200)

Thernstrom, Abigail (1985). Voting rights trap. *The New Republic.* 193(10), issue 3685. September 2: 21–23. (56)

Thernstrom, Abigail (1987). *Whose Votes Count? Affirmative Action and Minority Rights.* Cambridge, MA: Harvard University Press. (56)

Tribe, Lawrence H. (1978). *American Constitutional Law,* 1st ed. Mineola, NY: Foundation Press. (66)

Tufte, Edward (1973). The relationship between seats and votes in two-party systems. *American Political Science Review* 67: 540–547. (6, 44, 47, 175)

Tufte, Edward (1974). Communication. *American Political Science Review* 68: 211–213. (175)

U.S. Senate (1982). Report of the Committee on the Judiciary on S. 1992, Senate Report 97–417, 97th Congress, 2nd Session. Washington, DC: U.S. Government Printing Office. (50, 120, 196)

Voting Rights Act of 1965. 42 U.S.C. 1973 (1982). (p, 8, 61, 81, 121, 122, 127, 130, 133, 142, 166, 187, 203, 204, 243, 245)

Waller, R. J. (1983). The 1983 boundary commission: Policies and effects. *Electoral Studies* 2(3): 195–206. (140)

Ward, Norman (1967; 1985). A century of constituencies. *Canadian Public Administration* (March 1967): 105–122; reprinted in J. C. Courtney (ed.), Theories masquerading as principles: Canadian electoral boundary commissions and the Australian model. *The Canadian House of Commons: Essays in Honour of Norman Ward.* University of Calgary Press, 1985. (140)

Warren, Earl (1972). Past and present. *New York Times,* December 20, p. C. (13)

Warren, Earl (1977). *The Memoirs of Earl Warren,* New York: Doubleday, pp. 307–310. (13)

Weinstein, Harris (1984). Partisan gerrymandering: The next hurdle in the political thicket? *Journal of Law & Politics* 1: 357. (110)

Wells, David I. (1981). What criteria should be used in the establishment of legislative district boundary lines? Presented at National Conference on Government, Pittsburgh, PA, November 16. (6, 240, 289)

White, G. Edward (1982). *Earl Warren: A Public Life.* New York: Oxford University Press. (14)

Wollheim, Richard (1986). A paradox in the theory of voting. In R. M. Stewart (ed.), *Readings in Social and Political Philosophy.* New York: Oxford University Press. (142)

Wollock, Andrea J., ed. (1980). *Reapportionment: Law and Technology.* Denver: National Conference of State Legislatures. (46)

Young, H. Peyton (1988). Measuring the compactness of legislative districts. *Legislative Studies Quarterly,* 13(1) (February): 105–116. (167)

Court Cases

Assembly of the State of California et al. v. George Deukmejian, Attorney General et al., Sup. 180 Cal. Rptr. 297 (1982). (309)

Badham v. Eu (N.D. California, No. C–83–1126, dismissed April 21, 1988), certiorari denied for want of jurisdiction by the U.S. Supreme Court, October 1988. (9, 46, 50, 51, 55, 60, 62, 115, 118, 141, 142, 168)

Baker v. Carr, 369 U.S. 186 (1962). (p, 7, 14, 21, 51, 61, 64, 68, 69, 73, 74, 90, 95, 105, 113, 128, 147, 149, 150, 178, 179, 204, 241, 266)

Bandemer v. Davis, 603 F. Supp. 1479 (1984), S.D. Indiana. (*)

Bowers v. Hardwick, _____U.S. _____,106 S.Ct. 2841 (1986). (64)

Brown v. Board of Education, 347 U.S. 483 (1954). (77, 109)

Buckley v. Valeo, 424 U.S. 1 (1976). (107)

Chapman v. Meier, 420 U.S. 1 (1975). (113)

Citizens Against Rent Control v. City of Berkeley, 454 U.S. 290 (1981). (107)

City of Mobile v. Bolden, 466 U.S. 55 (1980). (35, 81, 84, 86, 103, 110, 111, 112, 120, 122)

City of Richmond, Va. v. U.S., 422 U.S. 358 (1975). (251)

Cleburne v. Cleburne Living Center, 473 U.S. 432, 105 S.Ct. 3249 (1985). (109, 112)

Colegrove v. Green, 328 U.S. 549 (1946). (12, 96, 105, 148)

Connor v. Finch, 431 U.S. 407 (1977). (46, 52, 113, 256)

Craig v. Boren, 429 U.S. 190 (1976). (78)

Davids v. Akers, 549 F 2d. 120 (9th Cir. 1977). (108)

Davis v. Bandemer, _____U.S. _____, 106 S.Ct. 2797 (1986), 92 L. Ed. 2d 85. (*)

Dunn v. Blumstein, 405 U.S. 331 (1972). (110)

Fortson v. Dorsey, 379 U.S. 433 (1965). (61, 96)

Gaffney v. Cummings, 412 U.S. 735 (1973). (17, 18, 19, 21, 91, 105, 110, 183, 196, 200, 291, 298, 316)

Gingles v. Edmisten, 590 F Supp 345 (1984), heard sub nom *Thornburg v. Gingles,* _____U.S. _____, 106 S. Ct. 2752 (1986). (56, 62, 293)

Gomillion v. Lightfoot, 364 U.S. 339 (1960). (19, 204)

Gray v. Sanders, 372 U.S. 368 (1963). (69, 70, 74, 106)

Harper v. Virginia Board of Elections, 383 U.S. 663 (1966). (110)

Holmes et al. v. Burns and the Rhode Island Board of Elections, Superior Court, Rhode Island CA No. 82–1727 (1982); previously denominated *R.I. Republican Party v. Friedmann*. (46)

Holmes v. Farmer, 475 A 2d 976 (R.I., 1984). (46)

Indiana Branches of the NAACP v. Orr, 603 F. Supp. 1479 (1984). (31, 58)

Karcher v. Daggett (I), 462 U.S. 725 (1983); 103 S. Ct. 2653 (1983). (6, 19, 20, 23, 32, 35, 36, 38, 40, 45, 91, 97, 114, 119, 120, 123, 125, 141, 150, 171, 172, 188, 203, 205, 206, 207, 208, 256, 277, 282)

Karcher v. Daggett (II), 466 U.S. 910 (1984). (84, 85)

Ketchum v. Byrne, 740 F. 2nd 1398 (1984) U.S. Ct. of Appeals, 7th Circuit cert. denied 105 S. Ct. 2673 (1985). (42, 43, 50, 51, 62, 103, 116, 196)

Kirkpatrick v. Preisler, 394 U.S. 526 (1969). (16, 150, 183, 188)

Kirksey v. Board of Supervisors of Hinds County, Mississippi 554 F. 2d 139, 5th Circuit, cert. denied, 434 U.S. 968 (1977). (56)

Korematsu v. United States, 323 U.S. 214 (1944). (78)

Kramer v. Union Free School District, 395 U.S. 621 (1969). (78)

Legislature of California v. Reinecke, 110 Cal. Rptr. 718 (1973). (297, 298, 299, 300, 301, 302, 304, 306, 316)

Lucas v. 44th General Assembly of Colorado, 377 U.S. 713 (1964). (13, 15, 71, 106)

Luther v. Borden, 7 How. [48 U.S.] 1 (1849). (68)

Mahan v. Howell, 410 U.S. 315 (1973). (17, 150, 277)

Major v. Treen, 574 F Supp 325 (1983). (42, 43, 50, 51, 56, 103, 116, 199, 201)

Marbury v. Madison, 1 Cranch. [5 U.S.] 137 (1803). (77, 105)

Metropolitan Life Insurance Co. v. Ward, _____U.S. _____, 105 S.Ct. 1676 (1985). (109, 112)

Mobile v. Bolden, see City of Mobile v. Bolden

Nevitt v. Sides, 571 F. Supp 209 (1978). (182)

New Orleans v. Dukes, 427 U.S. 297 (1976). (78)

Plyler v. Doe, 457 U.S. 202 (1982). (109)

Reynolds v. Sims, 377 U.S. 533 (1964). (3, 11, 12, 13, 14, 15, 16, 17, 18, 20, 21, 23, 30, 61, 62, 64, 65, 70, 71, 72, 73, 74, 75, 76, 77, 79, 80, 91, 105, 106, 107, 110, 128, 150, 186, 207, 256, 296)

Richmond v. U.S., see City of Richmond v. U.S.

Rogers v. Lodge, 458 U.S. 613 (1982). (50, 61, 110, 111, 112)

Roe v. Wade, 410 U.S. 113 (1973). (77)

Rybicki v. State Board of Elections, 574 F. Supp. 1082 (N.D. Illinois 1982). (60)

San Antonio Independent School District v. Rodriguez, 411 U.S. 1 (1973). (80, 109)

Slaughterhouse Cases, 16 Wall. [83 U.S.] 36 (1873). (109)

Thornburg v. Gingles, _____U.S. _____, 106 S.Ct. 2752 (1986). (4, 7, 9, 30, 31, 43, 50, 51, 54, 55, 57, 62, 103, 111, 112, 116, 119, 121, 123, 126, 127, 128, 131, 141, 198)

United Jewish Organizations v. Carey, 430 U.S. 144 (1977). (110, 196)

Washington v. Davis, 426 U.S. 229 (1976). (78, 79, 111)

Wells v. Rockefeller, 394 U.S. 542 (1969). (17, 150)

Wesberry v. Sanders, 376 U.S. 1 (1964). (12, 64, 69, 70, 74, 105, 106)

Whitcomb v. Chavis, 403 U.S. 124 (1971). (58, 110)

White v. Regester, 412 U.S. 755 (1973). (17, 50, 51, 96, 110, 301)

White v. Weiser, 412 U.S. 783 (1973). (18, 56)

WMCA v. Lomenzo, 238 F. Supp. 916, 925 (S.D.N.Y.) aff'd per curiam 382 U.S. 4 (1965) vacated, 384 U.S. 887 (1966). (58)

*These cases are cited so consistently throughout the text that we have not provided individual page cites.

Index

Page citations to author references and to court cases are separately listed in the References and Case Cites sections preceding this index. Page citations to individual Supreme Court justices and to redistricting in individual states are incomplete and must be supplemented by referring to the case cites. This index focuses on topic references.

A

At-large elections, 61

B

Bias (*also see* Gerrymandering, Swing ratio, Seats–Votes), 6, 8, 44, 47, 185-187, 217-219, 225-228, 304-305
Black, Hugo, 12, 69
Black representation (*see* Representation, black; *also see* Minority vote dilution)
Blacksher, James, 55
Brennan, William, 16, 54-55, 61-62, 84-85, 106, 149
Burger, Warren, 21

C

California (*also see* Gerrymandering, California; Redistricting, California; case cites to *Badham v. Eu*), 289-295
Master's Plan for (*also see* Districting criteria), 8-9, 206, 281-286, 289-295, 296-316, 301
Proposition 6 (1980), 308-309
Proposition 14 (1982), 309
Proposition 39 (1984), 310-311
Classifications (*see* Suspect classification)
Colorado (*see* Redistricting, Colorado)

Commissions (*see* Redistricting, commissions used in)
Communities of interest (*also see* Districting criteria), 6, 33, 153-154, 207, 215-217, 225, 228, 301-304
Compactness (*also see* Districting criteria) 6, 8, 9, 19, 33, 94, 138, 151-152, 167, 182-183, 199, 205-206, 214-215, 225-228, 229-231, 256-264, 281-288, 297, 302, 310
California, 281-288
Minority representation and, 139
Indiana, 255-265
Competition (*see* Political competition)
Computers (*see* Redistricting, computers use in)
Congress (*see* Redistricting, congressional; Gerrymandering (individual states))
Contiguity (*also see* Districting criteria), 182-183, 205-206, 297, 310
Cracking (*also see* Packing; Gerrymandering, techniques) 54, 185, 191, 195
Criteria for districting (*see* Districting criteria)

D

Declaration of Independence, 69
Dirksen Amendment, 150

*Asterisked items are topics cited too frequently to have individual page citations.